At Fault

The Florida James Joyce Series

UNIVERSITY PRESS OF FLORIDA

Florida A&M University, Tallahassee
Florida Atlantic University, Boca Raton
Florida Gulf Coast University, Ft. Myers
Florida International University, Miami
Florida State University, Tallahassee
New College of Florida, Sarasota
University of Central Florida, Orlando
University of Florida, Gainesville
University of North Florida, Jacksonville
University of South Florida, Tampa
University of West Florida, Pensacola

At Fault

Joyce and the Crisis of the Modern University

SEBASTIAN D. G. KNOWLES

University Press of Florida

Gainesville · Tallahassee · Tampa · Boca Raton

Pensacola · Orlando · Miami · Jacksonville · Ft. Myers · Sarasota

First cloth printing, 2018
First paperback printing, 2021

26 25 24 23 22 21   6 5 4 3 2 1

Library of Congress Cataloging-in-Publication Data
Names: Knowles, Sebastian D. G. (Sebastian David Guy), author.
Title: At fault : Joyce and the crisis of the modern university / Sebastian
    D. G. Knowles.
Other titles: Florida James Joyce series.
Description: Gainesville : University Press of Florida, 2018. | Series: The
    Florida James Joyce series | Includes bibliographical references and index.
Identifiers: LCCN 2017049114 | ISBN 9780813056920 (cloth : alk. paper) |
    ISBN 9780813068480 (pbk.)
Subjects: LCSH: Joyce, James, 1882–1941—Criticism and interpretation. |
    Education, Higher—Philosophy.
Classification: LCC PR6019.O9 Z6765 2018 | DDC 823/.912—dc23
LC record available at https://lccn.loc.gov/2017049114

The University Press of Florida is the scholarly publishing agency for the State University System
of Florida, comprising Florida A&M University, Florida Atlantic University, Florida Gulf Coast
University, Florida International University, Florida State University, New College of Florida,
University of Central Florida, University of Florida, University of North Florida, University of
South Florida, and University of West Florida.

University Press of Florida
2046 NE Waldo Road
Suite 2100
Gainesville, FL 32609
http://upress.ufl.edu

For Janette
again and always

—Hide fox, and all after.

Hamlet IV.ii.30–31

Contents

Figures

Acknowledgments

For moral support: Murray Beja and Ellen Jones, David Brewer and Rebecca Morton, Austin Briggs and Bunny Serlin, Julia and Rachel Falconer, Carl Faller and Mary Finnegan, E. Gordon Gee, Dave Gill, Jeremy Glazier and Andrew Aucoin, Cheryl Glenn, Helena Goscilo, Anna Grotans, Adam Hayward and Kelly Hong, Drew Jones and Leslie Lockett, Kevin Jones, Jackie Jones-Royster, Jay and Tim Knowles, Sam Knowles and Saskia Gent, Simon and Caroline Knowles, Sophie and Teddy Knowles, Valerie Lee, Hannah and Jim Mathison, Brian McHale, David Niwa, Matthew Platz, Wayne and Cathy Redenbarger, John Roberts, Donna Rocchi, Bonnie Roper, Allan and Ann Silverman, Clare Simmons, Scott and Sue Smith, Andrea Ward Ross, Tom and Carolyn Weber, and Bernard Wilburn and Julie Shuptrine. Above all, Janette.

For the introduction (The Centrifuge and the Outlaw): Alison Armstrong, William Catus, Alex DeTillio, Jeremy Glazier, Adam Hayward, Steven Kern, and Ciaran McMorran.

For chapter 1 (At Fault): Ben Acosta-Hughes, Christine Froula, Paul Gillingham, Robin Judd, Gregory Jusdanis, Jane Knowles, Tim Knowles, John McCourt, Ray Ockenden, Marc Randazza, Carole and Gordon Segal, Laurie Shannon, Robert Spoo, Kate Toller, Tom Weber, the students in OSU English H4590.06 (Proust, Joyce, and Mann), and the students in Northwestern English 312 (Dante and the Moderns). This chapter has been carefully edited by some exceptional readers, including Rachel Falconer, Jeremy Glazier, Adam Hayward, Janette Knowles, Wayne Redenbarger, and Ned Sparrow.

For chapter 2 (Philatelic Joyce): Austin Briggs, Catherine Gubernatis Dannen, A. Nicholas Fargnoli, and Nathan Weidenbenner.

For chapter 3 (*Finnegans Wake* for Dummies): Blake Hobby, Sean Latham, Michael Meagher, and all the students in English 863 (*Finnegans Wake*). Grateful acknowledgment is made to the *James Joyce Quarterly* for permission to include a revised version of "Finnegans Wake for Dummies," *James Joyce Quarterly* 46 (Autumn 2008): 97–112.

For chapter 4 (The True Story of Jumbo the Elephant): Austin Briggs, Erin Foley, A. H. Saxon, Tom Schneidermann and Julia Falconer, Mary Witkowski, and Jeffrey Wood. I would particularly like to thank Michael Groden, longtime professor at the University of Western Ontario, for keeping me posted of all things Jumbo for the last ten years or more—an envelope with another clipping always brightened my day. Thanks also to Ellen Carol Jones and Murray Beja, for permission to include a revised version of "The True Story of Jumbo the Elephant," *Twenty-First Joyce*, ed. Morris Beja and Ellen Carol Jones (Gainesville: University Press of Florida, 2004), 97–111.

For chapter 5 (Death by Gramophone): Graeme Boone, David Chinitz, Paula Marantz Cohen, Adam Hayward, Cheryl Hindrichs, Rick Livingston, Larson Powell, Tom Rice, Matthew Richardson, and Arthur Wrobel. This chapter includes a revised version of "Death by Gramophone," *Journal of Modern Literature* 27 (Autumn 2003): 1–13. © Indiana University Press, 2003. Thanks also to *ANQ*, for permission to reprint parts of "'Then You Wink the Other Eye': T. S. Eliot and the Music Hall," *ANQ* 11 (Autumn 1998): 20–32.

For chapter 6 (Siren Songs): Mary Davis, Josh Epstein, Rachel Falconer, Thomas Gurke, Blake Hobby, Nathan Mead, Michael O'Shea, and Patrick Reilly. Grateful acknowledgment is made to Murray Beja, co-editor of *Joyce in the Hibernian Metropolis*, for permission to include a revised version of "That Form Endearing: A Performance of Siren Songs; or, 'I was only vamping, man,'" in *Joyce in the Hibernian Metropolis: Essays*, ed. Morris Beja and David Norris (Columbus: Ohio State University Press, 1996), 213–36. Also to the *James Joyce Quarterly* for permission to reprint a version of my review of Josh Epstein's *Sublime Noise: Musical Culture and the Modernist Writer*, *James Joyce Quarterly* 51 (Summer 2014): 731–36.

For chapter 7 (Seeing the Joe Miller): Frederick Aldama, Alex Boney, Luca Crispi, Michael Groden, Geert Lernout, and John McCourt. An earlier version of a section of this chapter was published as *Seeing the Joe Miller: Humor Detection in* Ulysses, National Library Monograph Series, no. 12, ed. Luca Crispi and Catherine Fahy (Dublin: National Library of Ireland, 2004). Thanks also to Geert Lernout for permission to include a revised version of "Introduction," in *Joyce in Trieste: An Album of Risky Readings*, ed. Sebastian D. G. Knowles, Geert Lernout, and John McCourt (Gainesville: University Press of Florida, 2007), 1–9.

For chapter 8 (Performing Issy): Catherine Gubernatis Dannen, Finn Fordham, Richard Gerber, and John Gordon.

For chapter 9 (In Conclusion): Thanks to the acquisitions editors at the University Press of Florida, Amy Gorelick, Shannon McCarthy, and Stephanye Hunter, the excellent copy editor Penelope Cray, and the press's editor in chief, Linda Bathgate. A free pint to everyone whose foreword appears here: Richard Beckman, Kim Devlin and Christine Smedley, Edmund Epstein (in absentia), Michael Gillespie, Michael Groden, Alison Lacivita, Mary Lowe-Evans, Cóilín Owens, Vike Plock, Thomas Jackson Rice, Agata Szczeszak-Brewer, and Robert Weninger. Thanks also to all the other Joyceans whose work I've had the privilege of editing over the years (in order of appearance in the Florida James Joyce Series): George Cinclair Gibson, A. Nicholas Fargnoli, Jen Shelton, Andrew Gibson and Len Platt, Roy Gottfried, Dirk Van Hulle, Morris Beja and Anne Fogarty, Karen Lawrence, Marc Conner, Greg Winston, Daniel Ferrer, Sam Slote and André Topia, Matthew Kochis and Heather Lusty, Eleni Loukopoulou, and Jonathan Goldman. Thanks to the *James Joyce Quarterly* for permission to reprint "A Memorial Tribute to Zack Bowen," *James Joyce Quarterly* 46 (Spring/Summer 2009): 423–24. Thanks especially to Zack—I miss you.

Abbreviations

The following abbreviations are used throughout (all texts are fully identified in the works cited):

D	*Dubliners*
FW	*Finnegans Wake*
JJ	Richard Ellmann, *James Joyce*
JJA	*James Joyce Archive*
OCP	*Occasional, Critical, and Political Writing*
P	*A Portrait of the Artist as a Young Man*
Rosenbach	*Ulysses, A Facsimile of the Manuscript*
TWL	T. S. Eliot, *The Waste Land: A Facsimile and Transcript*
U	*Ulysses* (Gabler edition)
U-22	*Ulysses* (1922 edition)
U-61	*Ulysses* (1961 edition)

Unless otherwise specified, references to *Ulysses* are to the episode and line number(s) in the Gabler edition; references to *Finnegans Wake* are to the page(s) and line number(s) in the Viking edition. Paragraph breaks in citations from *Ulysses* are indicated by a slash (/).

Introduction

The Centrifuge and the Outlaw

1. The Outlaw

—Tell us a story, sir.
—O, do, sir. A ghoststory.

(*U* 2.54–55)

Joyce does everything he possibly can to put you off the scent, to conceal his value, to resist interpretation. Puzzlement is his essential starting point: the boy in "The Sisters" worries over his three words (*paralysis, gnomon, simony*) like a dog over a bone (*D* 1); the young Dedalus is fascinated by the sound of the word "Suck" and the sight of the word "*Fœtus*" (*P* 11, 89); Sargent, the schoolboy in Stephen's class in "Nestor," has trouble with his sums (*U* 2.128).[1] Bafflement is the default position in all the books: "Repeat" (*P* 204), says Lynch, not understanding the difference between pity and terror. "It skills not" (*U* 15.129), says Lynch again, unable to recognize Stephen's gestures for bread and wine. At the end of *Finnegans Wake*, Anna Livia speaks for her maker: "A hundred cares, a tithe of troubles and is there one who understands me?" (*FW* 627.14–15). At his wits' end in "Circe," Bloom speaks for his reader: "When will I hear the joke?" (*U* 15.3831). Finishing his limerick, Lenehan speaks for everyone in the room: "*I can't see the Joe Miller. Can you?*" (*U* 7.582). Think of a puzzled dog, hair and tail upright, nose to the wind. That is you.

Over the course of your reading experience, Joyce will leave clues for you to find your way. In the olfactory extravaganza that is *Ulysses*, he will provide bloody clouts for you to sniff, perfumed handkerchiefs, burned kidneys, lemon soap, soiled letters, and personal linen turned to the light for better viewing.[2] You begin, technically speaking, at fault. Joyce knows this: as Bloom tracks Stephen on a "Wildgoose chase" through Nighttown, just before feeding the dog in the street, he suddenly "*stops, at fault*" (*U* 15.635, 632–33). Strangely enough, there is a second reference to this unusual phrase in "Circe," and again in a canine context: the pack of bloodhounds chasing Bloom in "The Hue and Cry" are "*picking up the scent, nearer, baying, panting, at fault, breaking away*" (*U* 15.4330–31). "At fault," it turns out, is a term taken from fox hunting: to be "at fault," according to the OED, is to "overrun the line of scent owing to its irregularity or failure."[3] This is how Shakespeare used the term in "Venus and Adonis" in 1593: the "hounds [...] have singled [...] the cold fault cleanly out."[4] Only later in the seventeenth century did the term migrate from dogs to people, and come to mean "puzzled": "We are [...] at a fault," says the Reverend Wotton in 1626, "in the Hunter's term."[5] So Bloom is at fault in "Circe" not because he is guilty *but because he has lost his way*. Stephen is equally at fault in "Nestor" when he lets the fox of his riddle escape: his puzzled students have reached a "disappointed bridge" (*U* 2.39). The characters lose the scent: this is what it means to be "at fault." When Gerty MacDowell waves her handkerchief in Bloom's direction she is literally putting him back on the scent. One of the lovely things about the phrase "at fault," then, is that it doesn't mean "in fault" in the way we commonly take it to mean. "At fault" is incorrectly used in its common meaning of "having failed," for which "in fault" should be more properly used.[6] All of us have lost the scent.

What makes *Ulysses* such a maddening and satisfying experience is that the track is yours to find, and yours alone. There are six keys to reading Joyce, one for each sharp in the key of F# major (see figure 9.1 for a demonstration of the cycle of fifths, which will be more relevant later). Father Cowley chooses this dark and rich key for his accompaniment of Ben Dollard's trenchant rendition of "The Croppy Boy": "What key? Six sharps?" (*U* 11.996). First, you must understand the importance of transubstantiation: the Catholic Mass is Key #1. Second, you must understand the importance of history: Parnell and Home Rule is Key #2. Third, you must understand the importance of music: "When First I Saw," the principal song in "Sirens," is Key #3. Fourth, you must understand the importance of riddles: the Man in the Macintosh is Key #4. Fifth, you must understand the importance of character: Bloom's vision of Rudy is Key #5. Sixth, you must find the key that locks the door that only you can open. You are Key #6.

The sixth key, in my case, took a long time to find. It is error. By which I do not mean the intentional errors that are so deftly delineated in Tim Conley's *Joyces Mistakes*, or the transcription errors that Roy Gottfried catches so cleanly in *Joyce's Iritis and the Irritated Text*. Neither do I refer to my own delight in anachronisms and genetic manipulations recorded in *The Dublin Helix*. This book is more interested in the phrase that has been beautifully misread in Joyce's work: the question of being "at fault." Fritz Senn, says Matthew Creasy in his introduction to *Errears and Erroriboose*, "presents error as a universal failing, common to humanity" (Creasy 16). For Joyce and for all of us this is exactly right, though error is not merely, as Creasy suggests in the same essay, a means by which "unreliable characters evade their responsibilities and draw others into their misdemeanours" (Creasy 21). To be "human, erring and condonable" (*FW* 58.19), as HCE is at the moment of his trial in I.4 of *Finnegans Wake*, is not just to be condoned. It is to be already forgiven.

Guilt, betrayal, and mercy are the black, red, and white threads that weave themselves through the web of Joyce's writing. James Frazer, in "Farewell to Nemi," the final chapter of *The Golden Bough*, speaks of human thought as a "web woven of three different threads—the black thread of magic, the red thread of religion, and the white thread of science" (Frazer 855). Guilt is to mercy as black is to white, but betrayal is Joyce's religion.[7] The voice of Saint Peter is heard in the thrice-repeated denial at the bazaar in "Araby" ("O, I never said such a thing! [. . .] O, but I didn't! [. . .] O, there's a . . . fib!"—*D* 27). A wife's betrayal drives the plot in *Ulysses* and *Exiles*, and *Finnegans Wake* is riddled with Wagner's epic of betrayal, *Tristan and Isolde*. In that opera, a crucial subtext for the post-*Ulysses* Joyce, Isolde is betrayed twice by Tristan (killing her lover Morold, leading her to King Mark), the love potion betrays both lovers (it is not a healing potion, as he believes, or a death potion, as she believes), Tristan is betrayed by his trusted friend Melot (who leads King Mark to the place of the lovers' tryst), and the language of betrayal applies in the finest detail: when Tristan drains the poisoned cup Isolde cries "Betrug auch hier? / Mein die Hälfte!" [Betrayed even here? Give me my half!] (Wagner 56). King Mark himself, whose presence in *Finnegans Wake* is nearly as ubiquitous as that of Tristan or Isolde, has an extraordinary aria to betrayal that speaks of disloyalty as a poison (or "Gift") destroying his brain: "Dort mit der Waffe / quälendem Gift, / das Sinn und Hirn / mir sengend versehrt" [There with your weapon's tormenting poison, you have scotched and disabled my senses and my brain] (Wagner 86). As Finn is betrayed by Grania and King Arthur

("*Arthurgink*") by Guinevere ("*Everguin*"—*FW* 285.L2), "*Muster Mark*" (*FW* 383.01) becomes the *Wake*'s archetypal fallen hero, a broken king.

Robert Spoo has rightly suggested that Joyce is "obsessed with the dialectics of injury and remedy" in all his life and work.[8] The execution of "law and mercy" is Joyce's greatest role:

> WILLIAM, ARCHBISHOP OF ARMAGH
> (*in purple stock and shovel hat*) Will you to your power cause law and mercy to be executed in all your judgments in Ireland and territories thereunto belonging?
> BLOOM
> (*placing his right hand on his testicles, swears*) So may the Creator deal with me. All this I promise to do.
> (*U* 15.1479–85)

From the priest in "The Sisters" who has "something gone wrong with him" (*D* 10) to the man in Phoenix Park who may or may not have done something namelessly horrible in *Finnegans Wake*, Joyce's characters are always falling short of the mark. "He was too scrupulous always" (*D* 9) says one of the sisters about Father Flynn; "in my heart I had always despised him a little" (*D* 20), the boy says of Mahony after their encounter with the man in the field. Guilt is general all over Joyce's work, and human frailty is his greatest subject. But, in Joyce, it is more than just the falling. Humpty Dumpty is put back together again; Tim Finnegan rises from his wake. The beauty of Joyce is that through reading him we learn to make mistakes, and through them we learn to forgive ourselves.

"We are a generous people but we must also be just" says Mr. Deasy unjustly, to which Stephen replies "I fear those big words [. . .] which make us so unhappy" (*U* 2.262–64). Deasy is a fraud, Stephen is "not born to be a teacher, I think" (*U* 2.402), Sargent is hopeless at sums, Talbot stumbles over his recitation of "Lycidas" (*U* 2.79), and the boys outside can't even get a hockey game together without fighting: "Cochrane and Halliday are on the same side, sir" (*U* 2.190). That's in "Nestor" alone: outside of the schoolroom, Don Giovanni is sent to hell by the Commendatore, Bloom gets the words of the duet with Zerlina wrong, Lazarus misses his chance to come forth, Charles Stewart Parnell is unforgiven by the Catholic Church, for which the Catholic Church can never be forgiven by Mr. Casey, Icarus flies too close to the sun, and Mr. Duffy casts Mrs. Sinico from his mind after reading of her death, "his moral nature falling to pieces" (*D* 113).[9] All the characters in the Joycean universe are in the dock.

Stephen must "Kneel" before the prefect for his accidentally broken glasses (*P* 51), Bob Doran must marry the girl at the boarding house because her mother deals with "moral problems as a cleaver deals with meat" (*D* 58). The Mob in "Circe" calls for Bloom to be lynched and roasted, to which Bloom excitedly responds, "This is midsummer madness, some ghastly joke again. By heaven, I am guiltless as the unsunned snow!" (*U* 15.1768–69). And so he is, and so are all of us. This, the appreciation of human error, is the sixth key, the darkest key, F$^{\sharp}$ major. It is, again, the key of "The Croppy Boy," the song that will hold our attention in chapter 1: "Six sharps?" (*U* 11.996), says Father Cowley. It is this sixth key that allows us to experience *Ulysses* as the work of an outlaw.

When Joyce recorded himself on the gramophone in 1924, on equipment borrowed by Sylvia Beach from His Master's Voice, he chose a curious section to read. In "Aeolus," the *ponderous pundit* Professor MacHugh (*U* 7.578) delivers himself of a lengthy speech to a rapt audience in the newspaper office, ending with the following peroration:

> —*But, ladies and gentlemen, had the youthful Moses listened to and accepted that view of life, had he bowed his head and bowed his will and bowed his spirit before that arrogant admonition he would never have brought the chosen people out of their house of bondage, nor followed the pillar of the cloud by day. He would never have spoken with the Eternal amid lightnings on Sinai's mountaintop nor ever have come down with the light of inspiration shining in his countenance and bearing in his arms the tables of the law, graven in the language of the outlaw.* (*U* 7.862–69)

On Joyce's recording, the final beats (*"graven in the language of the outlaw"*) are declaimed with extraordinary relish. This is a text that has been twice "graven": once in the manner of an engraving, as a recording is engraved, and once as a text coming from beyond the grave. John F. Taylor's speech on the revival of the Irish tongue, which MacHugh quotes from memory, is both positive, as an example of fine diction from a bygone age, and negative, since Taylor died, as Moses did, without entering the land of promise: an engraving also has that dual distinction. It's curiously predictable, too, that Joyce mangles the text in several places on the recording, underscoring his delight in accident in all things. Joyce reads "*never have* led *the chosen people*" instead of "*never have brought*," and omits "*amid lightnings*" (Dachy): neither variation appears in any earlier version of the text. Though the tables of the Ten Commandments may be engraved in stone, there is nothing fixed about *Ulysses*, and as for *Finnegans*

Wake, there is always the sense that the text before us is only an approximation of what Joyce had in mind.

There are in fact only two recordings of Joyce's voice: the speech in praise of Moses from "Aeolus," made at Sylvia Beach's urging in 1924, and the end of "Anna Livia Plurabelle," recorded for C. K. Ogden in 1929.[10] These two selections have always had a pleasing complementarity. "Aeolus" takes place inside, during the day, in the company of men discussing language; "Anna Livia" takes place outside, by the River Liffey at dusk, in the company of washerwomen becoming myth. The stentorian tones of the orator in "Aeolus" do not brook compromise: when Joyce declares that Moses bears in his arms *"the tables of the law, graven in the language of the outlaw"* (*U* 7.868–69), nothing is left in doubt. The windy fluting notes of the women in the *Wake* place everything in doubt: the language chitters and flitters to an open close. If MacHugh's divine afflatus has the cadence of a Beethoven overture (*crescendo, marcato*), the washerwomen's descent into darkness is more like Debussy (*decrescendo, calando*). Here are male and female, agency and entropy, order and chaos, and "that's the he and the she of it" (*FW* 213.12).

In both recordings, Joyce allows his customary margin for error: we have seen that the ventriloquizing of MacHugh's rendition of Taylor's great speech is frequently inaccurate, and the *Finnegans Wake* reading (*FW* 213.11–216.05) differs from the printed text in several places, including a stunning drop of the lines "Night! Night!" six lines before the end (*FW* 215.36). Ellmann claims that the light in the recording studio for Joyce's reading at Ogden's Orthological Institute was so bad that he had to be "prompted in a whisper throughout" (*JJ* 617), though if this is true the prompts are undetectable on the recording. What Joyce had in mind on both occasions is made very clear by the readings: both texts are as much aural experiences as visual ones, and to read with the ear, or hear with the eye, is crucial to *Ulysses* and the *Wake*.

The decision to record the end of the "Anna Livia" section of *Finnegans Wake* (I.8) strikes everyone who hears it for the first time as a no-brainer: not only are these pages the most accessible in the text, in terms of narrative line, but they also show off to fullest advantage the importance of being Joyce. To understand *Finnegans Wake* you have to transform yourself into the kind of person who can understand it, and this generally means that it is necessary to become Joyce to the greatest extent that one possibly can. The recording allows us to become Joyce for a spell, to transform ourselves into tree ("Tell me, tell me, tell me, elm!") and stone ("I feel as heavy as yonder stone") as we listen to the play of

Joyce's "hitherandthithering waters" (*FW* 215.36–216.05). The reading is desperately funny ("Oronoko" comes unexpectedly out of a stretch and a yawn—*FW* 214.10), and Joyce plays the sound effects to the hilt, with brilliantly rolled *r*s, the sounds of bells and bats and birds, a nursery lilt, and a gorgeous dying fall. "*It seemed to me that I had been transported,*" as John F. Taylor says on the other occasion (*U* 7.830).

On the other occasion, the decision to engrave MacHugh's ventriloquism of Taylor's speech on the youthful Moses for posterity isn't as immediately obvious, especially to those who may have hoped for something lyrical from "Sirens" or "Penelope." Sylvia Beach writes of arranging for the "Aeolus" recording to be made, and the reasons behind Joyce's selection of the speech, in her memoir *Shakespeare and Company* (Beach 170–71). As Sylvia Beach remembers it, this was the perfect choice. No other section commands its audience so fully, from the opening "*Mr chairman, ladies and gentlemen*" (*U* 7.828) to the ringing declaration at the end. Joyce is always the poet and musician, balancing "*law*" and "*outlaw,*" stressing the final line for all its metrical worth. Above all, the text establishes Joyce as the visionary, coming down like Moses from Mt. Sinai, as the nationalist, speaking passionately through several screens in favor of the Irish language, and as the outlaw. Joyce writes from exile in an outlaw language as he participates in the outlaw creation of a new Irish literature; this, above all, is why his writing takes flight.

2. The Centrifuge

> As he grew accustomed to the great gallery of machines, he began to feel the forty-foot dynamos as a moral force, much as the early Christians felt the Cross. The planet itself seemed less impressive, in its old-fashioned, deliberate, annual or daily revolution, than this huge wheel, revolving within arm's-length at some vertiginous speed, and barely murmuring—scarcely humming an audible warning to stand a hair's-breadth further for respect of power—while it would not wake the baby lying close against its frame. Before the end, one began to pray to it; inherited instinct taught the natural expression of man before silent and infinite force.
>
> (Adams 380)

When Henry Adams visited Paris at the turn of the twentieth century, he heard the hum of a room full of dynamos, and it sounded to him like the future. He found himself "lying in the Gallery of Machines at the Great Exposition of 1900, his historical neck broken by the sudden irruption of forces totally new" (Adams 382). As part of what are habitually his final meditations of the day,

Leopold Bloom imagines "one sole unique advertisement to cause passers to stop in wonder, a poster novelty, with all extraneous accretions excluded, reduced to its simplest and most efficient terms not exceeding the span of casual vision and congruous with the velocity of modern life" (*U* 17.1770–73). This "novelty" is the novel he is in: passers have long stood in wonder at the singular advertisement that is the novel of Bloom and Stephen's day, their historical necks broken by the sudden irruption of forces totally new. Listening closely to the end of *Ulysses*, we may hear much the same thing that Henry Adams experienced in the Paris Exposition Hall: *Ulysses* is a dynamo, hurtling through space at vertiginous speed, barely murmuring, a huge wheel of infinite power. Though it is anything but simple, efficient, or casual, its present does not exceed the timespan of a single day and is congruous with the velocity of modern life. And like the forty-foot dynamos in the Paris gallery, *Ulysses* has a "moral force" (Adams 380).[11]

"Before the end, one began to pray to it" (Adams 380): the moment just before the end is always Joyce's primary focus. Bloom's "final meditations" (*U* 17.1769), in which the image of *Ulysses* appears, are penultimate to those of his wife. Joyce has little interest in exposition: his beginnings are re-beginnings, revolutions. The opening story of *Dubliners*, the first episode of *Ulysses*, the first part of *Finnegans Wake*: all these are less interesting than Gabriel's swoon, Molly's reverie, and Anna Livia's dying into the sea. Joyce's characters reflect and anticipate but rarely begin. "Telemachus" starts the book hesitantly: Buck Mulligan's "*Introibo ad altare Dei*" is thwarted by corporeal resistance ("A little trouble about those white corpuscles"), and we never visit the Martello tower again (*U* 1.05, 22–23). "Begin!" (*U* 11.63) says the conductor as the curtain comes up in "Sirens," but the summons is oddly placed, bracketed within the opening section.[12] "Begin to be forgotten" (*U* 6.872), Bloom thinks as the clay falls on Paddy Dignam's grave. Joyce's dynamo, the velocity of his method, is not a "radiant node or cluster [. . .] from which, and through which, and into which, ideas are constantly rushing" (Pound, *Gaudier-Brzeska* 92). Rather than moving centripetally, as Pound's vortex does, Joyce's method flies outward, turning and turning in a widening spiral, as Yeats' gyres do. It moves, as Adams says of his contemporary St. Gaudens, "beyond all" (Adams 387). It is a centrifuge.

Technically speaking, centrifugal force is an invented, or "fictitious," force that allows for a rotational frame of reference: it accounts for the perception of movement that Newton's laws of motion, which are based on an inertial, or nonmoving, frame of reference, cannot accommodate. It is calculated as

$$F = \frac{r\,\bar{\omega}^2}{g}$$

where F is the Relative Centrifugal Force, r is the radius of the object, $\bar{\omega}$ is the angular velocity and g is our old friend gravity, hurling objects earthward at "Thirtytwo feet per second per second" (U 5.44).[13] Bloom's thoughts in "Lotus-Eaters" on the natural buoyancy of human beings in the Dead Sea ("Couldn't sink if you tried") lead him to a fundamental equation in Joyce's world: "Law of falling bodies: per second per second. They all fall to the ground. The earth. It's the force of gravity of the earth is the weight" (U 5.39, 44–46). In the universe of Joyce's *Ulysses*, which is also governed by fictitious forces, objects can be located only by their relative frame of reference (r), are congruous with the velocity of modern life ($\bar{\omega}$), and are dependent on the law of falling bodies (g). Centrifugal force is radius times velocity squared over gravity:

$$F = \frac{r\,\bar{\omega}^2}{g}$$

What Bloom calls "the velocity of modern life" (U 17.1773) is Henry Adams' principal subject. The celebrated chapter on "The Dynamo and the Virgin," which gives this introduction its subtitle, leads to "A Dynamic Theory of History," which insists on acceleration of motion from equilibrium to "new equilibrium" (Adams 489): both mind and matter are moving as a comet moves, constantly in flight, constantly renewed. According to Henry Cabot Lodge, Adams' editor, in 1918, the original subtitle for *The Education of Henry Adams* was "A Study of Twentieth-Century Multiplicity" (Adams xxi): this is as good a definition of *Ulysses* as any. But Bloom's statement "They all fall to the ground" (U 5.45) is, for Joyce, more than a law of gravity. We are all fallen. "They all fall to the ground" is Gabriel's moment of *anagnorisis*, or recognition, as he hears the snow faintly falling and falling faintly "upon all the living and the dead" (*D* 225). "They all fall to the ground" is the overtone behind Bloom's valediction to "Poor Dignam!" (U 4.551) and the hideous revelation that sticks deep its grinning claws into Stephen's heart: "All must go through it, Stephen. More women than men in the world. You too. Time will come" (U 15.4182–84).[14] Joyce's centrifugal force is based on the law of falling bodies: all human beings are drawn by gravity to fault and error. Without that basic principle, Joyce's world would remain as virginal as Our Lady of Lourdes. With it, the characters in the Joycean universe begin to display their relative rotational force. "First we feel," says

Anna Livia at the end of *Finnegans Wake*, "then we fall" (*FW* 627.11). This is a miraculous line in the context of a book where nothing ever speaks true, where every page is mediated through semantic occlusion, and where no statement ever runs clear. The effect, as John Gordon has said, is axiomatic ("one of the *Wake*'s saddest axioms"—Gordon 142). The fundamental things apply.

Gretta Conroy and Gerty MacDowell are both fallen and feeling women, their frailties on full display. Their respective falls in "The Dead" and "Nausicaa" are instructive, since they take place on separate axes. Gretta Conroy falls in time, losing her innocence retroactively. Her previous relationship with Michael Furey has the cadence of a fairy story—"I am thinking about a person long ago," "It was a young boy I used to know" (*D* 220)—until her past catches up with Gabriel, and he plummets: "A vague terror seized Gabriel at this answer as if, at that hour when he had hoped to triumph, some impalpable and vindictive being was coming against him" (*D* 221). Gerty MacDowell falls in space, leaning back to reveal the arc of her unseen: "His hands and face were working and a tremour went over her. She leaned back far to look up where the fireworks were and she caught her knee in her hands so as not to fall back looking up and there was no-one to see only him and her" (*U* 13.694–98). The two Eves fall before their respective Adams: Gabriel discovers at the Gresham Hotel that he is no longer Gretta's First Man, and Leopold writes "I. [...] AM. A" (*U* 13.1258–64) in the sand with his stick. "A" stands for Adam, Aleph, and Alpha: on the same beach earlier in the day Stephen says "Put me on to Edenville. Aleph, alpha: nought, nought, one" (*U* 3.39–40). The dynamic force of each woman's fall from grace sends Gabriel Conroy and Leopold Bloom on a trajectory outward: they are nought, or "naught," cast out from Edenville. For Gabriel at the Gresham, "The time had come for him to set out on his journey westward" (*D* 225). For Bloom on the beach, it is time to push on: "Better not stick here all night like a limpet" (*U* 13.1211).

Centrifugal motion is an outward vector: Bloom knows that "at the termination of any allotted life only an infinitesimal part of any person's desires has been realised" (*U* 17.1761–62). Bloom's florin in "Ithaca," sent into the world for "possible, circuitous or direct, return" (*U* 17.984), has yet to reappear. This particular coin is worth a closer look: it was marked "in the summer of 1898" (*U* 17.980), and so has a portrait of Queen Victoria on the obverse side. The florin that Reuben J. Dodd paid the boatman for his son ("One and eightpence too much"—*U* 6.291), on the other hand, was likely to have been minted in the reign of Edward VII (1901–1910): if so, it was designed by George de Saulles and is famous among numismatists for its reverse side, with its device of Britannia gazing out to sea (Mackay 160). I have one from 1903 in front of me as I write, purchased at Spink's in Southampton Row for forty pounds. Allow me to describe it further. Britannia, statuesque in plumed helmet, is holding an aegis, or shield, sporting the Union Jack. In her right hand, she holds a trident in tribute to Poseidon: both Athena's plume and Poseidon's trident pierce the lettered edge that bears the legend "One Florin Two Shillings." Britannia is wearing a shimmering cloak that artfully fails to conceal the twin apples of her bosom, clearly shown in relief. Her cloak is carried seaward by a wind that blows from right to left, so that it *"simply swirls,"* like Milly Bloom's "pale blue scarf loose in the wind" (*U* 4.438, 435–36): Britannia is one of Boylan's "seaside girls" (*U* 4.282). The device on the reverse also includes a poop deck that displays the coin's date, behind which is the flat horizon of the sea, revealing within its waters a curved indication of what Bloom would call "nice waves" (*U* 11.300). The coin's liquidity, in Joyce's double sense of its "circulation on the waters of civic finance" (*U* 17.983–84), is represented by the waves of the sea before which Britannia stands. A more Joycean artifact, then, could scarcely be imagined.

The florin never finds its way back to Bloom's pocket, despite the "three notches on the milled edge" (*U* 17.981). The coin does return for us, as readers, and this is an important distinction. We may connect it to other two-shilling pieces in the Joycean canon, but the characters do not. In addition to the cost of Reuben J. Dodd's son, a florin is the payment for the morning's milk at the Martello tower ("We'll owe twopence"—*U* 1.458), the price of Bloom at auction in "Circe" ("A BIDDER / A florin"—*U* 15.3092–93), and the coin that the boy in "Araby" holds tightly in his hand as he makes his way to the bazaar train (*D* 26).[15] While the return of the florin is there for the Joycean reader to discover, for the Joycean characters all movement is relentlessly outward. For the readers of "Ithaca," circularity is permitted: we are invited to recapitulate the episodes of Bloom's day as rituals in the Jewish calendar (*U* 17.2043–58) or to compile the budget for 16 June 1904 (*U* 17.1455), and the resulting equations are as satisfactory as a circulating florin or the paternity of a particoloured clown (*U* 17.977). For the characters in "Ithaca," however, equanimity is hard-earned and near-achieved. "Ithaca" provides an ending for neither man nor woman: Stephen respectfully declines the invitation to stay (*U* 17.955), Bloom recognizes that the damage that Boylan has done is "irreparable" (*U* 17.2194), Milly has thrown her hat at a young student (*U* 4.399, 14.758), and Molly's soliloquy is about to take flight.

The movement through *Dubliners, Portrait, Ulysses,* and *Finnegans Wake* is centripetal for Joyce's readers, folding in on itself as the connections come clear. But for the characters—the boy in "Araby," the husband in "The Dead," the young artist in *Portrait,* the two companions drinking cocoa at the end of a long day in "Ithaca," Anna Livia at the end of the *Wake*—all movement is centrifugal. The clown in quest of paternity is not Bloom's son, and the florin never returns. Stephen plays *"the series of empty fifths"* (*U* 15.2073) on Bella Cohen's pianola, a sequence that arches out to the end of the world: "What went forth to the ends of the world to traverse not itself, God, the sun, Shakespeare, a commercial traveller, having itself traversed in reality itself becomes that self" (*U* 15.2117–19). (The fact that the cycle ends where it begins will be taken up in chapter 9.) The Odyssean journey is a movement from being to becoming: the self develops into that "which it itself was ineluctably preconditioned to become" (*U* 15.2120–21). Though the stuck flies copulate on the window pane at Davy Byrne's, piniment the past to the present, Bloom can never go back to his old self: "Me. And me now. / Stuck, the flies buzzed" (*U* 8.917–18). One of the commercial advantages of a modern centrifuge is that it can be used to separate isotopes: the twin isotopes of Bloom's former and present selves have similarly broken apart ("Or was that I? Or am I now I?"—*U* 8.608). Stephen has undergone an identical process: "I am other I now. Other I got pound" (*U* 9.205–06).

Shaking hands in farewell at the doorway of #7 Eccles Street, Bloom is the "centripetal remainer" and Stephen the "centrifugal departer" (*U* 17.1214). Their "(respectively) centrifugal and centripetal hands" form a "tangent," or the line through a pair of infinitely close points on a curve (*U* 17.1225, 1224). In Bloom's reflections, Molly's most recent suitor is "neither first nor last nor only nor alone in a series originating in and repeated to infinity" (*U* 17.2130–31), a series that continues "to no last term" (*U* 17.2142). Even at rest, the Blooms are moving forward:

In what state of rest or motion?

At rest relatively to themselves and to each other. In motion being each and both carried westward, forward and rereward respectively, by the proper perpetual motion of the earth through everchanging tracks of neverchanging space.

(*U* 17.2306–10)

Though the Blooms are at rest "relatively to themselves and to each other," they are carried "westward," as Gabriel Conroy, also in bed with his wife, travels westward in his mind at the end of "The Dead" (*D* 225). The "everchanging tracks" of the Earth's movement in "neverchanging space" provide precisely the rotational frame of reference in which a centrifugal force can be detected: what appears to be an inertial state is in fact an outward motion relative to the Earth's velocity.

Since the Blooms are at rest, the Coriolis force, which refers to bodies themselves in motion relative to a rotational frame, is not in effect as they fly through space. Both the Coriolis force and the centrifugal force are "fictitious forces," in that they are only perceived rather than real: we don't actually move forward when an airplane accelerates on takeoff, it just feels as though we do. Truth then exists in relation to perception, a principle that holds throughout all of *Ulysses* (see especially the separate vignettes of "Wandering Rocks," where every character is both perceiver and perceived). The earth rotates from West to East, and so the Blooms' motion, "each and both carried westward," is retrograde. Their journey westward is a journey ⍵est⍵ard, or subject to a squared velocity given as omega (ω^2), they are carried forward (*F*) and rereward (*r*), subject to the forces of Gea-Tellus (*g*). The black dot that closes "Ithaca" (*U* 17.2332), inked carefully according to Joyce's precise instructions, is essentially a forty-foot dynamo.[16] If you put your ear up close to it, as Henry Adams did in Paris three years before Stephen got there, you may be able to hear it spinning.[17] A "silent and infinite force" (Adams 380), it fails to wake the weary traveler, Leopold Bloom, sleeping like a baby against its frame. Molly Bloom, the woman who shares a birthday with the Blessed Virgin, is about to speak.

The clearest example of centrifugal force, and the one that everybody remembers from science class, is the effect of the earth's rotation on the shape of the earth: the centrifugal forces bulge at the equator where the radius is largest to form an oblate spheroid. Stephen knows this, even in his cups: walking (barely) upright "upon this oblate orange" he finds that his "centre of gravity is displaced" (*U* 15.4427, 4433). It is this professorial remark that Biddy the Clap and Cunty Kate applaud as having been delivered with "marked refinement" and "apposite trenchancy" (*U* 15.4444, 4446). "You should see him," Mulligan says, "when his body loses its balance. Wandering Aengus I call him" (*U* 10.1066–67); soon after displacing his center of gravity in his encounter with Private Carr, he falls to the ground, murmuring elliptically from a different Yeats poem that itself spirals outward to the "dishevelled wandering stars."[18]

In Joyce's notes to "Ithaca" there is a reference to the mathematicians "Lo-batschewsky" and "Riemann" (*JJA* 12:84), both references, according to Ciaran McMorran, originating from Joyce's reading of "Non-Euclidean Geometries" in Henri Poincaré's *Science and Hypothesis* (McMorran 23).[19] The note is transcribed by Phillip Herring as follows (Herring, ed., *Notesheets* 474):

Eucl. space no total curvature of spine ([M]illy)
Lobatschewsky   const. tot. curv. neg
Riemann   "   "   "   pos.

"Milly" is possibly a misreading for "Dilly" here, since Dilly Dedalus is the child with a posture problem in "Wandering Rocks": "Stand up straight, girl, he said. You'll get curvature of the spine" (*U* 10.662).[20] "[C]onst. tot. curv." stands for "constant total curvature," which can be either convex or concave. Negative curvature, which Joyce associates with the Russian mathematician Nikolai Lobachevsky, is hyperbolic or convex; positive curvature, which Joyce associates with the German geometrician Bernhard Riemann, is elliptical or concave. On another page of the "Ithaca" notesheets, we find the words "concave convex" just above "curvilinear," with "curvilinear" crossed out in blue crayon (Herring, ed., *Notesheets* 449, *JJA* 12:76). This concatenation of non-Euclidean terms can be traced forward to the printed text via the "curvilinear rope" beneath the "five coiled spring housebells" from which hang the "four smallsize square handkerchiefs" and the "three erect wooden pegs" between "two holdfasts" clamping "one pair of ladies' grey hose" (*U* 17.150–55). Five housebells, four handkerchiefs, three wooden pegs, two holdfasts, one pair of hose: there is a partridge, or a Poincaré, in this pear tree. Henri Poincaré, the source of Joyce's non-Euclidean mathematics, is concealed in the final dot of "Ithaca": in the 1922 edition of *Ulysses* the dot is square, or a "*point carré*" (McMorran 23).[21]

There is no evidence in the manuscripts or typescripts that Joyce ever intended the final dot of "Ithaca" to be square: he draws a circular dot in the placards (*JJA* 21:140) and calls for a "point [. . .] plus visible" in the page proofs (*JJA* 27:212) without specifying what would otherwise be an unusual shape. Nevertheless, the fact that it appears as a square dot in the 1922 edition (*U-22* 689) nicely lines up with the "square round" egg laid in the text just before the dot's appearance (*U* 17.2328) and with Bloom's thoughts of attempting to "square the circle," as Virag remembers in "Circe" (*U* 15.2401). Christine van Boheemen-Saaf, in *Joyce, Derrida, Lacan, and the Trauma of History*, speaks of the "large round/square dot" and the "squared-circular mark" (van Boheemen-Saaf 156), but that is mostly because the ambiguity amplifies her argument for the dot's double function. Though Joyce's Jesuit curriculum would never have permitted the discussion of non-Euclidean space (see Bradley 106), there are "ellipsoidal balls" in *A Portrait of the Artist as a Young Man* (*P* 192), and a mathematician who takes the Poincaré line, "projecting long slender fabrics from plane to plane of ever rarer and paler twilight, radiating swift eddies to the last verges of a universe ever vaster, farther and more impalpable" (*P* 191). Right from the start, Stephen Dedalus' world is vertiginously expansive:

> *Stephen Dedalus*
> *Class of Elements*
> *Clongowes Wood College*
> *Sallins*
> *County Kildare*
> *Ireland*
> *Europe*
> *The World*
> *The Universe*
> (*P* 15–16)

Putting Poincaré aside, the outward vectors of narrative movement in *Ulysses*, from the headlines in "Aeolus" to the interpolations in "Cyclops," from the trembling extension of Gerty MacDowell's straining back in "Nausicaa" to the increasing elliptical rings of "Oxen of the Sun," are Joyce's best indications of his centrifugal impulse. What begins as "compression, intensity" in Ezra Pound's evaluation of the first episodes in the *Little Review* becomes an unmoored object moving with such velocity that it can no longer be captured in an inertial frame.[22] After the fireworks display in "Nausicaa," Bloom's thoughts form a scattergram:

> O sweety all your little girlwhite up I saw dirty bracegirdle made me do love sticky we two naughty Grace darling she him half past the bed met him pike hoses frillies for Raoul de perfume your wife black hair heave under embon *señorita* young eyes Mulvey plump bubs me breadvan Winkle red slippers she rusty sleep wander years of dreams return tail end Agendath swoony lovey showed me her next year in drawers return next in her next her next.
> (*U* 13.1279–85)

Joyce mechanically thickens this paragraph as he writes, tying Gerty to Molly ("met him pike hoses"), Martha Clifford ("perfume your wife"), Mat Dillon ("breadvan Winkle"), *Sweets of Sin* ("frillies for Raoul"), William Wordsworth ("Grace darling"), Anne Bracegirdle ("dirty bracegirdle"), the Rock of Gibraltar ("*señorita* young eyes Mulvey"), and Jerusalem ("next year in drawers"). All these new vectors are added in the original manuscript to send the book flying in all directions (Rosenbach P364 L497–98 N381–82, *JJA* 13:242). Mairy has "lost the pin" of her drawers (*U* 13.803), and the text explodes like a grenade.

Some fragments of these ruminations we can trace: "next year in drawers" takes us to "Next year in Jerusalem" (*U* 7.207), as Rudolph Virag used to say, reading backward with his finger. The final fragment, "next her next," goes backward to Lessing's "*Nacheinander*" (*U* 3.13) and forward to Stephen's "Proparoxyton. Moment before the next, Lessing says" (*U* 15.3609). "Proparoxyton" refers to a stress on the antepenultimate syllable, as in the word "photography"; *Ulysses* is one great parable of the penultimate, a Pisgah sight of Palestine.[23] Stephen tells us so: "I call it *A Pisgah Sight of Palestine* or *The Parable of the Plums*" (*U* 7.1057–58). History may move to "one great goal" (*U* 2.381), as Garrett Deasy claims, but in Joyce, as for Moses on Mt. Pisgah, the goal is never reached. Mr. Deasy is wrong, then, not because history is a recurring nightmare, as Stephen suggests in the same conversation (*U* 2.377), but because an arrow never reaches its target, as Joyce everywhere insists. Return is impossible, from the very beginning: "Home also I cannot go" (*U* 1.740). Plumtree's incompleteness theorem, the inability for a character to reach resolution, is a fundamental principle in Joyce's works: "What is home without Plumtree's Potted Meat? / Incomplete" (*U* 17.597–98).[24] Joyce's position is always "Preparatory to anything else" (*U* 16.01).

A centrifuge is a detachment from magnetic force: "Better detach," Bloom thinks as he wonders about Molly's "magnetic influence" on his wristwatch in "Nausicaa" (*U* 13.980, 984–85). The final firework that concludes the display on Sandymount Strand falls haphazardly out of view, a monkey puzzle rocket disappearing beyond the curve of the rocks, "spluttering in darting crackles. Zrads and zrads, zrads, zrads" (*U* 13.933–34). Cissy Caffrey throws the ball along the sand and Tommy runs after it "in full career" (*U* 13.255). Gerty leans back watching the long Roman candle going up over the trees to beyond the point of no return: "he had a full view high up above her knee where no-one ever not even on the swing [...]" (*U* 13.728–29). All these are physical representations of the omega velocity of escaping force (ω), as is the "biscuitbox" that hurtles "through the atmosphere at a terrifying velocity" at Bloom's head at the end of "Cyclops" (*U* 12.1880–81).

The exploding text at the end of "Nausicaa" sends a further fragment forward with "next year in drawers" (*U* 13.1284), which refers not only to Virag's hopes for a sight of Jerusalem and to the drawers of which Mairy has lost her pin, but also to a set of child's drawings in a later drawer. "What did the first drawer unlocked contain?" (*U* 17.1774), asks the catechist in "Ithaca," and reveals in that drawer a collection of "diagram drawings" done by Papli's daughter (*U* 17.1776). Out of Bloom's drawer in Eccles Street tumbles yet another metaphor for *Ulysses* itself: a prophecy of Home Rule, pen nibs from Hely's, a Jewish Christmas card, a reverse letter cipher following the path of an ox in a field, erotic postcards, a penny stamp, a magnifying glass, a prospectus for The Wonderworker, and an hourglass "which rolled containing sand which rolled" (*U* 17.1787). Space (the sand on which Bloom writes his message) rolls in time (the hourglass in the unlocked drawer). The container contains the container that contains the thing contained, and all move through everchanging tracks of neverchanging space. It is no accident that Bloom opens the drawer immediately following his reflections on a "poster novelty [...] not exceeding the span of casual vision and congruous with the velocity of modern life" (*U* 17.1771–73). As we look closely at the objects in Bloom's drawer, at the florin that circulates through Dublin, at the other manifestations of the detritus of time placed as carefully throughout *Ulysses* as Stephen's ball of snot on a ledge of rock on Sandymount Strand (*U* 3.500), we come to an understanding of modernist memory. Memory is an hourglass that rolls, containing sand that rolls.

"These fragments I have shored" (*TWL* 146), says Eliot in his most centrifugal work; Leopold Bloom's meditations on utopia in "Ithaca" similarly allow him to put his "lands in order" (*TWL* 146). Bloom's wandering thoughts lead him to the unlikely prospect of the discovery of an object of unexpected monetary value, such as a precious stone, an antique dynastical ring, or three rare postage stamps (*U* 17.1679–83). The postage stamps, which we will examine more closely in chapter 2, are windows to an infinite world. Bloom is a philatelist, like his father-in-law before him: his schemes carry forward. He stands, so to speak, "with an unposted letter bearing the extra regulation fee before the too late box of the general postoffice of human life" (*U* 15.2778–80). "Philately" is, etymologically speaking, the love of being exempt from the obligation to come to a close (see chapter 2). Joyce's texts are philatelic in that they actively resist the *telos*. The desire to communicate imperfectly, to express desire to no fixed point, has always been with Joyce. The very first letter in the *Collected Letters*, from the Prefect at Clongowes Wood College to Joyce's mother on 9 March 1890, refers to another even earlier letter that the eight-year-old Joyce intended to send to his mother but apparently never reached its destination:

> My dear Mrs Joyce   Jim is getting a formidable letter into shape for you—if he has not already sent it. I attacked him, on getting your letter, for his silence. He met me by saying that he had written but *had not given the letter to be posted.*
>
> (*Letters* II:6, italics in original)

The promised letter is in the post: all of Joyce's writing, from the first to the last, is a sending forward.

Joyce's texts move in spirals; they repel perfection, rejoicing in that which is not fixed, refusing to end. This is true of *Dubliners*, which swoons and fades with Gabriel Conroy into a new gray and impalpable world, of *A Portrait of the Artist as a Young Man*, which goes to encounter reality of experience "for the millionth time" (*P* 253), and of *Ulysses*, which refuses the reader the satisfaction of a reconciliation between substitute father and substitute son, presenting a day of births and funerals in which nothing is settled and nothing resolved. The final words of *Ulysses*, "Trieste-Zurich-Paris / 1914–1921" (*U* 18.1610–11), trace the contrails of a man in flight in space and time, hurtling away from Dublin and 1904. As Stephen would say, Joyce has flown by those nets (*P* 203), and no text oscillates more wildly than *Portrait*, which bears Stephen's "weary mind outward to its verge and inward to its centre, a distant music accompanying him outward and inward" (*P* 103). The most pivotal departure in the Joycean canon, Stephen's diary entry at the close of *Portrait*, is a forgery: "to forge in the smithy of my soul the uncreated conscience of my race" (*P* 253). The margin of experience moves "for ever and for ever" for Stephen and Bloom. Ulysses, in Tennyson's "Ulysses," best explains the philatelic principle of Joyce's *Ulysses*:

> Yet all experience is an arch wherethrough
> Gleams that untravelled world, whose margin fades

For ever and for ever when I move.
How dull it is to pause, to make an end [...]!

(Tennyson 563)

Joyce's "Work in Progress," the working title for *Finnegans Wake*, is disposi-
tive in this regard. When St. Kevin determines the appropriate location for
his baptism, he sits in a bathtub in a water hole in a hut on an island in a lake
in Glendalough, "rafted centripetally" into a space that is its own "ventrifugal
principality" (*FW* 605.15, 17):

> on this one of eithers lone navigable lake piously Kevin, lawding the tri-
> une trishagion, amidships of his conducible altar super bath, rafted cen-
> tripetally, diaconal servent of orders hibernian, midway across the sub-
> ject lake surface to its supreem epicentric lake Ysle, whereof its lake is
> the ventrifugal principality, whereon by prime, powerful in knowledge,
> Kevin came to where its centre is among the circumfluent watercourses
> of Yshgafiena and Yshgafiuna, an enysled lakelet yslanding a lacustrine
> yslet, [....]

(*FW* 605.13–20)

Finnegans Wake is that "ventrifugal principality": the first explorer in these parts
is "The first exploder [...] in these parks" and Esau of Mesopotamia is "Essav
of Messagepostumia" (*FW* 606.23–24, 607.08–09). To explore is to explode;
the message is always "aposteriorious" (*FW* 83.11). Where "Ithaca" counts down
to zero, *Finnegans Wake* multiplies to infinity: "Wins won is nought, twigs too is
nil, tricks trees makes nix, fairs fears stoops at nothing" (*FW* 361.01–03).

What *At Fault* proposes to do is to rediscover the scent that Joyce has laid
down for us, track this philatelic gesture in Joyce, and examine the centrifugal
impulse in all his work. "Structurally, Joyce's works are like a pool," says Phillip Herring in *Joyce's Uncertainty Principle*, "a tossed stone sends ever-widening
circles that only stop at the shore's edge" (Herring, *Uncertainty* 180); Suzette
Henke speaks of "Telemachus" in terms of "widening circles" (Henke 4).[25] In
the notesheets for "Oxen of the Sun," Joyce famously sketched a diagram of
an ever-widening universe, where the history of English language and the development of human life are arranged in ever-increasing elliptical rings, each
corresponding to a month of gestation in the womb:

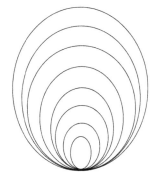

Figure 0.1. Joyce's ever-widening universe. Notesheets to "Oxen of the Sun": British Library Add. MS 49975 Folio 11r (*JJA* 12:23). Reconstruction by author.

These nine months are reciphered in the notesheets to "Ithaca":

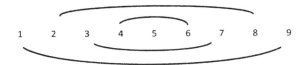

Figure 0.2. Numerical diagram. Notesheets to "Ithaca": British Library Add. MS 49975 Folio 25r (*JJA* 12:76). Reconstruction by author.

Immediately below this curious diagram, we find an invitation to take Joyce to the mathematical limit:

$$1 = \frac{1}{2} + \frac{1}{4} + \frac{1}{8} + \frac{1}{16} \sim \infty$$

Figure 0.3. Limit equation. Notesheets to "Ithaca": British Library Add. MS 49975 Folio 25r (*JJA* 12:76). Reconstruction by author.

We are all "at fault," and so must find our way. *At Fault* happily hunts through the Joycean universe for unexpected discoveries, from readings of fox hunting in "Circe" to the history of Jumbo the Elephant in "Cyclops" to readings of solfège in *Finnegans Wake*. Though Joyce is "dead nuts" on the retrospective arrangement as a theme (*U* 6.149), as Mr. Power says of Tom Kernan, his method is always and everywhere one that moves away from safety, toward error, beyond the nets of expectation. Though "Ithaca" is the home target, though "riverrun" (*FW* 3.01) is a beginning and an end, though the overarching theme of reincarnation and return is omnipresent in *Ulysses*, the vectors of Joyce's method point outward. That is the counterintuitive premise of this book. On one side of the equation, there is pattern, order, and the Logos: Wallace Stevens' "The Idea of Order at Key West" is the modernist exemplar of that approach, with its "rage for order," "Arranging, deepening, enchanting night" (Stevens 130). On the other side of the equals sign, there is randomness, chaos, and doubt: Stevens again provides modernism's finest example, with the ambiguous undulations of casual pigeons in "Sunday Morning" moving "Downward to darkness, on extended wings" (Stevens 70). The former approach was the subject of *The Dublin Helix*, my earlier and more closely patterned book, which presented the two strands of life and language in parallel. The latter approach is the subject of the present volume. My earlier reading imagined Joyce as a puzzle book, with each piece falling neatly into place. Now I see only the fall. In "The Dynamo and the Virgin," Henry Adams writes of the Great Exposition that he "haunted it, aching to absorb knowledge, and helpless to find it" (Adams 379). "He would have liked to know how much of it could have been grasped," he says, describing the sensation as "meditating chaos" (Adams 379). Like Henry Adams at the Paris Exposition, the author of this volume is "meditating chaos," and has reached a turning point in his thinking about Joyce and his relevance to our world. The dynamo has become a centrifuge; the virgin is now an outlaw.

Chapter 1, "At Fault: What Joyce Can Teach Us about the Crisis of the Modern University," takes us to the necessity of an institutional appreciation of error. A university must be a centrifuge: it is the job of higher education to take students out of themselves, to embrace risk, to search, as Emerson says, "for the extra."[26] Joyce points the way out of our current crisis of conformity. In chapter 2, "Philatelic Joyce," we start on the path, following Joyce's propensity for moving ever outward, his love of the absence of the *telos*. In chapter 3, "*Finnegans Wake* for Dummies," a way to open that hermetic text is suggested through a spiraled reading that maps Joyce's process of composition and follows the suggestion of Constantin Brâncuși in his "Symbol of Joyce":

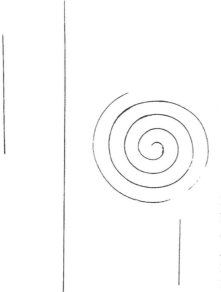

Figure 0.4. Constantin Brâncuși, "Symbol of Joyce." Digital image © Museum of Modern Art / Licensed by SCALA / Art Resource, New York. © Succession Brâncuși. All rights reserved, Artists Rights Society [ARS] 2017.

On the right side of figure 0.4 is an Archimedean spiral (see Israel 25); on the left, Euclid's parallel lines moving to infinity. Brâncuși's brilliant combination of the rock and the whirlpool is as good a way of entering the world of Joyce as any. In chapter 4, "The True Story of Jumbo the Elephant," we follow a trail from the wilds of Africa to a railway line near St. Thomas, Ontario: a reading of carnival elements in "Cyclops" developing from a single line in the text establishes that P. T. Barnum's elephant represents the excesses of empire and returns the reader to the fundamental levity of human nature as a principle of Joycean engagement. In chapter 5, "Death by Gramophone," we follow the path in another direction, and a wide-ranging study of the modernist fear of recording technology eventually settles on the tip of a gramophone needle. In chapter 6, "Siren Songs," all the songs in "Sirens" are exhumed from Joyce's text, forgotten to all but nineteenth-century-Irish-ballad enthusiasts, lost objects that have acquired the fourth dimension of time. In chapter 7, "Seeing the Joe Miller," the range of the hunt is still wider: Joyce's sense of humor is read through the catalogue provided by *Joe Miller's Jests*, and an analysis is provided of the neurological process of humor detection in the brain. In chapter 8, "Performing Issy," an outlaw reading of the "Night Lessons" chapter of *Finnegans Wake* pursues the elaborate conceit that the Earwickers' youngest child is announcing a baseball game between the Boston Red Sox and the Brooklyn Dodgers, taking *At Fault* as far from its point of origin as it can possibly go. The book then closes with a series of separate openings, each written to set off the work of another Joycean as she or he embarks on his or her own journey through the work of the master wanderer and adventurer.

This is a book that celebrates openness and engagement, and is everywhere concerned with Joyce's comic principles of empathy and delight. The words of the final chapter are offered as an invitation to further reading in Joyce, "the happy huntingground of all minds that have lost their balance" (*U* 10.1061–62). I have had the great good fortune to be the editor of the Florida James Joyce Series since Zack Bowen stepped down in 2004, and the job of an editor is to introduce things. Each foreword included in the conclusion is an image of something that Lucinda Leplastrier, one of the two title characters in Peter Carey's magical novel *Oscar and Lucinda*, would identify as a Prince Rupert drop. The Prince Rupert drop is "a solid teardrop of glass no more than two inches from head to tail" (Peter Carey 108); its salient feature is that it is both indestructible and immediately subject to collapse. A fourteen-pound sledgehammer will not break it, but, as Lucinda discovers to her delight, if you nip off the tail with a pair of blunt-nosed pliers, the whole thing will explode. Carey's book, like *Ulysses*, caresses its material objects at every step of the way, and it's worth taking a short detour to nineteenth-century Sydney to share in Lucinda's delight. The glass drop is an exquisitely distilled metaphor for Carey's book, which has a trick ending that snaps the plot in two:

You need not ask me who is Prince Rupert or what is a *batavique* because I do not know. I have, though, right beside me as I write (I hold it in the palm of my left hand while the right hand moves to and fro across the page) a Prince Rupert drop—a solid teardrop of glass no more than two inches from head to tail. And do not worry that this oddity, this rarity, was the basis for de la Bastie's technique for toughening glass, or that it led to the invention of safety glass—these are practical matters and shed no light on the incredible attractiveness of the drop itself which you will understand faster if you take a fourteen-pound sledgehammer and try to smash it on a forge. You cannot. This is glass of the most phenomenal strength and would seem, for a moment, to be the fabled unbreakable

glass described by the alchemical author of *Mappae Clavicula*. And yet if
you put down your hammer and take down your pliers instead—I say "if,"
I am not recommending it—you will soon see that this is not the fabled
glass stone of the alchemists, but something almost as magical. For although it is strong enough to withstand the sledgehammer, the tail can be
nipped with a pair of blunt-nosed pliers. It takes a little effort. And once it
is done it is as if you have taken out the keystone, removed the linchpin,
kicked out the foundations. The whole thing explodes. And where, a moment before, you had unbreakable glass, now you have grains of glass in
every corner of the workshop—in your eyes if you are not careful—and
what is left in your hand you can crumble—it feels like sugar—without
danger.

(Peter Carey 108)

One of the many pleasures of this paragraph is the way the meter follows
the meaning: the text rushes without punctuation to the impulse to smash the
object before it ("the incredible attractiveness of the drop itself which you will
understand faster if you take a fourteen-pound sledgehammer and try to smash
it on a forge"), and slows beautifully to a dying fall as the final sentence collapses into silence: "—and what is left in your hand you can crumble—it feels
like sugar—without danger." The forge we may recognize from the end of *Portrait*, and in the lyrical close there is a faint echo of the end of "The Dead." The
Prince Rupert drop holographically insists on both the presence and absence of
certainty: like Joyce's "forge" (*P* 253), it is both a creation and a counterfeit. The
glass is "a symbol of weakness and strength; it was a cipher for someone else's
heart" (Peter Carey 110). To Lucinda, it is an object that contains multitudes:

Lucinda was moved by something much more simple—grief that such
a lovely thing could vanish like a pricked balloon. But her feelings were
not unlayered and there was, mixed with that hard slap of disappoint-
ment, a deeper, more nourishing emotion: wonder.
It was very more-ish.

(Peter Carey 110)

It becomes abundantly clear that this symbol, this cipher, this layered source of
wonder and grief, is the dynamo of fiction itself. To Peter Carey, "glass is a thing
in disguise," "a liquid," "a joyous and paradoxical thing, as good a material as any
to build a life from" (Peter Carey 111). Joyce's joyous and paradoxical world is all

these things, too, and is certainly as good a material as any to build a life from. If Lucinda Leplastrier's sense of value can be extended to literary criticism, I would like this book to be "very more-ish." The major point of *At Fault* is that Joyce is to be enjoyed, that all Joycean readings are properly flights from the center, that comedy lies at the heart of all that Joyce does, and that if a text is truly atelic then a true reading of that work must take it out of its own bounds. But first we have to pick up the scent.

1 | At Fault

What Joyce Can Teach Us about the Crisis of the Modern University

1. Felix Culpa: Joyce and Error

> Except in directions in which we can go too far there is no interest in going at all; and only those who will risk going too far can possibly find out how far one can go.
>
> (Eliot, preface to Harry Crosby, *Transit of Venus*)

Let us start with the salutary example of teaching out of bounds. On the first fine day in April, it is my usual custom to take students on a walking tour of T. S. Eliot's *The Waste Land*. There is a logic to this: the poem is a journey, a music-hall performance, an act of ventriloquism, and a transgression of space. Students who have suffered a long winter gazing out at frozen lakes, as those in Evanston, Illinois, usually have, need to come out of hibernation, to walk and wander, to participate in the comedy of return. Ideally, we would be in London for this purpose, but any campus will do, and Northwestern's beautiful and hallowed spaces work better than most for an act of academic transgression.[1] The point of the exercise, besides the actual exercise, is that *The Waste Land* is a violation of poetic space and of poetic tradition. Like *Ulysses*, *The Waste Land* is a novelty that causes "passers to stop in wonder," an act of kinesis that is congruous with "the velocity of modern life" (*U* 17.1770–73). *Ulysses* and *The Waste Land* have in common, then, the act of wandering, of straying gleefully from the norm of their literary inheritance. Their paths are centrifugal.

And so, led by a student in the class who read the traveling sections of the poem while walking backward, we conducted a mock campus tour. I started things off by reading the opening invocation in Alice Millar Chapel, just before the parson came out to see what the devil was going on. In front of a sign marked "Private Property: No Trespassing" we found roots that clutch, and next to a red rock we watched our shadows rise to meet us in the afternoon sun. Says Virginia Woolf, "I refuse to allow you, Beadle though you are, to turn me off the grass [. . .] there is no gate, no lock, no bolt that you can set upon the freedom of my mind" (Woolf, *A Room of One's Own* 75–76): we picked up that clarion cry and ran with it, quite literally, across Sheridan Road. (I should hasten to say that we used the little red flags that allow for safe crossing.) We arranged a confrontation with Stetson ("You who were with me in the ships at Mylae!"—*TWL* 136), as a bemused police officer drove away in a state of perfect uncertainty about the legality of our proceedings. Then, of course, we went to the beach, where Cleopatra spoke to us from the top of a lifeguard chair: "The Chair she sat in, like a burnished throne, / Glowed on the marble [. . .] / Huge sea-wood fed with copper / Burned green and orange, framed by the coloured stone, / In which sad light a carvèd dolphin swam" (*TWL* 137). In this case, the chair was of distressed wood, and the dolphins had to be imagined in the far distance, but as Eliot distresses *Antony and Cleopatra*, turning Shakespeare's paean to the Egyptian queen into a misogynist tapestry of forced nature, so we had our moment of narrative subversion by water, the "No Lifeguard on Duty" sign neatly validating the force of our transgression.

Then it was on to the catamarans at the Northwestern Sailing Center, where two students playing Tom and Viv argued about nothing, as a gathering crowd of tourists from the Segal Visitors Center wondered what to make of it all. A music stand and a chair had been cunningly prepared by the instructor for the two performers reading a Cockney woman and the Bartender at the Bienen School of Music, the sailboat on the water through the window behind reminding us of the possibilities of *Damyata* provided by "the hand expert with sail and oar" (*TWL* 146). Ezekiel spoke to us from a withered stump of time, the typist met her young man carbuncular in a barbeque pit, the Rhine Maidens disported themselves in truly Wagnerian fashion, and Phlebas the Phoenician found an appropriate rock from which to declaim the "Death by Water" sequence (*TWL* 137, 141, 142, 143). Above all, it was April, it was just turning spring, and we were amateurs, in love with the text and the newly awakening world. By speaking of the Fisher King where it said "No Fishing" and of the Rhine Maidens where it said "No Swimming," we had brought a performance piece to rich and risky life, on a day when we were really supposed to be in class.

It is traditional for students at Northwestern to paint mottoes on rocks. Looking at my photographs of the event, I discovered an accidental message on the rock between two speakers in "What the Thunder Said." (The message is always on the rock in T. S. Eliot.) It read, in blue capital letters with the skyline of Chicago behind, "Never Settle." This has been the driving impulse behind all my teaching and all my work at every university I have ever taught. After a lifetime in academia, I have become familiar with the patterns of university life. And what I have seen, particularly in eight years as a university administrator, is a willingness for students, faculty, and especially deans and other college officers to settle. Let us agree, as Joyceans, that we are here in the academy to unsettle, to never settle, to always and at all times provoke the mind. This is something all of us must learn to do, from the lowest level of administration (the Provost) all the way up to the student reading poetry illegally from a lifeguard chair on a beach: we have to learn to embrace risk. But forces that tie these ambitions in increasingly Gordian and improbably constrictive knots are working powerfully against this necessary end. I hope by the end of this chapter to have provided some concrete examples of this quiescent acceptance of nontransgression. What is happening to American universities is not a gradual settling, as in the erosion of a limestone landscape. This is more like a flash freeze, a quick-setting concrete that has frozen the academy in place almost literally overnight. Think of the empty spaces where the bodies were in the lava of Pompeii. They represent, caught in negative space, screams of pain, howls of anguish, Goyaesque nightmare visions of living human beings incarcerated and calcified by an uncaring and protective layer of uniformity.[2] We have to rage against this. For the people in today's hollow tombs are not just professors. They are our students.

Joyceans, by their very nature, are transgressive people. We have conferences in Monaco in honor of Grace Kelly, in tobacco warehouses in Seville that were the inspiration for Bizet's *Carmen*, even one in Szombathely, Hungary, because Leopold Bloom's imaginary grandfather was born there. We embrace fictionality, turning Bloomsday into as real a day for the world of Joyce lovers as 221B Baker Street is a real address for the followers of Sherlock Holmes. We are teachers, we are performers, and we are risk-takers: Joyce models all three on our behalf. Stephen teaches us how to read *Ulysses* in "Nestor," as he guides Sargent through his sums: "Do you understand now? Can you work the second for yourself?" (*U* 2.161). The audience in the Ormond bar encourages Simon Dedalus to perform "M'appari": "Go on, Simon," "With it, Simon" (*U* 11.598,

653). Bloom silently urges Gerty MacDowell to risk leaning backward during the fireworks display, which she does, on account of his eyes:

> But there was an infinite store of mercy in those eyes, for him too a word
> of pardon even though he had erred and sinned and wandered.
>
> (*U* 13.748–49)

In this crucial text from "Nausicaa" you will find Joyce's three main verbs: "erred" and "sinned" and "wandered." Let's spend some time with this pivotal scene. Gerty MacDowell is sitting on Sandymount Strand on the evening of 16 June 1904 with her friends Edy and Cissy and the two boys Tommy and Jacky, who are dressed in identical sailor suits. There is a squalling infant also present, but we can ignore the noise from the pram for the moment. Gerty reveals herself to be pinched and strained and eager to please, as anxious as I am to get rid of the squalling baby, who is getting on her nerves, not to mention "the little brats of twins" (*U* 13.405–06). She turns her attentions to the man opposite her on the strand and hopes to be able to convert him: "Even if he was a protestant or methodist" (*U* 13.433–34). Well, he's Jewish, he's Leopold Bloom, and all he wants is a vision of knickers to take back home with him to Eccles Street. We do not discover until the second half of the episode that Gerty is lame, that Bloom has been masturbating, and that all this sentimentality is to be punctured by the tyranny of the real, as is the Joycean way. Bloom has sinned throughout the day, of course: he maintains an illicit correspondence with a nearly illiterate typist called Martha Clifford, he misinterprets the letters "I. H. S." on a priest's vestment as "I have sinned" or "I have suffered" (*U* 5.373), he fails to tell an anti-Semitic joke properly in a funeral carriage on the way to Glasnevin Cemetery (*U* 6.264–85).[3] He has erred and sinned and wandered.

How many of Joyce's characters are drawn to calamity! The boy in "Araby" realizes only too late that by paying a shilling entrance fee for the bazaar and reserving fourpence for the tram ride back home he has left himself just fourpence to buy something for Mangan's sister, and his eyes burn "with anguish and anger" (*D* 28). Gabriel Conroy puts his foot in it as he takes off his goloshes ("I suppose we'll be going to your wedding one of these fine days with your young man, eh?"—*D* 177), receives a sharp answer from Lily ("The men that is now is only all palaver and what they can get out of you"), and "coloured as if he felt he had made a mistake" (*D* 178). As if he *felt* he had made a mistake: in Joyce, it's not necessary to have actually done anything wrong; it's enough to feel that you have. Gabriel has wandered out of his depth. Later, as he was wrong about Lily, he will be spectacularly wrong about his wife: "I think I know what is the matter. Do I know?" (*D* 219). Gretta isn't sexually interested in him at all but is still carrying a torch for a boy who died for her in the snow long years ago. Both Gabriel Conroy and Michael Furey have erred by straying out of bounds. But this does not make them guilty; it only makes them human. First we feel, then we fall.

It is not just the priests and the prefects who dispose a rough and rigid justice on a heart bowed down. In every *Dubliners* story, a character sits in judgment on another and gets it wrong. "Do you think me an utter fool?" (*D* 87), asks Mr. Alleyne, to which Mr. Farrington astonishes himself by saying, "*I don't think that that's a fair question to put to me*" (*D* 89). "I'm asking for my rights" (*D* 147), says Mrs. Kearney, for which she is roundly abused by the Committee. In *Ulysses*, the Citizen hears Bloom speak simply and boldly of love ("Love, says Bloom. I mean the opposite of hatred"), nationhood ("Ireland, says Bloom. I was born here"), and persecution ("I'm talking about injustice, says Bloom") and determines that the only possible recourse is immediate crucifixion by biscuitbox: "By Jesus, says he, I'll brain that bloody jewman for using the holy name. By Jesus, I'll crucify him so I will. Give us that biscuitbox here" (*U* 12.1485, 1431, 1474, 1811–12). The words of the "Lacrimosa" from the requiem Mass have it exactly right (Britten v):

Lacrimosa dies illa	That day of weeping
Qua resurget ex favilla	When out of the dust arises
Judicandus homo reus.	The guilty to be judged.

The Day of Judgment does not refer to a day when "all humanity is judged," as some translations saccharinely have it, but to a day of reckoning for the guilty human being. "*Homo reus*": we are all already guilty.[4]

2. The Croppy Boy

> The voice of penance and of grief came slow, embellished, tremulous. Ben's contrite beard confessed. *In nomine Domini*, in God's name he knelt. He beat his hand upon his breast, confessing: *mea culpa*.
>
> Latin again. That holds them like birdlime.
>
> (*U* 11.1031–34)

As a way of bringing this together, I want to focus on one character who can stand for all these human beings racked with guilt and asking for forgiveness, all these broken souls who have erred and sinned and wandered, looking as Bloom did for a word of pardon in a world without mercy. The Croppy Boy makes a brief appearance in a song named after him at the end of the "Sirens" episode in *Ulysses*. In "Sirens" the songs are presented not as you or I would do it, setting the sung text off in indented italics as a separate temporal and spatial event, but interwoven into the text so that the music and its effect on the listener takes place simultaneously. The music makes what Leonard Bernstein calls "a direct hit":[5] it happens inside the text, with thought and sound so scrambled that you can't tell immediately which register you are listening to. In this respect, it most nearly approximates the condition of "aural eyeness" (*FW* 623.18) that prevails in *Finnegans Wake*. Most of the source texts for the soundtrack in "Sirens" are relics of a bygone age: it is a brave person nowadays who is willing to launch in public into "O My Dolores, Queen of the Eastern Sea" from the musical *Flora-dora*. "M'appari," the central Siren song, is well-known to admirers of Flotow's *Martha* and the recordings of Mario Lanza, but "Love and War" and "Good-bye, Sweetheart, Goodbye" are generally now known only to Joyceans, if at all. Thanks to the work of Ruth Bauerle in *The James Joyce Songbook*, it is now possible to resurrect these songs, and all but one of them are discussed in detail in chapter 6. The one missing is "The Croppy Boy."

"The Croppy Boy" has an interminable number of verses, and Joyce, who identified strongly with the main character in the song, loved to sing it at any available opportunity. Here are the first six:

"Good men and true in this house who dwell,
To a stranger bouchal *I pray you tell,*
Is the priest at home, or may he be seen?
I would speak a word with Father Green."

"The priest's at home, boy, and may be seen;
'Tis easy speaking with Father Green;
But you must wait while I go and see
If the holy Father alone may be."

The youth has entered an empty hall—
What a lonely sound has his light footfall!
And the gloomy chamber's chill and bare,
With a vested priest in a lonely chair.

"At the siege of Ross did my father fall,
And at Gorey my loving brothers all,

I alone am left of my name and race,
I will go to Wexford and take their place.

"I cursed three times since last Easter day—
At Mass-time once I went to play;
I passed the churchyard one day in haste
And forgot to pray for my mother's rest.

"I bear no hate against living thing
But I love my country above the King,
Now, Father, bless me and let me go,
To die if God has ordained it so."

(Bauerle 270)[6]

Joyce's lyrics differ slightly in words and versification (*U* 11.991–1074), but the song's presence is palpable beneath the text. Joyce has the boy forgetting to pray "for his mother's rest" (*U* 11.1042) before he insists on his rightful place at Wexford as the "Last of his name and race" (*U* 11.1064–65), rather than the other way around. The hall he enters is "lonely" (*U* 11.1021) rather than "*empty*," his footfall is "solemn" (*U* 11.1021) rather than "*lonely*." These are minor flecks in the birdlime. Bloom is listening to the accompaniment ("Chords dark," "Curlycues of chords"—*U* 11.1005, 1017) and to the words ("The priest's at home"—*U* 11.1016), processing music and text simultaneously. What is more, he is aware of the fact that he is analyzing music and text: "The sighing voice of sorrow sang" (*U* 11.1040); "Once by the churchyard he had passed and for his mother's rest he had not prayed" (*U* 11.1042–43). He forces himself to listen ("Listen") and watches others listening ("Bronze, listening, by the beerpull gazed far away") and is watched by a listening narrator: "Bloom listened. Richie Goulding listened" (*U* 11.1028, 1044, 1028). The waiter responds to the inaudible ("And by the door deaf Pat, bald Pat, tipped Pat, listened"—*U* 11.1028–29), and the narrator, too, hears things that are well out of earshot: "Tap"; "Cockcarracarra" (*U* 11.1010, 1048). Bloom "seehears lipspeech" as he stands up to go (*U* 11.1002) and projects his voice as the narrator does when he decides to stay: "Will? You? I. Want. You. To" (*U* 11.1096). He is transfixed both aurally ("But wait. But hear") and visually ("See her from here though") and meditates on the meaning of it all: "What do they think when they hear music?" (*U* 11.1005, 1110–11, 1049). We have reached a vortex in Joyce's text.

A "Croppy" is an Irish rebel, a Catholic and a peasant cropping the land (a "bouchal" is a herdboy): this ballad memorializes the Irish Rebellion of 1798, when the British yeomanry, aided covertly by the Catholic Church, brutally suppressed an uprising by Irish Republicans inspired by the successes of revolutions in America and France. The battles of the 1798 rebellion were mainly fought in County Wexford, in the southeast of Ireland, where Ross and Gorey are. The boy in the song doesn't know that the Catholic Church, shocked by the French capture of Rome, is working for the old enemy. His opening position is strikingly similar to the boy's in "Araby," who also enters a strangely empty and godless place, where he listens to the fall of the coins and hears the denial that, as we have heard, sounds strikingly like Saint Peter's (*D* 27). *In the song,* the emptiness of the hall is such that the vested priest, if he is a priest, sitting in his lonely chair, is hardly visible. *In Joyce's text,* we are in Wagner's "dark middle earth," hearing the "Lumpmusic" of "Embedded ore" (*U* 11.1006). *In the music,* we are in the subterranean key of F$^{\#}$ major, according to the gifted accompanist Father Cowley, who can apparently transpose at will (*U* 11.996). *In Bloom's mind,* the song reminds him of the blind stripling he helped across Dawson Street at lunchtime: "The sighing voice of sorrow sang. His sins. Since Easter he had cursed three times. You bitch's bast. And once at masstime he had gone to play. Once by the churchyard he had passed and for his mother's rest he had not prayed. A boy. A croppy boy" (*U* 11.1040–43). *In the narrator's mind,* "You bitch's bast" recalls the blind stripling's travels in "Wandering Rocks," when he reacted ferociously to Cashel Boyle O'Connor Fitzmaurice Tisdall Farrell crashing into him: "God's curse on you, he said sourly, whoever you are! You're blinder nor I am, you bitch's bastard!" (*U* 10.1119–20). That is a narrative connection, beyond Bloom's horizon, as is the boy's "Tap" that you hear in the text in percussive and persistent accompaniment to each verse of the song; the same blind boy is tapping his way to the Ormond bar to pick up the tuning fork he left on the piano. Because, of course, he's the piano tuner. In Joyce's calculus, a blind stripling would naturally be endowed with a prodigal sense of hearing, something that Odysseus, like Bloom, also requires as he passes the Sirens with his ears unstopped.

There are two things of additional interest here: "You bitch's bast" sounds as though it should be Bloom's recollection, but that cannot possibly be the case, since the phrase was expostulated at Merrion Square in front of the window of Mr. Bloom the dentist, a man who is both totally unrelated to Leopold and a long distance away from him, since Mr. Bloom the advertising man is at the time still at the bookstall on the banks of the Liffey (*U* 10.584). Later in the song, when the Croppy Boy dies, Bloom thinks "Dolor! O, he Dolores!" (*U* 11.1132), despite the fact that he didn't enter the bar until after "*O, Idolores, queen of the eastern seas!*" (*U* 11.226) was sung and couldn't possibly have heard the line. Further complicating matters, neither Lydia Douce nor Leopold Bloom has the text right: as anyone who has sung the song from *Floradora* would know (and there are about three of us left), "*my Dolores*" is the correct reading from the opera. These word errors open up a world. The songs are in the air. The text is going haywire. Joyce is out of control. Something is about to go terribly wrong.

Let's pause at this moment of maximum escape velocity and see what else is weighing us down. Who else is the Croppy Boy? Like the Croppy Boy, Stephen also refused to pray for his mother's rest: "You could have knelt down, damn it, Kinch, when your dying mother asked you" (*U* 1.91–92). He is also Robert Emmet, the boy hero of the 1803 rebellion, whose last words end the "Sirens" episode: "*When my country takes her place among […] Nations of the earth […] Then and not till then […] Let my epitaph be […] Written. I have […] Done*" (*U* 11.1284–94). Mr. Kernan makes this connection as he walks past St. Catherine's Church in "Wandering Rocks" and thinks "Down there Emmet was hanged, drawn and quartered," following up the thought with "Ben Dollard does sing that ballad touchingly. Masterly rendition. / *At the siege of Ross did my father fall*" (*U* 10.764–93). And in "Cyclops," Robert Emmet is metamorphosed into the Croppy Boy on his way to the gallows, in one of the funniest sections of the book. The high spirits of this passage are unsurpassed in any work of literature I know:

> The *nec* and *non plus ultra* of emotion were reached when the blushing bride elect burst her way through the serried ranks of the bystanders and flung herself upon the muscular bosom of him who was about to be launched into eternity for her sake. The hero folded her willowy form in a loving embrace murmuring fondly *Sheila, my own.* Encouraged by this use of her christian name she kissed passionately all the various suitable areas of his person which the decencies of prison garb permitted her ardour to reach. She swore to him as they mingled the salt streams of their tears that she would ever cherish his memory, that she would never forget her hero boy who went to his death with a song on his lips as if he were but going to a hurling match in Clonturk park. She brought back to his recollection the happy days of blissful childhood together on the

banks of Anna Liffey when they had indulged in the innocent pastimes of the young and, oblivious of the dreadful present, they both laughed heartily, all the spectators, including the venerable pastor, joining in the general merriment. That monster audience simply rocked with delight. But anon they were overcome with grief and clasped their hands for the last time. A fresh torrent of tears burst from their lachrymal ducts and the vast concourse of people, touched to the inmost core, broke into heart-rending sobs, not the least affected being the aged prebendary himself. Big strong men, officers of the peace and genial giants of the royal Irish constabulary, were making frank use of their handkerchiefs and it is safe to say that there was not a dry eye in that record assemblage. A most romantic incident occurred when a handsome young Oxford graduate, noted for his chivalry towards the fair sex, stepped forward and, presenting his visiting card, bankbook and genealogical tree, solicited the hand of the hapless young lady, requesting her to name the day, and was accepted on the spot. Every lady in the audience was presented with a tasteful souvenir of the occasion in the shape of a skull and crossbones brooch, a timely and generous act which evoked a fresh outburst of emotion: and when the gallant young Oxonian (the bearer, by the way, of one of the most timehonoured names in Albion's history) placed on the finger of his blushing *fiancée* an expensive engagement ring with emeralds set in the form of a fourleaved shamrock the excitement knew no bounds. Nay, even the stern provostmarshal, lieutenantcolonel Tomkin-Maxwell ffrenchmullan Tomlinson, who presided on the sad occasion, he who had blown a considerable number of sepoys from the cannonmouth without flinching, could not now restrain his natural emotion. With his mailed gauntlet he brushed away a furtive tear and was overheard, by those privileged burghers who happened to be in his immediate *entourage*, to murmur to himself in a faltering undertone:

—God blimey if she aint a clinker, that there bleeding tart. Blimey it makes me kind of bleeding cry, straight, it does, when I sees her cause I thinks of my old mashtub what's waiting for me down Limehouse way.

(U 12.635–78)

"That monster audience simply rocked with delight" (*U* 12.650–51): this is gleefully monstrous, a savage attack on colonial complacency and colonized acquiescence. The text has been quite literally colon-ized: in preparation for the boy's hanging the executioners have thoughtfully provided "various finely tempered disembowelling appliances" and "a terra cotta saucepan for the reception of the […] colon" (*U* 12.619, 621–22). All this, then, is in play as Bloom hears the first six verses of the song.

And there is still more. Bloom's own son is the Croppy Boy, the young Rudy, who died too young, and was the last of his race:

> All gone. All fallen. At the siege of Ross his father, at Gorey all his brothers fell. To Wexford, we are the boys of Wexford, he would. Last of his name and race.
>
> I too. Last of my race. Milly young student. Well, my fault perhaps. No son. Rudy. Too late now. Or if not? If not? If still?
>
> (*U* 11.1063–67)

Bloom is here technically at fault, as we have discovered him twice to be in "Circe" (*U* 15.632–33, 4331): he has lost the scent and is sniffing around to find the track, to restore his line, to find the patrilinear path. The false hope of "If not? If still?," the distant possibility of reunion with Molly, of a second son, of the continuation of the Bloom line from Virag to Rudolph to Leopold to a new male heir, is shattered by the music of what is about to happen next. "Bloom looked, unblessed to go. […] Low sank the music, air and words. Then hastened" (*U* 11.1076–81). It's what happens in the "music, air and words" that makes this moment so unbearable:

> *The priest said naught, but a rustling noise*
> *Made the youth look up in wild surprise:*
> *The robes were off, and in scarlet there*
> *Sat a Yeoman captain with fiery glare.*
>
> *"Upon yon river three tenders float,*
> *The priest's in one—if he isn't shot—*
> *We hold this house for our lord the King,*
> *And Amen, say I, may all traitors swing!"*
>
> *At Geneva Barracks that young man died*
> *And at Passage they have his body laid.*
> *Good people, who live in peace and joy,*
> *Breathe a prayer, shed a tear for the Croppy Boy!*
>
> (Bauerle 270)[7]

Note how cynical the captain is: his indifference to the outcome of his usurpation is breathtaking (*"The priest's in one—if he isn't shot"*). *"Amen, say I,"* blasphemes the captain, establishing that Man has ordained a fate that the boy was only willing to allow to God: *"our lord"* is now the English King. Note, too, how swiftly and impetuously the verdict is applied: from *"may all traitors swing!"* to *"that young man died"* there is barely time for breath. The moral of the story comes before the ink on the decision has dried; the administration is ferocious in its implacability. The robes of the ballad are off, and we see death in its naked glory. Fraud is unmasked. The captain is the devil in scarlet, with fiery glare: he says and is *"naught."*

It's useful to notice just how many layers of voicing are in this song. The narrator who bids us pathetically to breathe a prayer and shed a tear for the Croppy Boy is also the yeoman captain who doesn't even care if the priest is shot, and is also the boy who bears no hate against living thing, and is also the duplicitous man at the front desk who tells us that it's easy speaking with Father Green. This song has more narrative levels than Schubert's "Erlkönig": it is a kaleidoscope of conflicting perspectives, as polyphonic as Joyce's text itself. As Joyce said of the song, when providing singing instructions to his son, Giorgio, "When you sing it, be sure to hold the balance equal between the captain and the young man. The last stanza is sung on a solemn and impersonal note. The effect of this stanza, when rendered by a voice like yours, is electrifying. [. . .] Study every word of it and you will make it into a masterpiece" (qtd. in Bauerle 269). By the electrifying end of this masterpiece of a song, we don't know quite how we got to this terrible place. We only know that for the sake of three curses since Easter, a skipped Mass, a missed opportunity to pray for his mother, and a misplaced oath, a young man has been taken to the gallows. To misquote the Mikado himself, the punishment doesn't fit the crime (Sullivan, *Mikado* 172–79). And that is always Joyce's point.

3. At Fault: The University in Crisis

> Order in court! The accused will now make a bogus statement.
>
> (*U* 15.896–97)

The errors of a "man of genius," Stephen famously says in the National Library, "are the portals of discovery" (*U* 9.228–29). An appreciation of error, of the necessary mistakes that make us human, is the heart and soul of the humanist

enterprise. Life is full of mistakes, and so is literature, from the decision of Odysseus to taunt Poseidon's son to Emma Bovary's journey to Rouen to meet
her opera-loving friend. The fact that we are free to err and sin and wander
is the happy fault that propels our discipline, from Erasmus' *In Praise of Folly*
to David Mitchell's *Cloud Atlas*. The opening word of *Finnegans Wake*, "riverrun" (*FW* 3.01), has, as Fritz Senn has helpfully pointed out, the word "err"
inside it (Senn 59). In every wandering river there is a margin for error, as a
river is a flower (*flɔuɔ*: to rhyme with "rower") and a flower (*flauɔ*: to rhyme
with "hour"). The flow of language is also then the language of flowers or the
"language of flow" (*U* 11.298). The sight of the most famous flowers in English poetry, Wordsworth's daffodils, results from wandering "lonely as a cloud"
(Wordsworth 191). "To read is to wander," says Pascal Quignard in *The Roving
Shadows*: "Reading is errantry. [. . .] (Beware of knights errant! They are out for
adventure; they are drawn to calamity)" (Quignard 53). Edmund Spenser's *The
Faerie Queene* similarly plays between discourse and error in their etymological
senses, where, as Linda Gregerson writes, "'discourse' derives from *discurrere*
('to run back and forth') as 'error' or errancy derives from *errare* ('to wander')"
(Gregerson 92).[8]

Felix culpa: the happy fall motif is most clear in the fifteenth-century text
"Adam Lay Ybounden": "Ne had the apple taken been / The apple taken been
/ Ne had never our ladie / Abeen heav'ne queen" (Sloane Manuscript 2593,
British Library). Without **EVA** (the Fall of Man) there would be no **AVE** (the
Coming of Christ), a paradox central to Milton and *The Messiah*. The texts we
humanists all read are richly flawed and infinitely interpretable, from *Hamlet*'s
bad quartos to Auden's worse revisions of his poetry. And no one rejoices in
the fertility of language, the inability of a text to fix itself in the reader's ear and
eye, more fully than Joyce, where characters squint, letters fade, words are mis-
spelled as worlds, and in *Finnegans Wake*, the greatest moment of human error
is given not as *felix culpa* but as "foenix culprit!" (*FW* 23.16).[9] There are dozens
of variations on the happy fall motif in the *Wake*, each more delicious than the
last:

> O fortunous casualitas! (*FW* 175.29)
> O happy fault! Me wish it was he! You're wrong there, corribly wrong!
>   (*FW* 202.34–35)
> [. . .] felixed is who culpas does [. . .] (*FW* 246.31)

O felicitous culpability, sweet bad cess to you for an archetypt! (*FW* 263.29–30)

Hearasay in paradox lust. (*FW* 263.L4)

We are all "corribly wrong," especially in *Finnegans Wake*. We must be allowed to rise from our sins. To err is to divagate, to diverge, to divide, to take a glorious detour through the wilderness to search for the roots of language and find its flawed and fractured heart. To err is human: it therefore follows that the study of error is the proper subject of the humanities.

The Clerk of the Crown calls for order in the Carrollian universe that is Bloom's trial in "Circe" and announces: "The accused will now make a bogus statement" (*U* 15.896–97). I used to think that this line was the *nec* and *non plus ultra* of Joycean hilarity, but now I find it terrifying. Every crime in the modern university is punished, regardless of innocence or guilt. Our protectors have become our enemies, too eager to find fault in a system that finds no culpability felicitous, every phoenix a culprit. Joyce knows never to trust appearances—one of his first essays at the Belvedere School was titled "Trust not Appearances" (qtd. in *JJ* 36)—and his work is filled with people who see double, who look asquint, who find the truth at a slant. But in our higher courts of administration, optics reign. Like Joyce's priests, the officers of University Law are "too scrupulous always" (*D* 9) and have an infinite power, with their kangaroo courts, their complete disregard for process, and their total lack of empathy. One administrator in my experience was fond of saying that he would pray for faculty deaths in late spring to open up office and salary space for new hires. He is now chancellor at a major university. Another would refer to a certain department in his faculty as "The Island of Misfit Toys": that kind of exclusionary language should be instantly disqualifying. The university should be a place where eccentricity flourishes and is celebrated, not normalized out of existence.

Joyce has a lot to teach us in the modern university, if we would only listen to him. In the corporate world, if the matter is messy, it can just be resolved with money. In the university, money shouldn't be the primary motivation or the primary solution to anything. If a university is a place of learning, then mistakes must and will happen within it. That's how all of us learn. If learning is trial and error, then we've kept the trial and eliminated the errors. The modern university has lost its way: in its search for rectitude and the comforts of perception, it has failed to attend to its greatest and most vital purpose. Like Joyce's baying bloodhounds in "The Hue and Cry" (*U* 15.4331), the university is at fault in its most literal sense: the pack has lost the scent. In casually discarding the search for truth in favor of media perception and bottom-line economics, and in the very real fear, in the United States at least, of federal reprisals for perceived violations of Title IX of the Education Amendments of 1972, the university has jeopardized its right to lead the nations of the world. Worse still for the individuals involved in the current university system, by eliminating the "reasonable person" standard for Title IX complaints, the university has opened itself up to serious abuse of the protections afforded by decades of workplace policy. Truth, for a corporation, is quite simple: if it looks bad, it has to be removed. That is optics. But for a university to take such a cavalier attitude is to abdicate the value of learning itself.

Seven decades ago, as America debated whether to join the European War, an Englishman was inaugurated as president of Smith College. It was 17 October 1940. After the organ had played the "March of the Meistersingers" from *Die Meistersinger*, the Glee Club had sung the "Hallelujah Chorus," and Leverett Saltonstall, governor of Massachusetts, had said a few words of greeting, Herbert Davis, M.A. Oxon., rose to give the inaugural address. He spoke of defense, of liberty, of the need for faculty to teach honors classes as a central part of their teaching, and of the cultivation of a nucleus of students of first-rate ability through open scholarships. But above all, he spoke of the necessity of taking risks in university education:

> Education of any kind can never be a safe investment; it must always be something of a speculative venture. If it is worth anything at all, it must be a risky business. For by its very nature it must be an experiment in freedom. The life of the spirit must be a life of perfect freedom. If we really believe that the glory of man is in the powers of his mind and spirit, we must provide that freedom in which alone the mind can do its work. It is a farce to talk about the defense of freedom, unless we are ready to accept the fruits of freedom, and, in education, to recognize one chief purpose—to produce free spirits, and to let them work freely.
>
> In this time of the breaking of nations, with half the world at war, it is difficult enough to keep alive even the conception of that world of the spirit, in which there are no barriers of race or creed or nationality. Nevertheless as scientists and scholars and artists we cannot do our work

unless we can live in that world, where we may be free. And now here of all places in the world, we cannot be blind to this.

(Davis 29)[10]

I can hear him speak, though he died when I was five: Herbert Davis was my grandfather, and his ideas that guided Smith College through World War II are very much my own. "And now here of all places in the world" (Davis 29), here in the university, we must take risks, or we will never be free.

The evidence and the literature for an academic crisis is everywhere. Benjamin Ginsberg writes in *The Fall of the Faculty: The Rise of the All Administrative University and Why It Matters* of the "administrative imperialism" that is now choking the life out of the United States' greatest single contribution to human wisdom, the research university.[11] Terry Eagleton says in an essay for the *Chronicle of Higher Education*, "If the humanities in Britain are withering on the branch, it is largely because they are being driven by capitalist forces while being simultaneously starved of resources" (Eagleton, "The Slow Death of the University," 10 Apr. 2015: B9). The problem is simple: "when you hit a wrong note," Miles Davis is meant to have said, "it's the next note that makes it good or bad." The university writ large is so terrified of wrong notes that there is never any time to hear the next one. The human resources department at every academic institution has over time acquired total control over chairs, deans, and provosts, who have in turn lost sight of anything other than their own, or their university's, self-interest. Bureaucratic incompetence is a blind: the principal factor that explains the rise of the kangaroo courts and the loss of due process throughout the American university system is fear of litigation. If one false move can cost you your job, then there is no time to allow anyone to learn from their mistakes.[12] A university has a greater responsibility than a corporation to the question of truth, and to its inverse, the understanding of error.

Marina Warner writes in "Learning My Lesson" on 19 March 2015 of receiving correspondence, after her public resignation from a university post, that "reveals a deeper and more bitter scene in higher education than I had ever imagined. [. . .] Students, lecturers, professors from one institution after another were howling in sympathy and rage. [. . .] Cries also reached me from other countries, where the new methods have been taken even further; from New Zealand and Australia, above all; from Europe, especially the Netherlands, and from certain institutions in the US" (Warner 8). And what are these new methods? Departments "freighted to breaking point with imperious and ill-conceived demands from much higher up the food chain—from people who don't teach or do research at all" (qtd. in Warner 8). Warner warns us of the figure of Fraud, the face behind the boy in Bronzino's *Allegory with Venus and Cupid*, whose hands are the wrong way around and who holds a honeycomb in one hand and a venomous beast in the other (Warner 12). Accusing universities of fraud may be an extreme view: in a more conciliatory vein, Stefan Collini, in *What Are Universities For?*, writes of a "loss of confidence in the possibility of rational argument about the worthwhileness of various human activities" (Collini 108). Collini concludes that "the widely remarked public statement of these compelling and often devastating criticisms appears to have had little or no effect on policy-making. The arguments have not been answered; they have merely been ignored. [...] Those who make policy are just not listening" (Collini 116). We have been lulled by the "cruel optimism" Lauren Berlant speaks of as the undermining cause of university neglect: our "sense of self-worth" that "derives from doing something we believe in" is now profoundly at odds with "a hierarchical authority that is secretive, arbitrary, and ruthless" (qtd. in Gill 241).[13] Like the Croppy Boy, we have entered an empty hall. The university has become an abattoir. And those who suffer the most from the staggering weight of ignorance and inattention are obvious. As Marina Warner writes, "students are above all the victims" (Warner 10). When ignorance and intolerance meet, there is no remedy.

It's an interesting thought experiment to imagine the Croppy Boy as an extended analogy for the plight of the student or faculty member before the shadow justice system of the modern university. Let's say, for the sake of argument, that you do something wrong: you curse at someone, as the Croppy Boy did, or trespass against some human resources protocol placed there for the university's legal protection. You are both in fault and at fault: you are guilty and have lost your way. You expect to confess, as the Croppy Boy did, but instead you are hanged. You expect to be treated as a member of the academy, but the robes are off, and a cruel kind of justice is executed with breathtaking swiftness. Like the Croppy Boy, you *"bear no hate against living thing"* (Bauerle 270) but are faced with a yeoman captain with fiery glare. The university administration of today, as it was in Ireland at the time of the 1798 rebellion, is merciless, weaving a narrative of guilt and condemning souls to permanently blackened reputations before the ink on the decision has dried. The university has become, in its unquestioning acceptance of the accuser's testimony, and in its complete abandonment of any protections for the accused, once again a place of privilege and prejudice. And faculty, staff, and students, when they face judgment in the university system today, are horribly alone. I don't know if this has happened to you. I can bet that it has happened to someone you know. We are facing an old enemy, but the enemy is within our walls. In the song, the officer who has co-opted the role of the priest doesn't care if Father Green is alive or dead; similarly, there is an astonishing insouciance to modern university justice. A letter is placed in your file, an elegant piece of hand-wringing is performed, and then it's off to a better and safer future. Protestations are suppressed by a quick word against retaliation and the shame cycle of public opinion. The hanging of the Croppy Boy takes place offstage, leaving the rest of us to grieve, pray, and wonder. We have entered the world of silence and shadow.

Here would be the appropriate place in the sermon to provide data for you, cite the many scholars and columnists in this field from Hannah Arendt to Frank Donoghue to Nicholas Kristof, unroll some eye-glazingly dull statistics specially selected to prove my argument, flap my hands in an aggrieved manner, and we would all then have the same salutary but unsatisfactory experience from the choir-stalls.[14] But true to my chosen method I will instead provide a brief illustration from my own experience. Ramseyer Hall in Columbus, Ohio, was built as a school for children in 1932: it now houses the Ohio State School of Education. Over a doorway lintel is an extraordinary statement:

> PRIZE THE DOUBT
> LOW KINDS EXIST WITHOUT

The epigraph is remarkable on several levels. First, it shows an impressive knowledge of nineteenth-century poetry: it is a rare architect who chooses lines from Robert Browning's "Rabbi Ben Ezra," a poem, like Matthew Arnold's "Sohrab and Rustum," much beloved in its day but now almost entirely forgotten. Second, the phrase "low kinds" is deeply unsettling, in that it establishes a class structure based on intelligence, something that would never have been permitted in today's antielitist society. Third, the epigraph deliciously implies that those "without," or outside of the building, are themselves to be considered "low kinds." Fourth, the entrance is completely bricked up, suggesting that the university doesn't consider the lines to be a suitable path to education any more. In my first day back in the classroom at Ohio State after several years as an administrator, I took the twenty-five students in my Critical Writing seminar to the parking lot where these lines are carved. Thinking to tackle the problem of the university's intolerance for error head on, I launched into a passionate attack on entrenched opinions and soon got into a tangle. It doesn't matter, I said, whether you are prochoice or prolife, Democratic or Republican, progun or antigun, Tea Party or Green Party, Palestinian or Israeli, Shia or Sunni. I went too far: there were too many code words I had stepped on, too many prejudices exposed. A student wrote to me that evening to say that he would regrettably have to withdraw from my class because of my pointed remarks against a particular group, which he felt had been unfairly and deliberately targeted against him personally in a malicious and defamatory way. "Hmm," I thought, "classes have changed in the years since I've been out of them." I'm happy to say that a meeting over coffee led the student to change his mind about my approach, steer away from the conflict, and eventually become someone whose strident calls against university injustice I have been privileged to read and review. I have just written him a recommendation for law school.

That's all very well: I'm a professor with more than two decades of teaching behind me. What would I have done, I wonder, if I had been a new assistant professor starting my way up the tenure ladder? Would I be willing to take risks in an environment that has no tolerance for error? Would I have dared, as I once did, to have someone else pretend to be me on the first day of my classes at Ohio State, so that I could dress up like a punk, break into my own class, and read the student roster backward in a rhyming rap to the rhythm of Run-DMC? Would I have decided that it would have been better not to have the car radios of three students play the "Ride of the Valkyries," as I once did, at full volume on the lawn in front of the University Honors House? Would I risk spending six hours reading "Circe" aloud on a Thursday evening with my Joyce students, as described in chapter 8? No. I would be cautious and afraid. A student might reasonably object to the excesses of Joyce's excruciating pantomime, the person playing Stephen's mother coming out of the fireplace might have flashbacks to a third-degree burn suffered while they were toasting marshmallows at summer camp in second grade. We have lost the art of provocation; there is now an overwhelmingly negative value to risk-taking. Teachers should be *provocateurs*, unafraid to stir the pot. But we have slapped trigger warnings on *King Lear*—WARNING: EXTREME EYE-GOUGING; ADVANCED SENILITY; INSENSITIVITY TO ILLEGITIMACY; REAL DANGER OF HEARTBREAK—and treat young adults as if they were two-year-olds in need of padded helmets to walk down the stairs.[15] Ian McEwan puts the problem in a nutshell:

If my identity is that of a believer, I'm easily wounded, my flesh torn to bleeding by any questioning of my faith. Offended, I enter a state of grace. Should inconvenient opinions hover near me like fallen angels or evil djinn (a mile being too near), I'll be in need of the special campus safe room equipped with Play-Doh and looped footage of gambolling puppies. Ah, the intellectual life! I may need advance warning if upsetting books or ideas threaten my very being by coming too close, breathing on my face, my brain, like unwholesome dogs.

(McEwan, *Nutshell* 145)

A salutary if tendentious corrective to the current tendency to infantilize the student body was provided by the University of Chicago's letter to its students in August 2016, where the dean of students writes: "You will find that we expect members of our community to be engaged in rigorous debate, discussion, and even disagreement. At times this may challenge you and even cause discomfort."[16] That this statement was at all controversial is a sign of how far off the track we have wandered.

This is not the fault of the bubble-wrap generation, who grew up in the insulated world after 9/11: it is the fault of those who provide the bubble wrap. Jon Ronson, the author of *So You've Been Publicly Shamed*, writes that we run the risk of "creating a world where the smartest way to survive is to be bland."[17] Discovering that my order for a class hadn't arrived, I went in 2015 to the Student Book Exchange, the much beloved bookstore on High Street in Columbus, and asked if there were any extra copies of *Oliver Twist* ("Please sir—can I have some more?"). The bookseller and I went up to the attic to see if there were any left from previous orders and were both surprised to find that no one had ordered that text at Ohio State for twenty-eight years. "Because Fagin . . . ," as my students would say: it's much safer to stick with *Bleak House*.[18] I do believe in warning students that material may shock them, but if we are to lose *Lolita*, *Lady Chatterley's Lover*, Ovid's *Metamorphosis*, and *Oliver Twist* to the forces of sanctimony, then we will soon be steering clear of *Nineteen Eighty-Four* as well. A society that can select "post-truth" as its word of the year, as the *Oxford English Dictionary* did in 2016, has already become more Orwellian than it knows.

Francine Prose, who knows what it is to work in an academy and whose clear eye sees through everything, describes being on a review committee for a faculty member who misspoke at a departmental party and was then suspended without pay for two years for words he should never have allowed himself to say. She writes about the hearing as follows: "The tone was one of such civility and high moral seriousness that I could only assume I was the only person in the room tuned in to the disturbing static beneath all this calm inquiry: the only one hearing echoes of Victorian melodrama, of badly overacted student productions of Arthur Miller's play *The Crucible*" (Prose, "Hers; Bad Behavior"). Philip Roth, another novelist who knows what it is like to work in an academy, captures the puritanical spirit of recrimination better than anyone in *The Human Stain*. He speaks of "America's oldest communal passion, historically perhaps its most treacherous and subversive pleasure: the ecstasy of sanctimony" (Roth 2). But Francine Prose and Philip Roth are fabulists, artificers. What do lawyers make of the secret places where university judgment is carried out? Judith Shulevitz writes in the *New York Times* in February 2015 that universities are "squandering money and good will on their own all-too-easily second-guessed shadow justice systems" (Shulevitz, 8 Feb. 2015). From a judgment based on "clear and convincing" evidence (what Shulevitz calls a 75 percent likelihood), schools have moved to a determination of guilt based on a "preponderance of" evidence (a 51 percent likelihood), which has had a predictably negative effect on the successful prosecution of the actually guilty in a court of law (Shulevitz, 8 Feb. 2015). When cases are decided outside the media spotlight, and unlikely to go to trial, an even lower standard of proof is in play: the merest possibility of something *might* be true (a 1 percent likelihood) is enough to ruin a career.

Where is it written, outside of Arthur Miller's searing indictment of McCarthyism in *The Crucible*, that the accuser is "always holy now?" (Miller 77). Why should one person be wrongly accused in order to save the greater good? In the case of the very real scourges of campus rape and domestic violence, what is gained by marking texts that address these issues as unsafe for the classroom? Do we do the same for texts that address other forms of PTSD, such as Tim O'Brien's *The Things They Carried* or Elie Wiesel's *Night*? No. We must continue to teach *Tess of the d'Urbervilles*. "Leda and the Swan" is as important a modernist text as "Guernica." The university is not there to compromise. Here is the third page of every course I teach:

Sensitive Material

As someone who regularly teaches war literature to veterans and students on deployment, I take trigger warnings very seriously indeed. I firmly believe in the value of literature to disturb the expectations of all readers, and you would be a very strange person indeed not to have a visceral and negative emotional response to works like *King Lear* or *Tess of the d'Urbervilles*, let alone *Catch-22* or *A Clockwork Orange*. The texts chosen for my courses are not chosen for their shock value, but are part of a thematic approach that allows for all forms of literature to be studied in a safe environment. Texts may have classist positions (most British novels do), describe sexual assault (most Greek myths and the poems that come from them do), present racist or ethnic stereotypes (many Shakespeare plays and some Mozart operas do), and contain characters with suicidal inclinations (this is a plot line that saturates the modernist period). If any of these or other subjects are uncomfortable for you, you will find in this classroom a place where you can face that discomfort in an atmosphere of mutual respect, where ideas can be freely exchanged without censure of any particular point of view.

Literature ought to be disturbing, and its teachers should be—must be—firebrands. Otherwise the truth will go dark, and students will lose their way. The modern university is deranged, and we must stop its careering path.

E. F. Schumacher, the author of *Small Is Beautiful: Economics as if People Mattered*, writes in 1973 of the problem of universities in moral terms. What he says in that small but important book is worth remembering. "The essence of education," says Schumacher, "is the transmission of values" (Schumacher 75). Education gives us "a certain sureness of touch which stems from [. . .] inner clarity"; "Education which fails to clarify our central convictions [. . .] will then be an agent of destruction, in accordance with the principle *corruptio optimi pessima*" (Schumacher 88, 94). Corruptio optimi pessima: universities that fester smell far worse than weeds. Simon Leys writes in *The Hall of Uselessness* that "if I commit a crime, I hope to be judged by a judge who has read Simenon" (Leys, "Lies That Tell the Truth" 46). We can go further and say that if I have committed a crime or a misdemeanor in the academy today, I would hope to be judged by someone who has actually read a book.

In an intolerable irony, we are now judged within the university system by those whose training does not include the texts upon which human judgment is based, from the *Oresteia* to *Crime and Punishment*. Let us stipulate that if you just read Homer, Dante, Shakespeare, and Joyce, you will know all you need to know about what it means to be human. The classicism of this formulation should not invalidate it: if instead of a blind poet, a civil war veteran, a gay playwright, and a colonized exile you wish to substitute the authors of the *Popol Vuh*, *Pride and Prejudice*, *Mrs. Dalloway*, and the *Dream of the Red Chamber*, the result will be the same. Any four diverse, prolific, and highly gifted authors of any gender from any culture will do. The point is that if you don't study a literary tradition, you will know next to nothing about people. This is the real crisis of the humanities: that in losing the humanities we lose the ability to make informed decisions about the actions of human beings.[19] David Citino, Ohio's poet laureate, knew this; in "The World Without," his 1993 poem written for the twentieth-fifth anniversary of the College of Humanities at Ohio State, he imagines a world without the humanities, in ways that eerily predict the world of 2016:

> *Only disconnect*, the wisest advise.
>   *Who? Who?* we never think to ask,
>   but if we do, *I haven't a clue*
> becomes the fervent battle-cry—
>
> and better wars blossom daily.
>   Where are the old melodies to guard
>   like flames inside the windy heart?
> Every waving flag is new, shrill, red.
>
> Those different deserve their fate,
>   the primitive hiss of us.
>
>   (Citino)

David Citino died in 2005. The College of Humanities for which he wrote the poem from which these lines are taken no longer exists: it was folded into a larger organization some years later. The only thing David failed to predict in "The World Without" is that the red flag of hate would be a baseball cap worn by an American president. The "primitive hiss" is all too real; to be one of "Those different," in the age of tribalist politics, is to be denied the civil and social right to be human.

If you don't read *King Lear*, you don't know how to respond when your daughter tells you the improbable truth. If you don't read *Othello*, you won't understand that the handkerchief is harmless. If you don't read *Jude the Obscure*, you don't know that "The letter killeth" (Hardy, *Jude* 35), and if you don't read St. Paul's Second Letter to the Corinthians, you don't know that the next part of that book's epigraph is "but the spirit giveth life" (*II Corinthians* 3:6). If you don't read *A Passage to India*, you never wonder what actually happened in the Marabar Caves. Reading teaches us empathy; it gives us the ability to read character, to understand situations that come up every day in the real world, which includes the academic world.[20] "So, in the End, Why Read?," asks John Carey in *The Unexpected Professor*, and his answer is spot on target: "It encourages doubt" (John Carey, *Professor* 349). Every person should be made to read *Hamlet* and W. H. Auden's "September 1, 1939" before sitting in judgment on any other human being. How many of our appointed leaders at the university know that "We must love one another or die," the final line of the penultimate verse of "September 1, 1939" (Auden 246), was later changed to "We must love one another *and* die" (italics mine, see Hynes 384)? How many of their chief human resources officers would be able to explain the difference? And I would go further, and make this modest proposal: every administrator in every English-speaking university should have a thorough understanding of the works of James Joyce, up through and including *Finnegans Wake*.

Just as a test of your Empathy Quotient, take this short quiz. The answers are utterly impossible; give yourself a point if you recognize the question.

- ☐ Why does Odysseus fail to recognize his dog Argos?
- ☐ Must Iphigenia die?
- ☐ What does Hamlet mean by "Doubt truth to be a liar"?
- ☐ What is the value of a limestone landscape?
- ☐ Are you waving or drowning?
- ☐ To what do Kurtz's last words refer?
- ☐ What crime has Joseph K committed?
- ☐ Does Tess have anything to be ashamed of?
- ☐ Should Billy Budd hang?
- ☐ When does 2 + 2 = 5?

If you can think intelligently about more than six of these questions, you are wasting your time as an administrator: you should be an academic.

Those with the greatest empathy are often the quickest to discredit it. Ray Ockenden, a professor of German at Wadham College, Oxford, and the kindest man I know, listened patiently to my argument and said, "Empathy? That's what you've got?" Andrea Ward Ross, the best and most empathetic coworker I ever had, wrote back immediately on receiving a flyer advertising the lecture on which this chapter is based, saying, "Empathy is for losers." But think about it in Joycean terms. Who has the least empathy in *Ulysses*? Mr. Deasy: "Ireland, they say, has the honour of being the only country which never persecuted the jews. Do you know that? No. And do you know why? [. . .] Because she never let them in" (*U* 2.437–42). Who runs him a close second? Blazes Boylan, whose only moment of interior discourse in the entire novel occurs when he orders the fruit basket for Molly in "Wandering Rocks," looks down the cut of the shop assistant's blouse, and thinks: "A young pullet" (*U* 10.327).[21] Who else? The Citizen in "Cyclops": "By Jesus, I'll crucify him so I will" (*U* 12.1812). Farrington in "Counterparts," striking at his son: "I'll say a *Hail Mary* for you, pa, if you don't beat me" (*D* 94). The members of the program Committee for the Antient Concert Rooms in "A Mother": "That's a nice lady!" (*D* 148). To act without empathy in Joyce is to be, quite literally, "an impossible person!" (*U* 1.222). Buck Mulligan calls Stephen this after his apology is refused, and at least at that moment he is right: to be "an impossible person" is to fail in the act of personhood, to refuse to recognize another's value or position, to act entirely within one's own self-view. That is precisely the state of the modern university. We have to stop this absence of feeling from taking over the places that we love and the worlds that we live in.

For now I know what is wrong. Teachers must learn to take risks: our administrators have no tolerance for error. We are on a collision course. The modern university is "at fault": at a fault line, a place of tectonic shifting, where two opposite forces are crashing into one another. We have to say, with the Croppy Boy, "*I love my country*"—that is to say, the university—"*above the King*" (Bauerle 270). Otherwise, to pick up the opening thread of this chapter, a young student in sunglasses will never climb up a white lifeguard tower bearing the injunction "No Lifeguard on Duty" by a beach in Evanston, Illinois, to bend her copy of *The Waste Land* to the page that contains the words that begin "A Game of Chess" and read "The Chair she sat in" to a waiting audience of students trying to find their way. Otherwise, another young student will never prepare to do her Cockney accent as the friend of Albert and Lil, reading from her iPhone as a sailboat goes by on Lake Michigan, her face bright with happiness. The sun is shining through the School of Music. She has found the scent. Another student, reading from a music stand, is playing the Bartender in the same scene. He is saying something to her, to which we all need to pay particular attention:

    HURRY UP PLEASE IT'S TIME

    HURRY UP PLEASE IT'S TIME (*TWL* 139)[22]

I have done.

2 | Philatelic Joyce

1. The Collection of Stamps for Pious Purposes

This chapter owes its argument to a lady from Woodstock, Illinois, named Eleanor McClurkin. It was originally called "Stamp Craft in Joyce," but Nicholas Fargnoli, the organizer of the James Joyce Society lectures in New York, where this talk was first given, said that "philatelic" had a deliciously obscene ring to it and persuaded me to change it. I'm glad that he did, though I regretted to inform him, as Molly does, that there is "nothing smutty in it" (*U* 4.355).[1] My model is more Mrs. Mercer, the pious widow in "Araby" who keeps the boy's aunt company until her husband comes: "an old garrulous woman, a pawnbroker's widow, who collected used stamps for some pious purpose" (*D* 25).

Mrs. Mercer's collection of used stamps is part of the rummage pile of decayed objects with which the pages of *Dubliners* are littered: we can put her stamp collection on the scrap heap with the yellowing photograph of the priest that hangs on Eveline's wall (*D* 30), beside the equally yellowing pages of *The Devout Communicant* and *The Memoirs of Vidocq* left behind by the priest in the waste room behind the kitchen, along with his rusty bicycle-pump (*D* 21). The detritus of *Dubliners* has its own peculiar fragrance: an unhappy combination of "the odour of dusty cretonne" (*D* 29) from Eveline's window curtains, mingled with the faint scent of Mr. Duffy's "over-ripe apple" that still lingers in his desk (*D* 104).

It is not entirely clear what the pious purposes of collecting used stamps might be. The general understanding of the line in "Araby" is that these stamps are resold to collectors, with the profits going to the church. I was delighted to discover, after some research into twentieth-century Americana, that there is an alternative possibility:

Figure 2.1. Eleanor McClurkin, "Stamp Craft." Photograph by author.
With kind permission of the McClurkin/Weidenbenner family.

Here, you see that stamps have been artfully arranged as aesthetic objects, to signify a headboard, a footboard, a bedskirt, a teddy bear, and a child at prayer. The pious purpose is here married to the aesthetic one: the stamps have been converted from things in themselves to signs, as Bill Brown, the author of "Thing Theory," insists that things always inevitably are (Bill Brown 1–3). Bill Brown takes his cue from Jacques Derrida, who argues that the poet's job is to "make the thing sign" (qtd. in Bill Brown 3). No longer symbols of the successful transfer of information, the humble stamp has been removed from its privileged place in the right-hand top corner of the envelope and become a broken and repatched signifier of something else, as Duffy's overripe apple signals his fall from Paradise, as the rusty bicycle-pump anticipates the deflation of the spiritual inner tube of the boy in "Araby," as the withered religious objects scattered through the fifteen stories of *Dubliners* indicate the paralyzing effects of Catholic doctrine on turn-of-the-twentieth-century Dublin. "I could interpret these signs" (*D* 25), says the boy as his uncle lurches in, shortly after the departure of Mrs. Mercer: in the same way, we learn to become adept interpreters of

Joycean signs and symbols in our turn, reading piously (that's a bicycle-pump) and then impiously (no it's not; it's a Freudian symbol).

The kneeling child in figure 2.1 is an example of "Stamp Craft," a form of reappropriation that creates a new work of art through the human disposition of sensible matter. One of Joyce's early statements on aesthetics, from the Paris Notebook of 1903, speaks of the distinction between an object's original purpose and its rearrangement:

> Question: *Can a photograph be a work of art?*
> Answer: A photograph is a disposition of sensible matter and may be so disposed for an aesthetic end but it is not a human disposition of sensible matter. Therefore it is not a work of art. [...]

> Question: *Are houses, clothes, furniture, etc., works of art?*
> Answer: Houses, clothes, furniture, etc., are not necessarily works of art. They are human dispositions of sensible matter. When they are so disposed for an aesthetic end they are works of art.
> (*OCP* 104–105)

A useless object, like a used stamp, may be made useful and "disposed for an aesthetic end," exactly as in the case that the twenty-one-year-old Joyce discusses above.

The particular stamps in figure 2.1 were put together by Eleanor McClurkin, of Woodstock, Illinois, who published in 1959 a booklet, *How to Make Hand-Made Greeting Cards for Fun and Profit,* with a section on stamp craft. Like Mrs. Mercer, Eleanor McClurkin had a pious purpose in mind: she was the daughter of a Presbyterian minister and the pamphlet is distributed by a religious publishing house called The Lamp. Her work long postdates the world of late-nineteenth-century Dublin (as you can clearly see by the use of the NATO Commemorative Stamp) but according to Nathan Weidenbenner, a relative of the artist who was a student in my Joyce class in 2006, the McClurkin family had been doing this for generations, way back to his great-grandmother's sister in 1890, so I can at least attest to the practice being familiar to people in turn-of-the-twentieth-century rural Illinois. The art form of decoupage is seen everywhere in Victorian parlors, and in the arts and crafts movement of William Morris, finding its way into the collages of Juan Gris and Georges Braque and the works of Henri Matisse. Perhaps it led to the exploits of Mrs. Mercer. *Timbromanie,* or stamp mania, was in full force by the 1890s, with Queen Victoria keeping a collection for more than thirty years, and her grandson, who would later become King George V, serving as president of the Royal Philatelic Society in 1896 (Browne 163). It is not too far-fetched, then, to imagine the pawnbroker's widow in "Araby" cutting her stamps into works of pious art.

On the reverse of the framed artifact shown in figure 2.1 are two evocative lines:

STAMPCRAFT BY A HOMEBOUND ARTHRITIC
ELEANOR MCCLURKIN. WOODSTOCK, ILL.

Eleanor McClurkin's book has a further connection with the world of *Dubliners*, then, in highlighting the author's lifetime of paralysis: "During thirty-six years in a wheelchair (arthritis—if you're curious!) I've proved that one can be busy and happy just a-sittin' if fingers and brain are occupied" (McClurkin 1). This is good advice for the homebound citizens of *Dubliners*; more importantly, to create "something of beauty out of waste material" (McClurkin 10), as McClurkin puts it, is the Joycean way. Something as rudimentary as Lynch's basket, the object par excellence in *A Portrait of the Artist*, can be shown to have "*wholeness, harmony and radiance*" (*P* 212) if it is seen in the proper light. Think of all the bits of paper flying around the Dublin of *Ulysses* in 1904: the letters in Bloom's desk drawer (*U* 17.1799), the piece of the prize story in *Titbits* with which he wipes himself (*U* 4.537), the "strip of torn envelope" peeping out from under the pillow that indicates that Mrs. Marion Bloom has received a letter from her lover in the morning's mail (*U* 4.308), the letter on foot-and-mouth disease from which Stephen tears off the blank end to write some odd lines about a vampire (*U* 3.405), the throwaway announcing the return of Elijah that bobs down the River Liffey (*U* 10.294). These pieces of litter become radiant and achieve beauty because of what they signify beyond themselves: they have what Roland Barthes calls a connotative rather than a denotative function (Silverman 25–32). "Mother dying come home father" (*U-61* 42), as it is wrongly printed in the Vintage International edition, denotes the death of May Goulding; "Nother dying come home father" (*U* 3.199), as the telegram's text actually appears to Stephen in Paris, connotes the corruption of language. It is the disintegration of "Mother" into "Not her," the trouble with the corpuscles of language in expressing meaning, that makes the telegram a "curiosity to show" (*U* 3.198). The coffee advertisement that Ignatius Gallaher uses as a primitive fax machine to diagram the route of the Invincibles' escape after the Phoenix Park murders—"B is parkgate," "T is viceregal lodge. C is where murder took place. K is Knockmaroon gate" (*U* 7.659–62)—is no longer an advertisement for Bransome's coffee but a coded map signifying beyond itself, as the NATO stamp does in Eleanor McClurkin's kneeling child.

Words, in Joyce, always have this double function: it is the transfer, the act of transportation of meaning, that is of interest. Throughout *Ulysses*, the word is made flesh, the letters of the alphabet become incarnate, and objects are given a new transformative life. Clearly, letters and envelopes and postcards and the whole postal world of *Ulysses* are connected with this: the strip of torn envelope under the pillow connotes a wife's assignation (*U* 4.308), the card in Bloom's hat connotes the possibility of a husband's infidelity (*U* 4.70), as well as holding denotatively upon it the post office box number for Henry Flower at Westland Row (*U* 5.24), which will allow him to receive the letter that Martha Clifford writes (*U* 5.54), which will mistake the word "word" for "world" (*U* 5.295) and lead its recipient into a flurry of anxiety over whether he did in fact remember to tear up the envelope (*U* 5.300). (He did.) But the humble stamp plays a role in all this, too. Stamps are the quintessential double object: they are objects in themselves, fringed, rouletted, hinged or unhinged, colorful, collectible, a consummation devoutly to be wished. But a stamp is also a symbol of transmission, a passport to communication, a "gate of access" (*U* 14.1167). A stamp is an end in itself and a means to an end: it is both perfectly denotative and perfectly connotative. If any object has *integritas* (wholeness: it is itself and no other object), *consonantia* (harmony: it is square, perforated, lickable, perfectly formed), and *claritas* (radiance: its whatness is what gets your message across town), it is the stamp (*P* 212).

Let's look more closely at Martha's letter. Bloom recovers it from the postmistress at Westland Row and furtively checks the envelope:

> Henry Flower Esq,
> ℅ P. O. Westland Row,
>   City.
>   (*U* 5.62–64)

This is typed beautifully, as you might expect: his original advertisement, after all, was for a lady typist. He slips the letter into his pocket, leaving under the vigilant eye of a recruiting poster for the Royal Dublin Fusiliers, the regiment to which Major Tweedy, his wife's father, belonged. Opening the envelope in the darkness of his pocket, he draws out the letter, still in his pocket, crumples the envelope, and feels "Something pinned on: photo perhaps. Hair? No" (*U* 5.80–81). Hair is a better guess—it is a flower—but M'Coy interrupts the proceedings, delaying the presentation of the letter and its pinned object to us, and to Bloom, for several pages. Finally opening the letter itself within the pages of his copy of the *Daily Freeman* (a further concealment, a further framing), he hopes, as we do, to find the answers to all his questions:

> A flower. I think it's a. A yellow flower with flattened petals. Not annoyed then? What does she say?
>
> Dear Henry
>
> I got your last letter to me and thank you very much for it. I am sorry you did not like my last letter. Why did you enclose the stamps?

$$(U 5.239–43)$$

Why indeed? This letter seems to be raising more questions than it answers, a trend that continues as the letter progresses, or regresses:

> I am awfully angry with you. I do wish I could punish you for that. I called you naughty boy because I do not like that other world. Please tell me the real meaning of that word? Are you not happy in your home you poor little naughty boy? [...] So now you know what I will do to you, you naughty boy, if you do not wrote. O how I long to meet you. Henry dear, do not deny my request before my patience are exhausted. Goodbye now, naughty darling, I have such a bad headache. today. and write *by return* to your longing
>
> Martha
>
> P.S. Do tell me what kind of perfume does your wife use. I want to know.
>
> x x x x

$$(U 5.243–59)$$

What we want to know, besides the reasons for Bloom's attraction to a simpering illiterate when he has a highly sexed and intellectually curious reader in bed at home, is why *did* Bloom enclose the stamps? Does he mistakenly think that in Martha Clifford he has found a fellow philatelist? Do stamps conceal a lost language of love, the way that a yellow flower does? Are the stamps intended to pay for services rendered? Does Martha resent the implication that she may be otherwise too poor, too cheap, or too disinterested to spring for postage?

My money's on the first one. Bloom is a bit of a stamp man: it's what he shares with his father-in-law, whom Bloom approvingly remembers as having "had brains enough to make that corner in stamps. Now that was farseeing" (*U* 4.64–65). Major Tweedy's mythical stamp collection doesn't amount to much—Molly thinks of her English accent as "all father left me in spite of his stamps" (*U* 18.890)—but she remembers an American "talking stamps with father" (*U* 18.130), and it's not too much of a stretch to imagine Bloom doing the same. Stamps are connected with Major Tweedy, which is why Bloom looks up at his regiment in the post office after his guilty receipt of Martha Clifford's presumably stamped envelope. Both Martha and Molly meditate on the hidden meanings of stamps, Martha in her letter to Bloom, and Molly in her reading of Lieutenant Mulvey's letter in Gibraltar: "I never thought hed write making an appointment I had it inside my petticoat bodice all day reading it up in every hole and corner while father was up at the drill instructing to find out by the handwriting or the language of stamps" (*U* 18.764–67). Again, stamps are indirectly connected with Molly's father, and stamps are doing what they do best: signifying beyond themselves. Here they indicate through their placement (top center—"Yes"; bottom center—"No"; upside-down—"bring potted meat") an additional whatness, a greater radiance.

Stamps have always, since they were first designed, played a role in concealment: it wasn't until the introduction of the stamp that letters were contained in envelopes, so that all letters before that point were open to any reader. This led to the stealing of many letters, especially money-letters, which were simply, in the absence of any covering, money. The theft of letters was so rampant a crime in the eighteenth century that Ralph Allen, the man who revolutionized the postal system and the model for Squire Allworthy in *Tom Jones*, made it a hanging offense (Browne 31).[2] As a result, letters before the introduction of the stamp often contained secret devices and codes, like the cipher that Bloom uses to conceal the address of Martha Clifford in his kitchen drawer. Hermeneutics, the study of the interpretation of meaning, begins with Hermes, the messenger, and all acts of interpretation return to this root sense of the transfer of meaning through a message or a letter. Jed Rasula has reminded us, in his study of letter writing in *Finnegans Wake*, that to "explicate" literally means "to unfold" (Rasula 529), as one would unfold the pleats of a letter. Letters are always an expression of desire: Mulvey's stamp code, if he actually used one, sends Molly off to other languages of love ("the language of stamps singing I remember shall I wear a white rose"—*U* 18.767–68) that tie her further to the yellow flower on Martha's envelope, and to the stamps enclosed in the correspondence between Martha Clifford and Henry Flower.

Bloom's first thoughts of Major Tweedy in "Calypso" lead to this oddly truncated reverie:

> Stamps: stickyback pictures. Daresay lots of officers are in the swim too. Course they do. The sweated legend in the crown of his hat told him mutely: Plasto's high grade ha. He peeped quickly inside the leather headband. White slip of paper. Quite safe.
>
> $(U\ 4.67\text{--}71)$

Bloom's description of a stamp as a "stickyback" picture recalls Rowland Hill's definition when, as the Postmaster General, he first introduced stamps to the world: "a glutinous wash, which the bringer might by the application of a little moisture, attach to the back of the letter" (qtd. in Browne 51). Stamps are a "sweated legend," signifying as mutely as the message inside Bloom's hat. "Plasto's high grade ha" obscures the missing *t* through another signifying, and sweated-over, text, the white slip of paper ("Quite safe") that is placed stamplike over the legend in the hatband. It is this sweated legend that will allow him to retrieve the letter that will ask him why he enclosed the stamps, and in which the absence of a letter (the *t* of Bloom's high grade "ha*t*") will be restored by the addition of another (the missing *l* of Martha Clifford's "other wor*l*d"). In other words, words are other worlds, Bloom's hat tells us mutely: a word is flesh, a legend sweats.

2. Three Valuable Adhesive or Impressed Postage Stamps

The best evidence that Bloom is a stamp man, of course, is found in "Ithaca," where his reverie on a utopian existence leads him to thoughts of Bloom Cottage in Flowerville, "a thatched bungalowshaped 2 storey dwellinghouse of southerly aspect" (U 17.1504–05), equipped with a tennis court, a shrubbery, a humane beehive, a lumbershed full of eeltraps, and a lawnsprinkler with a hydraulic hose. To pay for all this extravagance, Bloom proposes to generate funds either slowly, through appreciation of income in a Building Society, or quickly, through a "rapid but insecure means to opulence [that] might facilitate immediate purchase" (U 17.1672–73). One such risky venture is a scheme by which a private wireless telegraph could relay the results of the Ascot Gold Cup before the betting windows close in Dublin. Another is the unexpected discovery of an object of great monetary value, such as three particularly valuable adhesive or impressed postage stamps, described as follows: "(7 schilling, mauve, imperforate, Hamburg, 1866: 4 pence, rose, blue paper, perforate, Great Britain, 1855: 1 franc, stone, official, rouletted, diagonal surcharge, Luxemburg, 1878)" (*U* 17.1680–83).

Faced with such an impressive array of useless information, I did what any self-respecting twenty-first-century Joycean would do: I bought them all on eBay. They cost about $67 all told, in 2007 American dollars.

Figure 2.2. Three valuable adhesive or impressed postage stamps. Private collection. Photograph by author.

This is, at least, as close as I could come to Joyce's descriptions (you will have to imagine the colors). On the left is a 7 schilling mauve perforate (imperforate stamps have smooth edges) from Hamburg, which was a free city only until 1870, when it was incorporated by Germany. Since the 7 schilling violet stamps were issued only in 1864 and 1865, Bloom must be in error: there are no 7 schilling stamps from 1866. The one pictured on the left in figure 2.2 is from 1865: had this been an imperforate stamp, it would have been worth thirty times its perforated equivalent. *Scott's Stamp Catalogue* of 1969 lists the imperforate 7 schilling mauve from 1865 as having a value of $90. Had it been a 9 schilling imperforate rather than 7, and *yellow* rather than mauve, it would have been worth six times more still, or $550: the 9 schilling yellow imperforate Hamburg 1864 or 1865 (canceled) is the most valuable stamp in the Hamburg collection (*Scott* II:521). Joyce, in any case, seems to have missed a step, or deliberately undercut Bloom's aspirations: his choices of stamps turn out not to be priceless after all, and the Hamburg one in his utopian trio does not actually exist.

In the center of figure 2.2, the 4 pence stamp with the cameo of Queen Victoria is a rose paper perforate from 1857. It is watermarked, with a large garter (referring to the size of the ring around the portrait). Had it been an 1855 on *white* paper, it would have had a smaller garter and been worth $850 uncanceled. So

Bloom appears to be right on the money with this one: except that the blue paper version, which he wants to find, is worth only a quarter of that. Bloom is off the mark again. (My purchase of such a particular stamp from a gentleman in California led the purveyor to ask if I had any further interest in philatelic purchases; I wrote to him to say that "I just needed this particular one since it appears—or something very much like it—in Joyce's *Ulysses* as one of the 'priceless' stamps that Leopold Bloom dreams of discovering." He wrote back to say, "I wish I could understand one word of what you are saying, but I am glad you are happy.")

On the right in figure 2.2, the stone (or bistre) 1 franc stamp with diagonal surcharge from Luxemburg is not what you see. The stamp on the right is lilac, not stone, and has the denomination of one centime, rather than one franc. Furthermore, it is from 1882, not 1878. Neither is it surcharged, with an overprint that changes or restates the value of the particular stamp, converting it "to a denomination or purpose not originally intended" (*Scott* I:viii). Disappointingly, it is not even rouletted, or separated with a tool that looks like a pizza-cutting wheel, or the "rowel of a spur" (*Scott* I:vi). (You get what you pay for on eBay.) Had this been the denomination I had wanted, with a diagonal surcharge, it would have still have been fairly worthless—but if it had been all of that and *from 1873*, rather than Bloom's specified 1878, it would have sold in 1969 for $1,200. So this is the one stamp that would actually have been worth something (though again, either Joyce or Bloom has the year wrong). The 1 franc Luxemburg from 1879 has a quality that Joyce could have also used: the "f" is sometimes printed as a "p" (as in "pranc"), an error that adds considerably to its value. Scott's catalogue warns the budding philatelist that "Excellent forgeries of [this stamp] are plentiful" (*Scott* II:777). So perhaps I was lucky.

Neither Bloom nor I apparently knows very much about stamps after all: something we share, perhaps, with Major Tweedy, who never did make much money on them, at least as far as Molly remembers (*U* 18.890). Joyce cobbled the information on the three valuable postage stamps from a stamp-collecting manual that he requested from Frank Budgen in November 1921, by which time *Ulysses* had been essentially completed:

> Dear Budgen: *Ulysses* is finished. [. . .] Will you please do poor *Ulysses* these last favours? I want:
>   any little handbook of fortune telling by cards
>   "   "   "   Brit. freemasonry

any catalogue of Whiteley's or Harrod's stores
   "   "   "   Tottenham Crt Rd furnishers
any bookseller's catalogue preferably old. [...]
Also if you can find it any little manual of stampcollecting.

(Letters I:177)

The handbook of fortune-telling serves as a guide for Molly's card play: "what was the 7th card after that the 10 of spades for journey by land then there was a letter on its way and scandals too the 3 queens and the 8 of diamonds for a rise in society" (*U* 18.1317–19). The guide to British Freemasonry assists with Bloom's murmuring of the Masonic oath: "swear that I will always hail, ever conceal, never reveal, any part or parts, art or arts" (*U* 15.4951–52). The store catalogues from Whiteley's and what we would now call Harrods help to furnish Bloom Cottage in Flowerville: "bentwood perch with fingertame parrot (expurgated language), embossed mural paper at 10/- per dozen with transverse swags of carmine floral design and top crown frieze" (*U* 17.1534–36). The bookseller's catalogue finds its way into the description of Bloom's present library: "(cover, brown leather, detached, 5 plates, antique letterpress long primer, author's footnotes nonpareil, marginal clues brevier, captions small pica" (*U* 17.1391–93). And the little manual of stamp collecting has its purpose, too.

There is sadly no evidence that young James Augustine Aloysius Joyce collected stamps in his youth. But I think—no, I am certain—that Joyce would have appreciated the three stamps in figure 2.2, wrong as they are, as collectible objects and that he would have equally enjoyed the adaptation of stamps into religious art for the pious purposes of Eleanor McClurkin. Objects in Joyce are a way of holding on to the past: they are sedimentary, occupying space and time. Like Bloom's potato, there is a memory attached to the stamps provided here. They come from 1865 (the mauve one on the left), 1857 (the rose one in the middle), and 1882 (the lilac one on the right): coincidentally the birthdates of Yeats, Conrad, and Joyce. As Joyce's letter to Budgen suggests, the precise nature of things matter intensely to Joyce, whether it be fortune-telling or freemasonry, bibliophilia or *timbromanie*. The accuracy with which information is recorded, the value of objects in themselves, is never to be underestimated in Joyce.

Bloom's stamps, in the terms of the sociologist Michael Thompson's *Rubbish Theory*, have a transient value at the time of their issue but by 1904 become something of durable value (Thompson 33).[3] "In our culture," says Thompson, "objects are assigned to one or other of two overt categories which I label 'transient' and 'durable.' Objects in the transient category decrease in value over time and have finite life-spans. Objects in the durable category increase in value over time and have (ideally) infinite life-spans" (Thompson 7). Objects are rarely unequivocal; category membership is determined by worldview, and a region of flexibility exists, which Thompson calls "rubbish," where an object can make the "seemingly impossible transfer [. . .] from transience to durability" (Thompson 9). The objects in Bloom's drawer have made this transition: they are durable rubbish (we all have a drawer like this in our kitchen). The objects within it have acquired a dimension of time as well as space: the catalogue moves backward in time from the child's drawings by Milly Bloom to his mother's cameo brooch; Bloom adds a fourth letter to the coded letters from Martha Clifford, arranging them in chronological order of reception. So it is that *Ulysses* records a transient period—approximately twenty hours in June 1904—and reimagines it to make it durable, to give it a density, a dimensionality it never had before.

Modernism in general is intensely engaged with the preservation of objects. T. S. Eliot's campaign to preserve St. Magnus the Martyr, the church where he served as a sidesman (or pew-minder), is the real reason he wrote *The Waste Land*.[4] Minta Doyle's search for her grandmother's brooch on the beach enlists the entire company of *To the Lighthouse*:

> her grandmother's brooch, the sole ornament she possessed—a weeping willow, it was (they must remember it) set in pearls. They must have seen it, she said, with the tears running down her cheeks, the brooch which her grandmother had fastened her cap with till the last day of her life. Now she had lost it. She would rather have lost anything than that! She would go back and look for it. They all went back.
>
> (Woolf, *Lighthouse* 120)

"They all went back": all the modernists return to look for the lost past. The nineteenth century is an ice age away from us, says Walter Benjamin, the patron saint of this kind of nostalgia: his angel of history looks backward as he rushes into the future, staring at the pile of debris that is history rising toward the sky (Benjamin, *Illuminations* 259). A collector annihilates an object's separate original function, converting it into a site of "practical memory" (Benjamin, *Arcades* 205): this is what gives an object its aura, its "object-code" (McCracken 131) by which meaning is made more visible.[5] Minta's brooch is more than a brooch:

"though it might be true that she minded losing her brooch, she wasn't cry-ing only for that. She was crying for something else" (Woolf, *Lighthouse* 121). The church of St. Magnus the Martyr holds an "Inexplicable splendour" (*TWL* 142): it is an object-code that we must crack.[6] As W. G. Sebald succinctly puts it in "Memo":

> Be sure
> not to look back
>
> Attempt
> the art of metamorphosis.
>
> (Sebald, Across the Land and the Water 6)

The work of W. G. Sebald has particular relevance here, especially the objects in the shop windows in Terezín that are photographed and lovingly recorded in *Austerlitz*:

> But even these four still lifes obviously composed entirely at random, which appeared to have grown quite naturally into the black branches of the lime trees standing around the square and reflected in the glass of the windows, exerted such a power of attraction on me that it was a long time before I could tear myself away from staring at the hundreds of different objects, my forehead pressed against the cold window as if one of them or their relationship with each other must provide an un-equivocal answer to the many questions I found it impossible to ask in my mind. What was the meaning of the festive white lace tablecloth hanging over the back of the ottoman, and the armchair with its worn brocade cover? What secret lay behind the three brass mortars of different sizes, which had about them the suggestion of an oracular utterance, or the cut-glass bowls, ceramic vases, and earthenware jugs, the tin advertising sign bearing the words *Theresienstädter Wasser*, the little box of seashells, the miniature barrel organ, the globe-shaped paperweights with wonderful marine flowers swaying inside their glassy spheres, the model ship (some kind of corvette under full sail), the oakleaf-embroidered jacket of light, pale, summery linen, the staghorn buttons, the outsize Russian officer's cap and the olive-green uniform tunic with gilt epaulettes that went with it, the fishing rod, the hunter's bag, the Japanese fan, the endless land-scape painted round a lampshade in fine brushstrokes, showing a river running quietly through perhaps Bohemia or perhaps Brazil? And then

there was the stuffed squirrel, already moth-eaten here and there, perched on the stump of a branch in a showcase the size of a shoebox, which had its beady button eye implacably fixed on me, and whose Czech name— *veverka*—I now recalled like the name of a long-lost friend. What, I asked myself, said Austerlitz, might be the significance of the river never rising from any source, never flowing out into any sea but always back into itself, what was the meaning of *veverka*, the squirrel forever perched in the same position, or of the ivory-colored porcelain group of a hero on horseback turning to look back, as his steed rears up on its hindquarters, in order to raise up with his outstretched left arm an innocent girl already bereft of her last hope, and to save her from a cruel fate not revealed to the observer? They were all as timeless as that moment of rescue, perpetuated but forever just occurring, these ornaments, utensils, and mementoes stranded in the Terezín bazaar, objects that for reasons one could never know had outlived their former owners and survived the process of destruction, so that I could now see my own faint shadow image barely perceptible among them.

(Sebald, *Austerlitz* 195–97)

Here is the list exhaustion familiar to readers of Joyce, but Sebald has in mind something of a riposte to the objects in Bloom's drawer. Instead of the safe haven of #7 Eccles Street, we are in a circle of hell. "One has the impression," says Austerlitz's mother's neighbor Vera, that photographs have "something stirring in them, as if one caught small sighs of despair [. . .], as if the pictures had a memory of their own" (Sebald, *Austerlitz* 182). When Austerlitz visits the town of Terezín, he takes photographs of door after door, all closed, all "obstructing access to a darkness never yet penetrated" (Sebald, *Austerlitz* 190). Four shop windows open to a world rescued from oblivion, revealing the crucial details of memory, the restoration of past experience. Twentieth-century objects are fetishized beyond their suspended immobility: the "ivory-colored porcelain" hero (Sebald, *Austerlitz* 197), always unable to rescue the innocent girl, stands as a rebuke to the unravished bride on Keats' Grecian urn. The *veverka* "forever perched in the same position" (Sebald, *Austerlitz* 197) becomes Sebald's great symbol, recovering its hoard in the newly fallen snow, tracking the past to save itself. "How indeed do the squirrels know, what do we know ourselves, how do we remember, and what is it we find in the end?" (Sebald, *Austerlitz* 204).

Austerlitz sees himself as a shadow in the frame, and Sebald is barely perceptible behind Austerlitz: we are a part of all that we have met. T. S. Eliot knew this:

> I have said before
> That the past experience revived in the meaning
> Is not the experience of one life only
> But of many generations—not forgetting
> Something that is probably quite ineffable:
> The backward look behind the assurance
> Of recorded history, the backward half-look
> Over the shoulder, towards the primitive terror.
>
> (Eliot, "Dry Salvages," *Poems* 194–95)

The thing always signs: it is never an object. When Walter Benjamin attempted to cross the Pyrenees in 1940, he held on to his black briefcase as if it was his life (qtd. in Buck-Morss 332). Dante Riordan's brushes (*P* 15) or Ignatius Gallaher's orange tie (*D* 70) are fossils that have evolved into a new nature; they enter a cabinet of curiosities, they are signs beyond themselves. "*An object falls*" (*U* 15.3594): the match that drops so tantalizingly into the text in "Aeolus" ("I have often thought since on looking back over that strange time that it was that small act, trivial in itself, that striking of that match [. . .]"—*U* 7.763–64) flares into life only when Bloom returns a box of matches to Stephen ("That fell. [. . .] Lucifer. Thanks"—*U* 15.3595–99), allowing the match to become a fallen Lucifer and to unite the protagonists in conversation for the first time. What Bloom's stamps signify is not just a rapid but insecure means to opulence but the far more durable value of the transfer of meaning, the recollection of the past, that is also the proud responsibility of these tiny beautiful colored squares.

3. The Real Meaning of Philately

> Now that was farseeing.
>
> (*U* 4.65)

Stamps have a future as well as a past: Bloom intends to sell them if he finds them, after all. Stamps are not just objects of history but symbols of transmission: and here the meaning of the word "philately," noted earlier, comes into play. Philately literally means "the love of not paying taxes," a fascinating but strangely unhelpful definition. The word comes from three Greek roots: *philos*, meaning love, *a-*, the prefix indicating the negation or lack of something, and *telos*, from *teleomai*: to complete, to execute, to bring to an end, to fulfill. One frequently fulfilled or completed action in Greek times was the payment of a tax, and so *teleos* or *telos* is a tax, or a fixed charge: a stamp is that which obviates the necessity of payment on receipt. It is a prepaying mechanism designed by Rowland Hill to prevent the world from suffering what happened to his mother: the dreaded "Postman's Knock."

Postal rates in the 1830s had soared beyond people's means, and all letters, not having stamps or envelopes, had to be paid for on receipt. Each letter was taxed on the distance it had traveled and on its size, and Hill, who reputedly was sent out of the house by his mother to sell a bag of clothes for a batch of letters, designed the stamp as an indicator that the tax had already been paid. The arrival of stamps with the penny black, designed by Hill himself, led to an explosive adoption of the idea worldwide: after Great Britain started things off in 1840, the second country to adopt the stamp was Brazil in 1843, with nineteen other countries following suit by 1854 (Browne 162). The stamp was an improvement on the previous system in several ways. Postmen no longer had to carry around large amounts of money, which, as we have already seen, made them less likely to be robbed or walk off the job. Postmen no longer had to wait to collect payment before delivering a letter, improving their delivery rate considerably: a test of the new method showed collectors delivering less than one letter a minute, while postmen with the new stamp method could deliver more than sixteen (Browne 50). But best of all, when the letter came to your door, you got it for free.

This is where the idea of Joyce as a philatelic writer really comes into play. Joyce's characters are always looking for ways of not paying for things: the inhabitants of the Martello tower fail to fully reconcile the account for ten mornings' worth of milk (U 1.458), and Hynes has owed Bloom three shillings for weeks (U 7.119). Joyce himself was famous for skipping out before paying the rent, but the I.O.U.s in *Ulysses* are not just flaws of character or plot devices: they are built into the way we read Joyce. Joyce is philatelic because he shows a love of preemption: all his writing casts forward. The white slip of paper that partially obscures the sweated legend in Bloom's high grade hat is given no explanation until he produces the card to collect Martha's letter from the Post Office in Dolphin's Barn (U 4.70, 5.54). The card is prepaid, as it were, anticipating the later transfer of meaning: it is a postage stamp, promising the reader a later receipt. These unexplained anticipations are part of the matrix of effects that Fritz Senn has called "dislocutions" (Senn 202), the adjectival form of which we could call philatelic.[7]

"Hades" is full of these promissory notes to the reader:

—What way is he taking us? Mr Power asked through both windows.
—Irishtown, Martin Cunningham said. Ringsend. Brunswick street.
    Mr Dedalus nodded, looking out.
—That's a fine old custom, he said. I am glad to see it has not died out.

(*U* 6.33–36)

What's a fine old custom? Taking the hearse through Irishtown? No—the text looks forward philatelically to what Simon, looking out, has seen before us:

All watched awhile through their windows caps and hats lifted by pass-ers. Respect. The carriage swerved from the tramtrack to the smoother road past Watery lane. Mr Bloom at gaze saw a lithe young man, clad in mourning, a wide hat.

(*U* 6.37–40)

And who is that? Bloom has processed the information before us—we are only given philatelic hints in the Hamlet hat and the funeral garb that stamp him for later (in this case, immediate, but still later) receipt:

—There's a friend of yours gone by, Dedalus, he said.
—Who is that?
—Your son and heir.

(*U* 6.41–43)

"Dedalus" is doubled here: it could refer to Stephen ("There's a friend of yours: Dedalus") or to Simon ("There's a friend of yours, Dedalus"). "Dedalus" is then impossible to read until Simon's response—"Who is that?"—establishes that the word philatelically addresses the intended listener rather than revealing the identity of the object in view.

—Was that Mulligan cad with him? His *fidus Achates*!
—No, Mr Bloom said. He was alone.
—Down with his aunt Sally, I suppose, Mr Dedalus said, the Goulding

faction, the drunken little costdrawer and Crissie, papa's little lump of
dung, the wise child that knows her own father.

Mr Bloom smiled joylessly on Ringsend road.

(*U* 6.49–54)

Why "joylessly"? What possible reason does the text give Bloom to despair? We
find out only later that is his own child, who never knew his father, his own little
lump of love, that flashes before him: "Full of his son. He is right. Something to
hand on. If little Rudy had lived. See him grow up. Hear his voice in the house.
Walking beside Molly in an Eton suit. My son. Me in his eyes" (*U* 6.74–76).
Bloom is joyless on Ringsend Road because his journey has reached the end of
the line before us, a circle, or Ringsend, that is not completed until the stamped
word "joylessly" finds its home in "Me in his eyes."

Something with a *telos* is looking for its end, as Odysseus does in his return
to Ithaca. The work that makes the highest virtue of the philatelic principle is
"Work in Progress," a book that is itself a dead letter. "[E]ver looked sufficiently
longly at a quite everydaylooking stamped addressed envelope?" (*FW* 109.07–
08), asks the announcer of Anna Livia's mamafesta, the letter around which
the *Wake* revolves as a purported exoneration of her husband's unspeakable
and unspecified crime. "Admittedly it is an outer husk" (*FW* 109.08): inside the
stamped addressed envelope is the item for which a stamp is always an advance
payment, the novel itself. As Wilhelm Füger says, "In *Finnegans Wake*, the letter and the novel can no longer be separated from each other, since the letter
actually *is* the novel" (Füger 412, italics Füger's). Inside of the letter of the novel
there is another letter, and "so each and so on to nolast term" (*U* 17.2141–42)
as Bloom thinks atelically of the series of his wife's imagined lovers. The post is
eternally delayed, Derrida says in *The Post Card*, as the word "post" implies: "il
n'est pas sûr que le sens du p.s. (postal service) soit lui-même assuré d'arriver à
destination, ni le mot poster" [it is not certain that the sense of p.s. (postal service) should assure us of a letter's arrival at its destination, nor the word "post"]
(qtd. in Benstock 184, translation mine). *Finnegans Wake* describes itself as a
"letter selfpenned to one's other, that neverperfect everplanned" (*FW* 489.33–
34): it deliberately and successfully fails to complete its expression, an arrow
that never reaches its target, a stamped envelope that can never be opened by
its imaginary addressee. Shem, the author, is the self and Shaun, the postman,
is the other: if *Finnegans Wake* is a tale of Shem and Shaun, then Shem is the
book's content and Shaun is its transfer.

These are the two senses of the stamp, an object in itself and an object of transmission, and these are the two senses of language in *Finnegans Wake*: the idea that everything is a carrier of meaning, descriptive and discursive, a subject that is also a signifying, a vehicle for itself. As Beckett famously has it: "His writing is not *about* something, *it is that something itself*."[8] Hanjo Berressem writes in "The Letter! The Litter!" that writing in the *Wake* "can be understood as a completely self-reflexive system" (Berressem 147): in the words of the *Wake*, "every word, letter, penstroke, paperspace is a perfect signature of its own" (*FW* 115.07–08). Jed Rasula hears "*l'être*" within "*lettre*" (Rasula 526): letters are epistolary, alphabetical, and a form of being. And that form of being is a state of desire: desire for meaning, for circulation, to forestall the dead letter box that Shari Benstock punningly calls an "*arrêt de mo(r)t*" (Benstock 184): an end of words (*arrêt de mot*) is a kind of death (*arrêt de mort*). "All the world's in want and is writing a letters" (*FW* 278.13–14), to quote the Postman's sister, Issy. She continues: "A letters from a person to a place about a thing. And all the world's on wish to be carrying a letters" (*FW* 278.14–16).[9]

What philately means most broadly is freedom, the love of being without boundaries, the ability to fly by the nets of "nationality, language, religion" (*P* 203), to send a letter for a penny black across the length and breadth of the kingdom, to wing one's words across the world. Philately is our fox: through it we escape paralysis, depart from Dublin, soar toward the sun, pay for a home in Flowerville, pass from County Wicklow through the River Liffey out into the sea. Joyce is always and only about the freedom that a stamp, an envelope, a letter, a word, a work of art can bring. If "Penelope" can be "the indispensable countersign to Bloom's passport to eternity" (*Letters* I:160), I am sure that Joyce, in designing his own passport to eternity, remembered to put a stamp on it.

3 | *Finnegans Wake* for Dummies

That's all very well—but how does one begin to become even conversant in the language of *Finnegans Wake*? It's a crucial question, and one that this chapter hopes to answer. Any first reading of *Finnegans Wake* resembles a novice's climb up a rock wall, secured precariously with footholds in the work of other Joyceans, undertaken by someone who is afraid to look down for fear of an almighty crash. As always, Joyce provides the analogy for the reader's experience in the *Wake*'s first page:

> The fall (bababadalgharaghtakamminarronnkonnbronntonnerronntu-onnthunntrovarrhounawnskawntoohoohoordenenthurnuk!) of a once wallstrait oldparr is retaled early in bed and later on life down through all christian minstrelsy.

> (*FW* 1.15–18)

"The great fall of the offwall" (*FW* 1.18–19) is the collapse of Wall Street, the great fall that Humpty had, the "pftjschute" (*FW* 1.19) of Finnegan and HCE, the fall of Icarus and Lucifer, the battles of Jericho and Waterloo, and the loss of Paradise. "Circe" has prepared us for this impregnation of language: "O! Weeshwashtkissinapooisthnapoohuck?" (*U* 15.3812–13) sings Marion Bloom in extremis, "Phillaphulla Poulaphouca / Poulaphouca" (*U* 15.3429–30) chants the Poulaphouca waterfall. We are "on the aquaface," fighting a "penisolate war" (*FW* 3.14, 3.06)—our battle is not the Duke of Wellington's, not yet, but with that slipperiest of foes, a language that swerves and bends as the River Liffey does in the *Wake's* circling sentence that closes and opens the book:

> A way a lone a last a loved a long
>
> the
>
> riverrun, past Eve and Adam's, from swerve of shore to bend of bay, brings us by a commodius vicus of recirculation back to Howth Castle and Environs. (*FW* 628.15–16, 3.01–03)

How is one meant to begin to comprehend this? Let me begin with a confession: in September 2003, after attending two decades of Joyce symposia, teaching more than a dozen courses on Joyce, writing a book entirely devoted to Joyce's work, and editing another, I still had not yet read *Finnegans Wake*. Worse, aside from desultory efforts with occasional reading groups, I had never even tried to. Thoroughly ashamed of this depressing state of affairs, I did the only thing I knew how: I wrote a song about my inability to read the *Wake*, set to the music of Bunthorne's aria from *Patience*. In that best of Gilbert and Sullivan's operettas, Bunthorne is a parody of Oscar Wilde, with a lot of Algernon Swinburne thrown in, and in his patter song he confesses his dislike of all things that are decadent, medieval, and Japanese. That seemed a fairly good description of the *Wake* as well, as far as I could tell, so I wrote this (to be sung to the tune of "If You're Anxious for to Shine"):

(Recit.)
Am I alone? And unobserved? I am.
Then let me own, I'm an academic sham.
My reading of the Wake's *a fake.*
Up to about page nine, I'm fine.
But the idea of reading every word's absurd.
Let me confess.
A languid love of Livia does not blight me,
Acronyms of HCE do not delight me,
I do not care for "thunderwords" and "Wellingturds,"
Everything one sees is in Chinese,
Even my attempts at the marginalia end in abject
  failure,
In short, my reading of the Wake's *an affectation*
Born of a morbid love of reputation!

(Verse 1)
If you're anxious for to shine in the high
    Joycean line
As a man of tenure rare,
You must get up all the germs of the neologic terms
And plant them everywhere.
You must lie about the phrases scattered through
    the text like daisies
For no clear reason why
Though they mean exactly zero you will always be
    a hero
If you can make them signify!

(Chorus)
And everyone will say
As you walk your mystic way,
"If this young man can read Finnegans Wake
Which is much too deep for me,
Why what a very singularly deep young man this
    deep young man must be!"

(Verse 2)
Be eloquent in praises of the very dull old pages
Only read by friends of Fritz Senn
And praise the ballad highly
(The one on Persse O'Reilly)
And leave the rest to them.
You must get all in a tizzy about Shem and Shaun
    and Issy
And they'll all give you a break
And if desperate start singing, just set the
    rafters ringing
With one more verse of "Finnegan's Wake!"

(Chorus)
And everyone will say
As you sing your mystic way,
"If this young man can sing 'Finnegan's Wake'

Which has too many notes for me,
Why what a very musically deep young man this
    deep young man must be!"

(Verse 3)
Then you must learn to be a niggler and prance
    among the sigla
Like Bishop or O'Shea
Don't read the book, just quote it, mine for epigrams, footnote it,
That's by far the simplest way.
Though the McCarthyites may jostle you will rank as an apostle
To the great non-reading throng,
You'll be one of the high elect
If you can drop Swiss German dialect
Into an after-dinner song!

(Chorus)
And everyone will say
As you bluff your desperate way,
"If he's trying to fake a book like Finnegans Wake
And can't fool even me,
Why what an unadulterated kind of fraud this total fraud must be!"

Performed at the traditional postbanquet entertainment at a Joyce Birthday conference in Miami in 2004, the song, called "Running Out of Patience, or Punthorne's Pride," was a problematic, even a professionally suicidal, thing for me to sing.[1] It was received with great applause, which was bewildering (I had, after all, done the postprandial equivalent of removing my clothes in public), until I realized that the audience thought I was making fun of *them*. "Brilliant, Sebastian," said Sheldon Brivic, "you've got that type down exactly." John Gordon shook his head sagely and said, "Skewered them nicely that time." "But," I protested, "the song is about me: I've never read the *Wake* either!" "Oh—very good," they said, still smiling: "That's quite excellent."

It was like something out of Lewis Carroll, or the first decade of twenty-first-century American politics (in retrospect, a more innocent time): a fraud myself, it was unimaginable that I could be taken for a fraud. Then things became still worse, as I was named as a member of the Board of Trustees for the International James Joyce Foundation and, finally, as its president. Chance the

gardener, in Jerzy Kosinski's excellent (and prophetic) film *Being There*, reaches
the presidency based on the innocuous nature of his platitudes about garden-
ing, all the time maintaining the IQ of one of the lesser vegetables.[2] Was this to
be my fate? No: I had to go and get properly dressed. And now, so can you.

I suppose the origin of all my trepidation concerning *Finnegans Wake* comes
down to the missing apostrophe in its title. I still remember the index finger of
my dissertation director, A. Walton Litz (and if there ever was a case of someone with more knowledge in his little finger than I would have in a lifetime of
studying Joyce, this was it), a finger resting over a typo on the pages I had laid
before him. "There's no apostrophe, Sebastian," he said, "in *Finnegans Wake*.
You're going to need to know that." He turned out to be right. At the end of my
graduate studies, before leaving for Ohio State University full of excitement at
the prospect of teaching the *Wake* (an undertaking I avoided zealously for the
next sixteen years), I met with Walt Litz again and asked him how I should begin. He sighed (he was always doing that) and gave me a selection of chapters
to read, which I wrote down on a napkin. I have it still. On one side, it lists the
books I would need to make sense of the *Wake*: Adaline Glasheen's *Census*, the
Skeleton Key, Clive Hart's *Structure and Motif*, and a new book by John Bishop,
Joyce's Book of the Dark (this was in 1987). On the other side, the text reads as
follows:

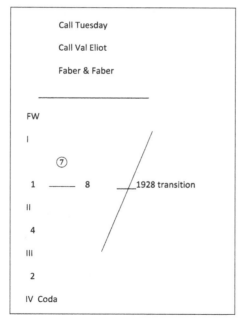

Figure 3.1. The Litz napkin.
Reconstruction by author.

There's a lot that's wrong with this picture.[3] To start with, there was no way a graduate student looking to publish compromising material on T. S. Eliot in the Paul Elmer More Collection at the Firestone Library in Princeton was ever going to call Valerie Eliot. Second, though the napkin reads "1928 transition," referring to the publication of the eight chapters of Book I in *transition* monthly, the episodes actually appeared from April to November 1927. And third, there is the advice itself:

- Book I chapters 1–8 (with an emphasis on I.7: the acridly autobiographical bit called "Shem the Penman")
- Book II chapter 4 (the first bit published in *transatlantic review* in 1924: four views of a dreamer dreaming of the Isolde love triangle)
- Book III chapter 2 (an odd choice, this one: the older brother Shaun preaching before his Rainbow girls)
- Book IV (the coda, or *ricorso*)

Looking back over this list, I think either Professor Litz was trying to sabotage me or I wrote them down wrong. Perhaps I was meant to have read not II.4 and III.2 but II.2 (the excellent bit with margins, marginally relevant footnotes, and white space everywhere) and III.4 (the only bit with a decent plot, where you can actually see what's happening, as the Earwicker family goes through a difficult night). But I did nothing, except to save the napkin for emergencies.

More than a quarter of a century later, my not having read the *Wake* had become an official emergency. Sporadic attendance at *Wake* reading groups had shown me that just reading the thing aloud in a bar isn't enough: without anything to frame the paragraph at hand, the point is utterly lost, and the reading descends into a cavorting in the ear, having the experience but missing the meaning. So I assigned myself a graduate seminar on the *Wake* for Spring 2004, whether I was ready for it or not, and had to develop a reading plan. Scaling the wall of I.1 right off the bat, as the Litz Napkin (as we must now call it) suggests, makes the first three pages of anyone's copy of the *Wake* look like Yeats' "Old Rocky Face" from "The Gyres," pitted with scars and pitons and marked with holds and crevices, all powerless to prevent the inevitable fall into the intolerable babble of the Museyroom. There had to be another way in.

Constantin Brâncuşi's drawing of Joyce, the drawing that greets the reader at the beginning of Ellmann's biography, gave me the key: his "Symbol of Joyce," with two parallel lines on the left and the Archimedean spiral on the right (see figure 0.4). The spiral is the clue: to get into *Finnegans Wake* you have to start in the middle and work your way out. Again, the path that Joyce presents us to escape the labyrinth is centrifugal, or "ventrifugal" (*FW* 605.17), as we have seen in St. Kevin's Matryoshka-like ablutions in "an enysled lakelet yslanding a lacustrine yslet" (*FW* 605.20). We move onward and upward, starting in medias res and following Joyce to the "utmost bound of human thought" (Tennyson 564). This is the solution to the *Finnegans Wake* paradox, which states that *Finnegans Wake* cannot be read except by someone who has already read *Finnegans Wake*. Why not, I thought as I prepared my syllabus, start with the easiest sections? We would read the book not in page order, or in the order of composition (though we found ourselves often in step with Joyce's writing process), but in order of difficulty, starting with what was generally agreed to be the easiest material, moving to the intermediate level, and finally attacking the hardest chapter of all. This "ski-slope" method of reading the *Wake* (where you bundle up carefully for the bunny slopes marked with green dots, let yourself take some turns and a couple of falls on the blue squares, and risk your neck on the black diamonds) allows the text to give the reader a sense of achievement as each level is passed (a sense it otherwise reserves to the final page) and the impression of real progress section by section. When learning how to play a piece of music, such as the Prelude in C from Bach's Cello Suite no. 3, you don't begin at the first bar and play through until you get it right. You have to learn how to play the cello first, moving through the bow hold, D major scales, Gustav Holst's "In the Bleak Midwinter," Bach's "Air on a G String," and only then can you crack the book open with the cello suites, which you stole from your brother who was given them by an old girlfriend long, long ago.

To be specific, the following reading plan is recommended for new readers of the *Wake*:

Round One
I.5: "Mamafesta" (104–25)
I.6: "Riddles" (126–68)
I.7: "Shem the Penman" (169–95)
I.8: "Anna Livia Plurabelle" (196–216)
II.4: "Mamalujo" (383–99)
III.4: "Dawn" (555–90)
IV: "Ricorso" (593–628)

Round Two
I.1–I.4: "HCE" (3–103)

II.1: "Children's Games" (219–59)
II.2: "Night Lessons" (260–308)
III.1–III.3: "Shaun" (403–554)

Round Three
II.3: "The Pub" (309–82)

This was the approach for a graduate seminar conducted at Ohio State University in Spring 2004, and what follows is a report on its success (the syllabus is included here in Appendix 3.1). The three-round method moved in outwardly radiating circles, like Yeats' widening gyres:

> We will begin with chapters that are either self-referential (the letter in I.5, the riddles in I.6), or that introduce plot elements (sunset in II.4, dawn in III.4, the final ricorso in IV), or that advance our sense of the main characters (Shem the younger brother in I.7, Anna Livia the mother in I.8). That will be our first round. We will then cycle back to the beginning (in true Wakean fashion) and read I.1, I.2, I.3, and I.4 (thereby putting HCE's punishment before his crime), II.1 and II.2 (those marvelous and childish sections of the *Wake*), and the three troublesome sections on Shaun, III.1, III.2, and III.3. And finally we will tackle the hardest and most rewarding chapter, II.3, which is the best example of *Finnegans Wake* as both montage (for eye types) and radio broadcast (for ear types), and itself tells a story (or a series of interwoven stories) three times, to mirror our three readings. So the method of our reading, round and round in threes, will be supported by the form of this extraordinary text.

This circular approach is well supported by *Wake* criticism, which since Clive Hart's chart of "Principal Counterpointed Cycles in *Finnegans Wake*" has been obsessed with circles (Hart 251). At the same time as we were reading three ways, ramping up slowly with the italicized peroration at the beginning of I.5 and finishing off at a tearing pace with the "*abnihilisation of the etym*" (*FW* 353.22) in the middle of II.3, we allowed four gospels to light our way into the Wakean darkness. These four texts, by disciples who have devoted a great part of their lives to making sense of the *Wake*, were: in the role of the Gospel of St. Matthew, Campbell and Robinson's *Skeleton Key*; in the role of the Gospel of St. Mark, William York Tindall's *Reader's Guide*; in the role of the Gospel of St. Luke, Glasheen's *Third Census*; and as the metaphysical gospel, in the role for which the author was named at birth, John Gordon's *Plot Summary*. Before reading any section of the *Wake*, we would read what these four texts had to say about it, in gospel order. The *Skeleton Key* is a World War II book, Tindall's is a hippie book from 1969 dropping jokes about LSD, Glasheen's third round through the census was completed in 1977, and Gordon's cold mad feary gospel was published in 1986: these four critics, from four different decades, became our four wise men (though one is a woman), our "Mamalujo" (*FW* 397.11) leading us through the book step by palimpsestic step.

And at the same time as we were reading the book four ways, through the secondary material (and we used McHugh's *Annotations*, too, as our St. Paul), and three ways, circling or spiraling around the text, we read the book in two ways, by day and by night. This course was offered before the publication of Edmund Epstein's *A Guide through* Finnegans Wake, which would otherwise have been perfectly suited for its purposes (see chapter 9). *Finnegans Wake* must (and this will be deeply controversial) be read sober, in the cold light of day, which we did in classtime, checking on plot elements, looking up references in the guidebooks, puzzling out the meaning of the text. But it must also (and this will not be controversial at all) be read at night, with the ear rather than the eye, preferably over a glass of something, to bring the sounds of the text to life. At our nighttime meetings, we allowed the text to wash over us as music, as soundscape, as a flow of language, more id than ego, more nightmare than waking. Our rules for reading throughout the course were as follows:

1. *discover* the key words in the passage;
2. *define* one or more of them to get Joyce's drift;
3. *brood* to let the associations animate the page.

The first meeting was cleverly designed to begin very dramatically with "In the name of Annah the Allmaziful, the Everliving, the Bringer of Plurabilities, haloed be her eve, her singtime sung, her rill be run, unhemmed as it is uneven!" (*FW* 104.01–03). The twenty students who showed up that first day (undergraduates and graduates from physics, Russian, Spanish, English, mathematics, education: a wonderful and necessary spectrum of the university) found references in Persian, Afrikaans, and Serbo-Croatian, sometimes all at once. And we argued: whether Joyce would have known about Popeye, or King Kong, or the discovery of Pluto, or the teddy as an article of ladies' lingerie (yes to all four), or the Kit Kat Club, or Seabiscuit, or the selling of Babe Ruth by the Boston Red Sox to finance the musical *No, No, Nanette* (maybe to all three), or Hell's Angels or Tweety Bird or the Kennedy assassination (no to all three).[4] Michael

Meagher, maddened by my inability to get the four provinces of Ireland right, made me a map, which not only clarifies the North-South-East-West axis of the provinces of the four old men but locates each county in *Finnegans Wake*-ese: in the province of "Moonster" (*FW* 389.05) we find the counties of "curries" (*FW* 595.13), "korps" (*FW* 595.10), and "waterfowls" (*FW* 595.12); in "Cannought" (*FW* 389.05) there is "rogues comings" (*FW* 595.16), "sly goings" (*FW* 595.16), and "goldways" (*FW* 595.14); in "Leanstare" (*FW* 389.05) we find "curlews" (*FW* 595.13), "awfully" (*FW* 577.15), and "wextward" (*FW* 245.08); and in "*Ulstria*" (*FW* 270.L4) there is "coffins" (*FW* 595.15), "armaurs" (*FW* 595.16), and "tantrums" (*FW* 595.15). (Translation: in the province of Munster, we find the counties of Kerry, Cork, and Waterford; in the province of Connaught, the counties of Roscommon, Sligo, and Galway; in the province of Leinster, the counties of Carlow, Offaly, and Wexford; in the province of Ulster, the counties of Cavan, Armagh, and Antrim.) Included on the Meagher Map is an inset on the Howth Castle and Environs area, listing as many versions of Chapelizod, the home of HCE and ALP, as the cartographer could find: "Shopalist" (*FW* 6.33), "Seeple Isout" (*FW* 7.28–29) "Shop Illicit" (*FW* 29.01), "Issy-la-Chapelle" (*FW* 80.36), "Cheepalizzy's" (*FW* 111.06), "Chapelldiseut" (*FW* 236.20), "Capel Ysnod" (*FW* 325.14), "Izd-la-Chapelle" (*FW* 334.36), "Ship-le-Zoyd" (*FW* 370.29), and "Capolic Gizzards" (*FW* 370.36). The map goes one step further to list, on the bottom left, every one of the class's students as they appear in *Finnegans Wake* (I'm "Attaboy Knowling" in *FW* 442.05).[5]

What appeared over the course of ten weeks' study was a book that grew with our understanding of it. As the stories in *Dubliners* grow in complexity from the three stories of childhood to the final statement of childhood, adolescence, maturity, and public life that is "The Dead," as the narrative matures in *Portrait* from baby talk to the voice of an artist, as *Ulysses* grows from innocent origins into a hybrid that no literary comparison could conveniently compartmentalize, so *Finnegans Wake*, in this tricyclic reading, is allowed to undergo a linear metamorphosis. Our first four weeks were a gradual unfolding, from the part Joyce said was accepted as the easiest (I.5: the "mamafesta"—*FW* 104.04) to the part that Bishop says is a good place to start (I.6: the riddles) to the part that all readers of *Ulysses* will recognize (I.7: the agonies of Shem as he reviews Joyce's life and work to date), to the part that everyone who reads the *Wake* wants to have read (I.8: the transubstantiation of prose into poetry at the end of "Anna Livia").[6] We learned from those four introductory sections about the text itself in the multiple metaphors for the *Wake* in I.5, about the characters through the riddles in I.6, about Joyce in I.7, and about language in I.8. The *"Tunc* page of the Book of Kells" appears in I.5 (*FW* 122.23) and provides, as many have noticed, an abiding metaphor for the book itself in its elaborate illumination of a simple vital scene, an embroidered screen that hides a temporary death ("Tunc," meaning "Then," is the first word of a verse in the Gospel of St. Matthew that refers to the crucifixion of Christ). Quite by accident, I found the page in a coloring book in my five-year-old's room, and the students took turns coloring it in on the first day, with results that are now, to my utter delight, found on the cover of the first number of the forty-sixth volume of the journal of record for Joyceans everywhere, the *James Joyce Quarterly*.[7]

By skipping to II.4 and III.4 we allowed ourselves the luxury of recognizing that there were things we didn't yet know, and weren't ready for, and could read the "Dream of King Mark" in the isolation in which it was originally published in the *transatlantic review*.[8] II.4, after all, doesn't follow II.3 or lead to III.1 in any way, and its insertion at this point is a useful reminder of some critical themes (betrayal, illicit love) and critical structures (the dream, the four-part perspective on the dream). Then there is nothing like skipping 150 pages of the *Wake* to keep one fresh, and it pays to be fresh for III.4, where HCE's pause at his daughter's door on the way to attend to a crying child is one of the scariest moments in fiction (*FW* 561), and the sight of the parents in rut from the rear view one of the funniest (*FW* 564): the whole of III.4 shows Joyce at his dazzling best. I.8, II.4, III.4, and IV are all final chapters in the Viconian cycle, chaotic chapters, but chapters of return, and when IV comes to a close in a flood, a millrace that sweeps down and out of sight, the current that pushes the reader to return to I.1 is irresistible, and we are washed up on the shores of I.1, like a drowning sailor reaching dry land.

Or quicksand, rather: Round Two is harder than the first. But we are ready for Kate and her Museyroom now: we know the verbal tics of the various characters, we have known the motifs already, known them all, and we know that HCE is guilty of something but we don't know what. It's somehow much more satisfying to discover that the crime is inconsequential after having seen its consequences, and we are now much more at ease with its uncertainty. The purposelessness of Mutt and Jute's vaudeville act in I.1 (*FW* 16–18) can be set against the perplexities of Muta and Juva in IV (*FW* 609–10), and the idea that I.2, I.3, and I.4 all rehearse the same scene over and over again is no longer foreign to readers at this second level. The children's games in II.1 and II.2 make a nice layer of jam between the bread of HCE's crime and trial in the first four sections of Book 1 and Shaun's three sections in Book III, with II.2, sitting roughly in the middle of the second reading, still retaining its vital function as a fulcrum for the book.

Round Two circles around a crime in a park involving one man ("the Haberdasher"), two girls ("the two Curchies"), and three soldiers ("the three Enkelchums in their Bearskin ghoats") (*FW* 51.14–15). There are as many theories as to the nature of the crime as there are human anxieties: this is the central fall, "Der Fall Adams" (*FW* 70.05). "Life," says Joyce deliciously, "is a wake" (*FW* 55.05): in "a wake" we are both alive and dead in a single collapsible space. "The house of Atreox is fallen indeedust" (*FW* 55.03), and "on the bunk of our breadwinning lies the cropse of our seedfather" (*FW* 55.05–08). The "seedfather" of HCE is the Croppy Boy, a "cropse" who is both crop and corpse, and also the copse in Phoenix Park where the fall has taken place. Like the Croppy Boy, HCE has succumbed to the essential indignity of misapprehension: both have been "subjected to the horrors of the premier terror of Errorland" (*FW* 62.25). "Errorland" is both Ireland and Alice's Wonderland, where Alice's fall leads to another trial: "Down, down, down. Would the fall *never* come to an end?," "*All persons more than a mile high to leave the court*" (Carroll 27, 156). Joyce's homage to Lewis Carroll is perfectly clear:

Thus the unfacts, did we possess them, are too imprecisely few to warrant our certitude, the evidencegivers by legpoll too untrustworthily irreperible where his adjugers are semmingly freak threes but his judicandees plainly minus twos. Nevertheless Madam's Toshowus waxes largely more lifeliked (entrance, one kudos; exits, free) and our notional gullery is now completely complacent, an exegious monument, aerily perennious. Oblige with your blackthorns; gamps, degrace! And there many have paused before that exposure of him by old Tom Quad, a flashback in which he sits sated, gowndabout, in clericalease habit, watching bland sol slithe dodgsomely into the nethermore, a globule of maugdleness about to corrugitate his mild dewed cheek and the tata of a tiny victorienne, Alys, pressed by his limper looser.

(*FW* 57.16–27)

Applying the three rules for reading of "discover," "define," and "brood," let's look closely at the passage above. *Tom Quad, gowndabout, clericalease habit*: we are in Oxford, and specifically in Christ Church, the home of a child photographer ("exposure of him," "flashback") called Charles Dodgson ("slithe dodgsomely," "maugdleness" for Magdalen, and there is in fact a roundabout, or "gowndabout," at the end of Oxford's Magdalen Bridge). *Madam's Toshowus, lifeliked, notional gullery*: we are in London, and our National Gallery is full of frauds and freaks, one of whom is *Martin Chuzzlewit*'s Sarah Gamp ("gamps, degrace"). *Aerily perennious*: Horace's "aere perennius" Ode, his eternal monument, is about to be found fleeting, as Horace's "Eheu fugaces" Ode will become "Eheu, for gassies" (*FW* 58.18) by the end of the next paragraph. *Legpoll, irreperible, judicandees*: we are in the law courts, where a deed poll is a leg pull, a statement is both irreparable and penetrating (Lat: *irrepere*, to penetrate), and the words of the *Dies Irae* from the requiem Mass remind us that "judicandus homo reus"—the guilty man is here to be judged. *Alys*: the "tiny victorienne" is Alice, Issy, and Isolde (Isolde's final transfiguration in the aria *"Mild und leise"* is lurking in the "mild dewed cheek"); she is also "a lys," a flower pressed by a "limper looser," or "tata" (Fr: pederast). *Kudos*: the rule of 1, 2, and 3 is everywhere in the *Wake*, and here the three numbers are cunningly concealed in "*one* ku*dos*; exits, *free*." These are the "unfacts," unwarranting our certitude, sending sol to the nethermore, turning kudos into escudos, corrugating our cogitations. Humphrey Chimpden Earwicker is "human, erring and condonable" (*FW* 58.19): the change in the regular acrostic pattern shows that we are first Human, second Erring, and third Condonable. That is always Joyce's order of things.

So now it's time for Round Three: off to the rarefied air of the Norwegian Captain, Butt and Taff, and HCE's gorgeous admission of guilt (*FW* 363.20–367.03). If I.3 allows for pardon, II.3 precludes it: Alice's innocence now crashes through the looking glass. HCE is gloriously unrepentant, confessing to whatever it is he is accused of:

> I am the catasthmatic old ruffin sippahsedly improctor to be seducint trovatellas, the dire daffy damedeaconesses, like (why sighs the sootheesinger) the lilliths oft I feldt, and, when booboob brutals and cautiouses only aims at the oggog hogs in the humand, then, (Houtes, Blymey and Torrenation, upkurts and scotchem!) I'll tall tale tell croon paysecurers, sowill nuggets and nippers, that thash on me stumpen blows the gaff off mombition and thit thides or marse makes a good dayle to be shattat. Fall stuff.

> (*FW* 366.22–30)

"Fall stuff" indeed: this is again Adam's Fall (with more than a hint of Falstaff). We have reached a "full stop": his speech is as conclusive as the dot at the end of "Ithaca." HCE admits to seducing the lilies of the field, gloriously spun from Luke 12:27 into "the lilliths oft I feldt," and to revealing the hog in the human: like Bloom in "Circe," HCE has "been a perfect pig" (*U* 15.3397). But, like Bloom, he is no more guilty than his "fellows culpows" (*FW* 363.20)—and by now we can hear the "felix culpa" in that defense. We have reached the "thides or marse": the Ides of March is a good day to be shot at by the "brutals and cautiouses" of the world.

II.3 is the last section of the *Wake* to be written: we have moved from innocence to experience and worked chronologically through Joyce's writing process (very roughly) as we have circled from round to round.[9] I.5 was written in 1924, III.4 was drafted in 1925, and parts of the Coda (St. Kevin at *FW* 604, Bishop Berkeley at *FW* 611) were the first bits written, so Round One is fairly early. I.1 was written after I.5 in 1926 and II.1 in 1930, so Round Two is roughly in the middle. II.3 was written very late, between 1933–1937, so Round Three comes at the compositional close. At the end of II.3, time is called, the pub closes, the bells of Sechseläuten chime (*FW* 379.27–30), and Joyce magically returns to very first bit of the *Wake* he wrote, way back in March 1923. Our third reading closes with the King Roderick O'Conor fragment (*FW* 380–82), where the innkeeper goes heel-tapping, drinking the dregs of all the booze in the bar, in one glorious rolling sentence that goes on for three merry pages, ending both the end and the beginning of the book. There is even a final envoi to speed us home:

> So sailed the stout ship *Nansy Hans*. From Liff away. For Nattenlaender.
> As who has come returns. Farvel, farerne! Goodbark, goodbye!
> Now follow we out by Starloe!
> (*FW* 382.27–30)

It's not a much better ending than "A way a lone a last a loved a long the" (*FW* 628.15–16), but at least we've stopped going around in circles.

And so, I give you a new beginning ("In the name of Annah the Allmaziful"—*FW* 104.01), a new ending ("Goodbark, goodbye!"—*FW* 382.30), and a new tailoring of a work that is "unhemmed as it is uneven" (*FW* 104.03). As I said in a final toast over a banquet of food items found in *Finnegans Wake* and provided by two students, surrounded by maps and mosaics provided by two others, after having heard a chorus of four students perform the last page and a half of the book from memory and having watched a movie based on the last chapter made by two more, I could never have imagined that coming to terms with the *Wake* could be so much fun. The students made it happen: through readings, references, laughter, sometimes just by the fact of their presence, hour after hour, they made this more than I ever dreamed a course on the *Wake* could be. Who could have imagined, I said, that this text could be so rich and so rewarding? A reflection of the world up to and including 1939, an almanac of the 1930s, alarmingly precise in its vision of the world that immediately follows it: a work of all times, at all times. And now, I said, speaking for myself most of all, we all know that we can read anything, that there is nothing on this earth, with sufficient application, that we will not be able to understand.

Appendix 3.1

English 863: Seminar in 20th Century British Literature

Finnegans Wake

Professor Knowles   Spring 2004

COURSE LOGISTICS:

   We meet on Thursday afternoons from 1:30–4:18 in Denney 213. There is an additional meeting of the class, optional and open to all, on Monday evenings from 7–10 p.m., at a site to be determined (probably Brazenhead's at 1027 W. 5th Ave.). (The Monday meeting on Memorial Day will be moved to Tuesday 1 June; the last Monday meeting in exam week will serve as the course's conclusion.) Office hours are Thursday mornings from 9–12 a.m. Appointments outside of office hours can be made in class, by phone (292–5786), or via e-mail (knowles.1@osu.edu). E-mail is likely to be useful throughout the course as a place for trying out questions, comments, and ideas.

COURSE DESCRIPTION:

   This is intended to be a truly nonthreatening look at an essential work of late modernism, and by far and away the most unread book in literature. *Finnegans Wake* has not been taught at OSU since the legendary Fritz Senn came from Zürich to do so in the early 1980s; the time has come for another shot. I have constructed this course after the fashion of the "Knitting/Microsoft Word for Dummies" books, ramping up slowly and finishing off at a tearing pace. No previous knowledge of Joyce, or of *Finnegans Wake*, is required. We will read the text four ways, then three, then two, then one, as follows:

   Reading 4 Ways
   We will be looking at this amazing text for 1) its response to history, 2) its use of the lyric voice, 3) its plot and character (if we can find it), and 4) its language and its world. We will unravel the mystery of the text with the help of four gospels, four critics who have devoted a great part of their lives to making sense of the *Wake*. In the role of Matthew, our first guide will be Campbell and Robinson's *Skeleton Key to* Finnegans Wake (a wartime book, first published five years after the *Wake* itself, in 1944). In the role of Mark, William York Tindall's *Reader's Guide to* Finnegans Wake (a hippie book, wonderfully funny, published in 1969). As Luke, Adaline Glasheen's *Third Census of* Finnegans Wake

(the hardest to find of all of them, done in three rounds and finished in 1977).
As the metaphysical gospel, John Gordon's Finnegans Wake: *A Plot Summary*
(the most readily available but the most idiosyncratic of the four, published
in 1986). These four, from four different decades, will be our four wise men
(though one is a woman), our "Mamalujo," as the book has it, taking us through
the book step by painful palimpsestic step.

Reading 3 Ways

And (in another breakthrough in *Finnegans Wake* reading studies), we will
read this book not in page order, or in the order of composition, but in order of difficulty, starting with the easiest material, moving to the intermediate
level, and finally attacking the hardest chapter of all. This "ski-slope" method of
reading the book will allow the text to give the reader a sense of achievement
(which it otherwise reserves to the final page) and a sense of real progress as we
proceed.

To be specific: we will begin with chapters that are either self-referential
(the letter in I.5, the riddles in I.6) or include clear plot elements (sunset in II.4,
dawn in III.4, the final ricorso in IV), or advance our sense of the characters
(Shem in I.7, Anna Livia in I.8). That will be our first round. We will then cycle
back to the beginning (in true Wakean fashion) and read I.1, I.2, I.3, I.4, II.1, II.2,
III.1, III.2, and III.3. That will be our second round. And finally we will tackle the
hardest and most rewarding chapter, II.3, which is the best example of *Finnegans
Wake* as both montage and radio broadcast (pick your eye/ear metaphor), and
itself tells a story (or a series of interwoven stories) three times, to mirror our
three readings, over three rounds of drinks (which by then we will all probably
need). So the method of our reading will be supported by the form of this extraordinary text.

Reading 2 Ways

At the same time, we will read the book by day and by night. *Finnegans Wake*
must be read sober, in the cold light of day, and we will do that in our regularly
scheduled class time, presenting material, checking on plot elements, looking up references, puzzling out the meaning of the text. It must also be read
at night, with the ear rather than the eye, preferably over a glass of something
to bring the sounds of the texts to life. At our nighttime meetings, we will not
so much examine as appreciate the text, allowing it to wash over us as music,
as soundscape, as a flow of language more allied to nonsense than sense, more
id than ego, more nightmare than waking. To join in these meetings you must

be twenty-one: I will also expect you to drink responsibly. Anyone visibly impaired will be driven home.

Reading Your Way

We may not finish. Along the way, somewhere, at some time, your head will explode. (I know mine did.) What will be interesting is to see when this will happen for each of you—in the first round, the second, or the third. We will get as far as we can along this path over the ten weeks, and if there is interest, we will continue through the summer in an independent study course until we are done. Know your limits—we will march through, but if you must stop, retire, retreat, kill the commanding officer, or go AWOL, that's all right. Just keep attending, and return to the parts you're most comfortable with, and work on them. It's all connected.

REQUIRED TEXTS:

All five are required, but not all five are available (there's a puzzle for you). Go to SBX to see what they could pick up (as of this writing, probably just the main text, Gordon, and Tindall). Take a look at Amazon.com and elsewhere (Half Price books?) to see what else you can find. All the secondary texts are on 2-hour reserve at the Main Library; Gordon, Glasheen, and Tindall are also in the ETC. I will xerox the opening pages of Glasheen for anyone who wants to make a copy of that useful section.

James Joyce, *Finnegans Wake*
Campbell and Robinson, *A Skeleton Key to* Finnegans Wake
Adaline Glasheen, *A Third Census of* Finnegans Wake
John Gordon, Finnegans Wake: *A Plot Summary*
William York Tindall, *A Reader's Guide to* Finnegans Wake

ASSIGNMENTS:

I will require each graduate student enrolled in the class for credit to assume ownership of one section in the first two rounds, which will mean that you will need to be prepared to lead a brief discussion on it, and then to write a short paper (5–7 pages) on some aspect of that section. At the end of the course, a third paper is required on either some aspect of chapter II.3 or some aspect of the whole. So three short papers for registered graduate students who are taking the course for credit.

Graduate auditors and undergraduates taking the course for independent study credit will be expected to write one short paper (5–7 pages) at one of the three opportunities to do so. Undergraduates do not need to attend the Thursday sessions, but are expected at the Monday sessions, and are welcome to join us on Thursdays. Auditors and regularly scheduled graduate students are expected at the Thursday sessions and are strongly encouraged to join us at the Monday sessions.

COURSE CALENDAR:

Round One

Th April 1	I.5: "Mamafesta" (104–25)
Th April 8	I.6: "Riddles" (126–68)
Th April 15	I.7: "Shem the Penman" (169–95)
Th April 22	I.8: "Anna Livia Plurabelle" (196–216)
Th April 29	II.4: "Mamalujo" (383–99) and III.4: "Dawn" (555–590)
Th May 6	IV: "Ricorso" (593–628)
M May 10	First paper (5–7 pages) due by the evening meeting

Round Two

Th May 13	I, 1–4: "HCE" (3–103)
Th May 20	II.1: "Children's Games" (219–59) and II.2: "Night Lessons" (260–308)
Th May 27	III, 1–3: "Shaun" (403–554)
T June 1	Second paper (5–7 pages) due by the evening meeting

Round Three

Th June 3	II.3: "The Pub" (309–82)
M June 7	Final evening meeting (all expected)
Th June 10	Third paper (5–7 pages) due by 4 p.m. in Denney 421

4 | The True Story of Jumbo the Elephant

> Love loves to love love. Nurse loves the new chemist. Constable 14 A loves Mary Kelly. Gerty MacDowell loves the boy that has the bicycle. M. B. loves a fair gentleman. Li Chi Han lovey up kissy Cha Pu Chow. Jumbo, the elephant, loves Alice, the elephant.
>
> (*U* 12.1493–96)

But did he? These lines are always deeply satisfying, showing the narrator at his scathing best, piling on the pieties of Bloom ("I mean the opposite of hatred"—*U* 12.1485) and the antipathies of the Citizen ("He's a nice pattern of a Romeo and Juliet"—*U* 12.1492) with equal abandon, throwing them both into the mincer.[1] The mock peroration to love, I was surprised to learn, has even found its way into the Yahoo Personals, where a desperate Joycean (can there be any other kind?) uses these very lines as an unlikely come-on, under the advertising heading "Tired of the bar scene?"[2] This citation not only gives the lie to Judge Woolsey, who famously claimed in 1933 that nowhere in the text does the effect of the book "tend to be an aphrodisiac" (*U*-61 xiv), it proves once and for all that the Internet and its users are oblivious to irony.

But to return to Jumbo. Jumbo the elephant was born in the African jungle, acquired by a Herr Schmidt for the Paris Zoo, and traded to the London Zoo in 1865 for a rhinoceros and a pachyderm to be named later. At his peak, he weighed seven tons, stood twelve feet high, and had a fondness for whisky. In the 1870s, Jumbo was a favorite of Queen Victoria, her son the Prince of Wales, and the young Winston Churchill. In March 1882, P. T. Barnum bought the elephant for £2,000 for his circus in America, an event that caused widespread panic. Children flocked to see the departing elephant (you will see them flocking in figure 4.1).

Figure 4.1. Cover of the *Illustrated London News*, Sunday, 18 Mar. 1882. © The Zoological Society of London. Reprinted by permission. Mathieson 17.

The *Times* of 9 March 1882 reported a gargantuan increase of 2,061 percent in daily attendance: "the total number of visitors for the day was 4,626, as against 214 for the corresponding Wednesday last year" (*Times*, 9 Mar. 1882: 6f). "The eagerness of children and young girls to ride on its back," said the *Illustrated London News*, "is beyond all precedent. There were 43,653 admissions last week" (*Illustrated London News*, 18 Mar. 1882: 254c). The *Times* also reported, to the presumed horror of its readers, that the superintendent of the steamship on which Jumbo was to sail, the *Assyrian Monarch*, had requested to be "provided with the means of killing the animal should such a necessity arise" (*Times*, 9 Mar. 1882: 6f), displaying the kind of scare tactics for which the paper has always been justly famous.

The elephant's sale was seen as a loss for all England and for its empire (figure 4.2). Retired colonels came out of the woodwork, as they always do at such moments, writing to the *Times* to reject the theory that Jumbo had "must," the disease that leads elephants to charge madly into crowds and kill people in zoos, for which A. D. Bartlett, the head of the Zoological Gardens at Regent's Park, had sensibly wanted to get rid of it. Though Major General Agnew of Belsize

JUMBO, THE PRIDE AND GLORY OF ENGLAND.

3

JUMBO, ENGLAND'S LOSS and AMERICA'S GAIN

Editorial from the London Telegraph, February 22d, 1882.

Figure 4.2. "Jumbo, England's Loss and America's Gain." Cartoon circa early 1882. Courtesy of the Bridgeport History Center, Bridgeport Public Library. Saxon, ed. 224.

Park Gardens, drawing on his thirty-four years of experience with elephants in Assam, could applaud the Council of the Zoological Society for taking "the wise step of getting rid of a very dangerous animal" (*Times*, 18 Mar. 1882: 5), George Bowyer claimed to the contrary that "any mahout or qualified keeper could control him" (*Times*, 16 Mar. 1882: 10b). Bowyer went further to compare the action of the council to a sale by the trustees of the British Museum of the Codex Alexandrinus.

The country went Jumbo mad: there were Jumbo cigars, Jumbo collars, Jumbo fans, and a Jumbo polka. "Why Part with Jumbo?" (words by G. H. Macdermott, music by E. J. Symons) was one of many popular songs written for the occasion (figure 4.3). Jumbo was imagined at the opera, at the bar, and even as an aesthete, after the fashion of Bunthorne in Gilbert and Sullivan's wildly popular operetta, *Patience*, which was still running at the time (figure 4.4). The Moore and Burgess minstrels advertised, on the day of Jumbo's departure, that their own "original Jumbo, who will never perform out of London, whom wild

Figure 4.3. "Why Part with Jumbo, the Pet of the Zoo." Song by G. H. Macdermott and E. J. Symons. © The Zoological Society of London. Reprinted by permission. Mathieson 22.

Figure 4.4. "Jumbo Aesthetic." Trade card, circa April 1882. Private collection. Published in A. H. Saxon, P. T. Barnum: The Legend and the Man (New York: Columbia University Press, 1989). Reprinted by permission. Saxon plates.

horses cannot tear from St. James' Hall, will make his entrée together with his keeper, Elephant William" (*Times*, 18 Mar. 1882: 1d). The London *Daily Telegraph* cabled Barnum on 22 February 1882 as follows: "EDITOR'S COMPLIMENTS. ALL BRITISH CHILDREN DISTRESSED AT ELEPHANT'S DEPARTURE. HUNDREDS OF CORRESPONDENTS BEG US TO INQUIRE ON WHAT TERMS YOU WILL KINDLY RETURN JUMBO" (Bryan 159), to which Barnum replied that £100,000 would be no inducement to cancel purchase. Dante Gabriel Rossetti died, as did Henry Wadsworth Longfellow, and a lunatic attempted to assassinate the Queen, but no one paid very much attention to anything else.

The departure of Jumbo for America, as recorded by the *Times'* society page of Monday, 27 March 1882, has a strangely familiar ring:

> By the 12 5 train from Fenchurch-street travelled Lady Burdett-Coutts to bid the great animal farewell. In her ladyship's saloon carriage were also Lord Tenterden, Lady Tenterden, Admiral Sir E. Commerell, Mr. Ashmead Bartlett, M. P., and Mrs. Ashmead Bartlett, Mr. Henry Wagner, Mrs. Scott, and Mr. Rendell. Mr. Vickers, a partner in the managing owners' firm (John Patton, junior) and Mr. Hosack travelled by the same train, and at Gravesend General Sir John and Lady Douglas and other visitors came on board, where the emigrants who had not joined on the previous day embarked, and Captain Wilson, the chief executive officer for the port, provisionally passed the vessel, leaving Captain Scone to make the final examination. The Baroness, who received a bouquet of sweet-scented violets from Mr. Vickers, went with her party to visit the elephant on the forward part of the 'tween decks, gave him his last bun, and wished him "Good-bye," expressing her opinion that he would find as warm friends in America as he had in England, and that he would be safe in the hands of Newman, with whom, as well as Scott, her ladyship shook hands. Lady Burdett-Coutts afterwards inspected the emigrants' quarters, and spoke to the poor people themselves, their Russian interpreter translating her remarks. When she passed them to go away the Jews pressed forward to kiss the hem of her garment, and they cheered her as she left. The Baroness left money to be employed in purchasing sweets and other trifling luxuries for the women and children. The Assyrian Monarch was gaily dressed out with bunting.
>
> (*Times*, 27 Mar. 1882: 10c)

"Blimey it makes me kind of bleeding cry, straight, it does" (*U* 12.676–77):
this is written with the same pathos and eye for social detail as the send-off for
the Croppy Boy in "Cyclops." Parnell was not there to see Jumbo off, because
he was in jail for the first and only time in his life: in the same edition of the
newspaper a small entry reads "Mr. Parnell has declined to write, unless under
very exceptional circumstances, letters from Kilmainham" (*Times*, 27 Mar. 1882:
10d). While Jumbo was caged on a steamer, "able by the wonderful flexibility of
his trunk to explore very fully by the touch the places immediately outside his
prison" (*Times*, 28 Mar. 1882: 11d), Parnell was in prison for protesting the 1881
Land Act. During the time of Parnell's incarceration, the Moonlighters, Parnell's phrase for the agrarian secret societies of Ireland, had taken over; murders
in Dublin were up 371 percent in the first quarter of 1882 (Lyons 177). Parnell
was released from Kilmainham on the day after Jumbo arrived in New York,
twenty-six days before the assassination of Burke and Cavendish in Phoenix
Park, on 6 May 1882.

Jumbo was both, then, a reprieve from and a representation of the problems
of empire. The call for the voiding of the contract with Barnum, seriously pur-
sued by the press, was brought up in Parliament on 11 March 1882 and "received
with cheers and laughter" (*Times*, 11 Mar. 1882: 6c), but it was sandwiched between two far more serious discussions of an atrocity committed in the Boer
War and a request for additional protection from members of the Irish National
Land League. (Perhaps not incidentally, a question immediately followed on
the reports of foot-and-mouth disease in a county in Cornwall, further linking
the Barnum episode to the historical background of *Ulysses*.) As the *Times* said
in its leader on the topic of 9 March 1882:

> For our own part, while we are sorry to part with a favourite, we cannot
> say that our zeal in Jumbo's behalf has kept pace with that of the many
> correspondents who have been roused by his wrongs. People who have
> no suspicion that the friendly relations between Russia and Germany
> have been endangered by Skubeleff's speeches, who have a vague idea of
> the Irish as a tiresome people, who are far from comprehending the issues
> raised by the appointment of the Lords' Committee, and who confess
> that they have not followed the discussion upon Parliamentary proce-
> dure, have taken a keen interest in Jumbo's destiny. Others have let fall
> the thread of public events while they gaped open-mouthed at Jumbo

reconnoitring his trolley. It is well enough that children should crowd in thousands to the Zoological Gardens, and, as a parting act of kindness, or cruelty, stuff the hero of the hour with buns innumerable. But it speaks volumes for the fundamental levity of adult nature that men have, for the last fortnight, given the first and foremost place in those of their thoughts which did not regard themselves, not to kingdoms and their destinies, but to Jumbo.

(*Times*, 9 Mar. 1882: 9e)

This, for the *Times* of 1882, or for the *Times* of any year, is quite wonderful. The newspaper agrees with Zack Bowen, and with Bakhtin, that the carnival spirit is a positive, regenerating force.[3] The comedy, played on a hyperbolic stage, is a distraction, as it is in "Cyclops," and a distraction from the same subject: the loss of a gigantic imperial dream.

But Jumbo was not just carnivalesque, he was in a carnival, and on his arrival in America his circus career took off. In six weeks he earned Barnum a third of a million dollars. Here he is (figure 4.5):

Figure 4.5. Jumbo the elephant with his keeper, Matthew Scott. Courtesy of the Bridgeport History Center, Bridgeport Public Library. Saxon plates.

Barnum advertised him as "The Colossus of the Old and New World," "The Universal Synonym for All Stupendous Things" (Bryan 162). And he did become the universal synonym for all stupendous things: it's because of this elephant that we have jumbo-size fries, jumbo shrimp, and the jumbo jet. Even his shit was jumbo-size, as seen by the size of the Jumbo-the-elephant sticker that a Puritanical librarian has placed on the photograph underneath the elephant's tail (figure 4.5).[4] Jumbo's arrival into small towns in America was compared to the coming of Christ: "The shouting at Jerusalem," according to his keeper, Matthew Scott, "for the 'Son of Man' when he rode triumphantly on an ass, could not have exceeded the shout that has gone up from the children of the United States as they have watched and waited by hours to get a sight of Jumbo" (qtd. in Saxon 297). The deity *is* a nickel dime bum show. Bloom is Ben Bloom Elijah and Jumbo is Jesus: both stories operate according to the principle of gigantism and parody, overkill and undercutting, Jumbo and the Jumbo sticker.

The end of Jumbo the elephant is tragic and affecting in the extreme (figure 4.6):

Figure 4.6. Jumbo the elephant lying dead after his collision with a goods train in September 1885. Private collection. Published in A. H. Saxon, *P. T. Barnum: The Legend and the Man* (New York: Columbia University Press 1989). Reprinted by permission. Saxon plates.

Here I must let *The True Story of Jumbo the Elephant,* a children's book from 1963, pick up the tale:

One evening, in September 1885, Barnum's circus had been visiting the town of St Thomas, Ontario, in Canada. As usual, the show had been packed and Jumbo had been the great success of the evening. The men were busy taking down the circus, getting ready to move on to the next stopping place. Most of the animals had already been loaded into their vans on the special train. Thirty-one lesser elephants who appeared with Jumbo were already safely aboard. Last of all, it was Jumbo's turn. He was led out, with his inseparable companion Tom Thumb [a smaller elephant], by his old friend Matthew Scott towards the grand "Palace Car."

To get to the car, they had to cross an old, unused piece of railway track; at least it had not been used for a long time. It disappeared round a large bend several hundred yards away from them, to join on to the Grand Trunk Railway. As Jumbo was making his stately way towards his car, without any warning, Matthew Scott heard the sound of an approaching train. He stood quite still for a moment, not knowing what to do, holding firmly on to Jumbo's chain. Jumbo pawed the ground nervously at the sudden noise. Suddenly, Scott was horrified to see an unexpected goods train appear round the bend of the supposedly unused branch railway line. He tugged frantically at Jumbo's chain and shouted for him to move. But Jumbo, by now quite terrified, braced his huge legs and would not move. The engine, moving very quickly, rushed down on them.

At the very last moment, Matthew Scott jumped aside. The engine hit little Tom Thumb on the back leg, throwing him down on the ground. Jumbo, standing right across the track, was hit by the full weight of the oncoming engine. His great bulk was hurled down with a terrifying crash. The engine itself was derailed.

At once there was noise and steam and confusion. People rushed to the scene. The dazed and frightened keeper picked himself up and went straight across to his old friend, lying there on his side. But one glance was sufficient for Matthew Scott to see the truth. Jumbo was dead. Blood was oozing from his great mouth. He had been killed at once, before he could possibly know what had happened.

The old keeper went down on his knees beside the dead elephant. His eyes filled with tears and, although knowing it was useless, he spoke to

Jumbo. He put his arms around the animal's great trunk and he remembered the frightened, skinny little creature who had arrived at London Zoo all those years before.

(Mathieson 37–39)

(It's hard to believe that these paragraphs were ever read to a child.) Jumbo's tragic death reminds us of the two great literary railway victims, Emily Sinico and Anna Karenina—though Jumbo's death cannot be the inspiration for the death of the latter, because Tolstoy's heroine threw herself under a train eight years earlier, in 1877.[5] It may also remind us of Joseph Merrick, who took up rooms in the London Hospital a year after Jumbo's death, and whose biography by Michael Howell and Peter Ford, *The True History of the Elephant Man*, pays silent tribute in its title to *The True Story of Jumbo the Elephant*. The town of St. Thomas, Ontario, built a statue in 1985 to mark the centenary of this occasion: it weighs 138 tons. More immediate attempts to capitalize on the elephant's death were made depressingly by Barnum himself, who exhibited both hide and skeleton of the elephant together, in a singularly disgusting attempt to recoup some of his losses, which were estimated at 50 percent of the total show's worth (figure 4.7):

Figure 4.7. "Double Jumbo." © Circus World Museum, Baraboo, Wisconsin.
Reprinted by permission. Saxon plates.

In "Double Jumbo," as this ghoulish exhibit was affectionately known, you have an exact match for the "Cyclops" theme of life in death and death in life: Barnum, like Bloom, is trying to downface you that dying is living. As Dignam's boots are preserved and resoled in the Blavatsky parody in "Cyclops"—"Before departing he requested that it should be told to his dear son Patsy that the other boot which he had been looking for was at present under the commode in the return room and that the pair should be sent to Cullen's to be soled" (*U* 12.366–69)—so Jumbo is reexhumed, both flesh and bone, sole and soul, a metempsychosis devoutly to be avoided.

To add insult to injury, Alice was brought over from London, the same Alice who had pined so much for Jumbo that people said, "Alice will be broken-hearted if Jumbo goes" (qtd. in Mathieson 23). Alice was exhibited in a widow's cap that was an exact replica of Queen Victoria's (Saxon 299). The elephant was tethered beside the remains of Jumbo, and billed, in a supreme example of deformitomania, as Jumbo's "widow." "His Majesty the King loves Her Majesty the Queen" (*U* 12.1498–99): everyone associated Jumbo with the Queen, not just because the Queen visited him with her son, but because they were both larger than life, both symbols of empire. The *New York Times* playfully reported in happier days that "the Queen would romp with him, rolling with him in innocent delight upon the turf. Later in life when the danger that her Majesty might by accident roll upon Jumbo and seriously injure him became too obvious to be disregarded, the Queen ceased […]" (Saxon 295).

To a shocked world the news of the death of Jumbo the elephant was as incomprehensible as the death of JFK or Princess Diana: as in the two latter-day cases, conspiracy theories sprang up as to the manner of his death. People said that Barnum had planned the elephant's death as a publicity stunt, an accusation that led Barnum to slap a libel suit on the newspaper that carried the story. Some said that the elephant was a drunkard, or suffering from a chronic disease, and needed to be disposed of. But the most startling, and most Joycean, theory was that he was killed for excessive flatulence. (Here the size of the Jumbo sticker in figure 4.5 should be recalled.) "The huge animal," says Barnum's principal biographer, "so stank up the circus that Barnum and his partners out of sheer embarrassment decided they had no choice but to do away with him" (Saxon 301).

Tram kran kran kran. Good oppor. Coming. Krandlkrankran. I'm sure it's
the burgund. Yes. One, two. *Let my epitaph be.* Kraaaaaa. *Written. I have.*
Pprrpffrrppffff.
Done.

(U 11.1290–94)

As Bloom waits for a passing tram, so Barnum, also an advertising man, waits
for a passing train on the Grand Trunk Railway.[6] Larry Quigle, the putative Barnum assassin in this theory, was meant to have been ordered to "shoot Jumbo
through the eye" (Saxon 301), ending Jumbo's Odyssean journey with a truly
Cyclopean gesture.

Jumbo's hide is preserved at Tufts College in Medford, Massachusetts, or
was, until the museum burned down in 1975, taking Jumbo's hide with it (figure
4.8):

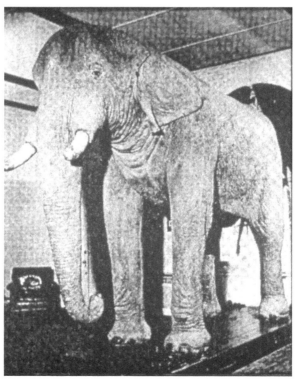

Figure 4.8. Jumbo's hide, displayed at Tufts College in
Medford, Massachusetts, until destroyed by a museum fire
in 1975. © Duette Photographers, Boston. Mathieson 40.

Tufts still calls its football team the Jumbos. The skeleton, the other half of "Double Jumbo," is found in the American Museum of Natural History in New York.[7] And Alice? Did Jumbo the elephant love Alice the elephant? Sadly, the answer is no. Jumbo showed no love at all to Alice, often instead menacing her angrily and violently (Saxon 293). The pining that Alice was meant to have displayed at Jumbo's imminent departure was more likely to have been a consequence of the unusual crowds outside her cage.

In "Circe" the Beatitudes mumble:

THE BEATITUDES
(*incoherently*) Beer beef battledog buybull businum barnum buggerum bishop.

(*U* 15.2241–43)

Though there is no evidence that P. T. Barnum ever buggered a bishop, he did practically everything else. He was a "businum," or businessman, and he did buy a bull, or bull elephant, and though "buybull" is a reference to the Bible, it also refers to buying the products of John Bull, or buying English. In buying Jumbo, the giant and mythological figure who bestrides two continents and one *Ulysses* episode like a colossus, Barnum bought English all right. Barnum's acquisition of Jumbo the elephant from the London Zoo in 1882 sent up a wail of lamentation through British society, a cry that was also, as the *Times* acutely observed, a celebration of the fundamental levity of adult nature. It was not Alice who loved Jumbo, in all the ways that "Love loves to love love": it was England.

H. G. Wells famously likened the syntactical contortions of the late Henry James to a hippopotamus intent on picking up a pea at all costs; if this chapter has had something of the same ponderous quality, it is because *Ulysses* requires an extraordinary and faintly ridiculous level of concentration.[8] *Ulysses* is an elephant in the zoological gardens of modern British literature, and we are its keepers. Sometimes, like Matthew Scott, we stand proudly and proprietorially at its head; sometimes, like the Puritanical librarian, we diligently place our sticker on its fundamentals; at other times, like P. T. Barnum, we are reduced to displaying its carcass. To know the whole of *Ulysses* is impossible. Instead, we must focus on an individual part, as in the fable of the blind men and the elephant, and by carefully following that single line of inquiry, a tiny piece of the whole, a fold and a wrinkle of its flesh, will be illuminated. That is the ever-widening path that Joyce affords his readers.

The preceding examination of a pea-size unit of Joycean meaning is an exemplum of this book's method. Jumbo the elephant didn't love Alice the elephant: how does one extrapolate from this? Maybe God doesn't love everybody after all, and perhaps Gerty is more interested in Cissy Caffrey than the boy that has the bicycle. Jumbo was sold under the eyes of a nation in March 1882: that same nation was beginning to lose control of colonies in Africa and Asia and was about to hear, in May, of an event that would galvanize the issue of Home Rule for Ireland, with the assassination of two of its government employees in a park in Dublin. Jumbo lived on after death, a ghostly carnival afterimage of himself: so does Paddy Dignam, and the beautiful May Goulding, but more than that, so does Queen Victoria. Jumbo the elephant, like Victoria, was a defining figure of the age, inhabiting a long-dead world of buns and violets on the *Assyrian Monarch*, of six-year-olds piling into the howdah for the *Illustrated London News*, a world that has been lost by 1904, along with the Fauntleroy suit that little Rudy would have worn, and the songs that are no longer sung around the Dedalus piano. And all that is still to be seen and heard in Dublin in 1904 has been lost by 1922, for Joyce, and for his postwar readers. It is up to the twenty-first-century reader to make these exhumations. This is the benefit of following a trail to see where it will take you: an inch can give you a mile; an incremental gain can open up a world. Sometimes, if one is in a carnival mood, the temptation comes to trumpet one's findings, overadvertising like a sideshow barker. For only then can Jumbo lumber through the undergrowth of "Cyclops," squash the narrative mockery that surrounds him, stand tall at seven tons against Bloom's eleven stone four pounds, and be recognized.

5 | Death by Gramophone

1. Eugene Jolas

> Put on poor old greatgrandfather. Kraahraark! Hellohellohello amawfullyglad kraark awfullygladaseeagain hellohello amawf krpthsth.
>
> (*U* 6.964–66)

This chapter exchanges Henry James' pea for H. G. Wells' periscope, and provides what James would likely dismiss as an outline of recorded history. Where Jumbo's examination was microscopic, the view here is macroscopic, following the example of Bloom in "Ithaca" when confronted by the spectacle of "The heaventree of stars hung with humid nightblue fruit" (*U* 17.1039). In both cases, this book's method is to follow a path to see where it leads. For the modern university to thrive, risks must be taken, whether in the classroom (as in chapters 1, 3, and 8) or in the world of research (as here, and in chapters 6 and 7). In chapter 4, we began with a single line of text and followed it through the maze. Here, we begin with a bird's-eye view of a critical problem and end with a splash.

Staring at the Milky Way, Bloom gives us whiplash. He provides a meditation of "involution increasingly less vast" extrapolating from "a single pinhead" (*U* 17.1057, 1063), accompanied by a meditation of "evolution increasingly vaster" (*U* 17.1042), entering the macroscopic level of time and space: "10 lightyears (57,000,000,000,000 miles)" (*U* 17.1047). Both the microbial level of involution and the astronomical level of evolution are fractal forms of argument: each parallels the other in charting the "incertitude of the void" (*U* 17.1015). The latter leads to the recognition that the allotted human life span of seventy years is "a parenthesis of infinitesimal brevity" (*U* 17.1055–56), the former to the realization of Zeno's arrow paradox: "dividends and divisors ever diminishing without actual division till, if the progress were carried far enough, nought nowhere was never reached" (*U* 17.1067–69). (Zeno, of course, appears in a book by Italo Svevo, Joyce's artistic companion in Trieste, in which the main character says that "it is essential to keep moving" [Svevo 287].) Both ways of seeing, the microbial and the astronomical, connect in what Virginia Woolf called "a rapid flight of the mind" (Woolf, "On Not Knowing Greek" 30) the concerns of an era with an object in extensive view.

The critical problem in this chapter is the modernist response to the machine age; the object is the gramophone. As mechanization introduced a world of sparkling certainty and certain death, the lost aurality of a prewar world is celebrated throughout modernist literature. More and more, the acoustic becomes the only real for Joyce; this is even more true of his partner in crime, T. S. Eliot, who serves as a secondary subject for Joyce's work throughout this book. If Joyce is the tonic of this book's argument, Eliot is the dominant, the V to his I (and there are five movements to *The Waste Land*, each given a roman numeral). The memory of the dead is modernism's first and last obligation, and nowhere more so than in the two works that stand in counterpoint to one another ever since their publication in the same year of 1922. But first we must roll back the years to a contested date in the history of technology, a decade before either Joyce or Eliot was born.

The evolution of the history of gramophone recording is meant to have begun on 12 August 1877, when Thomas Edison shouted "Mary had a little lamb" at a cylinder wrapped in tin foil, cranked the machine up again, and heard a reproduction of his voice. This version of Edison's breakthrough follows the date suggested by Roland Gelatt (Gelatt 22): Friedrich Kittler's extraordinary *Gramophone, Film, Typewriter* suggests that this event took place on 6 December 1877, but, as Roland Gelatt admits in *The Fabulous Phonograph*, any attempt to fix the date is "highly questionable" (Gelatt 22). 12 August 1877 is given as "the official date" (Gelatt 22) for anniversary purposes. The year 1877 happens to be the same one in which Henry Adams resigned his position as professor of medieval literature at Harvard College, renouncing "seven years of laborious banishment" (Adams 317) to become a journalist. Though "The Dynamo and the Virgin" is a response to the Paris Exhibition of 1900, its origins lie in the events of that earlier year. Adams' essay, as we have seen, provides both a critique of the new technology and an acknowledgment of the spirit of the engineer: his ambivalence toward the machine age, well documented by Cecelia Tichi in *Shifting Gears*, is shared by the modernist writers under review here (Tichi 137).

There are others who can claim to have invented the gramophone—Charles Cros had already shown how it was to be done before the French Academy four months earlier, and Scott de Martinville did much the same thing as Edison before Queen Victoria in 1857—but Edison was the first to take out a patent. "Speech has become, as it were, immortal," said Edison (qtd. in Kittler 21), who immediately foresaw many possibilities for his machine, some of which are still currently in use: the taking of dictation, the recording of books for the blind, the teaching of foreign languages, the reproduction of the last words of dying persons, and, most farsightedly, the potential for connecting his new device to the telephone, to make the telephone an auxiliary in the transmission of permanent and invaluable records (see Gelatt 29). (This idea of recording documents off the telephone wire by gramophone suggests that Thomas Edison was, among other things, the father of the internet.) Edison recorded on vertical cylinders and called his machine the phonograph; his main rival in the early days of the recording industry, Emile Berliner, used horizontal disks and called his invention the gramophone. Berliner had hopes similar to Edison's, foreseeing a time when "future generations will be able to condense within the space of twenty minutes a tone picture of a single lifetime: five minutes of a child's prattle, five of the boy's exultations, five of the man's reflections, and five from the feeble utterances of the death-bed" (Gelatt 62–63).

Right from its infancy, the gramophone is associated by both of its progenitors with the utterances of the deathbed and the recording of the dying. The gramophone as a musical device grew up quickly. Gianni Bettini's spider attachment in 1897 was capable of bringing several different vibrations to a single recording pin; by 1902 the quality of the singing had improved from obscure French baritones banging out the Toreador Song to Enrico Caruso's recordings in Milan. By 1909, when Berliner Gramophone introduced a model with a constant turntable speed, a spring motor, a new sound box, shellac disks, and an advertising campaign featuring a black-and-white fox terrier listening to His Master's Voice, the gramophone industry had reached maturity. During the same period, modernism also began to find its distinctive voice—"Prufrock's Pervigilium" was begun in 1910—and found itself in competition with the gramophone throughout its lifetime.

Modernism grew up alongside the gramophone: Rainer Maria Rilke remembers in "Primal Sound," an essay written in his thirties in 1919, that "It must have been when I was a boy at school that the phonograph was invented" (qtd. in Kittler 38) and compares the line carved by a phonograph needle onto a cylinder to the coronal suture of a skull (Kittler 40). T. S. Eliot, Virginia Woolf, Joyce, and D. H. Lawrence were all also children in the 1880s, developing as writers as the art of recording on both sides of the Atlantic became more sensitive. For them, and for later writers like Samuel Beckett, Aldous Huxley, and Graham Greene, the gramophone brought death, was a kind of death, the opposite of what they were writing for and a direct threat to their writing lives. Modernism embraces the audience, the speaker, the human connection. Far from creating the "Shock of the New," as Robert Hughes famously puts it, modernists were shocked by the new, afraid of this new technology and distrustful of its disembodied voice.

The clearest early statement of what was wrong with the gramophone comes from John Philip Sousa.[1] This is more than a little peculiar, since Sousa made a mint from early gramophone recordings: his pieces were short, vibrated both well and within defined parameters, and could be repeated ad nauseam, a necessary requirement in the early days when each performance could be copied onto only ten cylinders before having to be recorded again. Despite his commercial success in the new medium, John Philip Sousa warned in 1906, in "The Menace of Mechanical Music," of "injuries to music in its artistic manifestations by virtue—or rather by vice—of the multiplication of the various music-reproducing machines." "Sweeping across the country," says Sousa, "comes now the mechanical device to sing for us a song or play for us a piano, in substitute for human skill, intelligence, and soul" (Sousa 278). Sousa's condemnation establishes an unexpected connection with Joyce's Theodore Purefoy, who similarly accuses Bloom in "Circe" of employing "a mechanical device to frustrate the sacred ends of nature" (U 15.1741–42). Purefoy's magnificent line is usually taken to refer to the sacred ends of biology, but Purefoy's clear connection with the Man in the Macintosh allows for the possibility that the mechanical device of reproduction is a gramophone, the sacred ends are those of art, and the Man in the Macintosh is John Philip Sousa. Theodore Purefoy is dressed in an oilskin, after all, as he makes the accusation that Bloom, like the gramophone, is contra naturam; earlier, the Man in the Macintosh points a Purefoy-like finger at Bloom: "Don't you believe a word he says" (U 15.1561). Paddy Dignam puts us on the scent when he impersonates a familiar figure earlier in the episode:

"(*Paddy Dignam listens with visible effort, thinking, his tail stiffpointed, his ears cocked*)" (*U* 15.1251–52). As Thomas Jackson Rice has pointed out, Dignam here is a dead ringer for Little Nipper.[2]

In Sousa's "The Menace of Mechanical Music," the gramophone is a usurper in the Joycean sense, a mocking reproduction of all that is vital. "When a mother can turn on the phonograph with the same ease that she applies to the electric light, will she croon her baby to slumber with sweet lullabys, or will the infant be put to sleep by machinery?" (Sousa 281):

"*Will the infant be put to sleep by machinery?*"

Figure 5.1. F. Strothmann, illustration for John Philip Sousa, "The Menace of Mechanical Music," *Appleton's Magazine* 8 (September 1906): 280.

Sousa has good company in fearing for the soul of art in the age of mechanical reproduction: we will hear T. S. Eliot echo him exactly in a "London Letter" in 1922. Walter Benjamin sees in all forms of mechanical reproduction a loss or withering of aura, and occasionally betrays in his diction a vestigial longing for what has been eliminated (Benjamin, *Illuminations* 223).[3] Benjamin's Frankfurt associate Theodor Adorno goes further to suggest that the culture industry, including that of the phonograph recording, commodifies and petrifies a work's original authenticity (Adorno 43–48). Also by coincidence at Frankfurt, in a plenary lecture for the 1984 International James Joyce Symposium, Jacques Derrida calls attention to the gramophony of *Ulysses*: *Ulysses*, Derrida suggests, is both heard and read, reproduced by the ear and by the eye (Derrida, "Gramophone" 84). The gramophone that was developed by 1904, the year in which *Ulysses* is set, was both positive and negative: wax pressings of the recordings (positive) were transferred onto a stamping press (negative) to allow for their mass production (Gelatt 97). Bloom is in such a way gramophoned, doubled; his voice and his desires are both positive and negative, immediate and reproduced, real and parodied. In "Hades," Bloom imagines a graveyard filled with recording machines, to enable the bereaved to hear the voices of their loved ones: "Have a gramophone in every grave or keep it in the house. After dinner on a Sunday. Put on poor old greatgrandfather. Kraahraark! Hellohellohello amawfullyglad kraark awfullygladaseeagain hellohello amawf krpthsth" (*U* 6.963–66). In 1922, the year *Ulysses* was written, Darbycord Company "marketed its phonographs with this very purpose in mind" (North, *Reading* 27–29).

Joyce made two gramophone recordings, in 1924 and 1929; they are collected in a compilation wittily titled *James Joyce's Complete Recordings*, edited by Marc Dachy. The recordings have been discussed in the introduction; turning our attention to the CD booklet, we discover Eugene Jolas providing an accompaniment. Dachy explains in an introduction to this unexpected bonus that the English-language manuscript of Jolas' recollections of James Joyce was unearthed in an archive of materials relating to the *transition* review in the Paris home of Eugene's wife, Marie. The several versions of Jolas' "James Joyce" were collated and brought out in a French translation ("Sur James Joyce") in 1990; most of the material repeats and expands upon "My Friend James Joyce," Jolas' short piece in the *Partisan Review* on the occasion of Joyce's death, but the *Complete Recordings* is the only place with the extended version in the original English. Dachy reminds us that Joyce's "Work in Progress," appearing in *transition*'s inaugural issue in 1927, was a suitable fit for Jolas' review right from the start. The new journal, says Jolas, was to be "a linguistic laboratory where I strove to open new horizons" (qtd. in Dachy 6–7), and Joyce matched Jolas' rhetoric with linguistic action. The two became literary allies; Joyce's limerick on Jolas, which Dachy cites, is predictably excellent:

> There's a genial young poetriarch Euge
> Who hollers with heartiness huge:
> Let sick souls sob for solace
> So the jeunes joy with Jolas!
> Book your berths! Après mot, le déluge.
>
> (qtd. in Dachy 10)

The last line refers to Jolas' collection of poems, *Mots-déluge*, a coinage as suitable for Joyce as it is for his friend and editor.

The story of Joyce's acquaintance with Jolas is the story of the writing of *Finnegans Wake* and bears repeating here. Jolas' memoir begins with their first meeting at a dinner for Valery Larbaud in 1924 and ends with the publication party for the book on Joyce's fifty-seventh birthday in 1939. At the same time, the memoir covers the decade of *transition*, which played such a crucial role in bringing *Finnegans Wake* to light, beginning with the publication of the opening pages in issue no. 1 (April 1927) and ending with the Butt and Taff episode in its twenty-seventh and final issue (April–May 1938). The book's creation is strangely mapped onto the disintegration and destruction in Joyce's life and time: as one reads in Jolas' memoir of Lucia's descent into madness, and Europe's parallel fall, it is hard not to see the text and the world marching inversely toward their respective conclusions, one growing from nothing to publication and the other falling from something to despair. Brokenhearted at the thought of his sick daughter, Joyce says to Jolas: "And I am supposed to be writing a funny book . . ." (qtd. in Jolas 85). Jolas' narrative brings the "apocalyptic days" of late August 1939 to vivid life ("Gas masks were already obligatory, although the sky of Paris looked blue and cloud beflecked"—Jolas 103), so that the book and its backdrop become part of each other, and *Finnegans Wake* reveals itself as a lyrical expression of apocalypse.

Jolas also shows us Joyce's fascinations: we see him engrossed by the spectacle of Marshal Ferdinand Jean Marie Foch's funeral, "field glasses in hand, profoundly engrossed by the spectacle of the procession of dignitaries leaving the Invalides" (Jolas 31). We find him searching for Saint Laurence O'Toole's forgotten tombstone amid a heap of skeletons in the Department of Eu, Normandy (Jolas 42), suddenly racing for the railway station in Feldkirch, Lucia's mountain retreat, to watch the Orient Express pass by at seven thirty in the evening (Jolas 52), and writing a ballad to a turkey accidentally pitched in a gutter: "*Holy Poule, what's this I'm seeing*" (qtd. in Jolas 95). Above all, we see how Joyce mines the chance operations of his collapsing world, using all he saw to further the ends of his art. Jolas points out that Foch's funeral makes its way into the burial of HCE—"A mythological version of the funeral of another great little man (H. C. E.) was incorporated into *Work in Progress* shortly afterwards" (Jolas 31–32)—as does Laurence O'Toole's trip to the commune of Eu, in Normandy, to convert the heathen continentals ("Eu"—*FW* 307.26). When the Orient Express came to its scheduled ten-minute halt at Feldkirch, Joyce, says Jolas, "would ask me questions about the persons getting on or off the train, or he would listen to their conversations" (Jolas 53). Everything was grist to Joyce's mill: "Really, it is not I who am writing this crazy book," Jolas remembers him saying, "it is you and you and you and that girl over there and that man in the corner" (qtd. in Jolas 61). Speaking of the proofs of "Work in Progress" for *transition*, Jolas confirms this sense of Joyce's revelry in the accidental life of the text:

> For Joyce would improvise whenever something particularly interesting occur[r]ed to him during the reading, and occasionally even allowed a *coquille*—or typographical error—to stand, if it seemed to satisfy his encyclopaedic mills or appeal to his sense of the grotesque *hazard*.

(Jolas 30)

Jolas' recollection of Joyce is a memory piece, a way of preserving the history of Joyce's musical and literary world. Think of all the songs that Joyce has salvaged from the midden of history for us: "The Lass of Aughrim," "My Girl's a Yorkshire Girl," "Finnegan's Wake." Spending some time with the music in Joyce's "Sirens," as we will do in chapter 6, makes one wonder in quiet and satisfied amazement at Joyce's ability to bring these extraordinary songs to light, over the course of a century when they would have otherwise been doomed to be forgotten with all the other standards of Victorian parlor music. Though "Love's Old Sweet Song" has earned its unfortunate reputation as the Kumbaya of the Joyce conference meeting, the song is impossibly moving if done well. I'll always remember Robert Adams Day singing both verses at Newman House in

University College Dublin for the Thirteenth International James Joyce Symposium, in 1992, well into the twilight of a life that would soon come to a close, a man who never needed to be reminded of the quality and strength of music in the works of James Joyce. As Joyce recalls Taylor through MacHugh, as his recorded voice is the Master's Voice to which all of us must quizzically listen, as Jolas recalls Joyce through scraps of prewar memory, so the songs bring back to us the dear dead days beyond recall. "Mezha, didn't you hear it a deluge of times, ufer and ufer, respund to spond?" (*FW* 214.07–08).

2. Little Nipper

> Die, dog. Little dog, die.
>
> (*U* 11.1019)

Again, as with Jumbo the elephant, we have reached the land of the dead. But here our "gate of access" (*U* 14.1167) is aural rather than visual, the lyre of Orpheus rather than Aeneas' golden bough. The Orphic route is followed by all three of the great masterworks of European prewar nostalgia, *Ulysses*, *Swann's Way*, and *The Magic Mountain*, each of which uses aural cues to return to the underworld of a lost past. For Proust, the "petite phrase" from Vinteuil's violin sonata that obsesses Swann is presented live in salon concert: we are embedded in the aural world of the Second Empire.[4] The heart of musical longing is heard at the Verdurins', when a Chopin prelude performed for the Princesse des Laumes sends Madame de Cambremer into ecstasies:

> She had learned in her girlhood to fondle and cherish those long sinuous phrases of Chopin, so free, so flexible, so tactile, which begin by reaching out and exploring far outside and away from the direction in which they started, far beyond the point which one might have expected their notes to reach, and which divert themselves in those byways of fantasy only to return more deliberately—with a more premeditated reprise, with more precision, as on a crystal bowl that reverberates to the point of making you cry out—to strike at your heart.
>
> (Proust 471)[5]

For Joyce, who sets his clock back to 1904, the music hall has yet to be put out to pasture, but the gramophone that blares "The Holy City" over Stephen's playing on the pianola in "Circe" is a harbinger of an automated future (*U* 15.2115).

For Thomas Mann, who writes from the furthest distance (1925) and goes back to the most recent of all the three pasts (1907–14), the gramophone has fully arrived, and is a perfect medium into the world of the dead.

In *The Magic Mountain*, the gramophone leads those dying in the sanatorium to a musical underworld. When the machine appears at the close of the book in the proud hands of the Berghof's director, the narrator describes it with all the loving detail of a coffin salesman at a funeral parlor:

> It was a gramophone.
>
> We are seriously concerned that the term may be misunderstood, be associated with undignified and outdated notions, with an obsolete model that in no way does justice to the reality we envision here, the product of untiring advances in musical technology, developed to elegant perfection. My dear friends, this was no wretched crank-box, the old-fashioned sort with a turntable and stylus on top, plus a misshapen, trumpetlike brass appendage, the sort of thing you might have found at one time set up on a tavern counter to fill unsophisticated ears with nasal braying. This small cabinet, a little deeper than it was wide, was stained a dull black, had a silky cord that led to an electrical wall outlet, and stood on its special table in simple dignity—and bore no resemblance whatever to such crude, antediluvian machines. When you lifted the gracefully beveled lid, a well-secured brass rod raised automatically to hold it in place at a protective angle, and inside you saw, set slightly lower, the turntable with its green cloth cover and nickel rim, plus the nickel spindle that fitted into the hole of the ebonite disks. At the front on the right was a device like the dial on a clock for regulating the turntable's tempo, to its left, the lever that started and stopped it; at the rear on the left, however, was the sinuous, club-shaped nickel tube that had pliant, movable joints and ended in a flat, round sound-box equipped with a screw into which the needle was inserted. When you opened the double doors at the front, you saw a diagonal pattern of wooden louvers stained black—nothing more.

(Mann 627)

This object is both a Faustian wonder of modern technology along the lines of Henry Adams' dynamo and a coffin standing on its special table in simple dignity. Hans Castorp listens on Dr. Behrens' beautiful machine to Schubert's "Lindenbaum," and asks himself what lies behind the lied. In the shortest paragraph in the book, he receives his answer: "It was death" (Mann 642). Castorp then listens to the love duet between Radamès and Aida at the end of Verdi's opera, and pictures the cold facts of the scene: "Two people were being buried alive; their lungs full of the gases of the crypt, cramped with hunger, they would perish together, or even worse, one after the other; and then decay would do its unspeakable work on their bodies, until two skeletons lay there under those vaults, each indifferent and insensitive to whether it lay there alone or with another set of bones" (Mann 636).[6]

Every new form is romanced, as Mann's narrator romances the gramophone here, but sours as people discover the inherent weaknesses of the form.[7] For modernists, the primary weakness of the gramophone was that it was imitative, despite Victrola's bald protestations to the contrary. "The Victrola [...] is a musical instrument," said its company in 1917, "designed and built to meet its own requirements and not to *imitate anything*, for that would be bad art, bad mechanics, and bad judgment" (qtd. in Gelatt 157, italics Victrola's). This stunning display of corporate obliviousness to irony is also bad copy, for the whole function of the Victrola, and of the entire recording industry, is to simulate the real. Friedrich Kittler's analysis of modernism's distrust of the gramophone gives the B side of this argument, calling the gramophone "An invention that subverts both literature and music (because it reproduces the unimaginable real they are both based on)" (Kittler 22). For Kittler, the gramophone is not imitative but the thing that shows other art forms to be so: "The real takes the place of the symbolic" (Kittler 24). One can pursue Kittler's argument further by suggesting that the written text can never be as open as Umberto Eco or Robert Scholes would claim: a printed book is always bound by type, unable to change itself from reading to reading any more than the groove of a record is capable of rendering a different sound from hearing to hearing. But modernism, in its emphasis on bodily effort, strives toward orality, moving toward the original live form upon which narrative is based, whereas the recording industry moves away from the coughs and sinews of live music to a perfect, and perfectly unreal, reproduction. Aldous Huxley, who will be discussed later in this chapter, gives a perfect demonstration of this contrast in *Point Counter Point*. As another twentieth-century advertising campaign for the recording industry puts the question, "Is it live or is it Memorex?": the live performance is the ideal form, to which the tape recording acts as a simulacrum.

Even Little Nipper, the dog in the famous advertisement, was a double. Francis Barraud's painting of the fox terrier listening to Berliner's Improved

Gramophone was itself a re-covering of an earlier one that was first painted for and rejected by Edison, and behind the familiar horn gramophone can be detected a pentimento of Edison's earlier phonograph, with a recording cylinder much more suited to the subject of the painting (Petts 22):[8]

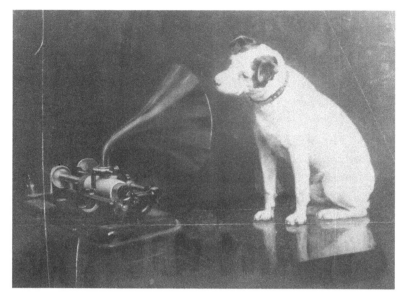

Figure 5.2. Francis Barraud, "Dog looking at and listening to a Phonograph" (1899). Public Record Office, The National Archives. Reprinted by permission. Leonard Petts, *The Story of "Nipper"* 22.

It's additionally useful to remember something that would have been immediately obvious to a Victorian audience for Barraud's painting: the dog's master is meant to be dead. The fox terrier is strictly at fault: the scent that has led him to his master's voice has betrayed him. In this case, the dog's master was in fact dead, and the painting of the dog was drawn from life: Nipper was listening to the recorded voice of the painter's brother (see Rice, *Cannibal* 116). The painting draws upon the subgenre of Victorian funeral painting that has animals in mourning for their owners, as in Landseer's *The Old Shepherd's Chief Mourner*, in which the loyal hound is the last to leave the graveside (see Rice, *Cannibal* 116). Barraud's painting is a pastiche comparable, at least in subject, to Hardy's "Ah, Are You Digging on My Grave?," in which the trope of the animal mourner is neatly reversed, since the dog is only looking for a place to bury his bone. Nipper himself died between the first and second versions of the painting and was buried beneath a mulberry tree in Kingston upon Thames.[9] As Bloom thinks cryptically during "The Croppy Boy": "Die, dog. Little dog, die" (*U* 11.1019).

T. S. Eliot, who is buried in a crypt in East Coker, took a predictably Tiresian attitude to the gramophone, as representative of the modern civilization from which he spent most of his writing life trying to escape. He ends his "London Letter" of December 1922 with a classic jeremiad:

> When every theatre has been replaced by 100 cinemas, when every musical instrument has been replaced by 100 gramaphones [*sic*], when every horse has been replaced by 100 cheap motor cars, when electrical ingenuity has made it possible for every child to hear its bedtime stories through a wireless receiver attached to both ears, when applied science has done everything possible with the materials on this earth to make life as interesting as possible, it will not be surprising if the population of the entire civilized world rapidly follows the fate of the Melanesians. You will see that the death of Marie Lloyd has had a depressing effect, and that I am quite incapable of taking any interest in any literary events in England in the last two months, if any have taken place.
>
> (Eliot, "London," Dec. 1922: 663)

Eliot here adds to the chorus of those who fear the Master's Voice supplanting the mother's voice at bedtime: the "infant lulled to sleep by machinery" is a vestige of the Virgin before the dynamo. But the passage from the December 1922 "London Letter" is additionally remarkable for at least three reasons.

First, "gramophones" is mistyped as "gramaphones," which, if it is Eliot's error, is either an accidental display of forgivable ignorance—given that Alexander Graham Bell had a graphophone, Frank Seaman made a zonophone, and Edison had a phonograph, all in Eliot's native America—or a deliberate misspelling to artfully decline knowledge of a newfangled item that has been in the public consciousness for at least twenty years and is by 1917 a $33 million industry. Either way, the misspelling is corrected when this essay appears in *Selected Essays* in 1930 (Eliot, "Marie Lloyd," *Essays* 408), and Eliot has no difficulty spelling the word in any manuscript or typescript version of *The Waste Land*, when the typist "puts a record on the gramophone" (*TWL* 141). So "gramaphones" must stand uncorrected as Eliot's version of "I do not like that other world" (*U* 5.245).

Second, the fate of the Melanesians has been brought to Eliot's attention by W.H.R. Rivers, the man who salvaged Wilfred Owen and Siegfried Sassoon, who observed in *Essays on the Depopulation of Melanesia* that if you give the Melanesians a gramophone, they quickly lose interest in life and their tribe collapses.[10] Rivers' *Essays on the Depopulation of Melanesia,* together with Bronisław Malinowski's *Argonauts of the Western Pacific,* announced in 1922 a new paradigm for ethnography that was social and participant-driven, a response to Frazer's sweeping armchair review of all mythologies in *The Golden Bough* (itself re-released in 1922). The connection with *The Golden Bough* and *The Waste Land* is evident from the outset (Eliot, *Poems* 70); Rivers' observations on the decline of primitive cultures when faced with modern technology also make their way into Eliot's "Fragment of an Agon":

> Well that's life on a crocodile isle.
> There's no telephones
> There's no gramophones
> There's no motor cars
>   (Eliot, *Poems* 118)

No problem with the spelling of "gramophones" there either.

Third, the person whose death Eliot is lamenting was a music-hall singer, Marie Lloyd. This leads us to an unsung figure of the modern period, who deserves top billing in this chapter as much as Eugene Jolas or Little Nipper. You will remember Tom Rochford with his infernal machine in "Wandering Rocks": "He slid in a disk for himself: and watched it shoot, wobble, ogle, stop: four. Turn Now On" (*U* 10.482–43). The gadget is a means of mechanically displaying what's up next at the music hall: for a time, then, Marie Lloyd must take the stage. M'Coy and Lenehan speak of Rochford's exploits as they pass "Dan Lowry's musichall where Marie Kendall, charming soubrette, smiled on them from a poster a dauby smile" (*U* 11.495–96): he has rescued a man who disappeared down a manhole, one of many traps in the cityscape that comprise the obstacle course that is "Wandering Rocks." So, in honor of Rochford's rescue, this chapter will follow the black-and-white fox terrier down a rabbit hole.

3. Marie Lloyd

Lydia Douce knows about Marie Lloyd: everybody does. "And your other eye!" (*U* 11.148), Lydia shouts in "Sirens," repeating the famous catchphrase from one of Marie Lloyd's songs (Cheshire frontispiece). Marie Kendall, the other music-hall Marie, has been given a thorough review by Garry Leonard, R. B. Kershner, and Cheryl Herr, and the Joycean reader would do well to turn to Leonard's *Advertising and Commodity Culture in Joyce*, R. B. Kershner's *Joyce and Popular Culture*, and Herr's *Joyce's Anatomy of Culture* to read more about the performative world of 1904 Dublin. In this section, which is an excursus of sorts, I want to look at Marie Kendall's more sophisticated namesake and examine what on earth T. S. Eliot might have had in common with Marie Lloyd, the hallowed mistress of the music hall. The music hall is a place of suggestion, and both Eliot and Joyce draw broadly from it. Sometimes the Joycean method of "silence, exile, and cunning" (*P* 247) is as appropriate for other writers as it is for Joyce himself.

T. S. Eliot wrote eight "London Letters" for the *Dial*, published in April, June, August, and October 1921 and May, July, September, and December 1922.[11] In his first "London Letter," Eliot establishes the familiar themes of all eight: admiration of the vitality of the lower classes, represented by the music-hall singer Marie Lloyd, disparagement of the dullness of middle-class culture, represented by the work of Mr. John Drinkwater, which is "dull, supremely dull" (Eliot, "London," Apr. 1921: 450), and self-advertisement of that paragon of the upper classes, himself. T. S. Eliot's essays are always more interesting for what they say about him than for what they say about the nominal subjects of the essays, whether the subject is William Blake (seeing man naked "from the centre of his own crystal"—Eliot, "William Blake," *Essays* 277), Joyce ("pursuing a method which others must pursue after him"—Eliot, "Ulysses, Order, and Myth," 483), Hamlet, whose problems with his mother seem to reflect Eliot's problems with his own ("Hamlet and His Problems," *Essays* 121–26), or the literary tradition, in an essay that establishes Eliot as the particular individual talent toward which European literature extends ("Tradition and the Individual Talent," *Essays* 3–11). But in the first "London Letter" Eliot directly insists on the connection between his subject, Marie Lloyd, and himself: "I am prepared to be accused," he writes, "of self-advertisement" (Eliot, "London," Apr. 1921: 451). The "London Letters" tell Eliot's audience a great deal about the author, and the story is one of music and class. The eight letters published in the *Dial* between April 1921 and December 1922 trace Eliot's brief flurry of public statements about the music hall and neatly follow the period of that art form's extinction. The music hall is commonly held to have faded into obscurity on or about the time of the death of Marie Lloyd, the subject of Eliot's final letter.[12]

Eliot foresees the fall of the halls in his first "London Letter" and predicts that the lower class, which Eliot professes to admire for its communal spirit, will become infolded into the knotted crowd of the middle: "Both middle class and lower class are finding safety in Regular Hours, Regular Wages, Regular Pensions, and Regular Ideas. In other words, there will soon be only one class, and the second Flood is here" (Eliot, "London," Apr. 1921: 451).[13] After Eliot, the deluge, and the one flicker of hope for a last civilization is a program at the Palladium: "the Palladium has at this moment an excellent bill, including Marie Lloyd, Little Tich, George Mozart, and Ernie Lotinga; and that provokes an important chapter on the Extinction of the Music Hall, the corruption of the Theatre Public, and the incapacity of the British public to appreciate Miss Ethel Levey" (Eliot, "London," Apr. 1921: 452–53). Eliot is deliberately slumming: he closes his letter with the delicious remark that Picasso "lies outside of my province" (Eliot, "London," Apr. 1921: 453), implying that while modern art may be beyond him, he's right at home with Marie Lloyd.[14] And I think this is because in Marie Lloyd he sees something of himself.

Little Tich, who took his name from the Tichborne Claimant (Short 61) and was famous for his big-boot dance (Mander 120), presented a music-hall equivalent of *The Waste Land* or *Ulysses*. In any given Little Tich number, one could expect patter songs in "French, German, Italian, and Spanish," arguments on "sundry philosophies and e'en upon the world's religions," and performances of "very remarkable feats in mathematics" (Newton 202). George Mozart's act included the playing of enormous numbers of musical instruments (Newton 224) and "acid sketches" of suburban life (Green 151). Ernie Lotinga had an act with a character called Drinkwater, allowing for the following Joycean interchange with a French lady called Madame Lablanc:

> *Lablanc*: Monsieur la Drink-Water?
> *Lotinga*: No, I never touch it—I only drink whisky.
> (Wilmut 99)

(The connection with the John Drinkwater of Monro's anthology *Some Contemporary Poets*, to whom we have heard Eliot refer in his first "London Letter," is probably a coincidence, since Lotinga's routine dates from the early 1930s.) Ethel Levey was the leading lady of "display revues" at the Hippodrome (Short 129): Eliot's second "London Letter" speaks of her further as a representative of the new breed of music-hall performer, in terms that curiously resonate with "Tradition and the Individual Talent." "She is the most aloof and impersonal of personalities" says Eliot Eliotically, "indifferent, rather than contemptuous, to-wards the audience; her appearance and movement are of an extremely modern type of beauty. Hers is not broad farce, but a fascinating inhuman grotesquerie; she plays for herself rather than for the audience" (Eliot, "London," Jun. 1921: 688). Ethel Levey herself, like the filamented mind of Eliot's platinum poet, remains "inert, neutral, and unchanged" (Eliot, "Tradition," *Essays* 7): the terms "indifferent" and "inhuman" are signs of her successful "escape from personal-ity" (Eliot, "Tradition," *Essays* 10).

Against this dead nettle of the new revue is the attachment and humanity of the music hall's Marie Lloyd, who was as beloved for the warmth of her per-sonality as for the attraction of her songs, and who made her audience, as Eliot wrote in one of the nicest things he said about anybody, "not so much hilarious as happy" (Eliot, "London," Dec. 1922: 661). Like Gabriel Conroy, her generos-ity was legendary (*D* 219): she would arrange for cabs and food for her chorus girls (Newton 100) and once bought the entire contents of an East End grocery to give them all away (Short 205). Like Molly Ivors, she could pluck a crow with the best of them (*D* 187): in her battle royal with the infamous music-hall man-ager Oswald Stoll, who dropped her off the program for the Royal Command Performance at the Palace Theatre on 1 July 1912 because of her role in a strike against his management six months before, Marie Lloyd promptly organized a rival program at the London Pavilion down the road, which she titled "a Com-mand Performance by order of the British Public" (Green 192).

Generous, indomitable, republican: a fourth characteristic that made her such a valuable representative, to Eliot, of the spirit of the lower classes was her gift for obscenity. As Chance Newton charmingly puts it:

> Many well remember that some of the smart ditties that our Marie war-bled were more or less tinged with squeezes from what the dear girl her-self called "the blue bag."
> There was really no need whatever (as I often told her) for an artiste so really gifted both in humour and the way of "putting it over," to descend to this ceruleanism of song.
>
> (Newton 96)

As with Eliot's poetry, the implications of Marie Lloyd's lyrics were to be in-ferred rather than directly received. When summoned before a committee charged with cleaning up the stage, she performed her songs straight, "without an inflection, a nod, wink, or smile" (Green 169), and the committee found

nothing offensive in them. She then sang the sentimental songs the committee's wives and children would be likely to sing at home and revealed depths of
depravity in them:

> Marie sang two of the popular ballads which were warbled at pretty well
> every musical evening at the time, when musical evenings were very pop-
> ular indeed. They were "Come into the Garden, Maud" and "Queen of my
> Heart." What she did with those songs was nobody's business; the men
> who wrote them would have been amazed; Alfred Lord Tennyson would
> probably have expired of heart failure. Every little word had a meaning of
> its own, when Marie so willed. Leaving the poor committee stunned and
> gasping, she wished the members good afternoon and swept out.
>
> (qtd. in Green 169)

"Every little word had a meaning of its own": this is vital for the connection with
Eliot, and of course also for Joyce, whose Mr. Browne says, quoting a now-lost
revue sketch, "*Now, Mary Grimes, if I don't take it, make me take it, for I feel I want
it*" (*D* 183). In the *New York Telegraph* as early as 1897, Marie Lloyd is quoted
as saying "if they want to turn and twist my meanings . . ." (qtd. in Cheshire
73): Lloyd's and Eliot's ambiguities operate on the same plane. Arnold Bennett
speaks censoriously of the same significant absences when reviewing Lloyd's
performance in 1910: "I couldn't see the legendary cleverness of the vulgarity of
Marie Lloyd. [. . .] All her songs were variations of the same theme of sexual
naughtiness. No censor would ever pass them, and especially he wouldn't pass
her winks and her silences" (qtd. in Green 135). Eliot's winks and silences in
The Waste Land are similarly suggestive. "Where other artists in the same line
needed an ell, Marie took only an inch. This, because she was a great enough
actress to make an inch do an ell's job, and sufficient of an artist to know when
the job had been done" (Green 265). Eliot shares this gift of giving an inch and
getting a mile: the excisions of "'The horror! the horror!'" (*TWL* 2) and the
couplet that originally ended the visit of the young man carbuncular to the
typist—"And at the corner where the stable is, / Delays only to urinate, and
spit" (*TWL* 47)—show Eliot, with the considerable help of Ezra Pound, paring
down the excesses of his poem to allow it to speak with a quieter force.

The presence of Marie Lloyd can be detected everywhere behind the poem
that appeared in the *Criterion* four days after her funeral. (The funeral was

Friday, 12 October 1922, and the poem appeared the next Monday.) Marie has been metamorphosed into the enigmatic woman on the sled in "The Burial of the Dead" ("Marie, hold on tight"—*TWL* 135),[15] her silences into the silence of the hyacinth girl ("I could not / Speak, and my eyes failed"—*TWL* 136), and the leer of the audience into *"Od' und leer das Meer"* [empty and waste the sea] (*TWL* 136).[16] Eliot's hyacinth girl—"You gave me hyacinths first a year ago; / They called me the hyacinth girl" (*TWL* 135)—may have originated in the flower-seller of music-hall comedy. The burlesque *Miss Esmeralda* (1887) presented a girl selling hyacinths, with the following delightful bit:

> *Customer*: How much are your hyacinths?
> *Sylvia*: Two shillings a bunch, Sir.
> *Customer*: Why, yesterday, they were a shilling.
> *Sylvia*: Yes, but they're *higher since.*
> (qtd. in Short 102)

Madame Sosostris, famous clairvoyante, is the next turn on: *The Waste Land*'s display of freaks and queens and psychics and hyacinth girls and cockney vaudeville acts gives the opening two sections of the poem the format of a variety show.[17] On any given night the music hall could offer crossdressers, performing seals, trick cyclists, living statues, and shooting exhibitions, rivalling *The Waste Land* or "Circe" in its gallery of grotesques. *The Waste Land* originally led off with the forgotten hits of "By the Watermelon Vine," "My Evaline," and "The Cubanola Glide" (*TWL* 125); the pantomime origins of "Circe" are clearly evident in Ellen Bloom's *"widow Twankey"* crinoline (*U* 15.283) and the *"cakewalk dance"* (*U* 15.425) of Tom and Sam Bohee.

One particular music-hall song in *The Waste Land* has got Marie Lloyd written all over it:

> O the moon shone bright on Mrs. Porter
> And on her daughter
> They wash their feet in soda water
> (*TWL* 140)

The spirit of Marie Lloyd is in that euphemism: somehow Eliot, like Lloyd, makes soda water the dirtiest thing in the world. Marie Lloyd was particularly gifted at this kind of disingenuity: her songs included "Our Lodger's Such a Nice Young Man," with the perfectly innocent line "At nights he makes the beds and does the other little jobs" (Kift 47), and "The Railroad Song," about which Lloyd, sounding suspiciously like Eliot, protested that the people "get clever and say it means all sorts of things. I can't help that, can I?" (Green 170). Judge for yourself: the English title of "The Railroad Song" is "She'd Never Had Her Ticket Punched Before," and the song begins:

> She arrived at Euston by the midnight train.
> But when she got to the wicket, there was someone wanted to punch
>   her ticket.
> The guards and the porters came round her by the score
> And she told them all that she'd never had her ticket punched before.
>
> (qtd. in Green 170)

The porters surrounding this unfortunate traveler recall another of Lloyd's railway hits, "Oh! Mr. Porter," the song that Eliot refers to indirectly in the sodawater song, and again in "Sweeney Agonistes": "The Queen of Hearts!—Mrs. Porter!" (Eliot, *Poems* 113).[18] It is in "Oh! Mr. Porter" that Lloyd most clearly reveals her gift for suggestive understatement:

> Oh! Mr. Porter, what shall I do?
> I want to go to Birmingham and they're taking me on to Crewe.
> Send me back to London as quickly as you can,
> Oh! Mr. Porter, what a silly girl I am.
>
> (qtd. in Green 171)

Molly Bloom can play the ingénue as well, as Lenehan gleefully recounts in "Wandering Rocks." During his musical turn in the ninth vignette, he and Molly start "singing glees and duets" (*U* 10.556) and end with a glorious bit of misdirection: "*And what star is that, Poldy?* says she. By God, she had Bloom cornered. *That one, is it?* says Chris Callinan, *sure that's only what you might call a pinprick*" (*U* 10.571–73). Of all the episodes in *Ulysses*, "Wandering Rocks" is the most set up like a music-hall revue, with its separate numbers and a grand finale.

At least one more music-hall song is concealed in Eliot's lines about Mrs. Porter and her daughter. "Oh, the Moon Shines Bright on Charlie Chaplin" accentuates the apparent cowardice of the eponymous hero, who left for California rather than fight in the war:

Oh, the moon shines bright
On Charlie Chaplin,
His boots are crackin'
For want of blackin'

And his little baggy
Trousers they need mendin'
Before we send him
To the Dardanelles.

   (qtd. in Green 231)

Eliot's disingenuous note to the soda-water line reads as follows: "I do not
know the origin of the ballad from which these lines are taken: it was reported
to me from Sydney, Australia" (Eliot, *Poems* 72). "Before we send him / To
the Dardanelles" perhaps explains why Eliot chose Australia as the place from
which this song was meant to have been reported to him, since Gallipoli is in
the Dardanelles, but the note, like so many of them, is a deliberate blind.[19] At
the time of the first publication of the notes to *The Waste Land*, for the New
York edition of 15 December 1922, Eliot has been talking about the music hall in
the *Dial* for more than a year and would be generally known to be familiar with
"Oh, the Moon Shines Bright," not needing to apply to Australia for his information. The footnote is a wink as wide as Marie Lloyd's (figure 5.3); the lines
are a "collocation"—as he says in the notes, with a similar wink (Eliot, *Poems*
74)—of two representatives of the music hall: "Oh! Mr. Porter" and "Oh, the
Moon Shines Bright on Charlie Chaplin."[20]

The Waste Land is a poem of London, as *Ulysses* is a novel of Dublin, and
Marie Lloyd, as H. M. Tomlinson has said, "was London" (qtd. in Green 267).[21]
Though Eliot mistakenly places her in the North of England in his second "London Letter" ("Marie Lloyd, if I am not mistaken, has a bit of a Manchester accent"—Eliot, "London," Jun. 1921: 687), he realizes his mistake by the time of
his funeral tribute in the eighth and last letter: "Marie Lloyd was of London—
in fact of Hoxton—and on the stage from her earliest years" (Eliot, "London,"
Dec. 1922: 661). In that letter, which is the original version of the "Marie Lloyd"
essay, there is a long paragraph quoted from a newspaper account of the funeral,
provided as evidence of Lloyd's enormous popularity with the lower class. That
section is deleted when it appears in *Selected Essays*, probably because it betrays

too great a knowledge of the world of the music hall for Faber and Faber's high-brow audience. In the earlier version, her popularity is attested by an extended wreath-count provided by an anonymous reporter:

> Tributes were also sent by Hetty King, Clarice Mayne, Clara Mayne, Little Tich, Arthur Prince, George Mozart, Harry Weldon, Charles Austin, Gertie Gitana, the Brothers Egbert, Zetta Mare, Julia Neilson, and Fred Terry, Mr and Mrs Frank Curzon, Marie Loftus, many of the provincial music-halls, the Gulliver halls, and dressers from most of the theatres, and many of Miss Lloyd's old school chums. . . .
>
> (qtd. in Eliot, "London," Dec. 1922: 659–60, ellipsis in original)[22]

All this sets up an elaborate distraction: the letter continues, "Among all of that small number of music-hall performers, whose names are familiar to what is called the lower class, Marie Lloyd had far the strongest hold on popular affection" (Eliot, "London," Dec. 1922: 660). First, "small number" is clearly wrong—not for nothing is "LITOTES" an anagram of "T. S. ELIOT." Second, "what is called the lower class" is a stunning piece of code-switching from an expert in the genre. And third, the claim that Marie Lloyd spoke directly to a working-class audience simply isn't true. At Sheffield, she was booed relentlessly, resulting in the following memorable outburst: "You don't like me, well I don't like you. And you know what you can do with your stainless knives and your scissors and your circular saws—you can shove 'em up your arse" (qtd. in Green 164). (To soothe his star attraction, the manager is supposed to have gone to her dressing-room and said, "They'll do what you say with the knives and scissors, [. . .] but can they be spared the circular saws?"—Green 165.) The East End didn't like the subtle songs that played so well up at the West End, preferring "up-front humor to sophistication"; according to Dagmar Kift, "she suffered quite badly from the shock of discovering that her style was not to the fancy of the working-class audiences in the East End" (Kift 170). "Our Marie" presented the mirror image of a working-class world, but it is an image more enduring to those, like Eliot, who cannot bear too much reality.

The moment when reality broke through the image came with the manner of her death, which is generally held to have taken place after a performance of her signature song, "It's a Bit of a Ruin That Cromwell Knocked About a Bit." Cromwell refers to the Cromwell Arms and signifies any pub; in the song, Marie Lloyd played an old woman rummaging through her handbag, staggering drunkenly about while a man who has stolen her purse asks her about the ruins of a local abbey. Performing it on 4 October 1922, she fell during the performance, to the great approval of the audience, and died three days later (Green 256). At fifty-two, she herself was one of the ruins of her song, knocked about by her husband, an Irish jockey called Bernard Dillon, whose beatings, under the influence of alcohol, led to her death. The song is neatly double in its mourning for a present ruin (the drunken singer ruined by the Cromwell Arms) and a past one (the abbey knocked about by Cromwell):

> In the gay old days, there must have been some doin's,
> No wonder that the poor old abbey went to ruins.

> (qtd. in Green 256)

In the song's yearning for the more vibrant church of the "gay old days," one can hear a faint echo of Paul Verlaine's line that immediately follows Mrs. Porter's washing ritual with her daughter: *"Et, O ces voix d'enfants, chantant dans la coupole!"* (*TWL* 140). The song begins "I'm very fond of ruins, and ruins I like to scan": Eliot ends his poem the way Marie bowed out of the music hall, with a man sitting down, trying to put his belongings in order. "Shall I at least set my lands in order? [. . .] These fragments I have shored against my ruins" (*TWL* 146), says the speaker; Marie sits, a "relic from a bygone age" (qtd. in Green 256), with an open handbag in the long grass, talking about the ruin of herself and of history and then leaving the stage for good.

Marie Lloyd was still alive when the last lines of *The Waste Land* were written, but Eliot, in his final "London Letter," recognizes the connection between the two farewells. He cites her final appearance in the essay:

> To appreciate for instance the last turn in which Marie Lloyd appeared, one ought to know already exactly what objects a middle-aged woman of the charwoman class would carry in her bag; exactly how she would go through her bag in search of something; and exactly the tone of voice in which she would enumerate the objects she found in it. This was only part of the acting in Marie Lloyd's last song, I'm One of the Ruins That Cromwell Knocked Abaht a Bit.

> (Eliot, "London," Dec. 1922: 661)

Marie Lloyd's gift is one of identity, of constructing a credible image of reality; Dennis Ryan speaks of her as "an objective correlative made flesh" (Ryan

37). This gift of exact imitation, Eliot says in his elegy to her, requires "selection and concentration" (Eliot, "London," Dec. 1922: 661): the art of poetry
and the art of the music hall have similar absolutes. For Eliot, this accuracy of
representation gives Marie Lloyd a "moral superiority" (Eliot, "London," Dec.
1922: 661–62), a morality based on aesthetics and sympathy. Dennis Ryan has
pointed out that Eliot uses *The Waste Land*'s three-part formula for grace (*Datta,
Dayadhvam, Damyata*: Give, Sympathize, Control) in his appreciation of Marie
Lloyd, using some form of each instruction in quick succession: "Marie Lloyd's
audiences were invariably *sympathetic*, and it was through that sympathy that
she *controlled* them. [. . .] No other comedian succeeded so well in *giving* expression to the life of that audience" (Eliot, "London," Dec. 1922: 660–61, italics
mine). It is worth noting that the giving, the sympathy, and the control are all
part of a shared compact between artist and viewer: Eliot's formulation applies
to his reader as well as his art. The success of his poem relies on his reader's
willingness to give (time, energy, and intellect), sympathize (with his conserva-
tive positions, or with the agony of his prisons), and control (the chaos of his
text). Marie Lloyd not only gave to an audience, she made her audience give
to her: Eliot's working man "was engaged in that collaboration of the audience
with the artist which is necessary in all art and most obviously in dramatic art"
(Eliot, "London," Dec. 1922: 662). The moral superiority of Marie Lloyd is one
that Eliot hopes to find in himself.

With the death of Marie Lloyd and the demise of the music hall, Eliot's
working man "will now go to the cinema, where his mind is lulled by continuous senseless music and continuous action too rapid for the brain to act upon,
and he will receive, without giving [. . . .] He will also have lost some of his interest in life" (Eliot, "London," Dec. 1922: 662). "Receive without giving": this is
why Eliot hates the cinema, the gramophone, the motor car, the modern world.
There is no pact between artist and viewer. In an obituary for Marie Lloyd, H.
G. Hibbert wrote, "it is not cruel to say that she dies opportunely [. . .] the
music hall is on the eve of a crisis" (Cheshire 75). With the arrival of radio and
the cinema, the music hall went into sharp decline, and Eliot predicts this in his
most Tiresian vein, following directly from Proust's epic lament from the end
of *Swann's Way*: "when every horse has been replaced by 100 cheap motor cars
[. . .]" (Eliot, "London," Dec. 1922: 663). In *The Waste Land*, civilization goes
the way of Rivers' Melanesia: Marvell's winged chariot is replaced by the horns
and motors of Mrs. Sweeney, Tiresias is replaced by Madame Sosostris, and the
thing that Tiresias must see is not the blinding of Oedipus by the wall of Thebes

but the typist home for teatime, a woman who after using machines for a living has mechanical sex in mechanical quatrains, following which she smoothes her hair with automatic hand and stoops, in a parody of Oliver Goldsmith, to put "a record on the gramophone" (*TWL* 141).[23]

Marie Lloyd, then, represents many things to Eliot. She is London, she is a vestige of a civilization that has been lost, and she is an image of the lower class, about which he is as anthropologically curious as Rivers is about the population of Melanesia. From the Chopin in "Portrait of a Lady" to "the stillness of the violin" in "Burnt Norton" (Eliot, *Poems* 8, 180), from *Preludes* to *Four Quartets*, Eliot has always been a poet with music in his ear. Marie Lloyd is the music behind *The Waste Land*'s "rhythmical grumbling" (qtd. in *TWL* 1). She is oblique and operates by silence and suggestion. Like Eliot, she is a ventriloquist, and in the accuracy of her imitations Marie Lloyd attains and allows a sympathy that is for Eliot a moral position. His interest in her is on the face of it surprising, given that the music hall is never mentioned in the first volume of his *Letters*, except for a retracted invitation to John Rodker to contribute "a rubric on cinema and music halls" for the *Criterion* in July 1922 (Eliot, *Letters* 540), and given that no other essay in his *Selected Essays* is even about a woman (the essay on Marianne Moore didn't make the cut), let alone a vaudevillian. But in one respect, his interest in her may be particularly revealing.

Also deleted from the December 1922 "London Letter" when it made its appearance in *Selected Essays* as "Marie Lloyd" was the final line:

> You will see that the death of Marie Lloyd has had a depressing effect, and that I am quite incapable of taking any interest in any literary events in England in the last two months, if any have taken place.
>
> (Eliot, "London," Dec. 1922: 663)

If any have taken place? The letter is actually dated November 1922 and appeared in the December issue of the *Dial*. What about the first issue of the *Criterion*, which came out in October 1922, with an unannotated version of *The Waste Land*? What about the prize in the *Dial*, news of which had certainly reached England by mid-November 1922?[24] What about the news, published in the *Liverpool Post* on 16 November 1922, that Eliot was the beneficiary of a scheme to keep him out of the working class entirely? The scandal of the Bel Esprit scheme had made Eliot particularly sensitive to issues of class at the time of writing his final "London Letter": he writes ruefully to Virginia Woolf on 4

December 1922 of receiving "four three halfpenny stamps" (Eliot, *Letters* 606) from a sarcastic well-wisher seeking to contribute to Eliot's financial independence. His renewed attention to Marie Lloyd may in fact be a response to the backfiring of Bel Esprit, as a way of reasserting his bankrupt credentials with the working-class world.

Like Joyce, Eliot is both a sponge and a sponger, and has created a cultural tradition that is a tree of sponges (or a coral reef): "Those are pearls that were his eyes" / "Five fathoms out there" (*TWL* 138, *U* 3.470). *The Waste Land* is the main literary event that has been taking place in the last two months of 1922, the period of which Eliot in his letter professes to be completely ignorant. The other thing that has been happening, of course, is *Ulysses*, which came out in a second edition on 12 October 1922. (We can safely assume that the Earl of Carnarvon's discovery of the tomb of Tutankhamun on 26 November didn't make the deadline: it would have been difficult even for Eliot to pretend ignorance of that.) For the last two months of 1922, it could be argued that the literary events in England have revolved to a great extent around Eliot himself, and once again, I think, Eliot is "prepared to be accused," as he wrote in the first "London Letter," "of self-advertisement" (Eliot, "London," Apr. 1921: 451). Eliot's professed inattention to these events shows him playing Marie Lloyd, winking with one eye while the other remains wide open. Marie Lloyd was as famous for what she

Figure 5.3. Alfred Bryan (1852–1899), caricature of Marie Lloyd. In "The Call Boy's Girls," a series of illustrations for an unidentified publication. Undated. Cheshire frontispiece, 75.

left out as much as for what she put in, operating by silence and suggestion. If anyone had what Walter Benjamin would call an aura, Marie Lloyd had, and her death, as her obituaries all said, was a sign of the end of vaudeville, as radio and cinema ousted the music hall.[25] *The Waste Land*, like Marie Lloyd, is a vaudeville act, an act of ventriloquism, and a work of silence and suggestion. One of Marie Lloyd's greatest hits, as Lydia Douce knows (*U* 11.148), was called "Then You Wink the Other Eye."

4. Mrs. Bundren

Winking the other eye is an essential character trait in Joyce's comedians: Simon Dedalus closes his left eye to imitate the "squint troubling" Corny Kelleher, saying in true vaudeville fashion, "Do you follow me?" (*U* 6.93–94). The joke in this case is obscure (the undertaker has apparently been saving money by cutting corners the way a tailor would), but that's precisely the point: not seeing the joke, as we will discover in chapter 7, is often Joyce's chosen comic mode. The "screwed" sailor in "Eumaeus" "shut his right eye completely" in imitation of Simon Dedalus demolishing "still a further egg" (*U* 16.396, 395, 400). Invited by Little Chandler to drink a health to the future Mr. and Mrs. Gallaher, Ignatius Gallaher "closed one eye expressively over the rim of his glass" (*D* 76). All these winkings and blinkings and nods are telling us one thing: we must read Joyce's text asquint. Robert Ball's *The Story of the Heavens*, a copy of which Bloom owns (*U* 17.1373) and thinks of as a "Fascinating little book" (*U* 8.110), tells us to "Close the right eye" in determining parallactically the position of a cloud (Ball 181–82, qtd. in Knowles, *Helix* 10).[26] So it is with all of Joyce.

   Like Marie Lloyd, Joyce works by silence and suggestion. Silence and cunning are two-thirds of Stephen Dedalus' defense against his home, his fatherland, and his church (*P* 247). Mr. Duffy reads the *Mail*'s report of the death of Mrs. Sinico "*Secreto*": "not aloud, but moving his lips as a priest does" (*D* 109). The boy in "Araby" suffers in silence, as does Eveline and Gabriel Conroy (*D* 28, 34, 223–25). In *Ulysses*, the narrator is the one whose silences speak volumes and who is in playful aspect most like Marie Lloyd. The narrator disappears entirely in "Circe," which ends with a moment of silence:

> (*Silent, thoughtful, alert he stands on guard, his fingers at his lips in the attitude of secret master. Against the dark wall a figure appears slowly, a fairy boy of eleven, a changeling, kidnapped, dressed in an Eton suit with glass shoes*

*and a little bronze helmet, holding a book in his hand. He reads from right to
left inaudibly, smiling, kissing the page.)*
BLOOM
(*wonderstruck, calls inaudibly*) Rudy!

(U 15.4955–62)

In direct contrast to Stephen's "ineluctable modality of the audible" (U 3.13),
here we hear the eluctable modality of the inaudible: silence has become
speech. It is next to impossible to perform this scene without verbalizing
Bloom's recognition, though the text clearly indicates that the name is to be
uttered "*Secreto.*"

The dynamo in the Paris Exhibition Hall has this extraordinary power of
silence: one begins to pray to it as the "natural expression of man before silent
and infinite force" (Adams 380). And here we must pick up the gramophone
needle again, for the silence of the gramophone is not just the silencing of the
music hall. It is the silence of death, the end of live art. After Eliot and Joyce,
the cry against recorded music in the modernist period becomes more strident.
"The loud speaker is the street walker of music" grumbles the reactionary critic
Constant Lambert in "The Appalling Popularity of Music" in 1934 (Lambert
239). Lambert, sounding very much like Eliot, claims that the gramophone is
the primary culprit for the present "age of tonal debauch" (Lambert 239) in
which the diffusion of musical culture makes the listener of a Bach concerto
experience "the faint nausea felt towards a piece of toffee by a worker in a sweet
factory" (Lambert 237).[27] Aldous Huxley, at the start of *Point Counter Point* in
1928, forces his reader to listen to the entirety of Bach's Orchestral Suite no. 2
in B minor and closes the book with a performance of the Heiliger Dankge-
sang, from Beethoven's String Quartet no. 15. The former program (the Bach)
is live, or as alive as a concert program can possibly be in a novel; the latter
(the Beethoven) is a gramophone recording. The difference between the two
is instructive. The Bach is performed by an Italian flautist, Pongileoni, who
blows glueily into his flute, the orchestra is all sweat and elbows, the audience
wriggles and fails to concentrate like the row of Schlegels at Beethoven's Fifth
in *Howards End*. Both Forster and Huxley emphasize the awareness of one-
self as audience, as part of a group, interacting with the performer: live music
forces this. The Beethoven, by contrast, is a slow dance of death, interrupted by
the turning of the disks. In the live performance, Lord Tantamount, a distin-
guished but slightly eccentric biologist who has been grafting legs onto frogs

in an evolutionary experiment, whispers "Bach?" ecstatically to his assistant as the sound of the orchestral suite makes its way through his ear into his brain (Huxley 32). In the recorded string quartet, the fortissimo chords just before the movement's coda are made to exactly coincide with the shots of Spandrell's assassins (Huxley 430). Live music is life. Recorded music is death. For Huxley, the case is closed.

For D. H. Lawrence, the lid may be closed, but the piano opens a passageway into the past:

> Softly, in the dusk, a woman is singing to me;
> Taking me back down the vista of years, till I see
> A child sitting under the piano, in the boom of the tingling strings
> And pressing the small, poised feet of a mother who smiles as she sings.

> (D. H. Lawrence, "Piano" 188)

Music for all these writers is memory, as it is for Proust and the little phrase of Vinteuil's violin sonata, for Joyce and the old sweet song of the concert performances given by Molly Bloom, for Eliot and his love of the comic songs of the dead Marie Lloyd.[28] And in all these cases the memory is a live one, a music of the body: a tingling string, a winked eye, a heaving bosom, the small poised feet of a mother who smiles as she sings. Modernism insists on live performance. Conrad presumes that his audience in *Heart of Darkness* will sit through a night on a smelly London river at low tide waiting for Marlow to get to the point, and Ford Madox Ford seats John Dowell's listener in *The Good Soldier* by an imaginary fireside. The "you" of "Let us go then, you and I" (Eliot, "Prufrock," *Poems* 3) rings throughout modernism: an audience is required. When Miss La Trobe puts a record on the gramophone at the end of her pageant in Woolf's *Between the Acts*, the audience snaps and breaks to its jagged rhythm:

> The tune changed; snapped; broke; jagged. Foxtrot was it? Jazz? Anyhow the rhythm kicked, reared, snapped short. What a jangle and a jingle! Well, with the means at her disposal, you can't ask too much. What a cackle, a cacophony! Nothing ended. So abrupt. And corrupt. Such an outrage; such an insult; and not plain. Very up to date, all the same. What is her game? To disrupt? Jog and trot? Jerk and smirk? Put the finger to the nose? Squint and pry? Peak and spy? O the irreverence of the generation which is only momentarily—thanks be—'the young.' The young, who

can't make, but only break; shiver into splinters the old vision; smash to atoms what was whole.

(Woolf, Acts 127–28)

The gramophone brings cacophony and disconnection; after a closing speech by the vicar, the audience disperses, but the gramophone gets the final word: "The gramophone gurgled *Unity—Dispersity*. It gurgled *Un . . dis. . . .* And ceased" (Woolf, *Acts* 140).[29]

Graham Greene, in *Brighton Rock*, gives the gramophone the last word again, and again it's the voice of death. Rose has lost her husband, the albino psychopath Pinky, but she is consoled by a recording that Pinky made for her on Brighton Pier in the days before he died. He told her that he put something loving on it, and so the book ends with Rose clutching the gramophone disk to her breast, walking "rapidly in the thin June sunlight towards the worst horror of all" (Greene 247). The book only ends there on the page: the text moves forward into the white space after the book is over, to complete its hideous circuit in the reader's imagination. For Pinky has recorded something truly horrible:[30]

"We haven't got a gramophone anyway. You won't be able to hear it. What's the good?"

"I don't want a gramophone," she said. "I just want to have it there. Perhaps one day you might be away somewhere and I could borrow a gramophone. And you'd speak," she said with a sudden intensity that scared him.

"What do you want me to say?"

"Just anything," she said. "Say something to me. Say Rose and—something."

He went into the box and closed the door. There was a slot for his sixpence: a mouthpiece: an instruction, "Speak clearly and close to the instrument." The scientific paraphernalia made him nervous. He looked over his shoulder and there outside she was watching him, without a smile. He saw her as a stranger: a shabby child from Nelson Place, and he was shaken by an appalling resentment. He put in a sixpence, and, speaking in a low voice for fear it might carry beyond the box, he gave his message up to be graven on vulcanite: "God damn you, you little bitch,

why can't you go back home for ever and let me be?" He heard the needle
scratch and the record whirr: then a click and silence.

(Greene 176–77)

"Graven on vulcanite": traces of the graven language of Joyce's recorded outlaw, and Edison's original sense of the applications of the phonograph, for the
purpose of preserving the sayings, the voices, and the last words of the dying member of the family. Pinky's message from the grave establishes that the
gramophone, like death, is a solitary object to be experienced alone. After the
gramophone plays in Huxley, Woolf, and Greene, there is always a dead silence.

"Have a gramophone in every grave," Bloom thinks in "Hades" (U 6.963).
"Put on poor old greatgrandfather" (U 6.964): the best available option for
the voice on the recording, since the name of Rudolph Virag's father is only
given as "Szombathely" (U 15.1868), is Julius Higgins, who is great-grandfather
on her mother's side to Milly Bloom (U 17.536). When the recording starts—
"Kraahraark!" (U 6.965)—and finishes—"krpthsth" (U 6.966)—the static
of the needle anticipates another machine in the text. The tram that interrupts Robert Emmet's funeral oration begins the same way—"Kraaaaaa" (U
11.1291)—and obscures a consonant cluster that parallels great-grandfather's
final croak: "Pprrpffrrppffff" (U 11.1293). Concealed among all the musical effects in that final sound is the famous acronym of the recording industry, "*ffrr.*"[31]
"Hellohellohello" (U 6.965), says the disembodied voice, directly quoting
Thomas Edison: "'Hullo!' Edison screamed into the telephone mouthpiece"
(Kittler 21). Joyce is joining a legion of modernist critics of the new technology, who increasingly recognize in the gramophone an enemy to the necessary
imperfections of their art. Even in his gramophone recordings, Joyce insists on
the language of the outlaw.

Nowhere is the loneliness of the long-playing record clearer than in Samuel
Beckett's *Krapp's Last Tape*. Krapp is recording the birthdays of his miserable
life, year by year, spool by spool. Krapp's tape, like Pinky's vulcanite, and the
cylinder in Barraud's original painting, reverts to Edison's first use of the gramophone as a recording device rather than a playing machine. As his name suggests, Krapp is in deliberate opposition to Proust's Swann, with the doubled last
consonant in both, one soaring on wings of memory to happy occasions well
remembered, the other sinking deeper into the mire of an irretrievable and rapidly forgotten past. The warmth and hope of Proust, the subject of Beckett's 1931

essay, is in *Krapp's Last Tape* turned grotesque, the cradle becomes the grave, the vessels that store each Proustian year are now spools, disks, and cylinders, the mechanics of memory. The spools are collected in nine boxes, five spools to a box, each spool recording the summation of a year. Where all the great musical moments in *Swann's Way* are captured live, the rare nonverbal sounds that Krapp manages to record are a popped cork, or *tape*, and a croaked "Evening Hymn": "*Ten seconds. Pop of cork. Ten seconds. Second cork. Ten seconds. Third cork. Ten seconds. Brief burst of quavering song*" (Beckett, *Krapp* 17). Besides being the sound of a cork in French, a "*tape*" is also the act of typing (mechanical writing), sex (mechanical reproduction), and recording (mechanical sound). Taken together, the spools record, as Emile Berliner imagined it, the "tone picture of a single lifetime," from child's prattle to boy's exultation to man's reflection to the feeble utterances of the deathbed (qtd. in Gelatt 62). Krapp begins the play searching for "Box . . . thrree . . . spool . . . five" (Beckett, *Krapp* 12), which contains the recording he made when he was thirty-nine, a recording that itself admits to "listening to an old year, [. . .] ten or twelve years ago." (Beckett, *Krapp* 15–16). The recordings are then embedded within one another: the new and possibly final recording, made at age sixty-nine, will also begin with a commentary on an old year: "Just been listening to that stupid bastard I took myself for thirty years ago, hard to believe I was ever as bad as that" (Beckett, *Krapp* 24). The embedding goes a level further: the thirty-nine-year-old Krapp listens to a Krapp in his late twenties who "Sneers at what he calls his youth and thanks to God that it's over" (Beckett, *Krapp* 17).

The recording cycle is vicious and unending, but stuck in the middle of box 3 spool 5 is something for which the latter-day Krapp is searching. "[S]uddenly," says the recorded Krapp, interrupting a description of lying on a woman in a boat, "I saw the whole thing. The vision, at last. This I fancy is what I have chiefly to record this evening, against the day when my work will be done and perhaps no place left in my memory, warm or cold, for the miracle that . . . (*hesitates*) . . . for the fire that set it alight. What I suddenly saw then was this, that the belief I had been going on all my life, namely—[. . .]" (Beckett, *Krapp* 20–21). But the live Krapp doesn't want to hear that bit and fast-forwards to the much more interesting part about the woman in the boat. The difficulty for any actor in this scene is that the fast-forwarding must be real. You can't just jab angrily at the tape player and wait for the technician to line up the next sound cue. The time it takes to fast-forward to the next line of the text that Krapp listens to—"great granite rocks the foam flying up in the light of the lighthouse and the wind-gauge spinning like a propellor, clear to me at last that the dark I have always struggled to keep under is in reality my most"—must be exactly the time it takes to complete the act of angrily fast-forwarding on a recorder (Beckett, *Krapp* 21). And when Krapp then curses, because the younger Krapp is still banging on about his epiphany, and fast-forwards again to—"unshatterable association until my dissolution of storm and night with the light of the understanding and the fire"—that must again take exactly the time it takes to complete the gesture (Beckett, *Krapp* 21). And when he curses *again*, because it's still not the bit he's looking for, and fast-forwards for a third time to "my face in her breasts and my hand on her," the gap from "fire" to "my face" is again not to be simulated (Beckett, *Krapp* 21). We know all this because Krapp then *rewinds*, back to a bit in between his second fast-forward and his third.

But he doesn't rewind far enough: the epiphany is missing. It's on the tape but absent in performance: recorded by the thirty-nine-year-old Krapp but forwarded past by a sixty-nine-year-old looking for the naughty bits. This is to a reader simply maddening, since it is possible to presume that "the whole thing" that the younger Krapp sees is the pay-off for the play, and Beckett chooses to have it remain absent, unreproduced. But to an actor, on another more alarming level, it must be nevertheless recorded, or something must, to get the time of the tape right. And it can't be gibberish, in case you make a mistake with the indicator and get "blah blah blah great granite rocks" or something. So the actor, or in this case the recorder, is in the unimaginable but perfectly Beckettian position of straining to complete a void, having to create something which will never be known, an absent presence, a lost aura, and under the additional pressure of having that never-heard text be the chief purpose of what Krapp had to record this evening, thirty years ago. The chasm between emotion and recollection is never wider.[32]

The transition from one medium to the next is always a kind of dying: Walter Benjamin suggests that the development of each art form requires a further one to meet its demands (Benjamin, *Illuminations* 239). When Douglas Fairbanks spoke for the first time on film he finally looked his age: talking pictures "saddled Douglas Fairbanks with a mortality that, in silent film, he had seemed to exist without" (Cohen 165). As modernism grew and made it new, it could see itself, like Prufrock, growing old. It could hear the snicker of the eternal, the singing of the mermaids, the metronomic precision of the gramophone. And so modernism drowns itself in human voices: modernism becomes desperately alive. Krapp loves his spools of time, but he's a negative example: all the great texts of modernism—*The Waste Land, Ulysses, Howards End, Women in Love, To the Lighthouse, As I Lay Dying*—all rage against the box, push the coffin lid open, insist on the voices of the living.

The gramophone, finally, is death because art is put in a box, a box into which you insert sixpence on a pier, a beautifully patterned dull black sound-box with wooden louvers, a box with your number on it, box 3 spool 5. Eliot and Joyce delight in not getting it perfectly right in endless manuscripts and typescripts, glorifying the process over the product, refusing to complete their work. There is always room for one more letter from Martha Clifford to place on the pile in the first drawer of Bloom's dresser: "What object did Bloom add to this collection of objects? / A 4th typewritten letter received by Henry Flower (let H. F. be L. B.) from Martha Clifford (find M. C.)" (*U* 17.1840–42). Lily Briscoe has her paint-box, which clicks one section shut of *To the Lighthouse,* but in that moment's nick the window to the book bursts wide open: the sound encompasses "in a circle for ever the paint-box, the lawn, Mr. Bankes, and that wild villain, Cam, dashing past" (Woolf, *Lighthouse* 87).[33] In *Howards End,* at the Queen's Hall concert of Beethoven's Fifth, Helen hears goblins, Tibby reads his score, Frieda listens only to classical music, and Margaret talks to the man next to her, with whose umbrella Helen will run off, resulting in her pregnancy and his death by falling bookcase: all these events are only possible as the result of a collective audience attending a live performance (Forster, *Howards End* 32ff).

The gramophone is a piece of machinery and, as such, is part of the new modern world that its writers, especially American writers, often glorify. From Walt Whitman's "body electric" and Eliot's "filament of platinum" to William Carlos Williams' "radiant gist," modern literature gleefully co-opts each new scientific discovery, each one, like the automated writing of Georgie Hyde-Lees, "come to give [them] metaphors for poetry."[34] But there is a dark side to modernism's fascination with machines. The gramophone, like Quentin's grandfather's watch in *The Sound and the Fury,* is the mausoleum of desire (Faulkner, *Sound* 76). William Faulkner's *As I Lay Dying* takes its reader past death, inside the coffin Cash has lovingly constructed for his mother, into the space where Addie thinks and breathes. At the end of *As I Lay Dying,* Anse introduces his brand-new wife to the family. As the book is wound up as tight as tight can be, with a punchline—"Meet Mrs. Bundren" (Faulkner, *Dying* 261)—that Faulkner said he had in his head when he started writing the novel, it's perhaps important to notice, in a book that has been obsessed with death in a box from the title on, that the new Mrs. Bundren is carrying something. In her grip she has a gramophone.[35]

6 | Siren Songs

1. From Silence to Solfège: A Solfa Fable

> Silence, all.
>
> (*U* 1.23)

If the gramophone in *As I Lay Dying* is the nadir of recorded sound in literature, then the live music sung in "Sirens" is its equal and opposite. That music will be the subject of this chapter, but first we must pause for a moment of silence. To be silent (*sileo*) is a different thing from merely holding one's peace (*taceo*). The verb *sileo* is to "be still," to make no noise, and to insist on the absence of noise. It describes the philosophical initiates known as the Silentes for their five-year silence during the period of Pythagorean instruction. The Latin verb *taceo* is said to derive from a Sanskrit root meaning "contentment": it simply means to "shut up."[1] It gives us taciturn, tacit understanding, and the Latin writer Tacitus. Virgil neatly contrasts the two in Book VI of the *Aeneid*:

> Di, quibus imperium est animarum, umbraeque *silentes*
> et Chaos et Phlegethon, loca nocte *tacentia* late[2]

The "umbrae silentes," or "silent shades," have no option in the matter: they are silent in essence. The "loca nocte tacentia," or "hushed places of night," have chosen to stay quiet: they are silent by choice. *Taceo* is a conscious withdrawal of noise; *sileo* is the inability to make it. When Tibby raises his finger to indicate the passage on the drum, he is silently commanding that the rest of the

Schlegels remain *tacet* (Forster, *Howards End* 34). *Ulysses* is crowded with "um-brae silentes," shades who "subsist in the silence," as Seamus Heaney translates the phrase (Heaney 29). "Aeolus" reveals "the silent typesetters at their cases" (*U* 7.163), "Proteus" ends with "a silent ship" (*U* 3.505), May Goulding utters "*a silent word*," as "*A choir of virgins and confessors sing voicelessly*" (*U* 15.4161–62). Often in this book of shades, silence is a sign of love rather than death: Bloom "stands silent" before Gerty, with a face "silent as the grave" (*U* 13.744–45, 691). Bloom's final bedtime kiss of his wife's backside is both anticipated and remembered in "silent contemplation" (*U* 17.2239, 2245). Silence is an active erotic force on the Hill of Howth: Molly wills him silently to come to her—"and then I asked him with my eyes" (*U* 18.1605)—and Bloom remembers that "She lay still" (*U* 8.910).[3] Silence, in the underworld of *Ulysses*, is a state of being.

After the narrator, the most voluble person in *Ulysses* is Molly Bloom, but her long monologue is of course actually silent, interrupted by the whistle of an occasional train and the music of the chamber pot: "Frseeeeeeeeeeeeeeeeeeeeee-frong that train again," "O Lord what a row youre making" (*U* 18.874, 1147). Her concern with the pronunciation of the words of "Love's Old Sweet Song"— "I hate that istsbeg" (*U* 18.876)—is unspoken, as is Bloom's anxiety about the nonexistent *voglio* in "Là ci darem": "Wonder if she pronounces that right: *voglio*" (*U* 4.327–28).[4] These two songs will be performed together at a later date:

—What are you singing?
—*Là ci darem* with J. C. Doyle, she said, and *Love's Old Sweet Song.*

(*U* 4.313–14)

Though the bedroom conversation sets the songs up from the start as crucial intertexts, they are sung mostly in the mind during the course of the day. Bloom has a crack at both in "Lotus-Eaters" (*U* 5.157–61, 227–28), and the imaginary Marion hums a phrase from the duet in "Circe" (*U* 15.351–53), but on the sound-stage of Dublin's outer world they remain as mutely suggestive as crumbs of potted meat, silent signifiers of the assignation at four o'clock.

"Silence, all" (*U* 1.23), says Mulligan: silence is all in *Ulysses*. It is also, as we discovered with Marie Lloyd in the previous chapter, the essence of music: a rest is often the most important note in any musical composition. The sound of silence acquires a physical presence in "Sirens": the seashell held to the ear gives a "silent roar" (*U* 11.936), taking us back to "Silent, oh Moyle, be the roar of thy water" from "Silent, O Moyle!" (Bauerle 158–60), the song that "throbbed deep and full" (*D* 48) in "Two Gallants."[5] Immediately following the sound of the seashell, the two barmaids are transformed into swans: "From the forsaken shell miss Mina glided to her tankards waiting. No, she was not so lonely archly miss Douce's head let Mr Lidwell know" (*U* 11.954–55). One glides, the other arches: they have both undergone the metamorphosis of Fionnuala in "Silent, O Moyle!," who was turned into a swan. The connection between shells, swans, and the silence of "Silent, O Moyle!" is made again in *Finnegans Wake*: "I wound around my swanchen's neckplace a school of shells of moyles marine to swing their saysangs in her silents" (*FW* 548.33–34). A "saysang" is a sea shanty and takes us back to Simon's singing in "Sirens": "Si sang," "The night Si sang" (*U* 11.779, 790–91). So Si, the singer of the Siren song, is in the silence: "It's in the silence after you feel you hear. Vibrations. Now silent air" (*U* 11.793–94). The isle is full of noises.

From silence to solfège: the word "Si" is many things—"is" backward, as in "God si Love" (Forster, *Passage* 284), "but" in French, "yes" in Italian, "Si" when Simon is singing—but it is also *Si*, the penultimate note of the solfège scale. Here are the eight syllables of that scale (*So* is often given as *Sol*, and *Si* as *Ti*):

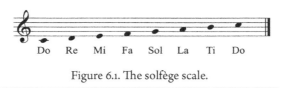

Figure 6.1. The solfège scale.

The syllables of the "solfa fable" (*U* 11.247) are endlessly interpretable in "Sirens":[6]

Do—Do, do,

Si/Ti—a fulldrawn tea,

La—Sonnez la

So(l)—That that was so.

Fa—Far. Far. Far. Far.

Mi—Sorrow from me

Re—. . . ray of hope is . . .

Do—Do, Ben, do.

Si is the leading tone in "Si sang," "silent," and "Siopold!" (*U* 11.791, 936, 752). The Joycean scale given here establishes *Do* as the tonic ("Do, do, they begged in one," "One body. Do. But do"—*U* 11.993, 908), which is another reason the episode ends as emphatically as it does with "*Done*" (*U* 11.1294). *Mi*, the parallel third, is heard in Mina Kennedy, and *Do*, the home key, is seen in Lydia Douce; *Re*, the second, can also be found in "pearl grey," "liver gravy," and "Last of my race" (*U* 11.67, 553, 1066). The sounding of "*La cloche!*" (*U* 11.415), or Lydia Douce's garter, becomes the sounding of the note *La* ("*Sonnez la*"—*U* 11.404), which is also the A of the tuning fork (*U* 11.313).

Finnegans Wake, of course, runs the "gamut," a word that literally means all the notes of the musical scale:

> I'd gamut my twittynice Dorian blackbudds chthonic solphia off my sin-gasongapiccolo to pipe musicall airs on numberous fairyaciodes. I give, a king, to me, she does, alone, up there, yes see, I double give, till the spinney all eclosed asong with them. Isn't that lovely though? I give to me alone I trouble give!
>
> (*FW* 450.17–24)

Here the music lesson is in Italian:

Do—I double give,
Si/Ti—yes see,
La—up there,
So(l)—alone,
Fa—she does,
Mi—to me,
Re—a king,
Do—I give,

"I give to me alone" (*FW* 450.22) is then a perfect triad, *Do-Mi-So*, with "I trouble give" (*FW* 450.22) rounding out the octave (*Do* doubled) at the top of the chord. Isn't that lovely though? There is another scale for us in II.2, a somewhat less savory one: "*Dont retch meat fat salt lard sinks down (and out)*" (*FW* 260.L3). This translates musically as follows:

Do—down (and out)
Si/Ti—sinks
La—lard
So(l)—salt
Fa—fat
Mi—meat
Re—retch
Do—Dont

The "wordchary is atvoiced" (*FW* 221.02): "Lad-o'-me-soul! Lad-o'-me-soul, see!" [*La, Do, Mi, Sol, Si*] (*FW* 221.01–02).

Silence is everywhere in *Finnegans Wake*, from HCE's beginning ("Hush! Caution! Echoland!"—*FW* 13.05) to ALP's ending: "For she'll be sweet for you as I was sweet when I came down out of me mother. My great blue bedroom, the air so quiet, scarce a cloud. In peace and silence. I could have stayed up there for always only. It's something fails us" (*FW* 627.07–11). Silence, for Anna Livia, is both death and the womb. The *Wake* is full of "sonorous silence" (*FW* 230.23) and reaches, at its apex, a moment of chaos and collapse:

    —Dovegall and finshark, they are ring to the rescue! —Zinzin. Zinzin.
    [...]
    —Slog slagt and sluaghter! Rape the daughter! Choke the pope!
    —Aure! Cloudy father! Unsure! Nongood!
    —Zinzin.
    —Sold! I am sold! Brinabride! My ersther! My sidster! Brinabride, good-bye! Brinabride! I sold!
    —Pipette dear! Us! Us! Me! Me!
    —Fort! Fort! Bayroyt! March!
    —Me! I'm true. True! Isolde. Pipette. My precious!
    —Zinzin. [...]
    —Now we're gettin it. Tune in and pick up the forain counties! Hello!
    —Zinzin.
    —Hello! Tittit! Tell your title?
    —Abride!
    —Hellohello! Ballymacarett! Am I thru' Iss? Miss? True?
    —Tit! What is the ti . . ?

SILENCE.

(*FW* 500.04–501.06)

Josh Epstein, in *Sublime Noise: Musical Culture and the Modernist Writer*, rightly regards this moment as the book's sonic climax. Hidden in the static is Richard Wagner (Bayreuth, Isolde), Jonathan Swift (Esther, Pepette), Danish (slog, tittit), German (Unser, fort), French (forain), Latin (aude), and Irish (sluagh), as well as a musical language.[7] Out of the "static babel" (*FW* 499.34) of these "zounds of sounds" (*FW* 499.27) we can faintly hear Joyce rising up the solfège scale:

Do—SILENCE.

Si/Ti—the ti . . ?

La—title? / Abride!

So(l)—Isolde.

Fa—Fort! Fort!

Mi—Me! Me!

Re—Rape the daughter!

Do—Dovegall

Silence is the *gam* and the *ut* of the *Wake*'s musical scale.

The hidden language of music, what Joyce calls a "chthonic solphia" (*FW* 450.17), has always been a part of the modern period. It was there as early as 1876, when Stéphane Mallarmé published "L'Après-Midi d'un Faune." As Robert Cohn has pointed out, that poem is artfully riddled with the "tone symbols of solfeggio" (Cohn 14): *La*, *Re*, *Mi* and *Fa* are all concealed in the title ("**L'Après-Mi**di d'un **Fa**une"), and the faun's opening invocation to his sirens foregrounds the penultimate note of the scale: (Mallarmé 38, solfège notes in bold for emphasis):

> Ces nymphes, je les veux perpétuer.
> > **Si** clair
> [These nymphs, I would make them permanent.
> > So clear]

The "Demon of Analogy," in which Mallarmé declares the death of the penultimate ("*La Pénultième* [. . .] *Est morte*"—Mallarmé 93), is back with a vengeance. During his afternoon, the faun searches for an italicized and completely mysterious *La*, the "there" of "qui cherche le *la*" (Mallarmé 39, italics Mallarmé's), ultimately declaring that he holds the *La* queen: "Je tiens **la** reine!" (Mallarmé 41). *La* is an overdetermined note in that poem (and especially in its musical setting by Claude Debussy): it is both "A" (*La*: the sixth note of the scale) and "the" (*la*: the definite article in French), both "here" (*là*: a place) and "hear" (*la*: a sound). Other echoes inhabit the modernist garden. The *So* of "**So** of course [. . .] there was nothing for it but to leave" that begins Virginia Woolf's *Jacob's Room* establishes that Mrs. Flanders has begun her letter on a note dominant to the tonic, in a book that waits for its resolution until the final page (Woolf, *Jacob* 1). The repeated *Do* of

                                                        'Do
'You know nothing? **Do** you see nothing? **Do** you remember
'Nothing?'

(*TWL* 138)

returns us to Eliot's tonic of "**O O O O** that Shakespeherian Rag" (*TWL* 138):
nothing will come of nothing, as *Do* returns to *Do*. In *The Waste Land*, nothing
is the answer to knowledge ("'**Do** / You know nothing?'"), sight ("'**Do** you see
nothing?'"), and memory: "'**Do** you remember / Nothing?'" (*TWL* 138). Eliot
and Joyce are our Aeneas and our Odysseus in the musical underworld, leading
us on a journey to silent shades.

At other times *Ulysses* has the radio dial turned well up: in "Aeolus," as Josh
Epstein has said, "Joyce explores the noise-music of the text-factory itself"
(Josh Epstein 176). Listen again to the fourth paragraph of that episode:

Right and left parallel clanging ringing a doubledecker and a singledeck
moved from their railheads, swerved to the down line, glided parallel.

(*U* 7.10–12)

In an inspired reading of this section, Josh Epstein writes that "The trams' 'parallel clanging' through the metropolis is patterned like a musical text" (Josh
Epstein 177) and shows how Joyce's parallelisms "orchestrate sounds as they
move through time," so that the only words that disturb the metallic ringing
of the soundscape "are the nouns—doubledecker and singledeck—which are
compelled to move, swerve, and glide as the sentence surges forward" (Josh
Epstein 177). This is absolutely right, as is Epstein's insistence that "Aeolus" is
a ballet, given the impossibly graceful exits and entrances of the episode's protagonists, the trams gliding in parallel in the opening number, and the headlines
barked like advertisements or poem titles through a megaphone (Josh Epstein
157). Returning to the original drafts and typescripts of "Aeolus," one hears how
the soundscape becomes cluttered over time: as the headlines vie for the listener's attention and the sound effects are built one by one into Joyce's accretive
text, so the clear signal of Joyce's recording of city life becomes progressively
distorted.

The reverse is true of *The Waste Land*: where for Joyce the process of revision
is the adding of noise, for Eliot the art lies in the silencing of it. Ezra Pound is

justly praised for his careful adjustment of the radio dial to eliminate distortion: "*Echt*" [true] is Pound's word in the margin for a signal that comes clear (*TWL* 41, 47, 51). To begin with "April is the cruellest month" (*TWL* 135) is to begin with a clear melodic line, as baffling and strange as the bassoon opening to *The Rite of Spring*. But listen to the drafts, or to the draughts ("'What is that noise?' / The wind under the door"—*TWL* 138). "First we had a couple of feelers down at Tom's place" (*TWL* 5), the first line of the first draft of *The Waste Land* that Eliot ever typed, is pure noise. A "feeler" is a drink—old Tom is "boiled to the eyes," and the scene ends with a race between two drunks down a London street after a night at the music hall: "When we got into the show, up in Row A, / I tried to put my foot in the drum, and didn't the girl squeal" (*TWL* 5). This is the stuff of the real: all the sweat of London is here, only to be wrung out by Ezra Pound in the final text. They lose Steve (who is thereby lost to all posterity—no one called Steve is permitted into the final version), demand women at a brothel without success, and then the cabman and a tailor run their race, with Mr. Donavan (whoever he is) holding the watch. "So I got out to see the sunrise," says the speaker, "and walked home" (*TWL* 5). So ends the immortal, and almost totally forgotten, opening to *The Waste Land*, from which the next line of the poem—"April is the cruellest month" (*TWL* 7)—follows logically as an observation by an exhausted and very hungover bon vivant about the London dawn.

And if this is true, that Eliot's impulse was to write a poem about London first and a poem about the world second, then it is in the first pages of the manuscript that this impulse finds its most urgent (and most obliterated) expression. *The Waste Land* manuscript's worst section, if you discount the drivel that was to have made its way into "Death by Water,"[8] is the peroration to London, with its "Phantasmal gnomes, burrowing in brick and stone and steel": "Some minds, aberrant from the normal equipoise / Record the motions of these pavement toys / And trace the cryptogram that may be curled / Within the faint perceptions of the noise / Of the movement, and the lights!" (*TWL* 31). Pound's comment just above this ("B[u]llS[hit]"—*TWL* 31) tersely explodes Eliot's painful apostrophe to his adopted city, as Eliot stumbles to find a voice:

> ~~daily feed~~
>   life   you kill and breed
> London, the swarming ~~creatures that you breed~~
> ~~Scampering Striving~~ Huddled ~~dazed~~ the concrete and the

~~Among half stunned beneath~~ / between ~~a heavy~~ sky
         stunned
[…]
        population
(London! your ~~people~~ is bound upon the wheel!)
   jerky motions   ~~poor cheap~~ pavement
Record the ~~movements~~ of these ~~huddled~~ toys
                 ~~tarnished~~
        cryptogram   may be curled
And trace the ~~painful, ideal meaning~~ which ~~they spell~~
~~Indistinctly~~ Vaguely
~~Doubtfully into~~ these faint perceptions
Within ~~this penumbral consciousness~~   of the noise

   (*TWL* 36–37)

This impressive pile of chicken scratch should reassure anyone considering poetry as a line of work. It is also the heart of the original poem, the one that Eliot wanted to write before Pound got to it: the manuscript page is number 1 (*TWL* 36). It's nearly impossible to decipher and was never typed. In it, we "trace the cryptogram which may be curled," whatever that means, and then the text disintegrates completely. Even the words are meaningless: we can make out "Doubtfully," "Indistinctly," "Vaguely" and at the very bottom, the words "penumbral consciousness" crossed out, with "faint perceptions of the noise" written on top. This is the noise, the "painful, ideal meaning," from which the signal of *The Waste Land* eventually sounds loud and clear. The "heart of light" (*TWL* 136) is silence: everything else is static. Like the cryptogram that imperfectly conceals the secret to Bloom's first drawer, this encrypted section of *The Waste Land* unlocks a world. But where for Joyce the method is accretion, for Eliot the method is deletion. Bloom's secret code began as a "reversed alphabetic cipher" (*JJA* 16:259) in the typescript; it is not until the page proofs that Joyce adds the words "boustrephodontic [*sic*] punctated [^quadrilinear] cryptogram" (*JJA* 27:195), along with a box of pen nibs and all the other detritus of Bloom's everyday life.[9] Eliot's "cryptogram" (*TWL* 36) is subtracted as Joyce's "cryptogram" (*JJA* 27:195) is added: both provide a solution, a key to the maze.

2. SATB: The Sirens Octet

For Joyce, the solution is music, and the key to the maze is "Sirens." Put all the wax in all the world in the ears of all the music critics of Joyce: they'll still listen for fugues in the episode. *Fuga per canonem*, a phrase guaranteed to make the eyes and ears glaze over of anyone who has ever read an essay on the subject, is the real Siren song for readers of the episode, as much as "When First I Saw" is the real Siren song for Bloom.[10] Joyce's advertisement of a fugue according to rule in the Linati Schema (*JJA* 12:174b) is a rhetorical flourish, a false grail that encourages the reader of the episode to become a listener, to concentrate on the aurality of Joyce. In Joyce, there is always a connection between the verbal and the aural, between words and music, between gold and bronze.

"Bronze by gold" (*U* 11.01): the words are an invitation. Like the Sirens they represent, they are themselves alluring. The "Sirens" episode is itself a seduction, drawing the reader into a world where text and music sound together, hinting at the possibility of a musical form. "Bronze" and "gold" are messengers of a multiple world, reinvented with each new context, each new chord. Bronze is not just the color of Lydia Douce's hair but also the color of her sunburnt skin ("Miss bronze unbloused her neck"—*U* 11.115), the metal for statuary ("A haughty bronze replied"—*U* 11.97), and the sound of bells: "they urged each each to peal after peal, ringing in changes, bronzegold, goldbronze" (*U* 11.174–75). Gold is not just the color of Mina Kennedy's hair but also the color of sunlight ("Miss Kennedy sauntered sadly from bright light, twining a loose hair behind an ear. Sauntering sadly, gold no more"—*U* 11.81–82), the light of the mirror ("With grace of alacrity towards the mirror gilt Cantrell and Cochrane's she turned herself"—*U* 11.214–15), the complexion of whisky ("With grace she tapped a measure of gold whisky from her crystal keg"—*U* 11.215–16), and the sound of laughter: "They threw young heads back, bronze gigglegold, to let freefly their laughter" (*U* 11.159–60). Bronze and Gold are two of the ages of humanity; a third, Iron, is hidden in the first sentence too, with a suggestion of a fourth in the ringing Steel: "hoofirons, steelyringing" (*U* 11.01). The phrase "Bronze by gold," falling under the weight of the several interpretations of its two signs, loses its lexical balance. Joyce, by overdetermining his opening phrase, is ensuring that it cannot be understood. Only then can it be heard; only then does the line approach the meaning of music.

The "by" of "Bronze by gold" has multiple resonances as well. The preposition can be the "by" of location, of *nebeneinander*, or the "by" of the passing of time, of *nacheinander*. In the first sentence after the opening warm-up on the keyboard, it is one and then the other: "Bronze by gold, miss Douce's head by [*nebeneinander*] miss Kennedy's head over the crossblind of the Ormond bar heard the viceregal hoofs go by [*nacheinander*], ringing steel" (*U* 11.64–65). The word "by" is literally multiple, in that it itself stands for the sign of multiplication. Bronze times gold; the two Sirens are commutative ("bronzegold, goldbronze"—*U* 11.175), working together in an enharmonic modulation that allows each to take the other's place: "Yes, bronze from anear, by gold from afar" (*U* 11.112), "Yes, gold from anear by bronze from afar" (*U* 11.338). The opening lines of "Sirens" have been briefly prepared for in the viceregal cavalcade that ends "Wandering Rocks," but in that instance bronze and gold have switched positions: "Above the crossblind of the Ormond hotel, gold by bronze, Miss Kennedy's head by Miss Douce's head watched and admired" (*U* 10.1197–99). The two are the mirror images of one another, as bronze is symmetrically reproduced in the gilt mirror of the bar:

> His spellbound eyes went after, after her gliding head as it went down the bar by mirrors, gilded arch for ginger ale, hock and claret glasses shimmering, a spiky shell, where it concerted, mirrored, bronze with sunnier bronze.
>
> (*U* 11.420–23)

Bronze and gold are concerted and mirrored as music and words are concerted and mirrored in "Sirens": without the one, you cannot have the other. These two things of opposite natures, word and sound, orality and aurality, are interdependent throughout Joyce.

Bronze is music, since Lydia Douce sings and Mina does not, trilling "*O, Idolores, queen of the eastern seas!*" (*U* 11.226). Gold is text, since Mina Kennedy reads and Lydia does not, reading at the same time as Lydia is singing: "Miss voice of Kennedy answered, a second teacup poised, her gaze upon a page" (*U* 11.237–38). Lydia gets the words wrong, singing "*Idolores*" for "*my Dolores*": she is a musician, not a wordsmith. Mina reads in silence ("In drowsy silence gold bent on her page"—*U* 11.312): she is a reader, not a sound effect. Words are as seductive as music in this episode, and "Sirens" is as full of paper as it is of song. During the singing of the "Croppy Boy," as Bronze fondles the barpull, and "the music, the air and words" (*U* 11.1081) sink to the point of confession and betrayal, Bloom imagines himself writing on Lydia's face: "Write something on it: page" (*U* 11.1086–87). In "Sirens," he purchases "Two sheets cream vellum paper one reserve two envelopes" (U 11.295), requests pen and ink from Pat, and writes to Martha as a lexical counterpoint to the singing from *Martha* after the song is completed.[11] The episode's final text is both gold and bronze: a text, the last words of Robert Emmet, that Bloom reads in a shop window, crossed with the music of Meyerbeer and the sounds of the street. In "Sirens," the two worlds of words and music coexist, and each world is represented in the opening two notes. These words, bronze and gold, are hair colors, precious metals, and metonyms, but they are also worlds, as Martha's confusion of "word" for "world"—"I do not like that other world" (U 5.245)—implies.[12]

The connection between the worlds of words and music, the multiplication of bronze by gold, is the only rule in "Sirens." Joyce's claim for "all the eight regular parts of a *fuga per canonem*," however, in his letter to Harriet Shaw Weaver, is not a complete blind (*Letters* I.129).[13] The eight parts, at least, can be readily assigned, and the results help to make sense of an episode that is otherwise a congeries of voices. Though there is a great deal of music in "Sirens," the overall effect, as both Pound and Weaver initially noticed, is not particularly lovely: "M'appari" must contend with Bloom's thoughts of Molly and Martha, "The Croppy Boy" competes with the beerpull and the doorknocker, and the episode collapses into cacophony. Joyce is very good at sounding lyrical: why not, then, have "Sirens" be another moment of musical grace, along the lines of the fall of the snow in "The Dead"?

It is when the voicing of the episode is distinctly heard that the sounds start to make sense. If you listen for eight parts, just as you would in a performance of an octet, the cacophony becomes polyphony and the voices blend together in clearly structured ways. (It is useful, too, to think of the Sirens singing in Plato's *Republic*, where the music of the spheres is voiced in eight parts: "and up above on each of the rims of the circles a Siren stood, borne around in its revolution and uttering one sound, one note, and from all the eight there was the concord of a single harmony"—Plato X.617b.) Since the Renaissance, eight vocal parts have been divided into two parallel sets of four lines: soprano, alto, tenor, and bass, each with its own identifiable range and timbre. In the octet given in figure 6.2, the world of music has four parts and the world of text has four parts, each with four distinct voices: soprano I (or S_1) is matched with soprano II (S_2), alto I (A_1) with alto II (A_2), and so on. The two parallel quartets are Bronze and Gold, since the episode persistently juxtaposes bronze and gold, setting them up in opposition ("bronze from anear, by gold from afar"), reversing their polarity ("gold from anear by bronze from afar"), and bringing them together:

"bronzegold, goldbronze" (U 11.112, 338, 174–75). Since Bronze is first in the opening formulation and since Lydia is the episode's most overtly seductive presence, Bronze is the first quartet. Since Gold comes after and since Mina is always reading, the written effects of the text fill out the second.

I: Bronze (Music)	II: Gold (Text)
S_1 = song	S_2 = conversation
A_1 = musical language	A_2 = narration
T_1 = onomatopoeia	T_2 = Bloom
B_1 = leitmotifs	B_2 = spondaic voice

Figure 6.2. The Sirens octet.

In the musical treble, or S_1 line, the songs sung in the bar sound clear above the rest: "The Shade of the Palm," "Goodbye, Sweetheart, Goodbye," "Love and War," "M'appari," and "The Croppy Boy." These five songs are the episode's melody, the most prominent notes, performed by the real musicians in the episode: Lydia Douce, Ben Dollard, Simon Dedalus, and Father Cowley. In the textual treble, or S_2 line, the conversation supplies the primary accompaniment to the music played at the piano. Just as the songs are all Siren songs, turning on love and betrayal, so the conversation is Siren conversation, referring to the basic themes of the Homeric myth: "He's killed looking back," "Am I awfully sunburnt?," "I won't listen" (U 11.77, 114, 132). Both treble lines are clearly heard and cleanly understood, often working in parallel:

—. . . *sweetheart, goodbye!*
—I'm off, said Boylan with impatience.

(U 11.425–26)

"*[S]weetheart, goodbye!*" is a sung line in S_1, pealing "in the treble clear" (U 11.397); "I'm off," is Boylan's line, apparently doubling the S_1 line. (Actually, as we will discover in the next section, Boylan's departure provides a sly inversion of the song text, since the singer in "Goodbye, Sweetheart, Goodbye" has decided not to leave his lover after all.)

Alto lines support the soprano melody: directly beneath the conversation, in the A_2 line, is the narrator, telling the story, commenting on the conversation ("said Boylan with impatience"—U 11.426). And directly beneath the singers, in the A_1 line, is the music of the narrative text, the language that supports the ecstasy of the final line of "M'appari":

> —*Come . . . !*
>
> It soared, a bird, it held its flight, a swift pure cry, soar silver orb it leaped serene, speeding, sustained, to come, don't spin it out too long long breath he breath long life, soaring high, high resplendent, aflame, crowned, high in the effulgence symbolistic, high, of the etherial bosom, high, of the high vast irradiation everywhere all soaring all around about the all, the endlessnessness. . . . . . .
> —*To me!*
>
> $$(U\ 11.744\text{--}50)$$

Both alto lines are narrative, and thus in parallel: A_2, the more textual one, places "miss Douce's head by miss Kennedy's head" (U 11.64) looking over the crossblind of the Ormond bar, but A_1, the more musical one, spins the hair of Mina Kennedy's head into a music trill: "Her wavyavyeavyheavyeavyevyevy-hair un comb:'d" (U 11.808–09).

Already Joyce has four distinct voices in horizontal and vertical parallel (A_2 with S_2, A_2 with A_1, etc.), but there are four more parts. Just below the narrator on the textual level, in T_2, is Bloom himself: "Why do I always think Figather? Gathering figs I think" (U 11.149–50). The narrator in A_2 has just given us the correct spelling of "Aaron Figatner's name" (U 11.149), so Bloom's misreading of it is a sign that he is as much a textual being as his wife is a musical one, gold to his wife's bronze. There is much more in "Sirens" and elsewhere to suggest this: Bloom buys stationery to write to his pen pal ("Two sheets cream vellum paper one reserve two envelopes when I was in Wisdom Hely's wise Bloom in Daly's Henry Flower bought"—U 11.295–96), he tries to "Remember write Greek ees" (U 11.860), and throughout the day he worries about strips of paper, writes in the sand, and puns on billboards and advertisements. His voice (T_2) and the narrator's (A_2) work together: "when I was in Wisdom Hely's" is an interpolation in a different register, T_2 assuming the melody from A_2. The same effect is heard in "By Bassi's blessed virgins Bloom's dark eyes went by. Bluerobed, white under, come to me. God they believe she is: or goddess" (U 11.151–52): here the T_2 line ("Bluerobed, white under") takes over directly from the A_2 line

("Bloom's dark eyes went by"). At other times, as in a musical octet, the two parts sing the same note, so that it is deliberately impossible to separate them:

> Wise Bloom eyed on the door a poster, a swaying mermaid smoking mid nice waves. Smoke mermaids, coolest whiff of all. Hair streaming: love-lorn. For some man. *For Raoul.* He eyed and saw afar on Essex bridge a gay hat riding on a jaunting car.

(*U* 11.299–302, italics mine)

This passage is literally equivocal, switching voices at several points within it. First, "Wise Bloom" is in the alto line. Then, "nice waves" is in the tenor line. But where does the alto line resume? If the switch from Bloom to narrator comes before "For Raoul," then the narrator in A_2 mimics Bloom's syntax in T_2—"For some man"—to undercut him with a reference to Boylan's correlative. But if the switch comes *after* "For Raoul," then the phrase becomes Bloom's association, revealing his awareness of Boylan's role as Raoul. We hear both, and we are supposed to hear both. The one reading is sympathetic, the other sardonic, and both occur at exactly the same time, in counterpoint to one another.

In T_1, just beneath the musical language of A_1 in figure 6.2, come the sound effects. The "Jingle" of Boylan's coins, the "Smack" of Lydia's garter, and the "Tap" of the stripling's cane (*U* 11.456, 413, 989) are as musical as the songs in the soprano line. Sometimes two notes sound together, as the sound of the fart ("Pprrpffrrppffff") does with the clang of the tram ("Krandlkrankran"), or the sound of the Liszt's Hungarian Rhapsody no. 2 ("Diddleiddle addleaddle oodleoodle") with the music of the chamber pot ("Hissss") (*U* 11.1293, 1290, 984, 984).[14] A riot of onomatopoeia heralds the moment of Molly and Boylan's assignation:

> [T_2] Chamber music. Could make a kind of pun on that. It is a kind of music I often thought when she. Acoustics that is. [T_1] Tinkling. [T_2] Empty vessels make most noise. Because the acoustics, the resonance changes according as the weight of the water is equal to the law of falling water. Like those rhapsodies of Liszt's, Hungarian, gipsyeyed. Pearls. Drops. Rain. [T_1] Diddleiddle addleaddle oodleoodle. Hissss. [T_2] Now. Maybe now. Before.
>
> [A_1] One rapped on a door, one tapped with a knock, did he knock Paul de Kock with a loud proud knocker with a cock carracarracarra cock. [T_1] Cockcock.

[T$_1$] Tap.
[S$_1$]—*Qui sdegno*, Ben, [A$_2$] said Father Cowley.
[S$_2$]—No, Ben, [A$_2$] Tom Kernan interfered, [S$_1$] *The Croppy Boy*. [S$_2$]
Our native Doric.
[S$_2$]—Ay do, Ben, [A$_2$] Mr Dedalus said. [S$_1$] Good men and true.

$$(U \, 11.979–92)$$

The bass parts of both quartets sound in the bottom register, barely notice-able, but providing an indispensable structure, a subterranean rhythm to the episode. There are two notes in the above example that have been sounded before: "Liszt's rhapsodies. Hissss," and "With a cock with a carra" (*U* 11.36, 38). These are the leitmotifs in B$_1$, drawn from two of the opening fifty-nine notes of the episode. From "Bronze by gold" to "Done" (*U* 11.01–62), these fifty-nine notes recur periodically, but not canonically, to provide a ground for the music quartet.[15] They are not words but phonemes, words stripped of their semantic value by virtue of having been divorced from their context in the opening sec-tion. They are the building blocks of the episode, all of them sonically active, all of them incomplete. The episode serves to make them whole, to weave the sound tapestry, to decipher the lost code of musical meaning.

B$_2$, the ground for the word quartet, is best heard by example in the opening of the scene:

[B$_1$] Bronze by gold, [A$_2$] miss Douce's head by miss Kennedy's head, over the crossblind of the Ormond bar heard the viceregal hoofs go by, [B$_1$] ringing steel.
[S$_2$]—Is that her? [A$_2$] asked miss Kennedy.
[A$_2$] Miss Douce said [S$_2$] yes, sitting with his ex, pearl grey and *eau de Nil*.
[S$_2$]—Exquisite contrast, [A$_2$] miss Kennedy said.
[A$_2$] When all agog miss Douce said eagerly:
[S$_2$]—Look at the fellow in the tall silk.
[S$_2$]—Who? Where? [B$_1$] gold [A$_2$] asked more eagerly.
[S$_2$]—In the second carriage, [A$_2$] miss Douce's wet lips said, laughing in the sun. [S$_2$] He's looking. Mind till I see.
[A$_2$] She darted, [B$_1$] bronze, [A$_2$] to the backmost corner, flattening her face against the pane in a halo of hurried breath.
[A$_2$] Her wet lips tittered:
[S$_2$]—He's killed looking back.

[A₂] She laughed:
[S₂]—O wept! Aren't men frightful idiots?
  [B₂] With sadness.

$$(U\ 11.64\text{–}80)$$

B₂ is a totally new voice, coming from nowhere. Out of the blue, or the "Bloowho" (U 11.86), comes a voice that is completely detached from anything else. Almost immediately, it is heard again:

[A₁] Miss Kennedy sauntered sadly from bright light, twining a loose hair behind an ear. Sauntering sadly, gold no more, she twisted twined a hair. Sadly she twined in sauntering gold hair behind a curving ear.
[S₂]—It's them has the fine times, [A₂] sadly then she said.
  [B₂] A man.
[A₁] Bloowho went by by [A₂] Moulang's pipes, bearing in his breast the sweets of sin, by Wine's antiques, in memory bearing sweet sinful words, by Carroll's dusky battered plate, for Raoul.

$$(U\ 11.81\text{–}88)$$

The narrator in A₂ picks up on B₂, underscoring who this unidentified man is. The bass voice in the word quartet will tell us as well, dropping the single word "Bloom" into the texture:

[B₁]—Imperthnthn thnthnthn, [A₂] bootssnout sniffed rudely, [A₁] as he retreated as she threatened as he had come.
  [B₂] Bloom.

$$(U\ 11.100\text{–}102)$$

"With sadness" / "A man" / "Bloom": B₂ stalks Bloom, creating his own line of commentary on Bloom's situation through the association of the conversation of the episode with Bloom's marital situation:

[S₂]—I won't listen, [A₂] she cried.
  [B₂] But Bloom?

$$(U\ 11.132\text{–}33)$$

[S₂]—O go away! [A₂] she said. [S₂] You're very simple, I don't think.
  [B₂] He was.

$$(U\ 11.204\text{–}05)$$

This voice generally speaks in spondees, two long strokes that complete and cauterize a thought, as "dead king" seals Mr. Casey's eulogy for Parnell in the Christmas dinner scene in *Portrait* (*P* 39), as "third stroke" puts the nail in the coffin of the scrupulous priest in "The Sisters" (*D* 1), as "Tight boots?" (*U* 13.771) punctures the narrative fantasy of the first half of "Nausicaa." B_2 is terminal and emphatic, hectoring and grave. Each time it appears, Bloom's compromised position is brought sharply back into focus:

[B_2] Of sin. (*U* 11.157)

[B_2] O'clock. (*U* 11.386)

[B_2] There was. (*U* 11.469)

Eight regular parts, then, provide a shape and a significance to what otherwise is musicological futility and textual anarchy. Every note of "Sirens," save one, can be assigned a part, and all parts overlap one another, as Lydia's hair is concerted and mirrored, bronze with sunnier bronze, in the golden mirror behind the bar. The one word that doesn't fit comes right after the opening; it is given to the conductor to begin the next section.

3. That Form Endearing: A Performance of Siren Songs

"Begin!"

    (*U* 11.63)

The business now at hand is to perform and discuss certain songs in and around the "Sirens" section of *Ulysses*, particularly Lionel's aria from Flotow's comic opera, *Martha*, a German song sung by Simon Dedalus in English and known to Bloom by its Italian title, "M'appari."[16] A great deal has been written about this and other Siren songs, and about their pertinence to Bloom's marital and extramarital situation, but by and large what has been written treats the songs as part of a Joycean text, not as individual pieces of music.[17] "It was the only language" (*U* 11.849), Mr. Dedalus says to the baritone Ben Dollard; he is speaking of Italian, but he is also speaking of music: "Blending their voices. God, such music, Ben" (*U* 11.852–53). This, the music of what happens, is the language of what follows.

The first song sung in the Ormond bar is sung a cappella, by Lydia Douce. It's "The Shade of the Palm," a tenor aria from the musical *Floradora*:

Gaily miss Douce polished a tumbler, trilling:
—*O, Idolores, queen of the eastern seas!*

(*U* 11.225–26)

This line establishes Lydia as a musical Siren, with her trill, as a sexual Siren, in her polishing off a tumbler, and as a singer of Siren songs, for the "*queen of the eastern seas*" leads us to Cleopatra, the Queen of the East, and Floradora is also a perfume, presumably containing some sort of man-luring pheromone. The text of the first verse of "The Shade of the Palm" is as follows:

There is a garden fair,
Set in an Eastern sea,
There is a maid,
Keeping her tryst with me
In the shade of the palm,
With a lover's delight,
Where 'tis ever the golden day,
Or a silvery night;
How can I leave her alone in this dream of sweet Arcadia?
How can I part from her for lands away?
In this valley of Eden,
Fairest isle of the sea,
Oh, my beloved, bid me to stay
In this fair land of Eden,
Bid me, belov'd, to stay

(Refrain)
Oh, my Dolores,
Queen of the Eastern sea!
Fair one of Eden,
Look to the West for me!
My star will be shining, love, when you're in the moonlight calm,
So be waiting for me by the Eastern sea,
In the shade of the shelt'ring palm.

(Bauerle 358–61)[18]

Cleopatra is a snake in the grass throughout "Sirens"; the color of the vice-roy's wife's dress is "*eau de Nil*" (*U* 11.67) and Bloom echoes Enobarbus' en-comium to Cleopatra as he avoids Boylan: "See me he might. The seat he sat on: warm" (*U* 11.342). *Antony and Cleopatra* is very much behind Joyce's use of this song, for "*Look to the West for me*" is precisely what Antony would be saying to Cleopatra, and "*Fair one of Eden,*" the preceding line, is transformed in "Sirens" to describe Lydia Douce as a "Fair one of Egypt" (*U* 11.383). As we have already seen in chapter 1, Miss Douce gets the line wrong twice: "*Idolores*" is incorrect, and there is only one "*sea.*"[19] With "*Idolores,*" Joyce is preparing us for Bloom's thoughts of the Croppy Boy ("he dolores!"—*U* 11.1132) and Molly ("shedolores"—*U* 11.734). Like "The seat he sat on," "Shedolores" is more likely to be Bloom's voice (T_2) than the narrator's (A_2), while "he dolores!" can be either. That Bloom misses Lydia singing this little snatch of song and thus can have no idea that he later is mirroring her mistake is one of many fascinating narrative irregularities in "Sirens," false notes that serve as cross relations do in the music of Thomas Tallis.

The next song, the first one played on the Ormond bar piano in "Sirens," is "Goodbye, Sweetheart, Goodbye." Before singing the song, Simon Dedalus raises the piano lid:

> Upholding the lid he (who?) gazed in the coffin (coffin?) at the oblique triple (piano!) wires. He pressed (the same who pressed indulgently her hand), soft pedalling, a triple of keys to see the thicknesses of felt advancing, to hear the muffled hammerfall in action.
>
> (*U* 11.291–94)

A tuning fork, left by the piano tuner on the piano, is sounded:

> From the saloon a call came, long in dying. That was a tuningfork the tuner had that he forgot that he now struck. A call again. That he now poised that it now throbbed. You hear? It throbbed, pure, purer, softly and softlier, its buzzing prongs. Longer in dying call.
>
> (*U* 11.313–16)

The A from the stripling's tuning fork is the 440Hz of a concertmaster, preparing the orchestra and the audience for the extraordinary performance to follow. And with Simon's preparatory actions a new narrative voice (A_1) is set free, the voice that plays musical chairs with syntax, that rings the changes on all possible puns before proceeding. The Sirens octet (figure 6.2) has many voices in many different registers: one can go further and assign them all separate timbres, as if they were orchestrated in the manner of Prokofiev's *Peter and the Wolf*. The songs themselves (S_1) one can assign to a voice and piano, the conversational voices (S_2) to the winds, the narrative voice (A_2) to the strings, Bloom's thoughts (T_2) to a solo clarinet, and the trenchant syllables that shadow Bloom on his way to the bar (B_2) to the double basses. The leitmotifs (B_1) wander in and out of the score like lost chords; and the onomatopoetic notes of keys, quoits, coins, knockers, tuning forks, garters, farts, bells, and whistles (T_1) all sound on percussion. The voice that raises the piano lid (A_1) is the quicksilver voice of musical language, released like music from a music box, sounding in the highest and merriest register of all, a glockenspiel played by a lunatic Mozart.

Where S_1 is strikingly cavalier in its attention to song lyrics, A_1 is unerringly accurate in its musical renditions. This is an important distinction: though Miss Kennedy (words) and Miss Douce (music) are apparently equal, Joyce knows to whom to award the prize. "Goodbye, Sweetheart, Goodbye" opens with four measures of triplet introduction, described by the Mozartean narrator as follows:

> A duodene of birdnotes chirruped bright treble answer under sensitive hands. Brightly the keys, all twinkling, linked, all harpsichording, called to a voice to sing the strain of dewy morn, of youth, of love's leavetaking, life's, love's morn.
>
> (*U* 11.323–26)

The performance of "Goodbye, Sweetheart, Goodbye" neatly circumscribes Boylan's brief appearance at the bar. The first verse goes like this:

> *The bright stars fade, that morn is breaking,*
> *The dew drops pearl each bud and leaf,*
> *And I from thee my leave am taking,*
> *With bliss too brief,* [etc.]
> *How sinks my heart with fond alarms,*
> *The tear is hiding in mine eye,*
> *For time doth thrust me from thine arms;*
> *Good bye sweet heart good bye!*

And then Bloom enters, hearing only the second verse. As Bloom enters, Boylan prepares to leave, and the mood of the song entirely switches. This is the second verse:

> *The sun is up, the lark is soaring,*
> *Loud swells the song of chanticleer;*
> *The levret bounds o'er earth's soft flooring,*
> *Yet I am here,* [etc.]
> *For since night's gems from heaven did fade,*
> *And morn to floral lips doth hie,*
> *I could not leave thee, tho' I said*
> *"Good bye sweet heart good bye!"*

(Bauerle 363–65)

The expected polarities are reversed: Bloom enters the bar in between the singer's reluctant decision to leave and his ecstatic decision to remain. Boylan is "off" (*U* 11.426) at the wrong time, leaving after the wrong verse. The song undercuts his intention, ironizing his departure.

The song's conclusion coincides with "*Sonnez!*" (*U* 11.412) as well as Boylan's departure, raising through the "smackable a woman's warmhosed thigh" (*U* 11.414) the offstage presence of Molly Bloom. The associations with Molly here are narrative, as is a minor lexical adjustment to the lyrics of the song. The second verse, it will be universally acknowledged, has in it some of the worst lines in all of nineteenth-century drawing room song. They serve Joyce's purpose well, however, for "*the levret,*" or hare, is figuratively both a mistress (from Shirley's *Gamester*: "Some wives will bid her husband's leverets welcome") and a spiritless person, thus combining in one word the hare-like Boylan, the mistress Molly, and the spiritless Bloom. The line "*And morn to floral lips doth hie*" is too horrible even for Joyce, and he changes "*floral lips*" to "*Flora's lips*":

> —Go on, pressed Lenehan. There's no-one. He never heard.
> —. . . *to Flora's lips did hie.*
>   High, a high note pealed in the treble clear.

(*U* 11.395–97)

This neat exchange from "*floral*" to "*Flora*" not only gives the moon a much more sensible place to hie to, if you're a moon, but also makes the association with Molly through the floral network that trails the Bloom family wherever it goes.[20]

Every song sung in the Ormond bar is threaded with every other through common reference to the Siren myth and to Molly Bloom (Knowles, "Substructure" 461). The next song, "Love and War," is no exception. The singer of "The Shade of the Palm" is dying to stay, the singer of "Goodbye, Sweetheart, Goodbye" cannot leave, and the soldier in "Love and War" sings "*I care not for or the morrow*" (*U* 11.552): all these paralyzed actions are consistent with the Homeric paradigm. Molly is "Dolores shedolores" from "The Shade of the Palm" (*U* 11.734), Bloom knows perfectly well where Boylan is off to after the performance of "Goodbye, Sweetheart, Goodbye" ("He's off. Light sob of breath Bloom sighed on the silent bluehued flowers"—*U* 11.457–58), and "Love and War" reminds Bloom of Molly's earlier reaction to Dollard's "belongings on show" (*U* 11.557). All the songs serve to underscore the centrality of Molly Bloom.

"Love and War" is a duet between a tenor, the lover, and a bass, the soldier. Big Ben Dollard begins with the tenor part by accident, with disastrous results:

> Over their voices Dollard bassooned attack, booming over bombarding chords:
> —*When love absorbs my ardent soul . . .*

(*U* 11.528–30)

He is quickly corrected by Father Cowley—"War! War! cried Father Cowley. You're the warrior" (*U* 11.532)—and moves down to the bass part:

> —So I am, Ben Warrior laughed. I was thinking of your landlord. Love or money.
> He stopped. He wagged huge beard, huge face over his blunder huge.
> —Sure, you'd burst the tympanum of her ear, man, Mr Dedalus said through smoke aroma, with an organ like yours.
> In bearded abundant laughter Dollard shook upon the keyboard. He would.
> —Not to mention another membrane, Father Cowley added. Half time, Ben. *Amoroso ma non troppo*. Let me there.

(*U* 11.533–41)

Again, this song is afforded a sexual significance and raises the question of what's taking place offstage. The broken tympanum announces the Virgin Mary, who, with Cleopatra, is one in the series of Bloom's Sirens later in the episode (the tradition that the Holy Spirit entered the Virgin through the ear, as the impregnating Logos, is not lost on Joyce). Lydia will later have a "Blank face. Virgin should say: or fingered only" (*U* 11.1086), and Mary, or Mairy, loses the pin of her drawers as Bloom writes to Martha Clifford (*U* 11.870). In "Lotus-Eaters," the Catholic Church is revealed to have a dangerously soporific effect: "Safe in the arms of kingdom come. Lulls all pain. Wake this time next year" (*U* 5.367–68). Passing "Bassi's blessed virgins" (*U* 11.151) on the way to the bar in "Sirens," Bloom thinks:

> Bluerobed, white under, come to me. God they believe she is: or goddess. Those today. I could not see. [. . .] All comely virgins. That brings those rakes of fellows in: her white.
>   By went his eyes. The sweets of sin. Sweet are the sweets.
>   Of sin.
>
> (U 11.151–57)

"Sirens" is a closely woven text: the weave is never closer than it is here. The bluerobed Virgin Mary leads to the rear view of the statues, Venus Callipyge, which leads to Raoul's mistress from *Sweets of Sin*. "I could not see" looks ahead to the blind stripling, and "Bluerobed, white under, come to me" brings us directly to the next Siren song, the last words of which are, as Bloom anticipates here, "come to me."

"M'appari" is first sung by Father Cowley in Italian to a seascape on the wall:

> —*M'appari tutt'amor:*
> *Il mio sguardo l'incontr . . .*
>   She waved, unhearing Cowley, her veil, to one departing, dear one, to wind, love, speeding sail, return.
>
> (U 11.594–97)

And then Mr. Dedalus takes a turn by himself, playing the song in its familiar key of D major:

> Mr Dedalus laid his pipe to rest beside the tuningfork and, sitting, touched the obedient keys.
> —No, Simon, Father Cowley turned. Play it in the original. One flat.

The keys, obedient, rose higher, told, faltered, confessed, confused.
Up stage strode Father Cowley.
—Here, Simon. I'll accompany you, he said. Get up.

(*U* 11.600–605)

Father Cowley strides upstage, Simon Dedalus rises, Cowley takes over the keyboard, and the piece moves up three keys, from D major, the traditional key in the English-Italian edition, to F major, the original key for the German aria as it appeared in Flotow's *Martha*, under the title "Ach so fromm." Simon Dedalus sings:

When first I saw that form endearing,
Sorrow from me seem'd to depart:
Each gracefull [sic] look, each word so cheering
Charm'd my eye and won my heart
Full of hope, and all delighted,
None could feel more blest than I;
All on Earth I then could wish for
Was near her to live and die:
But alas! 'twas idle dreaming,
And the dream too soon hath flown;
Not one ray of hope is gleaming;
I am lost, yes I am lost for she is gone

When first I saw that form endearing
Sorrow from me seem'd to depart:
Each graceful look, each word so cheering
Charm'd my eye and won my heart.
Martha, Martha, I am sighing
I am weeping still; for thee;
Come thou lost one Come thou dear one,
Thou alone can'st comfort me:
Ah! Martha return! Come to me![21]

"M'appari" is the central song of "Sirens": it is the musical heart of Joyce's book. When Auguste Morel was translating "Sirens" into French Joyce wrote to Harriet Shaw Weaver for the gramophone recording: "I want the *Martha* one for Mr Morel."[22] While it is sung Bloom is most literally Odysseus, gyving himself fast with a rubber band around his fingers. When it is over, Leopold and Simon are consumed into "Siopold!" (*U* 11.752), Stephen has one father, and the book, which is about the search of father for son and vice versa, is given its impetus for the rest of the day. Lionel, the lover who sings the aria in Flotow's opera, was originally included in "Siopold," according to Zack Bowen via Joseph Prescott via a Harvard proof sheet, which has the progression:

> Lionel
>> Leopold
>>> Simon
>>>> Richie
>>>>> ~~Richsiopold~~
>>>>>> Siopold[23]

After the song Bloom is "Lionel Leopold" (*U* 11.1261–62) and Dedalus is "Simonlionel" (*U* 11.1210), further tying them through Martha together. The tenor Giovanni Matteo Mario is singing "M'appari" throughout *Ulysses* (*U* 7.53–60): he appears in "Circe" as Henry Flower (*U* 15.2485), and Henry Flower sings "When first I saw," caressing on his breast "*a severed female head*" (*U* 15.2621, 2620). Bloom's daughter, Milly, is "Martha, thou lost one, Millicent, the young, the dear, the radiant" in "Oxen of the Sun" (*U* 14.1101–02), and Martha Clifford, the obvious parallel to Flotow's Martha, calls Bloom "Henry! Leopold! Lionel, thou lost one!" in "Circe" (*U* 15.753–54). Simon has lost the beautiful May Goulding, who is dead (*U* 15.4173–74). But Molly is the one Bloom has lost, the one who will not "Come. To me, to him, to her, you too, me, us" (*U* 11.754–55). Molly is at the center of all these songs.

  Martha takes place in the Middle Ages, in the reign of good Queen Anne—according to Flotow, who obviously had no idea what he was talking about. It is the story of two women, Lady Harriet and her friend Nancy (note the authentic medieval names), who are bored and decide to go to the fair dressed as servants, where they are sold to be chambermaids for Lionel and Mr. Plunkett. In the *Odyssey*, it is Odysseus who disguises himself as a servant, in the German *Verkleidungskomödie* the cross-class-dresser is usually a woman.[24] Dressed as a maid, Lady Harriet sings "The Last Rose of Summer," a song also referred to in "Sirens":

> And *The Last Rose of Summer* was a lovely song. Mina loved that song.
> Tankard loved the song that Mina.

'Tis the last rose of summer dollard left bloom felt wind wound round
inside.

(*U* 11.1176–79)

"The Last Rose of Summer" begins *"'Tis the last rose of summer, / Left blooming all alone"* (Bauerle 383), and it is clear that Joyce knew all about that *"blooming."* The thirty-first note on the opening keyboard is "I feel so sad. P. S. So lonely
blooming" (*U* 11.32). The fifty-second note is "Last rose Castile of summer left
bloom I feel so sad alone" (*U* 11.54). But it is not clear how Flotow passed this
song off as an original composition. The song was sung at his graveside; everyone seems to have assumed that he had composed it himself. It's lifted completely from Moore's *Irish Melodies of 1807*, where it was known as "The Young
Man's Dream," "The Groves of Blarney," and by other titles. Its history is extremely complicated: it was written either by a harper or a hedge schoolmaster
in the early nineteenth century, possibly as a parody of something else called
"Castlehyde." Joyce had a copy of Moore's collection, and so must have Flotow,
for in 1845 he beats the tune to death, scoring it for horns, for winds, for strings,
for full orchestra in the overture, until you think you'll go mad if you hear it
again. If you don't like the song, you're in for a lousy two hours. It's Sergeant
Cuff's favorite song in *The Moonstone*; Molly reads *The Moonstone* and has a
gynecologist called Collins. (Molly's gynecologist, it should be said, is not primarily modelled on Wilkie Collins but on Dr. Joseph Collins, the author of *The
Doctor Looks at Literature*.) So "The Last Rose of Summer" is a false song that is
actually Irish sung by a woman under a false name, disguised as a false servant,
falsely contracted to Lionel in a false landscape that is not really England. It's
perfect for Joyce. Lionel falls in love with the illusion, Lady Harriet escapes,
meets him hunting—"Got the horn or what?" (*U* 11.432)—and hounds him
off to prison, where Lionel (and this is the interesting part) has gone mad and
doesn't recognize Lady Harriet. He only recognizes her as Martha, so she puts
her peasant dress back on, and the opera ends with one more rousing chorus of
"The Last Rose of Summer" with the illusion maintained.

Martha, then, is an unauthenticated transumption of something Irish, a
cracked looking-glass in which is pictured a servant, Martha and not-Martha.
It is also, as Wilhelm Hübner has remarked, a comic opera obsessed with the
music of language: "Der Stil des Stückes kennzeichnet sich vornehmlich durch
eine besonders enge Verbindung zwischen Wort und Musik" [The style of the
musical numbers notably displays an extraordinary connection between the

words and the music] (Hübner 619).[25] At one point in the opera, Tristan, the buffo aristocrat, opens the window and asks for "Luft" [air], summoning a resounding blast from the wind instruments. Flotow's spinning scene is very much like Gilbert and Sullivan in its wordplay—"Mädchen" [maiden] rhymes with "Fädchen" [little thread], which rhymes with "Rädchen" [little wheel]— and Arthur Sullivan, in fact, edited the English-Italian edition of *Martha* that gave rise to the aria's popular name in the British Isles, "M'appari." An editor of Flotow's work, Edward Dent, has said that "there are many numbers in *Martha* which sound curiously like Sullivan" and even suggests that one song in the English-Italian edition not found in the original may have been actually written by him (Dent xvi). A 1990 review of a performance of the opera in New York makes the same comparison: "Now, for the first time since 1944 City Opera has disinterred 'Martha' (revived is hardly the word) in what appears to be a similar attempt to pass the work off as Gilbert-less Sullivan" (Oestreich). (This was not, needless to say, a rave review: set in a seaside carnival, the production "postured interminably," "pander[ed] to current American sitcom sensibilities," and ultimately "resembled nothing so much as a televised beer commercial.")

Hearing "M'appari" sung in English, one notices further similarities with the wordplay of Gilbert and Sullivan. First, though Sullivan is not responsible for it, the English translation turns the German into a patter song, especially at "Full of hope and all delighted." Second, the first four lines of the first verse are subtly different from the first four lines of the second—not textually, but in their emphasis, as in the famous song from Gilbert and Sullivan's *Patience*, "Long Years Ago," where placing a different emphasis on each word of the song's final line completely changes the meaning: [innocently] "*He* was a little boy!," [knowingly] "He *was* a little boy!," [indignantly] "He was a *little* boy!," [triumphantly] "He was a little *boy*!" (Sullivan, *Patience* 61–64). The first time that the four lines of "M'appari" are sung, you think Lionel is with her. The second time, you know he's not. The "*seemed*" of "*Sorrow from me seemed to depart*" (*U* 11.673) cuts the illusion dead; "*Charmed my eye*" (*U* 11.729) becomes the false charm of a Siren. It's a trick ending, as in "Goodbye, Sweetheart, Goodbye," except that here the twist is the other way, and the lover ends the second verse emphatically alone. Already, within the song, the impossibility of return is established. While Dedalus and Cowley are preparing to sing "M'appari," Richie Goulding whistles "*All is lost now*," from *La Sonnambula* (*U* 11.629). This, too, parodies the Odyssean *nostos* in defeating the promise of return, as Bloom himself recognizes: "Thou lost one. All songs on that theme" (*U* 11.802). The aria from *La*

Sonnambula acts as a prelude for Dedalus' more searing loss in *"Come...! [...] To me!"* (*U* 11.744–51), a distant accompaniment to the grander tragedy Bloom can only overhear.

Some numbers in Flotow's *Martha* sound curiously like Joyce. To return to the spinning scene: Harriet and Nancy, disguised as Martha and Julia, are forced to learn how to use the spinning wheel. "I can't spin," says Harriet, "Do it," says the evil Plunkett, "Like this," says the helpful Lionel, and Lady Harriet begins to enjoy it, trilling "Oh how lustig" over the grinding syncopation of the men singing "Brr, brr," imitating the sound of the rotating wheel. "Spin, spin," "Lick your finger," they cry, and Lady Harriet flies off the handle, reaching a high D, staccato in her excitement, "sending it flying with a will." They all pause for breath and Lionel asks, "So now you know how?" she says, "Yes thanks, here's a pass," and they're off again, laughing in exact time as Harriet rejoices at the "golden thread through my fingers," and everyone collapses in fits of helpless giggles on the floor (Flotow, act 2, Spinning-Quartet).

It's German comic romantic opera at its very worst, but it's also extremely Joycean in its overt sexuality, as coarse and comical as Lydia fondling the barpull. Sewing has been sex since long before Bovary pricked her thumb and Gretchen sat by the spinning wheel worrying about her boyfriend.[26] And let us not forget that *Faust* also has a quartet, which takes place in Martha's Garden, that for Ellmann *Ulysses* is an Irish *Faust* (*JJ* 265), that Faust the university student has many connections with Dedalus, that Gretchen's name for Faust is Heinrich, which is Bloom's assumed name when he courts his pen pal, who is called Martha, on whose letter he nearly pricks his finger—no, the thread between spinning and the eternal feminine begins, of course, with Penelope, weaving and unweaving her tapestry, which brings us back, by a commodious "vicus of recirculation" (*FW* 3.02), to Molly Bloom.[27]

During the singing of "M'appari," Bloom thinks of his wife, of the song, of Lydia, of Martha, and back to his wife. At the end, his thoughts race toward a union with all of these, with his wife, with the song, and with the singer, as he becomes consumed by the final soaring phrase. What I would do now, if I had a different kind of keyboard in front of me, is play "M'appari" again, singing only the lines of the song as they appear in Joyce's text. At the same time, I would read Bloom's thoughts, as they are recorded beside the lines of the song. The parallactic presentation of Joyce and Flotow would establish that Joyce has gone to some trouble to have Bloom's thoughts fit with the music that lies beneath his text.[28] Instead, I must resort to a written representation of what is essentially an aural analysis. It is not possible to reproduce here what is possible in performance, but figure 6.3 gives a rough idea. In figure 6.3, the entire text and the entire song are presented in tapestry form, weaving the central Siren song into the text of "Sirens." The italicized lines from "M'appari" are those also printed in *Ulysses*, quoted in the score exactly as they appear in *Ulysses*. The text of the rest of the song, not printed in the episode but heard nevertheless, is printed in the score in roman type. The parts of the Joycean text that are directly attached to the music have been overlaid or underlaid into the score. The rest of Joyce's text from "Sirens" follows lines 11.650–760 of the corrected text. Here's how it works:

Piano again. Sounds better than last time I heard. Tuned probably. Stopped again.[29]

harping chords of prelude

Dollard and Cowley still urged the lingering singer out with it.
—With it, Simon.
—It, Simon.
—Ladies and gentlemen, I am most deeply obliged by your kind solicitations.
—It, Simon.
—I have no money but if you will lend me your attention I shall endeavour to sing to you of a heart bowed down.[30]

By the sandwichbell in screening shadow Lydia, her bronze and rose, a lady's grace, gave and withheld: as in cool glaucous *eau de Nil* Mina to tankards two her pinnacles of gold.

The harping chords of prelude closed. A chord, longdrawn, expectant, drew a voice away.[31]

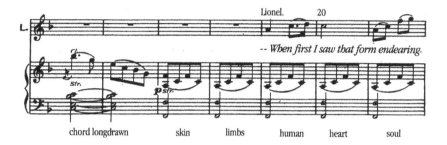

Richie turned.

—Si Dedalus' voice, he said.

Braintipped, cheek touched with flame, they listened feeling that flow endearing flow over skin limbs human heart soul spine.[32] Bloom signed to Pat, bald Pat is a waiter hard of hearing, to set ajar the door of the bar. The door of the bar. So. That will do. Pat, waiter, waited, waiting to hear, for he was hard of hear by the door.

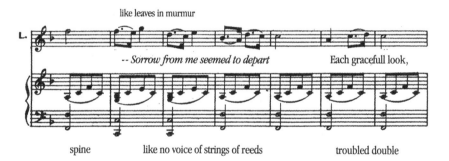

Through the hush of air a voice sang to them, low, not rain, not leaves in murmur,[33] like no voice of strings or reeds or whatdoyoucallthem dulcimers touching their still ears with words, still hearts of their each his remembered lives. Good, good to hear: sorrow from them each seemed to from both depart when first they heard. When first they saw, lost Richie

Poldy, mercy of beauty, heard from a person wouldn't expect it in the least, her first merciful lovesoft oftloved word.

each word so cheering Charm'd my eye and won my heart .   -- *Full of hope and all delighted* . . .

in octave   Jingle all delighted

Love that is singing: love's old sweet song. Bloom unwound slowly the elastic band of his packet.[34] Love's old sweet *sonnez la* gold. Bloom wound a skein round four forkfingers, stretched it, relaxed, and wound it round his troubled double, fourfold, in octave, gyved them fast.

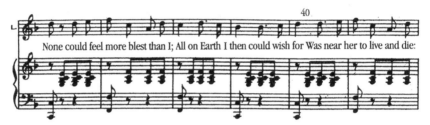

None could feel more blest than I; All on Earth I then could wish for Was near her to live and die:

Tenors get women by the score. Increase their flow. Throw flower at his feet. When will we meet? My head it simply. Jingle all delighted. He can't sing for tall hats. Your head it simply swurls. Perfumed for him. What perfume does your wife? I want to know. Jing. Stop. Knock. Last look at mirror always before she answers the door. The hall. There? How do you? I do well. There? What? Or? Phial of cachous, kissing comfits, in her satchel. Yes? Hands felt for the opulent.

Alas the voice rose, sighing, changed: loud, full, shining, proud.

-- *But alas, 'twas idle dreaming* ...   And the dream too soon hath flown; Not one --... *ray of hope* ...

Alas! The voice rose, singing, changed: loud, full, shining, proud.

Glorious tone he has still. Cork air softer also their brogue. Silly man!
Could have made oceans of money. Singing wrong words. Wore out his
wife: now sings. But hard to tell. Only the two themselves. If he doesn't
break down. Keep a trot for the avenue. His hands and feet sing too.
Drink. Nerves overstrung. Must be abstemious to sing. Jenny Lind soup:
stock, sage, raw eggs, half pint of cream. For creamy dreamy.

Tenderness it welled: slow, swelling, full it throbbed. That's the chat.
Ha, give! Take! Throb, a throb, a pulsing proud erect.

Words? Music? No: it's what's behind.

Bloom looped, unlooped, noded, disnoded.

Bloom. Flood of warm jamjam lickitup secretness flowed to flow[35] in
music out, in desire, dark to lick flow invading. Tipping her tepping her
tapping her topping her.[36] Tup. Pores to dilate dilating. Tup. The joy the
feel the warm the. Tup. To pour o'er sluices pouring gushes. Flood, gush,
flow, joygush, tupthrop. Now! Language of love.

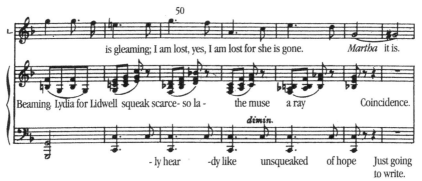

Beaming.[37] Lydia for Lidwell squeak scarcely hear so ladylike the muse
unsqueaked a ray of hopk.[38]

Martha it is. Coincidence.[39] Just going to write. Lionel's song. Lovely
name you have. Can't write. Accept my little pres. Play on her heartstrings
pursestrings too. She's a. I called you naughty boy. Still the name: Martha.
How strange! Today.

The voice of Lionel returned, weaker but unwearied. It sang again to Richie Poldy Lydia Lidwell also sang to Pat open mouth ear waiting to wait. How first he saw that form endearing, how sorrow seemed to part, how look, form, word charmed him Gould Lidwell, won Pat Bloom's heart.

Wish I could see his face, though. Explain better. Why the barber in Drago's always looked my face when I spoke his face in the glass. Still hear it better here than in the bar though farther.

Round and round slow.

First night when first I saw her at Mat Dillon's in Terenure. Yellow, black lace she wore. Musical chairs. We two the last. Fate. After her. Fate. Round and round slow. Quick round.[40] We two. All looked. Halt. Down she sat. All ousted looked. Lips laughing. Yellow knees.

Singing. *Waiting* she sang. I turned her music. Full voice of perfume of what perfume does your lilactrees. Bosom I saw, both full, throat warbling. First I saw. She thanked me. Why did she me? Fate. Spanishy eyes. Under a peartree alone patio this hour in old Madrid one side in shadow Dolores shedolores. At me. Luring. Ah, alluring.

with deepening yet with rising chords of harmony.

Quitting all languor Lionel cried in grief, in cry of passion dominant to love to return with deepening yet with rising chords of harmony. In cry of lionel loneliness[41] that she should know, must martha feel. For only her he waited. Where? Here there try there here all try where. Somewhere.

Alone. One love. One hope. One comfort me. Martha, chestnote, return!

It soared, a bird, it held its flight, a swift pure cry, soar silver orb it leaped serene, speeding, sustained, to come, don't spin it out too long long breath he breath long life, soaring high, high resplendent, aflame, crowned, high in the effulgence symbolistic, high, of the etherial bosom, high, of the high vast irradiation everywhere all soaring all around about the all, the endlessnessnessness. . . . . . .

Siopold!
Consumed.

Come. Well sung. All clapped. She ought to. Come. To me, to him, to her, you too, me, us.

—Bravo! Clapclap. Good man, Simon. Clappyclapclap. Encore! Clapclipclap clap. Sound as a bell. Bravo, Simon! Clapclopclap. Encore, enclap, said, cried, clapped all, Ben Dollard, Lydia Douce, George Lidwell, Pat, Mina Kennedy, two gentlemen with two tankards, Cowley, first gent with tank and bronze miss Douce and gold miss Mina.

Figure 6.3. Text of *U* 11.650–760 overlaid with Friedrich von Flotow, "M'appari." Excerpt from *Martha, or The Fair at Richmond*. Reprinted by permission of G. Schirmer, Inc. International copyright secured. All rights reserved. Bauerle 399–403.

"Words? Music? No: it's what's behind" (*U* 11.703). And behind this heady and beautifully timed sunburst are two important words, "spin," as in "don't spin it out too long" (*U* 11.746), which clearly ties the note back to Flotow's spinning-wheel scene, and "Come" (*U* 11.754). Leopold Bloom can never return to his wife, and his desire for return to Molly is the message of "Come. To me" (*U* 11.754). Molly Bloom is behind all these songs. She is the queen of the Eastern seas, the last rose of summer, the sweetheart in "Sweetheart, Goodbye." She is the flower of the mountain, Floradora, the Flora of "*Flora's lips*."

Her husband's pen name is Henry Flower, or "Enrique Flor" (*U* 12.1288), his real name is Bloom, his member is "a languid floating flower" (*U* 5.571–72), she kisses him among the rhododendrons, she will wear either a white rose or a red (*U* 18.1553, 1603), she's the Yorkshire Girl, whose name is "Rose, Rose, Rose." When "M'appari" appeared as a jazz tune some fifteen years after *Ulysses* was published, it was called "Flowers for Madame."

"Come" appears in many forms in "Sirens": as an injunction (Dollard's "Come on, Simon"), a phoneme (Molly's "kissing comfits"), and an abbreviation (Bloom's "Elijah is com.") (*U* 11.442, 691, 867). It is heard everywhere in the songs: "One comfort me," "See the conquering hero comes," "[comes] love's old sweet song" (*U* 11.742, 340, 681). Though the word is wrongly divided in the Vintage International edition as "*Co-me*" (*U-61* 275)—and indeed in the musical example above, which follows that edition—Gabler makes it clear that the word is to be syllabified as follows:

—*Co-ome, thou lost one!*
Co-ome, thou dear one!

(*U* 11.740–41)

This syllabification parallels the version that the tenor Mario sings in "Aeolus":

Co-ome thou lost one,
Co-ome thou dear one!

(*U* 7.59–60)

The additional exclamation mark in the first line of the "Sirens" version can be taken as an indication of a greater emotional commitment on Simon Dedalus' part, and the extra commas may be the result of his lack of professional training in sustaining the breathing over a long phrase. But what, in either case, is gained by the additional *o*? The music clearly requires some sort of separation between the syllables, but why "*Co-ome*" rather than "*Co-me*"? Joyce's division of the glowworm's lamp from "The Young May Moon" in "Lestrygonians" suggests the answer: "Glowworm's la-amp is gleaming, love" (*U* 8.590). What the glowworm possessed was, in manuscript, a "laamp" (Rosenbach P159–60 L211–13 N166–68), which was first mistyped as "lamp" in the typescript and then immediately corrected by the typist to the original "laamp" (*JJA* 12:312), then hypercorrected back to "lamp" for the placards, where it is amended by Joyce to "la-amp" (*JJA* 18:111), as it reads in the page proofs (*JJA* 23:157) and in both the Vintage International edition (*U*-61 167) and the Gabler edition.[42] Though "*Co-me*" is a sufficient indication to a singer to separate the word into two distinct parts, one for each of the two slurred notes on both occasions (F#-A in measure 78, D-F# in measure 80), this is not enough for Joyce. "*Co-ome*" overdetermines the sense of the word by raising the slag heap, Coombe Hill, and the sluts in the Coombe singing "*O, Mairy lost the pin of her drawers*" (*U* 5.281), which Bloom recollects in "Sirens" (*U* 11.870). What is clear is that Joyce is uncharacteristically precise in his musical effects at this point in "Sirens." Having cavalierly mistranscribed lines from "The Shade of the Palm," "Goodbye, Sweetheart, Goodbye," and other half-remembered songs, Joyce here takes a certain amount of trouble to ensure that the words and music fit. This kind of syllabic precision, then, invalidates the practice of taking the final "*Come!*" (*U* 11.744) up to the fifth, from B♭ to C, as certain tenors have allowed themselves the liberty of doing. The absence of a hyphen within the word clearly establishes unequivocally that the note is to be held and not raised.

Finally, some notes about Joyce's process of composition for this extraordinary scene are in order, since they reveal something of his musical intentions. The "Sirens" reading of the last phrases of "M'appari" began in manuscript as follows:

—*Co-ome, thou lost one!*
—*Co-ome, thou dear one!*
Alone. One love. One hope. One comfort me. Martha, [^chestnote], return!
—*Come [⸸] . . . !*
It soared, a bird, it held its flight, a swift pure cry, soar silver orb it leaped serene, to come, dont spin it out too long long breath he breath long life, soaring high, high resplendent, crowned, aflame, high in the effulgence [^symbolistic], high, of the etherial bosom, high of the vast irradiation, high, everywhere all soaring all around about the all, the endlessnessnessness.
—*To me!*

(Rosenbach P264–65 L355–56 N275–76)

Note that the two insertions in the manuscript, indicated here by carets, are linked to musical performance: one, "chestnote," is a directive to the tenor to sing with his diaphragm, the other, "symbolistic," is a comment on the nature of music in literature.[43] It was not until the second version of the page proofs approximately a month later that "Siopold!" was added between "—*To me!*" and "Consumed" (*JJA* 24:208–209). At the same time, in October 1921, Joyce made two significant alterations to the preceding paragraph:

> Quitting all langour Lionel cried in grief, in cry of passion [^dominant] to love to return with deepening yet with rising chords chords of harmony. In cry of lionel loneliness that she should know, must martha feel. For only her he waited. Where? [^Here there try there here all try where.] Somewhere.
>
> (*JJA* 24:192, 208)[44]

These two changes, marked here by carets, are again musical, tied directly to the music of "M'appari." At "dominant to love" we have heard the music move smartly into the dominant key (see measure 76 and note 41). "Here there try there here all try where" fits exactly with the harmonic chords underneath the voice (see measures 70–77 and note 41). As the "io" of "Siopold!" is not just an *i* from Simon and an *o* from Leopold but also the "io" of Lionel and the Italian for "I," so at the same time as he writes in this all-consuming word Joyce is strengthening the link between his text and Flotow's, between language and music. It is no accident that in simultaneous performance of the song and the text in 1992 it took as long for me to read the paragraph between "—*Come!*" and "—*To me!*" (*U* 11.744–51) at full speed as it did for the singer to sing the line. This is Joyce's answer to Shelley: the Joycean skylark soars on wings of premeditated art. "*One feels that one is listening,*" as Gabriel Conroy says in his review, "*to a thought-tormented music*" (*D* 192).

"Sirens" is a tremendously funny episode, with riotous sound effects, silly puns, bad mathematics and worse fugues, a *tour de farce* that mocks every character from "greaseabloom" (*U* 11.180) to bald deaf Pat: "Hee hee hee hee. He did not see" (*U* 11.1283). It is also unbearably sad. Listening to "The Croppy Boy," the next song sung at the bar, Bloom realizes that his son Rudy is dead, that his daughter, Milly, is in love with a Gentile, and that he cannot have another child:

> I too. Last of my race. Milly young student. Well, my fault perhaps. No son. Rudy. Too late now. Or if not? If not? If still?
>
> (*U* 11.1066–67)

This hope, this very false and painful hope of "If not? If still?," the desire for love, a true father, a true wife, a true son, is all compressed into "The Croppy Boy." The song has been the primary focus of chapter 1, so it will be enough here to review its connection to the other Siren songs in the episode. The boy is Bloom, the last of his race, is Stephen, omitting to pray for his mother, and is the blind stripling, tapping his way to the Ormond bar during the singing of the song, on his way back to pick up the tuning fork he left on the lid of the piano. The connections with Molly are obvious: thoughts of Molly are raging in Bloom's head as he listens to the song, and the tap of the blind stripling's cane is the "Cockcarracarra" (*U* 11.1048) on the door of #7 Eccles Street, the "Tap" of the barpull that Lydia caresses (*U* 11.1119), and the phonetic link to "tep," "tip," "top," and "tup," all activated as sexually descriptive verbs during the singing of "M'appari" (*U* 11.706–07). The betrayal of the false priest is Molly's, and the loneliness of the Croppy Boy is Bloom's.

While all this is going on in the bar, Molly is keeping her assignation with Blazes Boylan. It's a musical appointment as well, and presumably the songs Molly will take with her on the concert tour are rehearsed before or after anything else takes place, if anything does. Two songs lined up for the concert are the duet "Là ci darem" and "Love's Old Sweet Song." "Là ci darem" is, as we have discovered, a nonstarter in "Sirens": Bloom, though he is obsessed with the correct words of the song throughout the day, never wonders about that *voglio* in the Ormond bar. Cowley does play the *Don Giovanni* minuet before "The Croppy Boy," which would have been as good a moment as any for Bloom to think of Zerlina. But for "Là ci darem" to appear in an episode about maids and Sirens and music would perhaps be overkill: this may be a rare instance of Joycean restraint.

The final piece on Molly's program, "Love's Old Sweet Song," is really, if any song is, Molly's song. Bloom thinks of it as he hears "M'appari": "Love that is singing: love's old sweet song" (*U* 11.681). It should be sung at twilight, for obvious reasons, and it has to be sung at the end (Bauerle 243–47):

(Verse 1)
Once in the dear dead days beyond recall,
When on the world the mists began to fall,
Out of the dreams that rose in happy throng
Low to our hearts Love sung an old sweet song;

And in the dusk where fell the firelight gleam,
Softly it wove itself into our dream.

(Refrain)
Just a song at twilight, when the lights are low,
And the flick'ring shadows softly come and go,
Though the heart be weary, sad the day and long,
Still to us at twilight, comes Love's old song,
Comes Love's old sweet song.

(Verse 2)
Even today we hear Love's song of yore,
Deep in our hearts it dwells for evermore
Footsteps may falter, weary grow the way,
Still we can hear it at the close of day,
So till the end, when life's dim shadows fall,
Love will be found the sweetest song of all.

(Refrain)

7 | Seeing the Joe Miller

1. Wish You Were Here

To catch a fox, you have to take chances. Risk is part of what makes both Joyce and those who study Joyce tick; Joyce has a predictable unpredictability, and so does the Joycean. In an introduction to *Joyce in Trieste: An Album of Risky Readings*, I tried to explain what a risky reading actually does.[1] The piece was something of a risk in itself, in choosing to call out indirectly several of the members of the Joycean community and to poke fun generally at the timidity of academics. In the spirit of good-fellowship, I will not repeat that discourtesy here, but the risk turns out to be important: the term "poke fun," as we will discover in this chapter, is more telling than it may appear. The term "risky reading" is coined by Margot Norris, in her essay in *Joyce in Trieste*, "Risky Reading of Risky Writing" (Norris 36–53). In that essay, based on her plenary lecture for the 2002 International James Joyce Symposium, Norris unearths the original text of the postcard sent from Hester Stanhope to Molly Bloom, otherwise buried in the text of "Penelope" (*U* 18.613–23), here repunctuated for additional clarity (Norris 44):

Dearest Doggerina,

Just a p c to tell you I sent the little present. Have just had a

jolly warm bath and feel a *very* clean dog now -- enjoyed it.

Wogger wd give anything to be back in Gib and hear you

sing Waiting and In Old Madrid. Concone is the name of

those exercises. He bought me one of those new [???]

shawls, amusing things but they tear for the least thing.

Still, they're lovely I think, don't you? Well now, dearest

Doggerina, be sure and write soon. Kind [regards] to your

father, also Captain Grove. With love, yrs affly, Hester xxxxx

Figure 7.1. The Stanhope postcard (*U* 18.613–23).

This lays to rest the question of the postcard's impossible length: as the mock-up reveals above, the original postcard text isn't actually very long. It is Molly's memory and her interpretation of the written text—"some word I couldn't make out shawls," "kind she left out regards" (*U* 18.618–19, 623)—that prolong the *langue* beyond the postcard's *parole*.[2] What Norris does not mention is that at the plenary lecture from which her essay is taken, a man with a Macintosh (computer) suggested a simpler answer to the conundrum. It was not for nothing, this person said during the question period, that Hester Stanhope used "a p c" (*U* 18.614): if she was indeed using a personal computer, then all she would have needed to do to make the text fit on the card would be to change the size of the font.[3]

The transition from Hester's postcard to the personal computer is a great loss for literature, and for the one-way vector of emotion that literature is. At its best, a postcard is a record of hope and desire, as it is for Hester's note to Molly; at its worst, the postcard is a disaffected expression of regret, as in "Wish you were here." But in either case the postcard is charged with a peculiarly centrifugal energy: it is a message sent without the expectation of return. Like the stamp, the postcard is a quintessentially Joycean object. "[B]e sure and write soon" (*U* 18.622) says Hester in her postcard: this is not an order but a supplication. In the electronic version of the postcard, a reply is not only expected but demanded: the vector is returned, the outward energy is short-circuited. The e-mail message has all the time in the world: not so the postcard, which never makes such demands.

Joyce sends a postcard to his readers from Trieste in the middle of the "Night Lessons" section of the *Wake*:

> And trieste, ah trieste ate I my liver!

Figure 7.2. A postcard from Trieste (*FW* 301.16).

This is one of Joyce's classic riddles: the most obvious pun is on a line from Paul Verlaine, "triste, triste était mon âme" [sad, sad was my soul]. Replacing "*mon âme*" with "my liver," Joyce substitutes his own book for his soul, since "my liver" is also "*mon livre.*" Another pun allows Joyce's book ("*était mon livre*") to become Prometheus' liver ("ate I my liver"): Verlaine's *crise de foi* [crisis of faith] is Prometheus' *crise de foie* [crisis of the liver]. The *foi/foie* joke is an ancient one: it derives from Rabelais, referring to the bibliophagic tendencies of the prophets: "Jadis un antique Prophète de la nation Judaïque mangea un livre, et fut clerc jusques aux dens; presentement vous en boirez un et serez clerc jusques au foye" [Once a prophet of the Judaic nation ate a book, and became religious up to his teeth; now you may drink one and become religious down to your liver] (Rabelais, II:453). Verlaine's line is from "*Ariettes Oubliées*" [Forgotten arias]: Joyce's line is an aria to a place he could never forget. For Joyce, the answer to the riddle is the city that is his soul, liver, and heart. "And trieste, ah trieste ate I my liver" is a message from a place of several transformations, whether culinary (ate I/*était*), graphic (*triste*/Trieste), textual (*livre/âme*), or biological (liver/*livre*). And the source of that extraordinary vitality is Joyce's very strange sense of humor.

2. Humor Detection in *Ulysses*

Humor detection, we are reliably informed by a team of scientists from Dartmouth's Center for Cognitive Neuroscience, can be neurologically dissociated from humor appreciation. The former (getting the joke) is a cognitive function, associated with increased activation in the left posterior middle temporal gyrus (Moran 1057). The latter (actually finding the joke funny) is an affective function, associated with increased activity in the insular cortex. (This may explain why you haven't laughed yet at anything in this chapter.) What is particularly revealing about the left posterior middle temporal gyrus (together with its sometime companion, the right posterior middle temporal gyrus) is that this is the seat in the brain for semantic comprehension, the place where language tasks are performed (Moran 1058). What is particularly interesting about the insular cortex, the place where humor is appreciated, is that this is the area implicated in pain perception, the perception of disgust, and vomiting (Moran 1058).

From these premises, the following conclusions may be drawn:

#1.   Getting a joke is different from finding it funny;
#2.   A sense of humor depends on a sense of language;
#3.   Either jokes are painful, or pain is really funny.

The first statement is self-evident: we all know people (usually British people, and usually Victorianists) who look grave at a pun. The third statement is an essentially Joycean truth. But the second statement, the idea that a sense of humor depends on language, is deeply counterintuitive to anyone who has laughed at Charlie Chaplin falling nonverbally up the stairs or watched a preverbal baby burst into giggles at the threat of being tickled. Let us see how Dr. Joseph Moran and company explain this.

According to the authors of "Neural Correlates of Humor Detection and Appreciation," "Humor detection is critically dependent upon resolving incongruities" (Moran 1058), and in the context of humor detection the posterior temporal lobe and the inferior frontal regions act as a sort of one-two punch: the posterior temporal lobe brings up an existing paradigm, and the inferior frontal regions reconcile the new or ambiguous content with the stored paradigm. Thus the child compares the feigned attack of the mother to a recollection or instinctive image of an actual attack, and the silent moviegoer compares Chaplin's difficulty with banisters and carpets to the relative ease with which these obstacles are customarily negotiated. In the case of the Dartmouth study, the sources of the jokes were episodes from the American television shows *Seinfeld* and *The Simpsons*, and in all cases when jokes were appreciated by the test group of eighty-two college students, there was activity both in the left posterior middle temporal gyrus, where expectations are ("That's not what I expected!"), and in the left inferior frontal gyrus, where ambiguities are reconciled ("Now I get it!"). Turning to humor appreciation, the effects of laughter were found not only in the insular cortex, the area of visceral response ("Ow, that was funny!") but also in the amygdala, which is the site of memory processes ("I must remember that!").

It is vaguely reassuring to know that enjoying a joke is so complex and that scientists are working on this problem. But it is also of great interest to the Joycean to know that our ability to process language may have something to do with our development, as a species, of a sense of humor. The authors of the Dartmouth study conclude:

> In short, humor may have evolved from our separate abilities to understand language and respond emotionally. Curiously, the neural circuitry that permits mirth appears to be available to many animal species. What appears to be lacking in other species is the functional architecture necessary to resolve incongruities, and, as demonstrated by our results, comprehend humor. This critical dependence on circuitry involved in the semantic processing of language is perhaps what makes humor such a unique human characteristic.
>
> (Moran 1959)

For Joyce, we do not need to be so speculative: Joyce's humor rests squarely in his language. There are sight gags in *Ulysses*, of course, but the best of them (the moment when Bloom's sight of a woman lifting her petticoats in "Lotus-Eaters" is obscured by a passing tram; the parallel moment when Bloom's relief from the effects of the afternoon burgundy is accommodated by another tram) are turned into language games in Joyce's text: "Another gone" (*U* 5.136), Bloom sighs, referring to both the lost glimpse of stocking and the loss of Paddy Dignam; "Pprrpffrrppffff" (*U* 11.1293), he expostulates, sounding music as the tram goes by. The central gag in "Cyclops," that Bloom bet on an outsider to win the Ascot Gold Cup and then failed to buy drinks at Barney Kiernan's when Throwaway comes in at 20–1, is based on a lexical misunderstanding: "I was just going to throw it away" (*U* 5.534) says Bloom to Bantam Lyons, who has been asking about the race and wrongly thinks that he's been given a tip.

"Punning," said a gentleman to the notorious punster Mr. Henry Erskine, "is the lowest sort of wit." "It is so, answered he, and therefore the foundation of all" (Bellew 157). That joke is #770 in an expanded and expurgated edition of *Joe Miller's Jests* from 1865, and Joyce certainly knew of the eighteenth-century comedian Joe Miller, or at least of the book of jests that bears his name.[4] The original jokebook is a wonderful mirror of its time, full of ribaldry and cuckolds and priests and serving-maids, and a happy hunting ground for Joyceans. Rabelais is there, his boots greased for his journey to the next world (Mottley 7): as we saw in chapter 4, Joyce plays a similar joke with Paddy Dignam, who asks after the soles of his boots from the other world (*U* 12.369). A lady in *Joe Miller's Jests* is upset at the sign outside her lodgings that reads *The Cock and Leather-Breeches* and asks for it to be altered as follows: "I'll tell you how you may satisfy both me and my Daughters: *Only take down your Breeches and let your Cock stand*" (Mottley 7). The lady at #7 Eccles Street is a kindred spirit: Boylan knocks on Molly's door with a "cock carracarracarra cock" (*U* 11.987). Lenehan has a limerick on the subject of the Joe Miller:

—*There's a ponderous pundit MacHugh*
Who wears goggles of ebony hue.
As he mostly sees double
To wear them why trouble?
I can't see the Joe Miller. Can you?

(*U* 7.578–82)

Seeing the Joe Miller, or getting the joke, is the central readerly process of *Ulysses*. Every episode is built upon a joke, an essential incongruity for us to find incongruous with our posterior lobe, reconcile with our inferior frontal regions, experience as painfully funny with our insular cortex, and remember with our amygdala. Lenehan's limerick in "Aeolus" is inviting us to see, as the speaker of the limerick cannot, the Joe Miller, to participate in what a neurologist would call "humor detection."

And what is the joke of the limerick? That there isn't one. As I write this, if you will permit a brief excursion into the narrative present, I find this crucial absence so painfully funny that breath starts from my nostrils, my forehead wrinkles, and I turn away from the page trying to contain myself (Lord knows what my middle temporal gyrus is going through). Limericks, you see, are intended to be funny (our relevant stored knowledge of limericks provides useful examples of misers in caves or women riding on tigers or old men from islands off the coast of Massachusetts, all of whom experienced some kind of satisfactory setback). So when we come up to one in the offices of the *Freeman's Journal*, introduced with great fanfare by the bold headline "LENEHAN'S LIMERICK" (*U* 7.577), its five lines set in italics, we expect great things, only to be disappointed by the final line. This forces our inferior frontal regions into action, resolving ambiguities between our limerick expectations and the actual punchline, and we discover, if our inferior frontal regions are feeling cooperative at this particular moment, that this nonjoke, this riddle without an answer, this disappointed bridge, is exactly the game that Joyce has been playing and will continue to play throughout the book.[5]

What is a pier? To Stephen, baffling his pupils, it is a disappointed bridge (*U* 2.39). What is the answer to Stephen's other riddle in "Nestor"? A fox burying his grandmother under a holly bush (*U* 2.115). What kind of anagram of Leopold Bloom is "Old Ollebo, M. P." (*U* 17.409)? What sort of a cipher prints the solution before the problem: "Martha Clifford, ℅. P. O. Dolphin's Barn" (*U* 17.1798)?[6] When Bloom marks a coin on the milled edge for possible return on the circulating waters of civic finance, does it ever return (*U* 17.988)? Never. You might say that these bizarre sideways solutions, these broken pieces are just meta-jokes, along the lines of the one in the *New Yorker* I saw in the waiting room the other day: "A priest, a rabbi, and a minister walk into a bar. Bartender says, 'What is this, a joke?'" (Holt 184). You'd be right, and we've obviously been sharing the same dentist, but Joyce's best jokes are always meta-jokes, aiming both to please and to instruct. "*Can you?,*" the final words of Lenehan's limerick, is an invitation to us to make the effort to see the joke, or lack of it: we are encouraged to "*see double,*" as Professor MacHugh does. "*To wear them why trouble?*" is an important question in *Ulysses*: without the "*goggles of ebony hue,*" the trick glasses that allow us to see double, we will fail to see the joke, and thus fail to read the book. With them, a kaleidoscope of possibility opens before us.

According to Hugh Kenner, who heard this from Ezra Pound, Joyce's lament on the publication of *Ulysses* was that no one had either detected or appreciated his jokes: "If only someone, if only one reviewer, would say the book was *so damn funny* ..." (Kenner, "Comedian" 190). Robert Bell supports this reading, citing Arthur Power's interview with Joyce, where Joyce calls *Ulysses* "fundamentally a humorous work" (Bell 1). In one of the last things he ever wrote,

Kenner presents a brief for "Jim the Comedian," taking his title from Pound's sobriquet for Joyce in the *Pisan Cantos*: "these the companions: / Fordie that wrote of giants / and William who dreamed of nobility / and Jim the comedian singing" (Pound, "Canto LXXIV" 432–33). Read at the 2002 Trieste Symposium, "Jim the Comedian" calls for a new appreciation of the comic possibilities of *Ulysses*, and many have responded to that call.[7]

There is, in fact, a long tradition of appreciating the comic in *Ulysses*. Zack Bowen's Ulysses *as a Comic Novel* begins, as Moran does, with the acknowledged truth that "Of all living creatures only man is endowed with laughter" (a postulate first presented by Aristotle in *De Anima*) and proceeds to find the restorative function of comedy throughout Joyce's text (Bowen, *Comic Novel* v). For Bowen, the comedy of *Ulysses* manifests itself through mirth in funeral, pleasure in pork kidneys, and the laughing aspect of parody, in which everything is reborn and renewed. Bowen makes a distinction between humor and wit, allowing humor to be broadly defined as "the universal, even if perhaps a bit bizarre, incongruities of human life," and restricts wit to "the product of intellect, of language rather than action, of linguistic incongruities" (Bowen, *Comic Novel* 46). But wit, if the neurologists are right, and they usually are, has an original role to play: it's the ability to perceive linguistic incongruities in the human brain that hardwires us to detect humor in the first place, and sparks our reaction to incongruities of a more universal kind. The boy who laughs when his mother tickles him has been hardwired to find this incongruity between attack and feint amusing, and the audience who is still laughing at Charlie Chaplin falling up the stairs has been hardwired to match incompetence with competence. Arthur Koestler's 1978 essay on "Humour and Wit" argues that "the jester's riddles provide a convenient back-door entry, as it were, into the inner sanctum of creative originality" and reminds us that the sense of "wit" in English, French, and German is rooted in each case in something more profound: *witan* comes from the Sanskrit *veda*, or knowledge, *Witz* comes from *wissen*, to know, and *spirituel* can mean both witty and profound (Koestler 109).[8] For Koestler, wit is the realm of "bisociation," where "two mutually exclusive codes of rules" produce a comic effect (Koestler 112–13): this is what a metaphysical poet would call a conceit, a reader of Fitzgerald would call the sign of "first-rate intelligence," and a Joycean would call parallax.[9]

Parallax depends on incongruity: to identify the distance of a celestial body two separate readings must be taken and the results triangulated. Thus the book's main character, Bloom, is in a parallactic position with the book's title, *Ulysses*, and the incongruities between Bloom and Odysseus are left for the reader to resolve in all their comic possibility. Thus, the position of Gerty MacDowell as the object of Bloom's admiring gaze is in parallax with his later recognition of her as disabled ("Tight boots? No. She's lame! O!"—*U* 13.771), and the tumescence of the first half of "Nausicaa" is placed in tragicomic opposition with the detumescence of Bloom's postclimactic meditations. Thus the first three episodes of *Ulysses*, with a man in black (Stephen), a ceremony involving milk (the appearance of the milk lady), a passing cloud (which drives Stephen to thoughts of his mother), a usurper (the episode's parting shot), and an abandoned key (on Mulligan's chemise), are all in parallax with the second three episodes, where Bloom is also dressed in black (for a funeral at eleven), is also involved in a ceremony involving milk (feeding the cat), suffers under the same cloud, sees the bold hand of his usurper on the envelope to "Mrs Marion Bloom" (*U* 4.244), and leaves his latchkey "in the corresponding pocket of the trousers which he had worn on the day [. . .] preceding" (*U* 17.75–76). Stephen's walk along the Sandymount Strand in "Proteus" anticipates and deepens Bloom's adventures in "Nausicaa," and Stephen's question and answer in "Nestor" is mirrored and extended in "Ithaca": all these parallaxes *Ulysses* will truly deliver.

The two sides most clearly bisociated in *Ulysses*, the two ways in which we view the world, are the tragic and the comic. Identified throughout the book as the "grave" and the "gay," these are the terms by which Robert Bell, in his *Jocoserious Joyce*, first introduced the novel's readers to the "jocoserious sine curve" (Bell 84) of *Ulysses*. *Jocoserious Joyce* is a delightful and dazzling book and is also extremely convenient, in its thorough absorption of all previous works on Joyce and comedy, sparing you the trouble of reading them yourself. Bell finds in all the ballads, cons, and mismatches of *Ulysses* an endless source of revival and equilibrium; for Bell, Joycean comedy is virtually defined in Bloom's graveside meditation in "Hades": "Gives you second wind. New lease of life" (Bell 85, *U* 6.796). Sometimes the folly is "closer to self-demolition" (Bell 128), as in "Sirens," when the narrative risks losing control of the strings, and sometimes the joke's a dud ("Eumaeus," for all its admirers, has got to be the dampest squib in the fireworks show). Bell clearly establishes that through *Ulysses* the spirit of Buck Mulligan prevails, mocking, *toujours en pointe*, playing the fool with the malice and wisdom of the Fool in *Lear*, disappearing, as Bell says, when "the lessons of folly have been absorbed" (Bell 21). From the opening invocation ("*Introibo ad altare Dei*"—*U* 1.05), by which Dedalus' centrality is thoroughly usurped and the principles of mockery are permanently established, Mulligan sets himself up as the figure to watch, the form to follow. His raillery—"you fearful jesuit" / "Your absurd name" / "Kinch, the knife-blade" (*U* 1.08, 34, 55)—is exactly the voice we have been waiting for since Dedalus got away with the villanelle in *Portrait*; his mercurial movement from "bard" to "noserag" (*U* 1.73), from Swinburne to the "scrotumtightening" effects of seawater (*U* 1.78), from "You could have knelt down, damn it" to "*it's only Dedalus whose mother is beastly dead*" (*U* 1.91, 198–99), is exactly the reach the narrator will need and have throughout the course of *Ulysses*. Mulligan is created in the narrator's image: he holds at the book's opening the narrator's two main tools, mirror and razor, crossed over the bowl of lather that is, metaphorically, the book's feeble excuse for a plot (a plot that prominently features both soap and water). *Ulysses* is the kind of title Mulligan would come up with: from the book's opening gambit, the principles of incongruity are immediately in play.

3. Everybody's Book of Jokes

Each of the eighteen episodes of *Ulysses* has its own individual character, style, color values, and whatness; what they all share is a joke, an element of incongruity, around which the episode is built. Sometimes this joke can be a punchline, as in the case of Bloom's flatulent performance at the end of "Sirens," or the sound of the cuckoo clock that completes Gerty's final thought for her at the end of "Nausicaa" (*U* 11.1293, 13.1289–1306). Sometimes the joke is a riddle—"A. E. I. O. U.," thinks Stephen in "Scylla and Charybdis," Lenehan has an awful pun on *The Rose of Castile* in "Aeolus" (*U* 9.213, 7.588–91)—and sometimes the riddle cannot be solved: Stephen's holly bush riddle in "Nestor," Mr. Breen's postcard in "Lestrygonians" (*U* 2.102–107, 8.255–58).[10] Rather than provide a compendium of jokes in *Ulysses* (having tried this for the *Finnegans Wake* seminar discussed in chapter 3, I can attest to the fact that there is nothing more deadly than presenting one's own idea of hilarity to an unknown and suspicious audience), I have selected not the best but the most vital eighteen. While none of these may strike you as particularly funny, they are all meant to be funny to somebody, each in a different way. With the help of *Joe Miller's Jests* and other "right witty scholars" (*U* 14.202), we can see how each joke plays a central role in each episode and watch, since most of the jokes listed below are told by one character to another, both its detection and its appreciation. There are "1000 pages and a laugh in every one" (*U* 17.442) in *Everybody's Book of Jokes*, the book in which Bloom failed in his youth to find sufficient humorous allusions for the purpose of completing "a topical song" on "the events of the past" (*U* 17.417–18), and there are one thousand laughs in every page of Joyce's topical song on the events of the past, his harlequinade of old Dublin, his grand midsummer pantomime. Many jokes are told by the narrator, Mulligan-like, at the expense of a character: in "Sirens" we saw Bloom transformed to "Bloowho," "Bloowhose," and "Greaseabloom" (*U* 11.86, 149, 185), all in the space of time it takes him to walk down Wellington Quay. But if we look more closely at how characters make jokes a central part of their day, and how these jokes are received and played with in the text, then we will more nearly approximate the value of humor in Joyce's *Ulysses*.

> #1. Telemachus
> —I am not thinking of the offence to my mother.
> —Of what then? Buck Mulligan asked.
> —Of the offence to me, Stephen answered.
> (*U* 1.218–20)

In an episode dominated by Malachi Mulligan, who acts as a narrative stand-in until his voice is absorbed into the narration, it may seem willful to select a joke made by his adversary, a remark that is not on the face of it a joke at all. But we have seen Joyce's affinity for the nonjoke, and this is one of his finest. All of Mulligan's thrusts in the episode have to this point been parried: Mulligan has "pointed his finger in friendly jest" (*U* 1.35), thrust his hand into Stephen's upper pocket (*U* 1.67–68), skipped, showed, hopped, mounted, turned, attacked, and swept (*U* 1.30, 50, 64, 75, 86, 115, 130), pirouetting around Stephen like a lunatic fencing instructor. "Parried again" (*U* 1.152), Stephen thinks, "Drawing back and pointing" (*U* 1.145) after matching Mulligan's mirror jest—"The rage of Caliban at not seeing his face in a mirror"—with one of his own: "The cracked lookingglass of a servant" (*U* 1.143, 146). After a halt in the proceedings to catch their breath, the two combatants pick up their foils again, with Stephen making the first feint: "Do you remember the first day I went to your house after my mother's death?" (*U* 1.189–90). Mulligan frowns, Stephen pushes the point further ("You said [. . .] *O, it's only Dedalus whose mother is beastly dead*"), and allows a thrust ("I didn't mean to offend the memory of your mother"), which Stephen blocks ("shielding the gaping wounds which the words had left in his heart") and delivers the killer line ("[. . .] Of the offence to me"). At the moment of maximum weakness, Stephen delivers the "coup de la mouette," or seagull thrust (Eco 78). Buck Mulligan swings round on his heel, and the point is over (*U* 1.191–221).

There are several reasons why Stephen's reply is so satisfying. Stephen has been very much the straight man to this point, playing Laurel to Mulligan's Hardy, with the plump man in the dressing gown getting all the good lines: "A little trouble about those white corpuscles" / "Switch off the current, will you?" (*U* 1.22–23, 28–29). This has made Stephen the "dogsbody" (*U* 1.112), or underdog, giving him the advantage of sympathy; he has also shown no desire to win, giving him the advantage of surprise. His tactic—showing Mulligan a false opening, knowing that he would be unable to resist it—is ideally suited to his opponent and shows Stephen to be as good at the art of the conversational fencing match as he was, in lesser company, at University College in *Portrait*, and as he will be, in the company of real people, at the National Library in "Scylla and Charybdis." The riposte is, in fact, the first sign of life in Stephen, fulfilling the role of comedy in the novel, which is to act, as Robert Bell argued, as a "New lease of life" (*U* 6.796). By turning the direction of an offence from the dead to the living, Stephen vaults, Hamlet-like, out of the grave, becomes briefly and necessarily gay, and scores a palpable hit.[11] It's a giant leap for a small pronoun, but by moving from "my mother" to "me," Stephen signals to all concerned that he's back in the game.

#2. Nestor
—Pyrrhus, sir? Pyrrhus, a pier.
  All laughed. Mirthless high malicious laughter. Armstrong looked round at his classmates, silly glee in profile.

(*U* 2.26–28)

The importance of Armstrong's rather poor remark lies in its reaction, which is out of all proportion to the quality of the jest. Koestler asks us to bear in mind that

> laughter is a phenomenon of the trigger-releaser type, where a minute pull may open the tap for vast amounts of stored emotions, often derived from unconscious sources: repressed sadism, sexual tumescence, unavowed fear, even boredom: the explosive laughter of a class of schoolboys at some trivial incident is a measure of their pent-up resentment during a boring lecture.

(Koestler 117)

Just such a situation appears to be the case here; it is worth remembering that Moran, twenty-five years after Koestler, identifies the site of pain perception as the area lit up by the appearance of humor. Laughter, Koestler also reminds us, following Freud, is "aggression robbed of its purpose" (Koestler 114–15).[12] From the cartoons of Hogarth and Rowlandson (Koestler's examples) to *Seinfeld* and *The Simpsons* (Moran's test material), jokes have always required some "absence of sympathy with the victim of the joke" (Koestler 115). Hobbes expressly requires that laughter rise from "sudden glory" in us "by comparison with the infirmity of others"; Descartes believed that laughter is joy "mixed with surprise or hatred" (qtd. in Koestler 116, 115). Koestler argues that the aggressive tendency is always present in all forms of humor, like "salt in a well-prepared dish" that "would be tasteless without it" (Koestler 115).[13]

Armstrong's joke in Stephen's classroom is at the expense of two separate victims: Stephen, who recognizes that "In a moment they will laugh more loudly, aware of my lack of rule and of the fees their papas pay" (*U* 2.28–29), and language, which in one ambiguous syllable can encompass a forgotten victory at Asculum and the place where Dublin meets the sea. In two quick rounds, accompanied by diminishing laughter, the pier then becomes the place of adolescent battle between the sexes—"Kingstown pier, sir. [. . .] their bracelets tittering in the struggle" (*U* 2.33–38)—and a blessed way into Joyce's labyrinth:

> —Kingstown pier, Stephen said. Yes, a disappointed bridge.
> The words troubled their gaze.
> —How, sir? Comyn asked. A bridge is across a river.

$$(U\ 2.39\text{--}41)$$

Comyn is the only bright student in the bunch (he knows both the end of Pyrrhus and where they begin in "Lycidas"), and here Joyce is asking us to follow Stephen's star pupil and ask ourselves the same question. The words trouble our gaze: how is a pier like a disappointed bridge? Because it has failed to connect to the other side. Without using connections (Pyrrhus = a pier), all the piers in the novel will be disappointed, and the bridges between language and the world cannot be crossed.

Later in the episode, Sargent acts as Comyn's dim-witted reinforcement, standing in for the reader again as he asks his teacher for help with his algebraic equations. First, the reader of *Ulysses* is lost:

—Can you do them yourself? Stephen asked.

—No, sir.

$$(U\ 2.137\text{--}38)$$

Second, the reader of *Ulysses* gazes at the symbols on the page in paralyzed perplexity:

> Across the page the symbols moved in grave morrice, in the mummery of their letters, wearing quaint caps of squares and cubes.

$$(U\ 2.155\text{--}56)$$

Third, the reader, with the benefit of Dedalus' instruction, begins to work things out:

—Do you understand now? Can you work the second for yourself?

—Yes, sir.

$$(U\ 2.161\text{--}62)$$

Fourth and finally, we are abandoned to our own devices and can go and play field hockey if we want:

—It is very simple, Stephen said as he stood up.

—Yes, sir. Thanks, Sargent answered.

$$(U\ 2.174\text{--}75)$$

Ulysses is Sargent's book of sums, and Stephen in "Nestor" is standing in for Joyce. To connect Joyce to Homer, Bloom to Odysseus, God to a shout in the street, the young boy sniffling over his elementary equations to the Dedalus who broke his glasses earlier in life ("Like him was I"—*U* 2.168), the fox burying his grandmother to Stephen's guilt over the death of his mother ("Probably he killed her"—*U* 15.3610–11), the cloud that passes in "Telemachus" with the one that passes in "Calypso," with a similar depressing effect ("Ghoul! Chewer of corpses!"—*U* 1.278) / "Grey horror seared his flesh"—*U* 4.230), we must bridge the river, connect the dots, solve the equations, get the jokes. The pun is the place to start: not for nothing did Mr. Henry Erskine call punning "the foundation of all."[14]

But here I run the risk of playing the part of John Mottley's Country Parson on another occasion:

A Country Parson having divided his Text under two and twenty Heads, one of the Congregation went out of the Church in a great Hurry, and being met by a Friend, he ask'd him, whither he was going? *Home for my Night-Cap,* answered the first, *For I find we are to stay here all Night.*

(Mottley 11, italics in original)

At this rate, there will be no end to this discussion, for there are sixteen Joe Millers to go. What I will do is simply list the remaining jokes in episode order and hope to make my criteria for their selection clear over the remainder of this chapter. The list is admittedly highly subjective; each moment is selected not just for its comic value but for what it contributes to a general understanding of humor in *Ulysses*. Each one is an instructional game, a learning exercise. Since only one has been chosen for each of the eighteen episodes, some great favorites—the tree wedding in "Cyclops," the literary source of Stephen's imaginary girlfriend in "Circe," the expurgated language of the parrot in "Ithaca"—have been heartlessly ignored (*U* 12.1266–95, 15.4950, 17.1535).

#3. Proteus
—*Qui vous a mis dans cette fichue position?*
—*C'est le pigeon, Joseph.*

(*U* 3.161–62)

#4. Calypso
He tore away half the prize story sharply and wiped himself with it.
(*U* 4.537)

#5. Lotus-Eaters
Letters on his back: I. N. R. I.? No: I. H. S. Molly told me one time I asked her. I have sinned: or no: I have suffered, it is. And the other one? Iron nails ran in.

(*U* 5.372–74)

#6. Hades
—Yes, Mr Bloom said. But the funny part is. . . .

—And Reuben J, Martin Cunningham said, gave the boatman a florin for saving his son's life.

A stifled sigh came from under Mr Power's hand.

—O, he did, Martin Cunningham affirmed. Like a hero. A silver florin.

—Isn't it awfully good? Mr Bloom said eagerly.

—One and eightpence too much, Mr Dedalus said drily.

(*U* 6.285–91)

#7. Aeolus

—But my riddle! he said. What opera is like a railway line?

—Opera? Mr O'Madden Burke's sphinx face reriddled.

Lenehan announced gladly:

—*The Rose of Castile.* See the wheeze? Rows of cast steel. Gee!

(*U* 7.588–91)

#8. Lestrygonians

She took a folded postcard from her handbag.

—Read that, she said. He got it this morning.

—What is it? Mr Bloom asked, taking the card. U. P.?

—U. p: up, she said. Someone taking a rise out of him.

(*U* 8.255–58)

#9. Scylla and Charybdis

A. E. I. O. U.

(*U* 9.213)

#10. Wandering Rocks

She's a gamey mare and no mistake. Bloom was pointing out all the stars and comets in the heavens to Chris Callinan and the jarvey: the great bear and Hercules and the dragon, and the whole jingbang lot. But, by God, I was lost, so to speak, in the milky way. He knows them all, faith. At last she spotted a weeny weeshy one miles away. *And what star is that, Poldy?* says she. By God, she had Bloom cornered. *That one, is it?* says Chris Callinan, *sure that's only what you might call a pinprick.* By God, he wasn't far wide of the mark.

$$(U\ 10.566–74)$$

#11. Sirens
   Pprrpffrrppffff.

$$(U\ 11.1293)$$

#12. Cyclops
—By Jesus, says he, I'll brain that bloody jewman for using the holy name. By Jesus, I'll crucify him so I will. Give us that biscuitbox here.

$$(U\ 12.1811–12)$$

#13. Nausicaa
because it was a little canarybird bird that came out of its little house to tell the time that Gerty MacDowell noticed the time she was there because she was as quick as anything about a thing like that, was Gerty MacDowell, and she noticed at once that that foreign gentleman that was sitting on the rocks looking was

> *Cuckoo*
> *Cuckoo*
> *Cuckoo.*

$$(U\ 13.1299–1306)$$

#14. Oxen of the Sun
He was laying his hand upon a winejar: Malachi saw it and withheld his act, pointing to the stranger and to the scarlet label. Warily, Malachi whispered, preserve a druid silence. His soul is far away. It is as painful

perhaps to be awakened from a vision as to be born. Any object, intensely regarded, may be a gate of access to the incorruptible eon of the gods.

(*U* 14.1162–67)

#15. Circe
STEPHEN
[. . .] Enter, gentleman, to see in mirror every positions trapezes all that machine there besides also if desire act awfully bestial butcher's boy pollutes in warm veal liver or omlet on the belly *pièce de Shakespeare*.
BELLA
(*clapping her belly sinks back on the sofa, with a shout of laughter*) An omelette on the. . . . Ho! ho! ho! ho! . . . omelette on the. . . .

(*U* 15.3907–12)

#16. Eumaeus
—Know how to keep them off? he inquired generally.
    Nobody volunteering a statement he winked, saying:
—Glass. That boggles 'em. Glass.

(*U* 16.484–86)

#17. Ithaca
Then?

He kissed the plump mellow yellow smellow melons of her rump, on each plump melonous hemisphere, in their mellow yellow furrow, with obscure prolonged provocative melonsmellonous osculation.

(*U* 17.2240–43)

#18. Penelope
I hate that confession when I used to go to Father Corrigan he touched me father and what harm if he did where and I said on the canal bank like a fool but whereabouts on your person my child on the leg behind high

up was it yes rather high up was it where you sit down yes O Lord couldnt
he say bottom right out and have done with it

$$(U \, 18.106\text{--}11)$$

From these jokes, riddles, and comic moments in *Ulysses* certain aspects of
Joycean humor can be identified. First, the joke often depends, as was the case
three times in Stephen's classroom, on audience reaction: Freud says, "A joke
[...] *must* be told to someone else" (Freud 143, italics Freud's). Bloom's halt-
ing attempt to tell a funny story (#6) at the expense of the moneylender (and,
by traditional association of that profession with Jews, at his own expense)
is botched several times, before being picked up and delivered superbly by
Martin Cunningham, and then topped by Simon Dedalus, whose unexpected
punchline is received with explosive appreciation from Mr. Power: "Mr Power's
choked laugh burst quietly in the carriage" (*U* 6.292). Lenehan's riddle (#7) ties
the Irish composer Michael Balfe's opera onto the train tracks of language and
provides an image for the parallelism of the pun itself in "Rows of cast steel" (*U*
7.591): the tracks of the railway line form an equals sign, as well as an illustration
of Euclid's parallel postulate. The riddle is received with mock enthusiasm by
Mr. O'Madden Burke, forcing Lenehan to turn to physical comedy to prolong
the moment:

> He poked Mr O'Madden Burke mildly in the spleen. Mr O'Madden
> Burke fell back with grace on his umbrella, feigning a gasp.
> —Help! he sighed. I feel a strong weakness.
> Lenehan, rising to tiptoe, fanned his face rapidly with the rustling
> tissues.
>
> $$(U \, 7.592\text{--}96)$$

Lenehan's recounting of the midnight ride of Molly Bloom (#10) falls similarly
flat—M'Coy gives only a thin smile, leaving the rest up to the highly developed
insular cortex of the raconteur:

> Lenehan stopped and leaned on the riverwall, panting with soft
> laughter.
> —I'm weak, he gasped.
> M'Coy's white face smiled about it at instants and grew grave.

$$(U \, 10.575\text{--}78)$$

Stephen's Mulliganesque conclusion to a bravura piece of "Parleyvoo!" (*U* 15.3898) in "Circe" (#15) elicits a better response from Bella Cohen than any of his theorems did in the library episode, giving us the book's most enthusiastic response to any telling of any joke during the day (*"clasping her belly sinks back on the sofa, with a shout of laughter"*). By contrast, "Eumaeus" gives us that most dangerous and mostly deadly kind of joke (#16), where the laughter, if there is any, is wholly at the teller's expense. Murphy's line, which he intends to be taken at face value, boomerangs, and immediately Bloom becomes suspicious of "our friend's *bona fides*" (*U* 16.498).

Humor appreciation, then, depends on the audience or test subject group; so too does it depend on its target. We have established that a joke is a malicious event and that the place where humor is appreciated (the insular cortex) is also the site of pain perception, disgust, and vomiting, and so it is always important in Joyce to see who the joke is on. Stephen's signature joke from "Proteus" (#3), an imaginary conversation between Joseph and the pregnant Virgin, translates roughly as follows: "—Who put you in this cursed [*fichue*] position? / —It was the pigeon, Joseph." Here, it is Joseph in the line of fire, and by extension all cuckolds in the text; the fact that "*fichue*" translates more literally as "fucked-up" broadens the target area in its unsentimental attack on the Christmas story, as does the Holy Ghost's unflattering appearance as a pigeon. When Bloom wipes himself with *Matcham's Masterstroke* (#4), the writing of Mr. Philip Beaufoy is in the target sights, and, as collateral victims, both the reading and writing of literature as a dignified occupation. Where Stephen's joke gleefully fleshes out the Word, in Bloom's action the word is flushed, made deeply and literally subordinate to flesh. ("Flushed" is not to be taken literally here: Bloom takes the prize-winning story from an old number of *Titbits* into an outhouse.) Someone is "taking a rise" out of Mr. Breen with the mysterious postcard in #8, and though the point of attack is obscure (what "U. P." may actually mean is a riddle still unsolved), the morning's mail has claimed yet another victim. (The three pieces of mail delivered to #7 Eccles Street, together with the one sent to Henry Flower to the postbox on Westland Row, unsettle Bloom for the rest of his day.) The word always wars with flesh in *Ulysses*: these are the two great antagonists, right from the start, where "Stately" and "plump" (*U* 1.01) do battle together.[15]

In "Cyclops," with "By Jesus, I'll crucify him" (#12), the word wins. The Citizen's attack on Bloom is a classic Irish joke, right from the pages of *Joe Miller's Jests*. In the *Jests*, whenever the Joe Miller revolves around faulty logic, or where the speaker fails to realize that what he has said is either logically impossible or self-defeating, an Irishman is always called for:

> #39. An Irish lawyer of the Temple having occasion to go to dinner, left these directions written, and put in the key-hole of his chamber door: I am gone to the Elephant and Castle, where you shall find me; and if you can't read this note, carry it down to the stationer's, and he will read it for you.
>
> (Bellew 8)

> #299. A certain Irishman making strong love to a lady of great fortune, told her, He could not sleep for dreaming of her.
>
> (Bellew 58)

> #490. An Irishman and an Englishman falling out, the Hibernian told him if he did not hold his tongue, he would break his impenetrable head and let the brains out of his empty skull!
>
> (Bellew 100)

> #652. A gentleman indisposed, and confined to his bed, sent his servant to see what hour it was by a sun-dial, which was fastened to a post in his garden. The servant was an Irishman, and being at a loss how to find the time, carried the sun-dial to his master, saying, Arrah, now look at it your-self: it is indeed all a mystery to me.
>
> (Bellew 135)

The poison in these jests is obvious, and it is a crushing irony that Joyce blasts the bigot with a language joke of the kind under which the Irish had suffered for more than a century. The narrator is getting into the act, and in "Nausicaa" we find a completely gratuitous attack on Bloom (#13), via Gerty's memory of an unlikely cuckoo clock well out of the scene's otherwise unbroken line of vision. The narrative humiliations have begun that will provide so much of the comic impulse for "Circe."[16]

If the two essential elements of humor appreciation are its audience and its target, the two essential elements of humor detection are language and incongruity. Just as a joke must be both directed (at a target) and received (by an audience) to be found funny, so it must be detected (compared with stored experience, generally semantic) and integrated (reconciled with that experience) to be understood. All the jokes discussed so far have involved language in some way, usually hinging on the ambiguities of a single word: "*pinprick*" (#10), "*Cuckoo*" (#13), "crucify" (#12), "*pigeon*" (#3). Joyce's richest jokes are language jokes: "Come forth, Lazarus! And he came fifth and lost the job" (*U* 6.678–79).[17] The key to humor detection, it is to be remembered, is "reconciling ambiguous semantic content with stored knowledge" (Moran 1058); first the stored information is brought forward (comes forth) from the posterior temporal lobe, and then the resulting ambiguities are reconciled (comes fifth). Stored experience is the thing that "comes forth" in any language joke: we first hear, if we have been brought up speaking any Western language, the cycle of vowels in "A. E. I. O. U." (#9), and we may hear "Iesus Nazarenus Rex Iudæorum," if we have been brought up as altar-boys, in "I. N. R. I." (#5). But then something "comes fifth": A. E. becomes the poet philosopher George Russell, whose pseudonym is Æ, to whom Stephen owes a pound (I.O.U.); I. N. R. I. becomes an acronym for "Iron nails ran in." Letters are developing a life of their own; "Iron nails ran in" galvanizes the Word, reminding us of Christ's flesh at the end of his life as much as "*fichue position*" reminds us of Christ's beginning. "In Hoc Signo," one of two possible readings of "I. H. S.," is to Bloom either "I have suffered" or "I have sinned." The other Latin reading of the acronym is "Jesus Hominum Salvator" (Gifford 94): it is interesting to see the sign that Bloom doubly misinterprets as an outsider is itself subject to multiple interpretations within the Catholic Church. Moreover, as we may remember from the Vision of Constantine (see chapter 1), one of the orthodox readings of "I. H. S." is an affirmation of the certainty of the sign—"By this sign [you shall conquer]"—further indicating the slippage of this and all signs in the Joycean bathtub: "ONLY ONCE MORE THAT SOAP" (*U* 7.221). "In Hoc Signo" then becomes a singularly apt reading for a liturgical text with multiple signifiers: the sign itself is a four-way symbol of salvation, suffering, sinning, and naming. It's no wonder, then, that Bloom can't get the world right. The words are wandering before his eyes.

"Pprrpffrrppffff" (#11) comes forth as a fart and comes fifth, when the reader/listener recognizes that the noise is a musical performance, made up entirely of musical dynamic and expressive markings (*piano—forte—rallentando*). These, not coincidentally, are the three musical markings Joyce cites particularly in reference to "Sirens": "It is a fugue with all musical notations: *piano, forte, rallentando*, and so on" (qtd. in *JJ* 459). *Rallentando* (slowing) is more usually abbreviated as "*rall.*," as *ritardando* is more usually abbreviated as "*rit.*" or "*ritard.*," but "*r*" can also indicate a rallentando, as it may do here. There is also "*rf*" for *rinforzando* (strengthening), since the best-known use of *rinforzando* as a dynamic mark is in Wagner's *Die Meistersinger*, to which Joyce compared "Sirens" favorably (qtd. in *JJ* 459), but "*r*" always precedes "p" in the Bloomian note. Another distant musical possibility for "*r*" is *ripieno* (fuller), though that is also an irregular abbreviation of the Italian word. Perhaps all three should be considered to be in play: the fart is slowing (*rallentando*), strengthening (*rinforzando*), and ripening (*ripieno*) as it oscillates from *pianissimo* to *fortissimo*, with a triumphant quadruple *forte* at the close. Like "Iron nails ran in," the fart made music is an example of the word made flesh, an opera fashioned from another intersection with a tramway line.

When Molly asks her husband what metempsychosis means, coming across the word in her bedside reading, the question is incompletely rendered: "Met him what?" (*U* 4.336). It is only later, during the singing of "The Croppy Boy," that Bloom remembers her spelling the word out: "Met him pike hoses. Philosophy. O rocks!" (*U* 11.1062). Joycean jokes are a substitution of the real ("met him pike hoses") in place of the abstract ("metempsychosis"), giving concrete life to language. This central substantiation, the celebration of the object, is what makes Joyce's world spring to life, from the "rubber prickles" (*U* 4.183) on which Bloom lays his three pennies to pay for his morning kidney to the "nothandle" (*U* 4.333) by which Molly holds her morning cup of tea. The bottle of Bass in "Oxen of the Sun" at which Bloom stares so intently is Joyce's shining symbol of this process (#14). As Bloom fixes his eyes on the scarlet triangle on the label of the beer bottle before him at the National Maternity Hospital, Malachi Mulligan lays down Joyce's primary postulate: "Any object, intensely regarded, may be a gate of access to the incorruptible eon of the gods" (*U* 14.1166–67). This is a phrase that should be tattooed on every practicing Joycean. Through Bloom's intense regard, the two cheeks of Molly's rump become the twin hemispheres of a mortal man's material world (#17). Through our intense regard, every letter in *Ulysses*, whether stitched on a priest's garment ("I. N. R. I."), sent as a telegram ("Nother dying"), written by a pen pal ("I do not like that other world"), plastered on a wall ("POST NO BILLS / POST 110

PILLS"), or circulated through Dublin ("H. E. L. Y. S."), can change and cohere in new and unpredictable patterns (*U* 5.372, 3.199, 5.245, 8.101, 8.126). "Nother dying come home father," as we saw in chapter 2, is the telegram Stephen receives in Paris that sends him home to his mother's deathbed; the misprint is wrongly corrected to "Mother" in the Vintage International edition (*U-61* 42). "I do not like that other world" is Martha Clifford's mistake in the letter that Bloom receives in "Lotus-Eaters"; the misprint is rightly uncorrected in both *U-61* (77) and the Gabler edition, allowing the word to become a world. The admonition in "Lestrygonians" to "POST NO BILLS" loses a diagonal from the *N* and a bottom circle from the *B*, raising the possibility that the billsticker Boylan is giving a venereal dose to Molly, requiring one of Hy Franks' "110 PILLS" (*U* 8.101). Wisdom Hely's, the printing firm, advertises its wares by a procession of men in hats: both the *Y* and the apostrophe *S* are having difficulty keeping up: "Y lagging behind," "apostrophe S had plodded by" (*U* 8.126–27, 155). All these are forms of lexical parallax, forcing us to see double, as MacHugh's limerick instructs us. "If you see Kay" (*U* 15.1893), the song the prison gate girls sing, turns "F-U-C-K" into a phonetic acrostic; language is procreating all the time. Joyce's words, his letters, his language, all have an infinite variety. Letters clip and kiss in a beautifully patterned dance.[18]

I've saved the best joke (#18) for last, and for Molly Bloom, whose wit too often goes unnoticed. Molly is, like Bloom and Stephen, quick to notice the value of words—"your vagina he called it I suppose thats how he got all the gilt mirrors and carpets" (*U* 18.1154–55)—and their comic possibilities: "asking me had I frequent omissions where do those old fellows get all the words they have omissions" (*U* 18.1169–70). Names are a constant source of delight in "Penelope"—"Mrs Opisso in Governor street O what a name Id go and drown myself in the first river if I had a name like her" (*U* 18.1466–67)—and this is hardly surprising given Molly's opening salvo on Paul de Kock in "Calypso": "Nice name he has" (*U* 4.358). Joke #18 ("I said on the canal bank like a fool") is deeply satisfying on many levels, working just the way Dr. Moran tells us it does. Our expectation, after "he touched me father," is a prurient one, already titillated by Father Corrigan's unconventional response. (He has no business asking "where": small wonder that he appears in the list of Molly's suitors—*U* 17.2134–35.) So as our posterior temporal lobe lights up with the possible areas where Molly may have been touched (including her posterior, which has been lovingly kissed at the end of the previous episode), we are pleasantly surprised by the incongruity of "canal bank," which we rapidly reconcile in our inferior

202 · AT FAULT

frontal regions (which are good at language tasks) by recognizing that "where" is deliciously ambiguous, and that both answers, "bottom" and "canal bank," are correct. Moving over to the insular cortex, we recognize in a painful, or at least visceral, reaction that the reconciling of this ambiguity is a pleasurable experience, and we laugh. Part of the pleasure of this moment in the text lies in connecting Molly's body to the city of Dublin: the single object (the site of the touch) has become a gate of access to a greater geography (the site of the book). The word "where" opens upon a world. And finally, if we know our *Joe Miller's Jests*, the joke rejoins an old friend in our amygdala, or memory banks. Because just such a joke, making the same substitution of the geographical for the anatomical, appears as #753 in Bellew's edition of *Joe Miller's Jests*:

> #753. Sir Charles F——received a severe injury one day in stepping into his cabriolet. Whereabouts were you hurt, Sir Charles? said Sir Peter L——; was it near the vertebræ? No, no, answered the baronet, it was near the Monument.
>
> (Bellew 153)

8 | Performing Issy

1. Outlaw Readings of *Ulysses*

The best way to understand *Ulysses* is to read it aloud. On a train from Copenhagen to Helsinki in 1979 I asked an Irishman to read "Penelope" to me, rewarding him with a beer from the restaurant car after each sentence. Molly Bloom immediately made perfect sense: the episode punctuated itself in front of me. During a twenty-four-hour reading of *Ulysses* in 1990, two fraternity boys came to the door of the student residence where the reading was taking place and asked if they could read. Actually, what they apparently said was "Got any weed?," but I misunderstood them and ushered them to the reading area, sitting one of them down in the reading chair. Though his friend left quickly, that one stayed for a whole episode: I like to think that the reading from "Hades" gave him a natural high. At another overnight reading in 2004, an Irish doctoral student in mathematics and I ended up reading "Cyclops" as adversaries, with him reading the narrative and me reading the interpolations. I have a sharply British accent, the kind that gets me associated with villains in motion pictures (think *Die Hard*, *Titanic*), and interrupting his graceful brogue with the scathing and heartless wit of the parodist felt like the act of imperialism that it clearly was meant to be. Over three decades of teaching, I have become adept at the dark arts of the all-day reading of *Ulysses*, and of its mousetrap version, the evening reading of "Circe." Here are the rules for both:

Knowles Rules for an All-Day Ulysses *Reading*

1. The reading begins at 6 p.m. on a Saturday and ends at 4 p.m. on a Sunday. The following shortcuts are permitted:
    a. For "Oxen of the Sun," everyone in attendance reads one page simultaneously, to create a Babel of languages, and to save time.
    b. Instead of reading "Eumaeus," everyone yawns very loudly.
    c. It is not necessary to attend the whole thing—everyone comes for whichever part interests them the most. Estimated times for episodes are as follows (based on a "Turn Now On" poster maintained by the timekeepers at our first reading in 1990):[1]

6:00 PM	Telemachus
6:47 PM	Nestor
7:13 PM	Proteus
7:56 PM	Calypso
8:32 PM	Lotus-Eaters
9:11 PM	Hades
10:20 PM	Aeolus
11:21 PM	Lestrygonians
12:44 AM	Scylla and Charybdis
2:05 AM	Wandering Rocks
3:20 AM	Sirens
4:30 AM	Cyclops
6:18 AM	Nausicaa
7:55 AM	Oxen of the Sun
8:15 AM	Circe
11:40 AM	Eumaeus (omitted)
11:41 AM	Ithaca
2:00 PM	Penelope

Figure 8.1. Estimated times for a *Ulysses* reading.

2. At midnight, there is a break for spaghetti, and at 8 a.m., breakfast is served. The reading must be continuous: one person must be in the reading armchair reading a page of *Ulysses* throughout the reading. Everyone reads from their own copy, if available: variations in editions are always appreciated. Food suggestions are as follows:

   a. Kidneys for breakfast, naturally, fried with onions. If the butcher at the farmer's market asks you, "Are these for your dog?," do not make the mistake of saying, as I did, "No, they're for my students . . ."

   b. Strawberries and cream, for the appropriate moment in "Circe" (*U* 15.3805).

   c. Any other Joycean foodstuff found in Alison Armstrong's excellent *The Joyce of Cooking* (gorgonzola, porksteak, Yorkshire pudding, seedcake, etc.).

3. Rules for reading: as in Alice's trial (Carroll 158), begin at the beginning of each page, go on until you come to the end, and then stop (with the omissions given in #1 above). The unit of reading is a single page, with the following exceptions:

   a. "Aeolus" should be divided up by headline, with a new person taking over at each section.

   b. "Wandering Rocks" should be divided by vignette, with the final cavalcade (*U* 10.1176–1282) read in the round sentence by sentence.

   c. "Sirens" should be read in its entirety by one person who understands something about music.

   d. "Cyclops" should be read adversarially, with one half of the room reading the narrative turn and turn about and the other half reading the interpolations turn and turn about.

   e. For "Circe," see the instructions below.

   f. For "Ithaca," the instructor should be the catechist and the students should answer the questions in a circle. Lists should be read *sequuntur* (each person reading in quick succession around the room).

   g. For "Penelope," eight people should be chosen to read a sentence each. The word "yes" should be chanted in unison whenever it appears. The words "Trieste-Zurich-Paris 1914–1921" (*U* 18.1610–11) are not to be spoken.

Additional Rules for an Evening "Circe" Reading

1. The part of the narrator is given to the instructor, who reads the stage directions and the part names. All other roles are assigned at random, with the following exceptions:

   a. The role of Private Carr must always be played by a British person, or if no British person is available by someone with a hot temper and a profane and vulgar temperament.

    b. The roles of Mrs. Yelverton Barry, Mrs. Bellingham, and The Honourable Mrs. Mervyn Talboys (U 15.1013–1119) must always be played by men.

    c. The role of Rudy should be assigned by the instructor to the person with the highest Empathy Quotient (see the quiz in chapter 1).

    d. It is helpful to have people perform languages (such as Stephen's Latin, and the Hobgoblin's and Mr. Maginni's French—U 15.77–84, 2159–63, 4045–4104) with which they are completely unfamiliar.

    e. By contrast, the people playing the Retriever (U 15.4753–66) and the Horse (U 15.4877–99) at the conclusion of the episode should be able to make plausible animal sounds.

    f. If anyone shows a particular talent at a role (especially Bloom at trial [U 15.774–890] or Bella as Bello [U 15.2834–3218]), that person should be encouraged to keep reading the part for as long as they are able to stand it.

2. All attendees must perform: there are no bystanders. Begin by seating yourself in a circle and taking whatever role appears as the order of reading proceeds clockwise. Read that role for one round only, taking on a new one as your turn comes up again, with the exceptions given above.

3. The following cuts are encouraged:

    a. Virag and the Cardinal (U 15.2311–2741). Virag is a certain buzz-kill (there is a moment when Bloom speaks for everyone in the room when he says "I am going to scream"—U 15.2455); omitting this lengthy section allows for a collective renewal of energy with the arrival of Bella Cohen. With this cut in place, the episode takes approximately four hours to perform: otherwise it is closer to five.

    b. If other cuts are needed: the first trip to the inner world (Rudolph and Ellen, Mrs. Breen) is comparatively slow going (U 15.252–576); cutting this section will give the class the pleasant illusion that things will move swiftly over the course of the evening.

    c. Bello's section may start to become unperformable as it moves to the deeper reaches of Joyce's fetishistic universe; you may skip after Bello's uncorking to the Sins of the Past (U 15.2963–3026), or even, if there is a shortage of time or an excess of prudery, to the recovery of Bloom's potato (U 15.2963–3498). The episode can then be read in three hours flat.

4. The following sections should be read *sequuntur*, with each person taking one semantic unit in turn:
   a. The members of the processional van (*U* 15.1411–36).
   b. The various acts in Bloom's political campaign (*U* 15.1600–15).
   c. The people in the Hue and Cry (*U* 15.4336–61).
   d. The birds of prey (*U* 15.4667–69) and the duelists (*U* 15.4682–88) at the End of the World.

5. The following sections should be read in unison:
   a. The prayers of the Daughters of Erin (*U* 15.1941–52).
   b. The Sins of the Past (*U* 15.3028–40).
   c. The Voices of All the Damned and the Blessed (*U* 15.4707–13).[2]

6. At the appearance of Stephen's mother (*U* 15.4157), someone should cut the lights, which can come back on at "Police!" (*U* 15.4254). The final scene should also be performed with the lights dimmed. It is helpful to have a keyboard available for Stephen's cycle of fifths (*U* 15.2072–73) and the performance of "My Girl's a Yorkshire Girl" (*U* 15.4026–4150), if anyone can play it.

7. It is crucial that Bloom does not actually say "Rudy!" (*U* 15.4962) but that all present are able to hear him mouth the word. The person playing the character of Rudy, chosen according to principles outlined in #1c above, should be placed out of the reading space in another realm—via Skype, through an outdoor window, or separated by glass paneled doors (if available).

All that is very well (and in my experience, it's often quite good indeed), but what of *Finnegans Wake*? How does one read that one aloud? I've made a start at suggesting how this might be done in chapter 3, by dividing sessions up into day readings, with the reference texts, and night listenings, in the round at a pub. One such night session, in the basement of a pub called the Brazenhead in 2006, went so well that it's worth trying to re-create here. It casts "Night Lessons" as a baseball game and suggests that James Joyce was a closet Red Sox fan. As with the musical tapestry in chapter 6, rather than explain how it works, it's better just to perform it.

2. Night Baseball

It is a truth universally acknowledged that "Night Lessons," the second chapter of the second book of *Finnegans Wake*, is one of the most difficult sections of the book to understand. Contributing to that difficulty, at least for reading groups, is the problem that the section presents in reading aloud. The heavily marginal- ized and footnoted text of II.2 (*FW* 260–308) resists live performance like no other part of Joyce's published work. Do you stop at the footnotes, diving down and resurfacing with each ordinal number? Are the marginal headlines in capi- tals to be read before each section, as you would in "Aeolus," or simultaneously, in a different register? What voice is used for the marginal headlines in italics, and when do these interjections enter the reading? Make no mistake: this sec- tion is intended to be performed. When parts of it were published separately in 1937, the title was *Storiella as She Is Syung* (*FW* 267.07–08, Tindall 172). Like the scene in the Ormond bar, this story is to be sung, or "syung" (*FW* 267.08). But how?

The visual diagrams, as always in Joyce, give us a clue. The geometry prob- lem in "Night Lessons" (*FW* 293), which has been connected with everything from Irish land development to Anna Livia's labia, gives us the four corners of a foreshortened baseball diamond. The hand-scrawled hieroglyphs at the end of the section (*FW* 308) look like nothing else as much as base-stealing signals from a third-base coach. And if you make the admittedly arcane assumption that each page of "Night Lessons" represents the top or bottom half of an in- ning in a baseball game, you will discover, in the top of the seventh, the musical interlude that regularly accompanies a seventh inning stretch:

Figure 8.2. The musical notes in "Night Lessons" (*FW* 272.L2).

Four musical notes from the organist (B-C-A-D) precede an advertisement for "*Seidlitz powther for slogan plumpers*" (*FW* 272.L3) and an anthem, "*Hoploits and atthems*" (*FW* 272.L4), which is quite possibly "Take Me Out to the Ballgame." I put it to you, then, that the first twenty pages of "Night Lessons" can be played, sung, and read as a baseball game. And not just any baseball game but a game between the Boston Red Sox—"redcoatliar[s]" (*FW* 264.n3)—and the Brooklyn Dodgers—"the catched and dodged" (*FW* 285.09)—sometime before the sale of Babe Ruth—"Our bright bull babe" (*FW* 562.22)—to the New York Yankees (or "new yonks," as "jake, jack and little sousoucie" sign their "youlldied greedings" [*FW* 308.22, 24, 17]). Such a reading would cast a new light on the exonerating letter in I.5, "originating by tranship from Boston (Mass.)" (*FW* 111.09–10). True, the Catholic Mass is a plausible origin in itself, as John Gordon points out (Gordon 147), and the *Boston Evening Transcript* is a reliable newspaper, as T. S. Eliot observes (Eliot, *Poems* 20), and the "original hen" who dug the letter up is more likely to be Harriet Shaw Weaver (*FW* 110.22).[3] But that letter, it is established in the introduction to the Museyroom, is found in Kate's knapsack along with "boaston nightgarters and masses of shoesets" (*FW* 11.22–23). Why the literary interest in leggings from Massachusetts? Why indeed?

Each of the first twenty pages of "Night Lessons" has at least three footnotes on each page, both verso (away team, first up on the left-hand side) and recto (home inning, at bat on the right-hand side).[4] Issy is taking score: the footnotes can be read as entries in a scorer's chart, recording the success of each batter. She records the hits, runs, bunts ("Punt[s]"—*FW* 263.n2), errors, steals ("Skip one"—*FW* 271.n2), and hits by pitch: "Bhing, said the burglar's head"—*FW* 261.n4. There are always three outs, and then the other team comes to bat on the next page. Sometimes Issy provides color commentary ("we were always wholly rose marines on our side"—*FW* 264.n3), but she always watches the game from the sidelines. Her role in the children's game is to comment and keep score, providing "Real life behind the floodlights" (*FW* 260.n3).[5] After the "Punt," or bunt, in the bottom of the 2nd (*FW* 263.n2), we have "two fingers," or a split-fingered fastball, in the bottom of the 3rd (*FW* 265.n2), a "pull," or a hard hit to right, for the third out in the top of the 4th (*FW* 266.n4), a "sinfly," or sacrifice fly, in the bottom of the 4th (*FW* 267.n3), and a "halfwayhoist," a double, from the fourth batter in the top of the 5th (*FW* 268.n4).[6] By this time, Perfidious Albion ("Porphyrious Olbion, redcoatliar"—*FW* 264.n3) is winning, with the Irish seeking "to dodge the gobbet" (*FW* 277.26–278.01). The Red Sox and the Trolley Dodgers, the "catched and the dodged" (*FW* 285.09): it's the English versus the Irish all over again.[7]

"Making it up as we goes along," says Issy, describing the second batter in the top of the 5th (*FW* 268.n2), and you might agree with her on this, but innings and outings are everywhere in the opening of "Night Lessons." "All be dood" (*FW* 264.n1) is an easy out, as is "turn to find out" (*FW* 265.n2), "skewer that old one and slosh her out" (*FW* 267.n5), and "The gaggles all out" (*FW* 270.n1). "Inn inn! Inn inn!" cry the fans under the influence of "Bacchus" (*FW* 262.27), as "The babbers ply the pen," warming up in the bullpen (*FW* 262.28).

The umpire speaks from the italicized margins. He rings the batter up in the top of the 1st, on a vicious sinker that the overweight batter couldn't reach (this sequence is also in solfège, as diagrammed earlier in chapter 6): *"fat salt lard sinks down (and out)"* [*Fa, Sol, La, Si, Do*] (*FW* 260.L2). And he calls the batter out at the plate in the bottom of the 2nd: *"Smith, no home"* (*FW* 263.L2). The sounds of baseball are everywhere in the crowd: *"Tickets for the Tailwaggers"* (*FW* 262.L4), *"Move up, Mackinerny!"* (*FW* 264.L2). *"Swing the banjo, bantams"* the crowd implores (*FW* 262.L1), only to fall into despair (this is the Red Sox, after all): *"bounce-the-baller's blown to fook,"* they cry, as "his flutterby" is "netted" (*FW* 262.L1, 262.13–14). (There is a Trinity College in Connecticut that has called its athletics teams the Bantams since 1899.)

We are a place "leased of carr and fen" (*FW* 264.16): this is Fenway Park, with Finnegan or "Fen-Again" at bat. *"Bags. Balls"* cries the umpire at the top of the 3rd (*FW* 264.L1), an umpire who speaks with a pronounced Brooklyn accent: *"Bet you fippence anythesious there's no puggatory, are yous game?"* (*FW* 266.L1). Are we game? You bet we are: and when Babe Ruth comes up to bat in the 4th, we begin to have a sense of the stakes. "I believe in Dublin and the Sultan of Turkey" (*FW* 266.n1) says Issy, announcing Babe Ruth, the Sultan of Swat. He's up again in the top of the 9th, "ever in those twawsers and then babeteasing us out of our hoydenname" (*FW* 276.n1): it's another weak pop-up from the Babe in trousers. Babe Ruth, of course, is the person—"O, foetal sleep! Ah, fatal slip!" (*FW* 563.10)—whom the Red Sox famously sold to the Yankees in 1920, the fatal error that cursed them throughout the rest of the twentieth century: "plenty of preprosperousness through their coming new yonks" (*FW* 308.20–22). If you are a die-hard Red Sox fan (and there used to be no other kind), you also know that the team's owners sold the Bambino to finance a Broadway musical, *No, No, Nanette*, a musical that is meant to have flopped while Babe Ruth went on to glory.[8] This is something *Finnegans Wake* also knows: "meekname mocktitles her Nan Nan Nanetta" (*FW* 567.14–15), the second gospeler says at the scene of the crime where the "bull babe" (*FW* 562.22) is sleeping. "Before born babe bliss had" (*U* 14.60), says Joyce in "Oxen of the Sun," writing in 1919, a year before the actual event: with the casting off of the blessed babe, the Red Sox were plunged into everlasting night. This is Fenway Park's original sin, or, as it is written in the book of the 2nd inning, its "original sun" (*FW* 263.27). The sacred text of "Night Lessons" continues: "Securely judges orb terrestrial. *Haud certo ergo*. But O felicitous culpability, sweet bad cess to you for an archetypt!" (*FW* 263.27–30).

There are archetypal falls in these fens and some spectacularly good fielding ("Securely judges orb terrestrial" is a particularly well-judged fly ball out). "Is a game over? The game goes on" (*FW* 269.21–22), says a hitter in the bottom of the 5th. The relief pitcher in the top of the 6th has "A spitter that can be depended on" (*FW* 270.19) and equally recognizable footwear, at least to a modern audience: "Nike with your kickshoes on" (*FW* 270.24). "As they warred in their big innings" (*FW* 271.22–23): as it was in the beginning, yes, but in the beginning was baseball, and God saw that it was good. There are other games in Joyce's compendium: Marco Sonzogni has argued convincingly for the relevance of rugby, tying *FW* 335.15–23 to the *haka*, or Maori war dance, that was written for the 1924–25 European tour of the All Blacks, New Zealand's rugby team, citing the connection with Joyce's sister Margaret Alice, who became a nun in Christchurch, New Zealand (Sonzogni 15). The *Wake's* many connections to *Alice in Wonderland* (not least with Charles Dodgson, the primary figure hiding behind the "dodged") may suggest that the game in II.2 is more properly croquet: "Though Wonderlawn's lost us for ever. Alis, alas, she broke the glass! Liddell lokker through the leafery, ours is mistery of pain" (*FW* 270.19–22). The "King Willow" paragraph in III.4 cites an entire cricketing team from *Wisden's Almanac*, suggesting that the game is very likely to be cricket. Concealed in this glorious section are the following cricketers: *Tyldesley*—"tyddlesly wink" (*FW* 583.35); *Studd and Stoddard*—"as he studd and stoddard" (*FW* 583.36–584.01); *W. G. Grace*—"for the grace of the fields" (*FW* 584.11); *Jessup*—"wide lickering jessup" (*FW* 583.33), and many others. Also the following cricketing terms: *LBW* [Leg Before Wicket]—"elbiduubled"; *cover, point, wicket, batter*—"duffed coverpoint of a wickedy batter"; *stumps*—"druv behind her stumps"; *boundary, yorker*—"rising bounder's yorkers"; *innings*—"tickled her innings"; *bails*—"a flick at the bails"; *bowling*—"old tom's bowling"; *duck*—"break his duck"; *MCC* [the Marylebone Cricket Club], *googly*—"the empsyseas run googlie"; *declare, Ashes, test match*—"Declare to ashes and teste his metch!"; *bye, caught, slips*—"bye and by caught in the slips"; *maiden, Oval, over*—"a maiden wellheld, ovalled over"; *crease, pads*—"with her crease where the pads of her punishments ought to be"; *Howzat, no-ball, bat*—"how's that? Noball, he carries his bat!"; *not out*—"ninehundred and dirty too not out" (*FW* 583.26–584.25, see Tindall 298–99). But you will also find concealed in the cricketers' paragraph the words "red" and "socks" (*FW* 584.02, 16).

According to the box score, the time of the "big inning" (*FW* 271.23) is the bottom of the 6th. The organ plays the notes "B.C. [. . .] A.D." (*FW* 272.L2,

272.13–14), it's the top of the 7th, and there's just time to get some beer before they stop serving: "Foamous homely brew, bebattled by bottle, gageure de
guegerre" (*FW* 272.28–29). In "*Hoploits and atthems*" (*FW* 272.L4), we hear the
traditional anthem sung during the 7th inning stretch, but also "Up guards and
at 'em," as the Duke of Wellington said at the Battle of Waterloo: the eternal battle between the contraries has begun again. "Bull igien bear and then bearagain
bulligan" (*FW* 272.29–30): the Wall Street Crash is here retaled, retailed, and
retailored. It's "Staffs varsus herds and bucks vursus barks" (*FW* 272.31): we are
back with Humpty Dumpty and Tweedledum ("old Grumbledum's walls"—
FW 273.01), Mutt and Jeff ("mutts and jeffs"—*FW* 273.18), Bruno of Nola and
Kevin O'Nolan ("nolens volens, [. . .] brune in brume"—*FW* 271.20–21), but
we are also in the middle of one hell of a baseball game. Fenway Park, after all,
has a famous wall of its own, known as the Green Monster. And then the Boston
fans make their first unmistakable appearance: "*Curragh machree, me bosthoon
fiend*" [Love of my heart, my Boston fans!] (*FW* 273.L1). Later in the section
the source of the letter is revealed, and again it's a familiar address: "Ask for
bosthoon, late for Mass" (*FW* 301.05).

By this time it's the top of the 8th (*FW* 274), and the relief pitcher comes on
to get out of a jam: "*As Shakefork might pitch it*" (*FW* 274.L4). To be precise,
there are four at-bats in this inning, each marked by a footnote number (*FW*
274.n1–4):

[1] Go up quick, stay so long, come down slow. [*out*]

[2] If I gnows me gneesgnobs the both of him is gnatives of Genuas. [*double*]

[3] A glass of peel and pip for Mr Potter of Texas, please. [*intentional walk*]

[4] All the world loves a big gleaming jelly. [*double play*]

"[C]ome down slow" is a lazy fly ball, "the both of him" is a double, and the
alliteration of "peel," "pip," and "Potter" indicates a three-ball count that was
allowed to go to four (the fourth *p* in "please") to put another man on base so
as to allow the force at second. Shakespeare then comes on in relief and gets a
badly needed double play ("out, vile jelly!") with a murderous forkball ("bare
forked animal").[9] By the top of the 9th—"Bats that?" (*FW* 276.20)—it's getting late: "And still here is noctules" (*FW* 276.23). Finnegan's up again, lugging
his lumber to the batter's box, looking for a pitch in his wheelhouse to hit: "At
Tam Fanagan's weak yat his still's going strang. [. . .] Larges loomy wheelhouse
to bodgbox[7] lumber up" (*FW* 276.22–28). A swing and a miss, says Issy in the
seventh footnote: "A liss in hunterland" (*FW* 276.n7). Shakespeare, batting for

himself in the bottom of the 9th, works a steal in his own inimitable fashion—
"And a ripping rude rape in his lucreasious togery" (*FW* 277.n2)—but the
theft of Lucretia is to no avail: "Will ye nought would wet your weapons, war-
riors bard?" (*FW* 277.n3). The "dodge[rs]" (*FW* 277.26) and the "redbanked
profanian[s]" go into extra innings (*FW* 277.n7).

So now it's the top of the 10th. The visiting team loads the bases but ends up
empty-handed (*FW* 278.n1–6):

[1] Gosem pher, gezumpher, greeze a jarry grim felon! Good bloke him! [*hit*]
[2] And if they was setting on your stool as hard as my was she could beth
her bothom dolours he'd have a culious impressiom on the diminitive that
chafes our ends [*hit by pitch*]
[3] […] I'll do that droop on […] [*drops in for a hit with the infield pulled in*]
[4] […] if it's one of his I'll fearly feint as swoon […] [*flyout*]
[5] […] And when you're done push the chain. [*lineout*]
[6] With her modesties office. [*strikeout*]

There is a seventh footnote here—"Strutting as proud as a great turquin weg-
gin […]" (*FW* 278.n7)—which can be interpreted as the natural expression
of a closer getting out of a jam, as well as a further reference through Tarquin
to Shakespearean villainy.[10] The "fenmen" (*FW* 278.20) have failed. It's time for
the final play of the game. It's the bottom of the 10th on page 279, and for the
first time there's only one footnote, and it is a monster, at thirty-seven lines long
(*FW* 279.n1). No page up to this point has had any less than three footnotes, and
each has been restricted to short commentary of one to four lines. It's the end
of the game, in one single massive at-bat. And you know what that means, don't
you. That's right: a walk-off home run. The Dodgers have beaten the Red Sox in
extras, with Bill Shakespeare, called up to pitch in relief, getting the win.[11] The
legendary pitcher, Cy Young, who pitched for the Red Sox until 1909, is tagged
with the loss: "Storiella as she is syung" (*FW* 267.08). Pandemonium.

"Do you believe your own theory?," asks John Eglinton (*U* 9.1065–66) after Stephen's Shakespearean lecture in the National Library, to which Stephen
promptly answers "No" (*U* 9.1067). The fact that there's has never been a moment when Babe Ruth ("the Sultan"—*FW* 266.n6) and Cy Young ("syung"—
FW 267.08) played on the same Red Sox team strongly suggests that this odd-
ball reading of the first section of II.2 is as much a delusion as Stephen's French
triangle in "Scylla and Charybdis." That the Boston Red Sox and the Brooklyn
Dodgers have always played in separate leagues may also give us pause, though

as it happens there was an exhibition game played in New Orleans on Saturday, 7 April 1918 between the Boston Red Sox and the Brooklyn Dodgers that did go into extra innings, and Babe Ruth did in point of actual fact pitch in that one, giving up three hits over nine innings and going 2-for-4 at the plate. You could look it up.[12]

The students of my *Finnegans Wake* seminar were frankly skeptical, as I had them read the footnotes in a radio commentator's voice, the left margins in the voice of a home-plate umpire, and the right margins in the voice of a stadium announcer. They were admittedly unclear about when it was their turn to come up to bat, and what was a hit and what was an out (it helps to have an adjudicator for these things). But they were already past the threshold, through the wardrobe, down the rabbit hole, lost in the funhouse, committed to the play of the text in *Finnegans Wake*. "Let's play two!" they cried, as Issy pauses for breath on *FW* 280, the only page in "Night Lessons" without a footnote, and then resumes the game for another fourteen innings. What we have managed to do, when students read this way, is bring the text to new life.

This may be what Issy calls a "fortuitous fiction" (*FW* 279.n1), straight out of left field,[13] but it is important for three reasons. First, by limiting the range of meaning to the national pastime, we control the difficult. Its parameters are reduced, the puzzle of reading the book becomes arithmetic rather than logarithmic, trivial rather than quadrivial. That, to return to Stephen's three-part formulation of the qualities of universal beauty, is *integritas* (*P* 212). Second, by dividing the text into discrete units, each page a half inning, each inning with a series of outs, and each out with a series of at-bats of strikes and balls, the infinite is made finite. That is *consonantia*. And third, by bringing the text to life with different voices, accents, and registers, we give it a plot line, and there is suddenly the thing that is missing in so much of Joyce's work: suspense. Will Gabriel Conroy flub his speech? Will Molly sleep with Boylan? Will HCE ever atone for his crime? Nobody really cares, least of all Joyce. But for a moment, as the ball flies off the bat and arcs into the stands, and as Issy rises to watch it go, we are given (or we have stolen) a precious moment of *claritas*. Lynch would agree—he compares Stephen's argument to a flying arrow reaching its target: "—Bull's eye! said Lynch, laughing" (*P* 212).

Just as the only way to truly understand baseball (or cricket) is to witness a game, so the only way to appreciate II.2 is to live it and read it aloud. Something is at stake, undetermined forces are at war, and someone is on the sidelines taking all this down in a secret notation that is next to impossible to decipher.

Why shouldn't it be baseball? What is, otherwise, your explanation for the big giant footnote on page 279? Something has been won, and some game is being played: why shouldn't it be the circular game that Joyce would have known as rounders? As we saw in chapter 3, some Wakean connections will always be spurious (bluetooth, hogwarts, grassy knoll), and some connections will always be real (Baird's television set, the Crimean war, Bruno of Nola). But some connections lie in between, postulates that cannot be proven, significances that shimmer. "In the buginning is the woid, in the muddle is the sounddance" (FW 378.29–30): Finnegans Wake is a pharmakon that is both word and void, a poison that is its own remedy.[14] Meaning exists in the permeable membrane between the possible and the impossible: in the muddle, the sound dances.

These outlaw readings of Ulysses and the Wake are At Fault's best demonstration of the risks that teaching must require and make the clearest case for Joyce as the solution to the crisis of institutional conformity. "Pastimes are past times" (FW 263.17): turning the first twenty facing pages of "Night Lessons" into an epic ballgame allows Finnegans Wake to become, for a moment, the pastime that it has always wanted to be, a pastime of past times, a record of the great game of history. Properly played, the reading game takes about 2½ hours, with at least twenty-one students each taking on a clearly defined role (nine batters on each side reading a sentence each on alternate pages, the radio commentator reading the footnotes, the umpire reading the left margins, the stadium announcer reading the right margins). Through such a performance, the dead text is made alive: "We vivvy soddy. All be dood" (FW 264.n1). True baseball fans will thrill to the unexpected encounter with Satchel Paige in the bottom of the 4th ("whose slit satchel spilleth peas"—FW 267.11), they will groan at the failure of the pinch hitter in the 5th ("the greater the patrarc the griefer the pinch"—FW 269.24–25), and above all, they will keep score, right until the final at-bat: "The game goes on" (FW 269.22).[15]

Here, finally, is how the game ends. First, there is the pitch on the right, which is clearly a splitter: "MODES COALESCING PROLIFERATE HOMOGENUINE HOMOGENEITY" (FW 279.R1). Then, there is a long at-bat before the ball flies centrifugally out into space (FW 279.01–09):

[Batter up] and the face in the treebark feigns afear. [Strike 1] This is rainstones ringing. [Ball 1] Strangely cult for this ceasing of the yore. [He steps out of the batter's box, feeling the chill in the autumn air] But Erigureen is ever. [And now a word from our sponsor] Pot price pon patrilinear plop, if the osseletion of the onkring gives omen nome? [*Close! A long fly ball, down the right field line, just foul. The count goes to 1–2*] Since alls war that end war let sports be leisure and bring and buy fair. [*Another ball—all square at 2–2*] Ah ah athclete, blest your bally bathfeet! [*The batter skips athletically out of the way of a curve ball, low and outside. Full count*] Town-toquest, fortorest, the hour that hies is hurley. [*It's getting late: past midnight. Never knew such silence. The hurler hies, but it's another foul ball. Count remains full at 3–2*] A halt for hearsake.[1] [*It's going, going, gone!*]

And the commentator rises up in her radio booth to report to us for "hearsake," for her sake and for our sake, for the sake of her listeners and for the sake of our ears, for the ache of our hearts and the ague of our years.[16] Issy blossoms into her finest role, with a broadcast that takes us right to the heart of *Finnegans Wake*. For with footnote #1, on page 279, in the bottom of the 10th inning, *Finnegans Wake* becomes pure radio.

The description of the game-winning hit itself (*FW* 279.n1) is fully thirty-seven lines long. It is a moment out of time, of infinite expansion. The ball first leaves the bat ("Come, smooth of my slate, to the beat of my blosh") and is watched by "morrow fans" as it skies into the upper deck ("verbe de vie and verve to vie, with love ay loved have I on my back spine and does for ever"). "Wait till spring," says the announcer: the Red Sox have lost again. The batsman, having "learned all the runes of the gamest game ever," takes "A most adventuring trot" to commemorate his four-bagger: "all heartswise and fourwords." As he rounds the bases—"Sago sound, rite go round"—his thunderbolt is praised to the skies: "(remember all should I forget to) bolt the thor." The Dodgers win the pennant: "Don't be of red, you blanching mench!" Truth wins over fiction: "For tough troth is stronger than fortuitous fiction." We return to the womb, to home plate, to our mighty mother, to the place where we began: "Amum. Amum. And Amum again."

Hooray! Whrrwhee!

9 | In Conclusion

A Series of Forewords

You'll remember from this book's introduction the tiny piece of glass from *Oscar and Lucinda* that holds itself perfectly together until the end is snipped off, at which point the "whole thing explodes" (Peter Carey 108). I'd like, by way of a conclusion, to provide a dozen Prince Rupert drops, each approximately a page long, to send the vectors flying. The centrifugal force of Lucinda's unbreakable glass sends the projectile outward in all directions, but by returning here to the object so lovingly described in Peter Carey's book, the patient reader of this one is given the satisfaction of return. At the end of the last chapter we witnessed a similar paradox: a home run ball leaves the park (centrifugal force), allowing the player to enact the principle of return by touching all the bases (centripetal motion). This little parable, repeated on baseball diamonds every season, presents the Joycean dilemma exactly. Joyce's method is centrifugal, but his theme is always centripetal: though he goes for the long ball, he will always return home. "Amum. Amum. And Amum again" (*FW* 279.n1), Issy chants at the end of her impossible footnote, sounding a bit like T. S. Eliot at the end of *The Waste Land*: we all go back to "Amum." When Stephen "*repeats once more the series of empty fifths*" (*U* 15.2073) on Bella Cohen's pianola, he goes to the far end of the universe—"What went forth to the ends of the world" (*U* 15.2117)—but then he comes back:

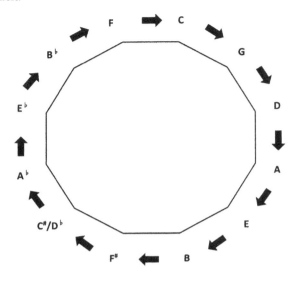

Figure 9.1. The cycle of fifths.

The cycle of fifths is a series of twelve keys that has no ending, looping upon itself indefinitely: from C (no sharps or flats) to G is a fifth, adding a sharp in the key signature, and so to D (2 sharps) and A (3 sharps) and E (4 sharps) and B (5 sharps) and F♯ (6 sharps, as we know by now), and C♯/D♭ (7 sharps/5 flats) and A♭ (4 flats) and E♭ (3 flats) and B♭ (2 flats) and F (1 flat), that will bring us back to C. As Stephen struggles to say in the brothel: "the greatest possible ellipse. Consistent with. The ultimate return" (*U* 15.2111–12). To end a centrifugal argument is not, then, a contradiction in terms:

> We shall not cease from exploration
> And the end of all our exploring
> Will be to arrive where we started
> And know the place for the first time.

> (Eliot, "Little Gidding," *Poems* 208)

Or to put it in the musical terms of the Chopin prelude performed by the Princesse des Laumes, there are sinuous phrases capable of "reaching out and exploring far outside and away from the direction in which they started, far beyond the point which one might have expected their notes to reach," only to "return more deliberately [...] to strike at your heart" (Proust 471).

In "Ithaca," the reader arrives exactly where Bloom started, at the left (larger) hob of the range in the kitchen at #7 Eccles Street. Bloom puts the kettle on for Stephen primarily as a mark of hospitality. By relinquishing his right to the moustache cup and providing an extraordinary measure of cream in his guest's cup of cocoa (*U* 17.361–65), Bloom levels the playing field between the two and shows the generosity of spirit that is fundamental to the Joycean enterprise. The phrase that Gretta bestows upon her husband, "You are a very generous person, Gabriel" (*D* 219), can stand as a motto for all Joyceans. As series editor, my job has been similar to Bloom's act of putting on the kettle, tapping the current "by turning the faucet to let it flow" (*U* 17.162). And flow it has, in work that celebrates in Joyce what Bloom admires in water: Joyce's universality, the vastness of his projection, his unplumbed profundity, his capacity to dissolve and hold in solution all soluble substances, his weight and volume and density (*U* 17.185–228).[1] What Robert Adams Day beautifully called "Joyce's AquaCities" (Beja and Norris eds., *Hibernian Metropolis* 3–20) is everywhere in evidence in each of the sixty-four books published in the Florida James Joyce Series between 1994 and 2016.[2]

The hallmark of a good Joycean reading, I have always felt, is the strange ability to read generously, to make something wonderful out of nothing. This is a gift Joyce had in overplus and one that his three main characters in *Ulysses* all share. Bloom stares at a label on a bottle of Bass, Molly listens to a distant train, Stephen identifies the number of masts on a passing ship (*U* 14.1181–82, 18.874, 3.504–05): each is an acute observer of the richness of the world. This quality of perceptual abundance has been the guiding principle of the series in which this book appears. The track to follow is endless: there is no limit to Joycean study. We are uncovering the Joycean universe, which is ever expanding. If ń is the number of Joyceans, and *J* our understanding of Joyce, as the number of Joyceans reaches infinity the equation for Joycean scholarship is as follows:

$$\lim_{n \to \infty} (J)^n$$

Figure 9.2. The unbounded limit of Joyce studies.

The sequence is divergent, yielding $J^1 + J^2 + J^3$ and "so on to no last term" (*U* 17.2142). The Joycean scholar is "neither first nor last nor only nor alone in a series originating in and repeated to infinity" (*U* 17.2130–31). This is exactly, after all, what it means to be a number in a series: the world of Joyce scholarship is unbounded, originating in and continuing to infinity. A foreword must be an invitation to that world: it requires a careful distillation of an author's tens of thousands of words and many more thousands of hours of work into an editor's two or three paragraphs. A foreword must also move forward: it is that arch wherethrough gleams the margins of criticism, which fade "for ever and forever" as we move. At its best, a foreword is both playful and serious, writing at its most centrifugal, reaching beyond itself, a florin cast on the waters, a postage stamp, a throwaway.

Of the sixty-four books that have appeared in the Florida James Joyce Series at the time of this writing (September 2016), I have had the great good fortune to serve as editor of twenty-eight, one for each of Issy's "twentyeight bows of curls" (*FW* 283.n1), one for each of the twenty-eight phases of the "Lunar Sisters' Celibacy Club" (*FW* 92.24–25). They have been written on every conceivable subject "immarginable" (*FW* 4.19): I have chosen twelve here, one for each note in the chromatic scale, appearing in the order that they were published in the series. Like the preludes of Bach or Chopin, each of the books has been written in a particular key, allowing each to take its place in the musical cycle of fifths (see figure 9.1). Though the forewords included below are selected because they best demonstrate the centrifugal impulse in my own writing, all the books in the series widen our knowledge of Joyce. The cycle returns home with a memorial tribute to the previous editor, Zack Bowen, who has done more to show us the way than anyone I know.

"Research, teaching, and service, these three: but the greatest of these is research." Giving workshops on promotion and tenure at the beginning of this century, I would always begin with this line, a parody of the words of St. Paul's triumvirate of "faith, hope, [and] charity" (*I Corinthians* 13:13). I have tried to show here how the university can expand its definitions of research to include a wide range of interdisciplinary approaches, how university teaching can be taken out of the classroom to inspire students with what is truly original and new, and how the service that administrators provide to their universities must travel beyond the bounds of corporate hesitation and institutional cowardice. But I now think that the greatest thing that a university provides is precisely what is properly debarred from consideration in tenure decisions: collegiality. It is not necessary, or even desirable, for faculty to be friendly, or well-disposed, or particularly likeable. But it is a vital obligation of every university to provide a place of collegial friendship, a community of scholars. A college (*col-legere*) is literally a place where people read together. That is what the Joyce community has been to me, especially in the years since the Ohio State University failed to heed its own inscriptions. That university's dishonor, and its disgrace, is more than made up for by the friendships I have made with scholars in the Joycean world. This book is written for all the Joyceans I know: here are some of the best of them.

> *If this be error, and upon me proved*
> *Then no editor ever lived, and no reader ever loved.*

1. Richard Beckman, *Joyce's Rare View: The Nature of Things in* Finnegans Wake (Gainesville: University Press of Florida, 2007).

Joyce's Rare View is a looking-glass book in at least three ways: it takes a wonderland trip down the rabbit hole, it holds the mirror up to Medusa, and it sees things darkly, not face to face. The approach, as someone probably said to Alice, Perseus, and St. Paul, must be precisely determined. In Beckman's capable hands, the fall down the hole is exhilarating, the angle at which Beckman reflects the Medusa of the *Wake* is exactly right, and the face of God (or at least His backside) is fully revealed. The idea of this book, that Joyce in *Finnegans Wake* is best seen as working from behind, whether behind what we see, behind the tapestry, or behind the text in so many other ways, is rich and right. The rare or rear view works throughout *Finnegans Wake* as a way of reading the man who shot the Russian General, Moses, various Kantian noumenalists from the druid to Bishop Berkeley, and HCE himself. It also connects to the retrospective arrangement in *Ulysses*, the parallel obsessions of Bloom and Molly with "bottom" as word and idea, and the importance of seeing things askance, or at an oblique angle, that has been vital to Joyce ever since Ignatius Gallaher squinted at Little Chandler from behind the rim of his glass of whisky.

As Beckman says in his excellent introduction, *Finnegans Wake* "must be read with a kind of moody alertness" (Beckman 1) and this precisely describes the quality of his own book. Nothing escapes Beckman's extraordinary eye, whether it be the tapestries of Polonius and Cardinal Newman, the etymologies of Wakean words, the language of flowers, the importance of interjections, or the exquisite contrast between Botticelli and Rembrandt. When it comes time for Beckman to ring the changes on a particular idea, the sound is as loud, complete, and joyful as a full peal of Grandsire Triples: the word "tube" is taken through plumbing and the Pompidou Center to the canals of Dublin and the body to the Euston tube station and Eustachian tubes to tubes of perception and peeping Toms. There are sentences that are so well-written that the greatest pleasure I can give you here is to quote them directly: "HCE's wide arse is the seat on which our society sits" (Beckman 7). "If undergarments and underworld are akin, then Proserpina knew the terrain before Pluto dragged her there" (Beckman 155). "Homer was so called because he was a homing pigeon. The *Iliad* and the *Odyssey* are in this sense tales of a Taube" (Beckman 104). Beckman has written a wonderfully wise book, with a critical and sensitive eye, a book that delights in close reading and holds everywhere a philosopher's detachment from his subject. And there are passages that are so gloriously filthy, in the awakening of all that lies deep in the *Wake*'s subconscious, that the result is something like reading Huysmans' *Là-Bas* for the first time. It is an infernal journey that *Joyce's Rare View* traces, beyond question, but with Beckman as our unflappably Virgilian guide the result is something heavenly, predicated on the possibility of Paradise.

2. Thomas Jackson Rice, *Cannibal Joyce* (Gainesville: University Press of Florida, 2008).

Ronald Reagan will be remembered for many things, but the thing that sticks out in my mind is his fondness for jellybeans. Our fortieth president shared a sweet tooth with another world leader, King Edward VII: in "Lestrygonians" the latter is revealed on his throne, "sucking red jujubes white" (*U* 8.04). The comfits of the King are clearly meant to be discomfiting: the King and his empire are bleeding the colonies white, draining the blood from the red areas of the map. At the end of "Circe," the King's at it again: a red jujube turns white in his phosphorescent face as he *"levitates over heaps of slain"* (*U* 15.4476). Edward VII is a cannibal: his colonization, in Rice's excellent phrase, is colonic.

   The connection of presidential jellybean and imperial jujube has been made possible by Rice's brilliant exploration of Joyce's digestive capacity. No one is better in this business than Rice at the precise overview, the detailed and comprehensive analysis of a theme. If you or I were to be set the topic of the cannibal theme in Joyce, we might think of the return of Stephen's mother, the Eucharist, and the limerick on the reverend Mr. MacTrigger. Perhaps we might include Swift's *A Modest Proposal* and the near-anagram of Caliban and say something about Joyce's cannibalization of earlier literature in "Oxen of the Sun." But Tom Rice also shows us that Gabriel Conroy derives his name from a Bret Harte novel inspired by an account of the snowbound Donner party. Rice connects the cannibal trope in fairy tales to the ogres, trolls, and witches of *Dubliners* and gives us the etymology of cannibalization (from World War II) and cannibal (from 1492) and makes both relevant to Joyce. He finds traces of vampirism in Stephen's villanelle and calls *Finnegans Wake* a literary and linguistic incorporation that is intended to be the reader's breakfast. Everything from Shylock to seedcake is thrown into the maw, until suddenly all of Joyce is about consumption. When Rice arrives at the moment of truth in the Gresham Hotel, as Gabriel asks his innocent question about the nature of Michael Furey's death—"Consumption, was it?" (*D* 221)—we reach, like Gabriel, the last moment of our innocence, and our souls swoon with the new possibilities of Rice's reading.

Rice has other fish to fry: *Cannibal Joyce* is not just a study of alimentary aspects in Joyce's writing but an investigation of all the ways in which Joyce can be considered an agent of cultural transfer. Joyce's detachment from his native language as a Berlitz instructor in Pola and Trieste allowed him to manipulate and eviscerate the word: Rice shows us how the linguistic instability of *Finnegans Wake* is anticipated in the first pages of *Dubliners*. Language is let loose in *Ulysses*: a punning analysis of adverbial modifiers in "Scylla and Charybdis" valuably underscores the comedy of that episode and includes the worst pun on Bakhtin's name that I have ever come across. For Rice, *Ulysses* is a mincer: when Stephen minces Mr. Deasy's words, just after the letter-writer has smugly said, "I don't mince words, do I?" (*U* 2.331), we are given both a reading strategy and an essential clue to the Joycean method. *Ulysses*, in its cannibalization of literary and mythological tradition, is a reprocessing of all that has come before. And then Rice turns his attention from language and the literary past to the technological present, and in a series of dazzling essays he places Joyce squarely in the middle of a postwar avant-garde that embraces the new technologies of sound reproduction, photography, cinema, television, and radio. For Joyce, who predicts the atrophying effects of television on the interpreting mind (Rice, *Cannibal* 157–59), the embrace is pythonic: one must consume or be consumed. This is one of the rare books where the subject and the author find their perfect match: the consumption theme is a rich and rewarding approach to Joyce's work, and Rice has given us, in witty and lucid readings of a range of texts, a banquet of ideas to savor.

3. Mary Lowe-Evans, *Catholic Nostalgia in Joyce and Company* (Gainesville: University Press of Florida, 2008).

Of the three recent books in the Florida James Joyce Series on Joyce and Catholicism, *Catholic Nostalgia in Joyce and Company* has the widest reach. Where Cóilín Owens focused on "A Painful Case," allowing Mr. Duffy to stand as a representative for all of Joyce's spoiled priests, and where Roy Gottfried carried the theme of misbelief through all of Joyce's writings, Mary Lowe-Evans explores the general implications of the modernist crisis in Catholicism, establishing Joyce as the seminal figure for a century of Catholic literature.[3] These three texts represent a third wave in Joycean Catholic studies, after William Noon, J. Mitchell Morse, and Robert Boyle opened the subject up between 1958 and 1978, followed by the revisionist work of feminist scholars such as Frances Restuccia, Christine Froula, and Beryl Schlossman in the 1980s and 1990s. Lowe-Evans provides a vital historical context for Joyce's ambivalence toward the religion of his childhood: we see through the smokescreen of Joyce's anti-Catholicism and find the hard diamond of his unassailable belief in the soul. Joyce's nostalgia for Catholicism is doubled: it is both the ache of return and the pain of going back, a double-edged formulation that is an essential part of the Joycean aesthetic (*amor Matris*, the love of the Mother of God, is both subjective and objective genitive).

Joyce is a double agent in the Catholic company of twentieth-century literature, too: Thomas Merton found the sermon in *Portrait* so compelling that he took it straight, styling himself after Stephen in his own confessions. F. Scott Fitzgerald's story "Benediction" appeared in the same year as "Nausicaa" (1920), and Lowe-Evans finds a fascinating point of connection between them: both find release in a weird combination of religion, sexuality, and medicine, through the unlikely pairing (in both texts) of the host-bearing monstrance of the Catholic Church with the electromagnetic vibrator of modern obstetrics. A stranger pairing cannot be imagined: but these parallactic points are neatly triangulated in Bernini's *Ecstasy of St. Teresa* and in Joyce's incamination of St. Teresa's transverberation in *Finnegans Wake* ("It vibroverberates upon the tegmen"—*FW* 249.15). Flannery O'Connor and Joyce are then found to share an erotic Mariolatry that runs counter to papal pronouncements on the subject and has something to do, as it always seems to in these cases, with the authors' relationships with their own mothers. "The Madonna is not pleased when she is put above her son," says Pope John XXIII in 1959 (qtd. in Lowe-Evans 156), but in Lowe-Evans' reading, Mother always knows best.

4. Edmund Lloyd Epstein, *A Guide through* Finnegans Wake (Gainesville: University Press of Florida, 2009).

This is a masterful study of the *Wake*, by one who has lived with the book for many ages, who communicates his understanding of the book with clarity and enthusiasm, and who leaves us with a richer sense of the possibilities of this impossible text than any critic since William York Tindall. Like Tindall, Epstein is a right witty scholar, having the rare gift of a happy turn of phrase, which makes his companionship through the *Wake* that much more welcome. The opening pages of Epstein's introduction should be mandatory reading for anyone embarking on *Finnegans Wake* in a graduate seminar, a reading group, or on one's own. Expanding on the same expository ideas at wider and wider reaches, the guide then moves deeper and deeper into the text, like the embryonic diagram Joyce made for "Oxen of the Sun." Each ripple, each reach of the oar, takes us further into the watery center of the *Wake*. The division of Joyce's text into modes of space (almost all of Book I, Book IV) and modes of time (the more temporally explicit sections in Books II and III, where the book moves chronologically from twilight to dawn) is especially helpful for those searching for a traditional narrative in the *Wake*. Epstein's synopses of particular episodes are likewise invaluable; this book is an ideal guide for any reader. *A Guide through* Finnegans Wake will be a book that every Joycean will want to own and will become a mainstay of the Florida James Joyce Series.

Epstein tells an old joke from *Punch*, wherein a literary gent stands before the sea and declaims, "Roll on, thou deep and dark blue Ocean, roll!," to the delight of the girl on his arm: "Oh Harold, you marvelous man! It's doing it!" (Edmund Epstein 160). One could say the same of Epstein's book, which makes one want immediately to turn to the *Wake* and watch it work its magic.

5. Vike Martina Plock, *Joyce, Medicine, and Modernity* (Gainesville: University Press of Florida, 2010).

Joyce had a pathological attraction to prescriptions of all kinds, particularly medical ones. The rich and varied use of contemporary medical material in his work has not yet received its due, especially given Joyce's original aspirations as a "Trinity medical," in the disparaging terms of the Mabbot Street Bawd (*U* 15.86). In many respects, the "Ithaca" questioner is less a catechizer in the Jesuitical tradition than he is a medical diagnostician, probing the body of a sick patient. The overarching paradigm for *Ulysses* is diagnosis: what ails Mr. Breen, or Stephen? More to the point, what ails Dublin and the modern world? Is *Ulysses* the "strong draught" (*U*-61 xiv) that John Woolsey famously called it in his 1933 decision to permit the book's publication, or is the book itself a symptom of disease?

Vike Plock has the answers for us and is especially good at the nosological classification of Joyce's various pathologies, from alcoholism (in *Dubliners*) to masturbation (in *Portrait*), obstetrics (in "Oxen of the Sun") to neurasthenia (in "Eumaeus"). By linking Farrington's paralysis with the physiological theories of Cesare Lombroso and the psychological *dédoublement* of Pierre Janet, "Counterparts" acquires a depth of field it has previously lacked. In a synaptic reading of "Eumaeus," Plock maps out the nerve-endings and neuroses of that episode, all carefully presented within the historical framework of the state of neurological science at the time. The work of Santiago Ramón y Cajal, arguing for contiguity rather than continuity in neural transfer, for which he won the Nobel Prize in 1906, becomes a crucial fragmentation to add to the collection of modernist crack-ups, along with the atom (Bohr), the psyche (Freud), time (Bergson), and the body (shrapnel). Plock's study of the state of contemporary gynecology places many of the book's curiosities in historical perspective: Mrs. Bellingham's remark, "Vivisect him" (*U* 15.1105), can now be usefully connected to the rhetoric of the feminist and antivivisectionist Frances Power Cobbe.

What results is a gleaning of Joycean afflictions, and a book that clearly lays out, with surgical precision, the many ways in which Joyce's work is indebted to turn-of-the-twentieth-century medicine. One might call this book, after Rembrandt's study of Nicolaes Tulp, *The Anatomy Lesson of Dr. Plock*: like Rembrandt's painting, Plock's study of one man's revolutionary work with a scalpel is itself a work of art.

6. Michael Groden, Ulysses *in Focus: Genetic, Textual, and Personal Views* (Gainesville: University Press of Florida, 2010). [Working title: Ulysses *from Monument to Mobile.*]

The turn to autobiography, or "life-writing," in academia has value only in proportion to the general conclusions that can be drawn from the particular narrative, and just as all young intellectual would-be artists can see themselves in Stephen Dedalus, so all budding Joyceans can see themselves in Michael Groden, who has had the Zelig-like ability to be involved in seemingly every great Joycean event of the past quarter-century. It was Michael Groden who was handed over the keys to the Joycean kingdom as a graduate student in Grand Central Station, and his story of how he ended up as the primary editor of the sixty-three volumes of the Garland Archive, still the single greatest printed resource for any scholar of any writer, is itself worth the price of admission. It was Michael Groden who served on the front lines of the Gabler Wars and lived to tell the tale, and again Michael Groden who was called in September 2001 to ask if he could help identify what are now known as the National Library of Ireland Manuscripts. Throughout the extraordinary story of his literary life, Groden keeps us grounded with a wry and self-deprecating wit: after his dissertation director tells him that his original idea for a thesis will never fly, Groden reports, "I spent about a month after that meeting lying in bed or sitting in a chair staring at a wall" (Groden 71). It is enormously reassuring, for instance, to come upon an admission by the general editor of the *James Joyce Archive* that "even after putting the reproductions together, I can't find specific passages in them" (Groden 89). And editors everywhere will rejoice to learn that only when the bound copies of the page proofs for "Oxen of the Sun" arrived at Garland Press did someone finally notice that the title page read "Oxen *in* the Sun" (Groden 89).

We are in the witches' kitchen, with the cauldron of Joyce's *Ulysses* coming to a boil: as the text reaches its perfect state, Groden has equally valuable insights to share about the process by which a text is created. This book is three things: a record of the growth of Joyce studies from 1970 to the present day, a record of the genesis of the field of genetic criticism, and a testament to the evolutionary development of a Joycean. And it is more than all these: Groden reports his observations with such felicity that as much pleasure comes from the presentation of the material as from the material itself. Again and again, Groden takes well-known points and phrases from the Joycean canon and recasts them so that they are resorted and restored, reversed and reserved. Love is not so much the "word known to all men" but "the means by which the Word was made known to all men" (Groden 31). Stephen's thoughts on history in "Nestor"— "But can those have been possible seeing that they never were? Or was that only possible which came to pass?" (*U* 2.51–52)—become the first musings of a genetic critic. The "Parable of the Plums" is read as Stephen's greatest work of art in the book, an anecdote that is itself a parable of the need for interpretation. Reading the section genetically, Groden calls attention to Professor MacHugh's smile, which comes and goes in the drafts "like *Alice in Wonderland*'s Cheshire Cat's grin" (Groden 67). Balanced by the headlines ("ANNE WIMBLES, FLO

WANGLES"—*U* 7.1070–71) and the parallel lines of motionless trolleys bound
for or from points around Dublin, Stephen's parable is memorably described as
a "mobile" (Groden 66), in which Nelson's Monument and all that surrounds
it are suspended for a moment in time. A mobile is a work of art that is "still
and still moving," as Eliot says in *Four Quartets*: *Ulysses in Focus* has the same
kinetic facility. In its breathtaking attention to detail, it has the stillness of a violin; in its constant search for new dimensions of reading in *Ulysses*, it is a moving
distillation of a lifetime's devotion to Joyce.

7. Agata Szczeszak-Brewer, *Empire and Pilgrimage in Conrad and Joyce* (Gainesville: University Press of Florida, 2011). [Working title: *Profane Pilgrimage.*]

Conrad and Joyce: I like to think of them as Corley and Lenehan in "Two Man-
darins," an imaginary short story from a lost collection called *Modernists* (which
also features D. H. Lawrence as Bob Doran, W. B. Yeats as Little Chandler, and
T. S. Eliot as Gabriel Conroy). In that story, the two unlikely companions wander through the turn-of-the-twentieth-century universe, maddeningly unclear
in their discourse and intentions, searching for a transcendence to which they
are both pathologically averse. It is Agata Szczeszak-Brewer's great achievement
that she can see through her authors' smokescreens, can tolerate their para-
doxes and hypocrisies, and can flick them into focus with a clear and dispas-
sionate eye. Szczeszak-Brewer marches them up the hill, through a subtle and
sympathetic reading of Conrad's teleological and hegemonic ambitions, and
marches them down again, through a freewheeling engagement with Joyce's
subversive attitudes to the colonialist enterprise. The resulting dyad gives us
Conrad and Joyce as a combined Penelope figure, first weaving (Joseph Conrad, conquering the day) and then unweaving (James Joyce, unconquering the
night). By considering the characters in Joyce's and Conrad's work together,
we now see that Don John Conmee and Inspector Heat are cut from the same
cloth, as are, from a more variegated bolt, the Harlequin and Buck Mulligan.
Dedalus has a marked resemblance to Decoud; Leopold Bloom and Nostromo
share, in their stealth and circularity, the habits of the flaneur. We now understand how "The Dead" shares a swooning uncertainty with *Lord Jim* and why
the most important thing about the first part of *Ulysses* is that it ends, as *Heart
of Darkness* begins, with a ship.

Above all, Szczeszak-Brewer has provided depth and balance for the outward odysseys of all the journeyers in Joyce and Conrad and, by extension, of all the pilgrims in modernism from Rachel Vinrace to the fisherman of "What the Thunder Said": each outward journey now has its inward counterpart, a voyage in every way the equal of the journey in the world. The act of colonialization has been internalized, with deep and useful results. Conrad and Joyce, through the work of this important study, have been shown to be two things of opposite natures depending on one another, as the imagined on the real. To be able to bring such opposites together requires art as well as scholarship: *Empire and Pilgrimage* is a work of both clarity and grace.

8. Robert K. Weninger, *The German Joyce* (Gainesville: University Press of Florida, 2012). [Working title: *Elective Affinities.*]

Effi Briest's father had a favorite phrase, as Robert Weninger reminds us at the end of his introduction: "ein weites Feld" [a wide field] (Weninger 9). It was his way of dismissing the incomprehensible, and as such has made its way into the lexicon of useful German phrases beside *Schadenfreude*, *Lebensraum*, and *Schlimmbesserung* (the act of making something worse by improving it). The study of Joyce's reception history in Germany is truly *ein weites Feld*, and in Robert Weninger we have a scholar with the historical and critical range to scan the entire ground.

Within these pages, you will find not only an exhaustive review of Joyce's direct influence on German literary production in the twentieth century (what Weninger calls *rapports de fait*) but also an examination of those elective affinities, or intertextual echoes, that defy categorization, as when Goethe, Rilke, and the Dadaists appear to be writing in the key of Joyce. The dynamics of reception are never so compelling as here: on the one side, the march of Nazism across the landscape of German ideas gives real urgency to the terms of the debate; on the other, the shifting requirements of Marxist ideology establish *Ulysses* as the most important literary work of the twentieth century. To critics of both the left and the right, *Ulysses* is "entartete Kunst" [degenerate art]; it is Weninger's great gift that he can find a balance between so many one-sided arguments and steer his craft safely past the Fascist rock and the Marxist whirlpool. He shows us Bloch's corrective to Lukács' rejection of *Ulysses*, and Brecht's defense of the book as more populist than the work of Thomas Mann. He points out that

Ulysses, despite being blacklisted in Nazi Germany for its lack of "any healthy ethically racial bond," was allowed to stay in print in Germany until April 1939, an act attributed to "commercial cynicism" (Weninger 54, 56). The subject of these critiques is the real story: *Ulysses* becomes, as Weninger suggests, a defining space for critics of all political persuasion. Oscillating between the *nacheinander* (Weninger's phrase for relations that are real and take place in time) and the *nebeneinander* (textual simultaneities that take place out of time in literary space), *The German Joyce* is a masterwork of sustained analysis, assured writing, and careful conviction.

Three things are clear as a result of this book. First, if Joyce can come under attack from both Marxists and Fascists, then he must be doing something right. Second, if Fitzgerald is right that the test of a first-rate intelligence is to be able to hold two opposing ideas in mind at the same time, then Weninger passes that test. And third, we now know that Joyce's connection with German literature and criticism is a rich field for scholarly study; it has taken an expert gardener to make the flowers bloom.

9. Cóilín Owens, *Before Daybreak: "After the Race" and the Origins of Joyce's Art* (Gainesville: University Press of Florida, 2013).

"After the Race" is, after "Eveline," the second shortest story in *Dubliners* and generally taken to be the slightest. What Cóilín Owens has done is more than rehabilitate this minor story; he has revived the far more important question of Joyce's origins as an artist. *A Portrait of the Artist* never really told us anything about how Joyce learned to become the genius that he was: Owens shows us how Joyce took the clay of his material life, whether biographical, philosophical, religious, literary, cultural, technological, or political, and learned to sculpt. Through gloriously close readings of the world of Dublin at the time of the Gordon Bennett Cup in 1903, we are given a window into Joyce's creative process and into Ireland's promise of a new dawn. It is not for nothing that the last line of "After the Race" is "Daybreak, gentlemen!" (*D* 42).

"After the Race" is an ur-story, a bronze spearhead in the sand, and Cóilín Owens is our Schliemann, an archaeologist carefully brushing off the dust to reveal a work of telling significance, of proto-Joycean capabilities. With the bravura of Monsieur Dupin in "The Purloined Letter," he shows us that this nexus of Joycean effects has been hiding in plain sight, skipped by generations of critics as a subpar effort on the way to "Two Gallants." He shows us the crucial intersection of the race course with the sites associated with the life and death of Robert Emmet, he tracks the automobilists' wild career over the historical scenes of Irish paralysis, he shows us the implications of the Pauline close to Emmet's famous speech ("*I have* [. . .] *Done*"—*U* 11.1292–94), he displays how the text's obsessive doubling makes it truly a work of "Doublends Jined" (*FW* 20.16), he hears a theosophist hum in the silent ministrations of Villona, and he leads Jimmy Doyle through an Dantean inferno, bringing us out of darkness to admire the stars.

Cóilín Owens' work is quite literally groundbreaking. Through this "top-typsical reading" (*FW* 20.15) of "After the Race" and its afterlife in *Ulysses* and *Finnegans Wake*, we are shown the rest of the Joyce iceberg, the world that lies below the surface of every one of his texts. The fact that any part of that world still remained to be discovered is simply astonishing.

10. Alison Lacivita, *The Ecology of* Finnegans Wake (Gainesville: University Press of Florida, 2015).

Once in a blue moon a work comes across an editor's desk that promises to shape the work of a generation. **H**ere **C**omes **E**cocriticism, led by **A**lison Lacivita, **Ph.D.** Lacivita has created an exquisite **chapel** in her study of the *Wake* and the natural world; the intertwining vines of genetic study and ecocritical reading **pleach** together in an intricately braided text that is a veritable ar**chipela**go of new and hidden discoveries. It is as if James Frazer had actually done his homework: this is *The Golden Bough* for the ecocritical age, an inspirational and breathtakingly original reading that is everywhere supported by close critical engagement with the text. This book provides a necessary redress to the legions of critics who require Joyce to be an urban writer in Aesopian dualism against the Irish Literary Revival, a town mouse against the country mice of Yeats and Synge, out in their pampooties to murder him. Joyce may have played that distinction up in a particolored way ever since his departure from Dublin, but Alison Lacivita isn't fooled and returns James Joyce to the green world where he belongs, leading us to fresh woods and pastures new.

In undergraduate exams on *Ulysses*, I have been known to set two simple questions from the "Ithaca" catechism: "Did he fall?" and "Did it flow?" (*U* 17.90, 163). What follows constitutes the single best possible answer to both questions at once. Lacivita is concerned with nothing more nor less than our post-Edenic existence, and the way that we may make our return to Paradise.

Did it flow? Yes, it certainly did: the watery sources of all Joyce's work are revealed in all contexts—genetic, cultural, political, physical, literary, geographical. From paleobotany to poststructuralism, from partridges to peatbogs, from
polar bears to Poulaphouca, we are given an encyclopedic topology of the leg-
ible landscapes of the *Wake*, including a welcome disquisition on the influence
of gaslight on paraheliotropic trees. Lacivita does more than shore up the presence of the River Liffey in the *Wake*; her reclamation of an entire subject from
the silted waters of the *Wake* makes her at once a charitable mason, a landscape
architect, and a hydroengineer.

In Joyce, genetic criticism and environmental scholarship are neatly aligned
in ways that make *Finnegans Wake* a perfect study for Lacivita's general argument. Over time and through space *Finnegans Wake* developed like nothing
else in literature, allowing Lacivita to shuttle effortlessly between the growth of
the text and the text's love of growing things. By the end of Lacivita's book, we
come to realize that *Finnegans Wake* allows infinite space to explore the nutshell
of the natural world. But that does not make Joyce's work unique; *Finnegans
Wake* just makes the ecocritical argument better than any text ever written.
This is the unique quality of Lacivita's scholarship: she makes *Finnegans Wake*
a representative work rather than a singularity, a great tree of life instead of a
radioactive stone only to be approached in a hazmat suit with a Geiger counter.
"Allalivial, allalluvial!" (*FW* 213.32). "Environs" (*FW* 3.03) has been hiding in
plain sight. Lacivita is our Lucretius, and *The Ecology of* Finnegans Wake our *De
Rerum Natura*: through her marvelous work, we are drawn closer to the stars.

11. Michael Patrick Gillespie, *James Joyce and the Exilic Imagination* (Gainesville: University Press of Florida, 2015).

"Each exilic experience is as unique as the experience of any human life" (Gillespie, *Imagination* 10). Perhaps this is obvious, but sometimes it takes a critic
with the special gifts of Michael Gillespie to hit what Lynch would call the
"Bull's eye!" (*P* 212). I have some personal interest in the subject, leaving England at thirteen for the brave new world across the Atlantic, and so does Gillespie, who glances beautifully at his own family's part in the Irish diaspora:
"when my grandfather left Achill Island" (Gillespie, *Imagination* 16). So does
Bloom, of course, and so does Joyce, and so do all of us. As the introduction
shows, in a far-ranging study of the exile theme from Emile Zola to John Ford,
from Joseph Conrad to Thomas Mann, exile is a "word known to all men"

(*U* 15.4192–93). What Michael Gillespie brings to the long-worn subject of modernist exile is a double vision of sharpness and sensitivity, which is at once unafraid to take on the foolishness of received critical opinion and deeply attuned to the folly of the human heart. Time and again, Gillespie gives us a less cynical, less hierarchical reading of the text, whether it is in a new validation of the intensity of Mr. Duffy's mourning, a new appreciation of the solicitude of the sisters of Reverend Flynn, or a new and warmer light shone on the machinations of Mrs. Mooney and Mrs. Kearney. This is a deeply sympathetic reading, but it is also coldly unafraid to tackle the prescriptive tenets of Joycean criticism, from the literary bases for Ellmann's biographical pronouncements to the standard readings of Stephen's encounter with Cyril Sargent in "Nestor." With this book, Michael Gillespie returns empathy to the center of Joyce's world, which (as any reader of *Ulysses* comes to understand) is its rightful place.

The idea of the book, that Joyce's personal experience of exile was shot through with ambivalence to his native Ireland, an ambivalence that expresses itself in both his life and his work as hostility and sentimentality in equal measure, is everywhere compelling. The oscillating perspectives of rancor and nostalgia perfectly map onto the exilic authors and characters that Gillespie discusses and provide the reader with a clear path right to Joyce's doubled heart. This book is written clearly and sensibly, unblinkered by theoretical commitments, and achieves exactly what it intends in providing a timely and useful intervention in Joyce studies. This is an open work in the best sense: welcoming, evenhanded, and open-minded. What results is nothing less than a vital rehabilitation of Joyce's prose work.

12. Kimberly J. Devlin and Christine Smedley, eds., *Joyce's Allmaziful Plurabilities: Polyvocal Explorations of* Finnegans Wake (Gainesville: University Press of Florida, 2015).

Thomas Tallis' great forty-voice motet *Spem in Alium* is a masterwork of Renaissance polyphony; *Finnegans Wake*, by contrast, is perhaps best understood as a claustrafork of Mishrashnist preverbosity. In the Tallis motet, each part requires utter and complete concentration in itself, and only by putting the sum of its parts together can the motet speak in all its exquisite cross relations. *Finnegans Wake* also requires utter concentration on a single line, whose meaning is made manifest only when taken as part of a chorus of plurabilities. Each chapter of *Finnegans Wake*, as Kimberly Devlin and Christine Smedley clearly establish, requires a separate voice to sing in its own register, and only by joining all seventeen chapters into a polyvocal whole can the text resonate in all its confounding glory.

And what voices they are! Enda Duffy sounds a trumpet, making a clarion call to action by interpreting the book's title as an imperative ("Finnegans Wake!") in his reading of the politics of II.3. David Spurr argues as sinuously and subversively as a clarinet in his serpentine reading of the countergospel in II.4. Margot Norris has such a gift for intonation in her reading of the "Anna Livia" section of I.8 that all her sentences sound perfectly in tune, like three French horns. Sean Latham's switched-on study of game theory for the question time in I.6 sounds for all the world like a virtuoso synthesizer playing Bach. Vicki Mahaffey brings the book to a beautiful close with her reading of the Ricorso in IV, where the final lines of her essay sound like the singing line of a cello, bowing up and down across the string. The seventeen writers in this volume have been perfectly chosen for their command of the material, yes, but also for their particular timbre, their particular approach and style. This is what made "Our Exagmination . . ." such an ideal introduction to "Work in Progress" and what makes *Joyce's Allmaziful Plurabilities* such an ideal introduction to *Finnegans Wake*: each approach is discrete and singular, allowing the eager but baffled member of the Wakean audience to discover several different ways into the music of the text. Each author has found a perfect pitch, and the whole chord now sings together.

Finnegans Wake is, according to this book:

a. a node or vortex from which and through which and into which ideas are constantly rushing
b. a circular dance for narrative power in the style of Jane Austen
c. a game which teaches you how to play itself as you proceed level by level
d. a gathering of the limbs of Osiris
e. a set of Matryoshka dolls in which each character is nested within another character
f. all of the above and more

The answer, of course, is "f." These seventeen gifted critics have "come to give you metaphors" for *Finnegans Wake*, to borrow Yeats' immortal phrase from his introduction to *A Vision* (Yeats 8). There is the metaphor of the relay, which turns out to be the perfect approach for what Devlin and Smedley in their introduction call "The Prodigal Text." For Sean Latham, the book is in pieces and is best learned through "chunking" (95); Tim Conley's reading of the atmospherics in I.3 suggests that any slice of *Finnegans Wake* will reveal by synecdoche the greater whole, in the manner of a Mandelbrot set. *Polyvocal Explorations* gives us the source code, to use Latham's helpful analogy, for each chapter, the core data from which we can all build our own varying and contradicting readings. The relay metaphor gives us a further way in. There is a word relay in I.6 that takes us from birth to death, letter by letter (*FW* 142.35–143.01):

BORN for
LORN in
LORE of
LOVE to
LIVE and
WIVE by
WILE and
RILE by
RULE of
RUSE 'reathed
ROSE and
HOSE

But then the path bifurcates, giving us two separate outcomes:

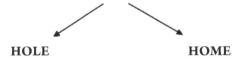

HOLE   **HOME**

One way leads to death, the place of our beginning, and the other leads to life, and all the comforts of an abode of bliss. Like Milton Bradley's *Game of Life* (and you will see that both "LIKE" and "LIFE" were possibilities in the word ladder), *Finnegans Wake* can lead us to the Poor Farm or to Millionaire Acres, to "HOLE," which completes a circular trajectory from birth to the grave, or to "HOME," completing a separate circuit from birth to marriage and return. Joyce characteristically gives us both answers: "by rule of ruse 'reathed rose and hose hol'd home" (*FW* 142.36–143.01). Through this allmaziful book, we reach the wreath and the rose, finding both hole and home. *Spem in alium*: there is, after all, hope in others.

"A Memorial Tribute to Zack Bowen." *James Joyce Quarterly* 46 (Spring/ Summer 2008): 423–24.

We've lost him, surely: the only Joycean of the Western World. Zack wrote many books: his compendium of *Musical Allusions in the Works of James Joyce* (1974) is, with Ruth Bauerle's *Songbook*, the origin of all study of Joyce and music. *Ulysses* as a Comic Novel (1989) is the most compelling use of Bakhtin I know: when Zack Bowen spoke of the carnivalesque, he spoke authoritatively. *Bloom's Old Sweet Song* (1995), his marvelous set of essays on Joyce and music, has a hidden acrostic: he was the **B-O-S-S**, both as editor of the Florida James Joyce Series, a position he held from 1995 to 2004, and as the president of the International James Joyce Foundation from 1996 to 2000. His work on *Padraic Colum* (1970), *Mary Lavin* (1975), and the two cultures of *Science and Literature* (2001) established him as a polymath, writing freshly and fervently about subjects and writers who mattered to him, so that they could matter to us.

But he was more, far more, than the sum of his bibliographic parts. The tributes that flew around the Joycean circuits on the news of his death bear witness to a life well lived: he was the great connector, the person who created, as chair of the Department of English at the University of Miami from 1986 to 1996, what was arguably the greatest concentration of Joyceans in one department that the world will ever know. Testimonials on e-mail, on Facebook, in the *Miami Herald*, in the *Newestlatter*, speak of Zack Bowen having brought marriages together, lifting people from the depths of academic despair, setting right and sending forward career after career. He was, as Nicholas Fargnoli has said, "the most well-liked of all Joyceans"—and if all this is sounding a trifle Homeric, let me remind you of Zack's plenary lecture at the Trieste Symposium in 2002, "Plato, Homer, and Joyce: Involving Orientalism, a Smidgeon of Smut, and a Pinch of Perverse Egotism," in which Homer's "seamy epic" is revealed for the first time as the true source of Joyce's comic wisdom. My favorite memory of that symposium was the question time after Zack's talk, which swiftly descended into a careful cross-examination of Penelope's virtuous intentions, with interruptions from Fritz Senn, who wanted to know the score of the football match going on at the same time. As Zack said at the end of his talk, speaking of his hope for a solution to the riddles of *Finnegans Wake*, "Whatever that involves, I know in my heart and mind that it will be funny" (Bowen, "Plato, Homer, and Joyce" 64).

And funny he certainly was: I have a whole drawerful of his lyrics to comic songs that we did together. What songs they were! "Three Crumbs in the Bedsheets," with the chorus "Make it Bloom / Only Bloom / Make it Bloom." "Bloomusalem," set to the tune of "The Holy City," the finest bit of parodic writing I know. We sang duets together: Zack was the Don Giovanni to my Zerlina, the Donald Flanders to my Michael Swann, the Oliver Hardy to my Stan Laurel. That I was ever able to be a part of the great comedy act that is Joycean studies is entirely due to this wonderful man, whose personal generosity to me, as to everybody, was literally unbounded. Every highlight of my academic career can be in some direct way traced to something Zack Bowen did for me. And what is so stunning is that this is not in any way unusual: everyone who knew him was touched by the gift of his unconditional love.

Zack Bowen is one of very few Joyceans who will be remembered long after we are all gone, not just for his extraordinary scholarship—and there is abundant evidence of that—but because of his indispensable humanity. We are better people for having known him, and now our world—what Michael O'Shea calls "the Zack-less universe"—has become that much smaller. This is a very Ulyssean predicament. Give me the old world where men like Zack strode like giants, give me a world of gongs and trams, of music-hall turns and petticoats, of Roman candles and far-off trains, give me the empathy and hospitality of Leopold Bloom. All these things Zack loved, and we will always love him for it.

Zack was larger than life: one-time used car salesman, owner of houses on Key West and Martha's Vineyard, perennial carrier of a box of cherry cough drops, deliverer of performative gestures that only he could get away with: he was, one can say without exaggeration, the "Chairman of the Board." I have said many times that I would give a great deal to hear him sing "Our Way," his great defense of Leopold Bloom, sung in a beseeching tenor that burst its way through all your Puritanical reservations, one last time. He first sang it in a *Ratskeller* in Zürich at the Fifteenth International James Joyce Symposium in 1996, with me trying desperately to keep up on the keyboard. Here, by way of conclusion, is that perfect song. Who else but Zack would recognize the rhyme of "drooped" and "pooped" as precisely the right tone for the occasion? None of Gabriel Conroy's banquet indecision plagued him (*D* 179), nor did he recoil from indiscretion. If, like the Nymph of the Bath, you should blanch at words that are not in your dictionary (*U* 15.3279), you can always do as she did, and put your fingers in your ears. . . .

Leopold and Molly Discussing Closure with the Scholars
(sung to the tune of "My Way")

And now the dawn is come
And we have reached the final section,
Our struggle's not resolved
And life is nothing like perfection,

So now what can we do
To force a closure to this June day
Perversion's hardly new
And love's not our way.

We've had our share of sex,
Vicarious and narcissistic,
And thought of even more,
including straight and sodomistic,

It's late and we are pooped
And Bloom's erection's in a drooped way,
We offer only "yes":
Perplexing wordplay.

O there were times we think you knew
That you bit off more than you could chew
But through it all, the joy and gall,
Of fading news about it all,
To hear our call, and have a ball,
Discussing our way.

What does it mean to you
This orgasmic affirmation?
To fill your hollow lives
With memories of satiation?
Perhaps all you can do
Is symposiaze on what we did say
And earn your living through discussing our way.

For what are we? What have we got?
Some jingling quoits, a chamberpot,

To say the words we truly feel,
And nothing much, with sex appeal,
The record shows that no one knows
If we did it Our Way.

    (Bowen, "Our Way")

Notes

Introduction: The Centrifuge and the Outlaw

1. He's not the only one in mathematical difficulties: Bloom, like Sargent, is perplexed by algebra ("The figures whitened in his mind, unsolved"—*U* 4.141–42), and Stephen had his issues with the subject as a boy: "They had big voices and big boots and they studied trigonometry. That was very far away" (*P* 17).

2. *Bloody clouts*—"shows coyly her bloodied clout" (*U* 15.373); *perfumed handkerchiefs*—"Yes. That's her perfume" (*U* 13.1007); *burned kidneys*—"There's a smell of burn" (*U* 4.380); *lemon soap*—"Ah no, that's the soap" (*U* 13.1043); *soiled letters*—"to soil his letter in an unspeakable manner" (*U* 15.1071); *personal linen*—"wrong side up with care" (*U* 15.3288). The Nymph of the Bath is particularly upset about that last one.

3. "Fault," *n.*, 8a. *Oxford English Dictionary*. Online database accessed 11 Jun. 2015.

4. William Shakespeare, "Venus and Adonis" (11.692–94), qtd. in "Fault," *n.*, 8a. *Oxford English Dictionary*.

5. H. Wotton, *Reliquæ Wottonianæ*, 1626, qtd. in "Fault," *n.*, 8b. *Oxford English Dictionary*.

6. "With still greater impropriety," the phrase "at fault" is "frequently employed," sniffs Mr. Fitzedward Hall in the original *New English Dictionary*, "by American and occasionally by English writers in the sense of 'in fault,'" ("Fault," *n.*, 8c. *Oxford English Dictionary*).

7. See most recently James Alexander Fraser, *Joyce and Betrayal* (London: Palgrave, 2016).

8. Robert Spoo, "Injuries, Remedies, Moral Rights, and the Public Domain," *James Joyce Quarterly* 37 (Spring/Summer 2000): 333, qtd. in Goldman, ed., *Legal Joyce* 943. See also *Joyce and the Law*, ed. Jonathan Goldman (Gainesville: University Press of Florida, 2017).

9. *Don Giovanni*—"a cenar teco" (*U* 8.1080); *Zerlina*—"Voglio e non vorrei" (*U* 4.327); *Lazarus*—"And he came fifth and lost the job" (*U* 6.679); *Charles Stewart Parnell*—"Poor Parnell! he cried loudly. My dead king!" (*P* 39); *Icarus*—"Pater, ait" [Father, help me] (*U* 9.954).

10. See *James Joyce: The Complete Recordings*, ed. Marc Dachy, with an introduction by Eugene Jolas (Sub Rosa: Aural Documents SR60). Jolas' introduction is discussed further in chapter 5.

242 · Notes to Pages 8–13

11. This highly romanticized idea of objects having a moral life derives from Wordsworth's *Prelude*, to which Henry Adams' autobiography is greatly indebted: "To every natural form, rock, fruit or flower, / Even the loose stones that cover the highway, / I gave a moral life: I saw them feel" (Wordsworth, *Prelude*, Book III, qtd. in Dyer 115).

12. The spacing in the original typescript of "Sirens" (*JJA* 13:59) establishes that "Begin!" always ended the opening section rather than beginning a new one. In that typescript, the sizeable space between "Begin!" and the return of "Bronze by gold" contains the mysterious word "Chartrain," twice underlined (*JJA* 13:59). I had hoped that this would refer to the Chartres School of Neoplatonists, Macrobius and William of Conches among them, who held that a singing Siren was assigned to each of eight spheres, creating a single harmony, since that reading would support the argument for an octet in that episode (see chapter 6), but the word is disappointingly just a printer's signature. See Plato's *Republic* X.617b and E. Jeauneau, "Macrobe, Source du Platonisme Chartrain," *Studi Medievali* 3a, no. 1 (1960): 3–24, qtd. in Kupke 426.

13. Actually 32.174 ft/sec^2, but who's counting. This jocoserious equation of Joyce's Relative Centrifugal Force is offered in homage to Adams' similar effort in "Vis Nova": "The automobile alone could unite them in any reasonable sequence, and although the force of the automobile, for the purposes of a commercial traveller, seemed to have no relation whatever to the force that inspired a Gothic cathedral, the Virgin in the twelfth century would have guided and controlled both bag-man and architect, as she controlled the seeker of history. In his mind the problem offered itself as to Newton; it was a matter of mutual attraction, and he knew it, in his own case, to be a formula as precise as $s = \frac{g\,t^2}{2}$ if he could but experimentally prove it" (Adams 469). Please note that this chapter does not serve as an introduction to Joyce and physics: for discussions of chaos theory and quantum mechanics in Joyce, see Thomas Jackson Rice, *Joyce, Chaos, and Complexity*, Jeffrey S. Drouin, *James Joyce, Science, and Modernist Print Culture*, Michael Patrick Gillespie, *The Aesthetics of Chaos*, and Andrzej Duszenko, "The Joyce of Science: Quantum Physics in *Finnegans Wake*."

14. May Goulding's peculiar line, "More women than men in the world," mirrors Bloom's thoughts in "Hades": "One must outlive the other. Wise men say. There are more women than men in the world" (*U* 6.545–47). The two lines are parallactic, triangulating on the song from which the phrase is taken, "Three Women to Every Man" (Gifford 116), which raises the specter of outliving the dead.

15. The circulation of the florin through the waters of his work is the reason, perhaps, for Joyce's lowering the value of Bloom's contribution to civic finance from the half-crown (two-and-a-half shillings) originally in the Ithaca notesheets to a florin (two shillings): "LB put a marked ½ crown in circ." (*JJA* 12:72, see Herring, ed., *Notesheets* 427).

16. Joyce instructed his printer Darantiere to ink the period well: "un point bien visible" (*JJA* 21:140). The dot is missing or wrongly printed in some editions: see below, and Knowles, *Helix* 135.

17. The Great Exposition took place in 1900; Stephen's flight to Paris has been dated to 1903 (see Kenner, "The Date of Stephen's Flight," *Ulysses* 161–63).

18. W. B. Yeats, "Who Goes with Fergus," from which Stephen quotes at the end of "Circe": ".... shadows ... the woods / ... white breast ... dim sea" (*U* 15.4942–43).

19. McMorran goes further to suggest that the Romanic transliteration of Lobachevsky's name indicates that Joyce has read Poincaré in a 1905 translation by Walter Scott (McMorran 23).

20. The mark that can be either an *M* or a *D* on line 86 of the thirteenth page of the "Ithaca" notesheets (*JJA* 12:84, see Herring, ed., *Notesheets* 474) is decipherable as the latter, yielding the more plausible "Dilly," through comparison with Joyce's helpful alphabet cipher at the start of the notesheets for "Ithaca" (*JJA* 12:73). When writing at speed, as he presumably is in working out the reverse alphabet for the cryptogram in Bloom's drawer, Joyce makes a capital *D* that looks something like the letter scrawled after "curvature of spine" (*JJA* 12:84). Herring's misreading, if it is one, has also perplexed Drouin: "Euclidean space (empty, infinite, 'straight') is somehow contrasted with the curvature of Milly's spine" (Drouin 114).

21. See also "Thanks eversore much, Pointcarried!" in the geometry lesson from II.2 in *Finnegans Wake* (*FW* 304.05). McMorran also connects curvilinearity with "Penelope," which is meant to be "amplitudinously curvilinear" by comparison with the "mathematico-astronomico-physico-mechanico-geometrico-chemico" rectilinearity of "Ithaca": see Joyce's letter to Claud Sykes from Spring 1921 (*Letters* I:164, McMorran 115). For more on Joyce's investigations into non-Euclidean geometry, see Rice, *Chaos* 52–81.

22. "It looks to me rather better than Flaubert," says "one critic of international reputation" in the opening advertisement for *Ulysses* in the *Little Review* (March 1918): 3. This critic can be none other than Margaret Anderson's foreign editor Ezra Pound, who compares *Ulysses* to *Bouvard et Pécuchet* a few months later (*The Future* 2.6 [May 1918]).

23. See Stéphane Mallarmé's lament on the death of the penultimate in "Le Démon de l'Analogie" [The demon of analogy]: "*La Pénultième* [...] *Est morte*" (Mallarmé 93). In this prose poem, "*La Pénultième*" ends the verse and "*Est morte*" "detaches itself from the fateful suspension, trailing uselessly off into the void" (Mallarmé, trans. Henry Weinfield 93). For more on Mallarmé and the penultimate, see the discussion of solfège in chapter 6.

24. Plumtree's incompleteness theorem is a restatement of Zeno's arrow paradox, about which more in chapter 5; Gödel's incompleteness theorems, on the other hand, indicate the formal unprovability of recursive systems.

25. From Suzette Henke, *Joyce's Moraculous Sindbook*: many thanks to Alison Armstrong for bringing this to my attention. See also the recent study in Columbia's Modernist Latitudes Series by Nico Israel, *Spirals: The Whirled Image in Twentieth-Century Literature and Art* (2015).

26. Emerson actually tells his readers on "Self-Reliance" *not* to search beyond themselves, citing Beaumont and Fletcher: "*ne te quaesiveris extra*" (Emerson 127). But as I had occasion to tell the freshmen in 2005 in a convocation speech at OSU, "I'm here to tell you that Emerson was wrong."

Chapter 1. At Fault: What Joyce Can Teach Us about the Crisis of the Modern University

1. This essay, which was first given as the 2015 Carole and Gordon Segal Lecture at Northwestern University, owes a great debt to many people (see acknowledgments) but especially to both classes of English 368 during my time as the Carole and Gordon Segal Visiting Professor of Irish Literature at Northwestern in Spring 2015. Participating in *The Waste Land* Tour 2015 were Matt DeGregorio, Rebecca Ehlers, Charles Foster, Anna Luy Tan, Tiffany Sevilla, Xindi Song, Andréa Swanson, and Jack Wilson.

2. "[A] special plaster mix is poured into the skeleton's cavity and left to harden for 48 hours. [. . .] [S]cientists don't know what type of skeleton they've unearthed until the liquid plaster has hardened." Meg Weaver, "Human History on Display at Pompeii," http://intelligenttravel.nationalgeographic.com/2010/04/14/human_history_on_display_at_po/. Accessed 18 Apr. 2015.

3. In the case of the letters "I. H. S." Bloom has good reason for his confusion; "I. H. S." means neither of the two things he thinks it does but can actually mean at least two other things: "Iesus Hoc Salvator" and "In Hoc Signo." Just to muddy the waters still further, "I. H. S." can also be the first three letters of the Greek Christogram, "IHSOYS," while the Chi-Rho, a second image of Christ, was seen by Emperor Constantine before the Battle of Milvian Bridge in 312 C.E., leading to the phrase "In Hoc Signo Vinces" (By this sign we shall conquer). For more on this overdetermined crux, see the discussion of joke #5 in chapter 7.

4. "Reus" is the Latin for "guilty," as "actus reus" is a guilty act before the law, displaying "mens rea," or criminal intent. The apocalypse, as everyone from Hieronymus Bosch to Samuel Beckett knows, is not a separation of sheep and goats but a simple statement that we are all goats (or, at the very least, sheep who have gone astray). That's why everyone in the choir sounds so terrified when they sing the "Dies Irae," whether the *Requiem* is by Mozart, Berlioz, Verdi, or (perhaps especially) Benjamin Britten.

5. "An F sharp doesn't have to be considered in the mind; it is a direct hit." 1958 telecast qtd. in "An Affair to Remember," *Newsweek* 29 (Oct. 1990): 80.

6. I have omitted stanzas 4 and 9 in the discussion that follows. They read like this: Verse 4—"*The youth has knelt to tell his sins. / 'Nomine Dei,' the youth begins; / At 'Mea culpa' he beats his breast, / And in broken murmurs he speaks the rest*"; Verse 9—"*With fiery glare and with fury hoarse, / Instead of a blessing he breathed a curse: / "Twas a good thought, boy, to come here and shrive / For one short hour is your time to live'*" (Bauerle 270). Neither verse scans very well, and both first lines idly recycle text from the stanza preceding.

7. Variations in this part of the text include "Geneva barrack" (*U* 11.1131) for "*Geneva Barracks*," "was his body laid" (*U* 11.1131–32) for "*they have his body laid*," and "drop a tear" (*U* 11.1140) for "*shed a tear*."

8. Linda Gregerson acknowledges the work of the Spenserian critic Patricia Parker in this connection; Jorie Graham makes a similar point in *The Errancy* (Graham 112).

I am indebted to Jeremy Glazier for bringing these parallels to my attention. See also David Hayman, "Forms of Folly in Joyce: A Study of Clowning in *Ulysses*," *ELH* 34 (1967): 260–83.

9. See Andrew J. Mitchell, "Writing the Fortunate Fall: '*O felix culpa!*' in *Finnegans Wake*" (*James Joyce Quarterly* 47 [Summer 2010]: 589–606). The best statement of the virtue of error is found in Paul Proteus' letter in Kurt Vonnegut's *Player Piano*: "That there must be virtue in imperfection, for Man is imperfect, and Man is a creation of God. / "That there must be virtue in frailty, for Man is frail, and Man is a creation of God. / "That there must be virtue in inefficiency, for Man is inefficient, and Man is a creation of God. / "That there must be virtue in brilliance followed by stupidity, for Man is alternately brilliant and stupid, and Man is a creation of God" (Vonnegut 285–86).

10. This impressive salvo deliberately challenged its contemporary audience in several ways, not least with the musical selections from Wagner and Handel, and was very much against the isolationist sentiment of the time. Herbert Davis was also the editor of the Oxford English Novels, a Swiftian, and the instructor of a feared course in bibliography at Oxford in the 1950s that required all graduate students to manually typeset a page of print on the Clarendon Printing Press in his office on the corner of Broad Street.

11. Qtd. in Matthew Abraham, Rev. for *Portside*, 30 Mar. 2016, http://portside.org/2016-03-30/fall-faculty-rise-all-administrative-university. Accessed 22 May 2016. Jon Wiener supports this argument in *The Nation*, writing in May 2014 that the ratio of faculty appointments to administrative ones at Ohio State University from 2010 to 2012 was 45:670. See https://www.thenation.com/article/what-makes-ohio-state-most-unequal-public-university-america/. Accessed 31 Oct. 2016.

12. A case in point: during my brief tenure as chair of the department, a man of great learning was dismissed for saying the wrong thing. And then he died. Before he died I went to his bedside and sat with him, and his rabbi, and with another man, the husband of a dear friend in the Department of History. At his funeral the other man compared the three of us, each one of us who had come from our own place, to Job's three friends, Eliphaz the Temanite, Bildad the Shuhite, and Zophar the Naamathite, for we "had made an appointment together to come to mourn with him and to comfort him" (*The Book of Job* 2:11). His last message to me ended with the line "make it worth it." This book has been an attempt to make it worth it.

13. Lauren Berlant, says Rosalind Gill, "may be helpful [. . .] in showing how such passionate investment (e.g. in the myth of the academic good life) allows us to survive, whilst simultaneously making things worse" (Gill 241). Marina Warner cites Berlant's idea of "cruel optimism" in her essay, "Learning My Lesson" (qtd. in Warner 10).

14. Hannah Arendt's "The Crisis of Education" was published in 1954 but is still used as a guide to common sense in the classroom, for better or worse. Frank Donoghue's *The Last Professors* (Fordham, 2008) makes the case for alarming trends in the declining professoriate, and Nicholas Kristof writes frequently on this topic for the *New York*

Times. The topic has become fashionable in the mainstream press: see also Laura Kipnis, *Unwanted Advances* (2017).

15. One company who makes such baby helmets is called Thudguard©, who began copyrighting its name in 2001. The baby-helmet boom then almost exactly coincides with the age of the student population under review here.

16. John (Jay) Ellison, dean of students, The University of Chicago, letter to the incoming class of 2020. https://chicagomaroon.com/2016/08/24/university-to-freshmen-dont-expect-safe-spaces-or-trigger-warnings/. Accessed 29 Aug. 2016.

17. Jon Ronson, *So You've Been Publicly Shamed*, qtd. in the *New York Times Book Review*, 19 Apr. 2015: 13.

18. And as for following "Consider Yourself," from Carol Reed's film version of *Oliver Twist*, with "Every Sperm is Sacred," its most compelling parody, forget about it: you'd be run out of town. *Oliver Twist*, dir. Carol Reed (1968); *Monty Python's The Meaning of Life*, dir. Terry Jones (1983).

19. Schumacher from *Small Is Beautiful* again: "what do I miss by not knowing Shakespeare? Unless I get my understanding from another source, I simply miss my life" (Schumacher 80). Shakespeare reveals to us, this profoundly well-read economist tells us, "the *inner* development of man, showing the whole grandeur and misery of human existence" (Schumacher 80).

20. As Clive James writes, there is another criterion, for which Joyceans are perhaps better prepared than anyone: "Those who lack humor are without judgment and should be trusted with nothing" (qtd. in Martin Amis, rev. of *There Is Simply Too Much to Think About: Saul Bellow's Nonfiction, New York Times Book Review*, 27 Apr. 2015). See also Julianne Chiaet, "Reading Literary Fiction Improves Empathy," *Scientific American*, 4 Oct. 2013 (http://scientificamerican.com/article/novel-finding-reading-literary-fiction-improves-empathy). Accessed 7 Nov. 2016.

21. I have Enda Duffy to thank for this, an observation made in a Princeton Seminar back in 1985 and never forgotten.

22. Though the edition in the *Dial* and later versions (Eliot, *Poems* 58–59) have "ITS" for "IT'S," the discarded apostrophe is a transcription error. The typescript (*TWL* 18–20) and the first edition published by Boni and Liveright in 1922 (*TWL* 138–39) both clearly include the apostrophe each time the phrase appears. See Pichaske 151–63.

Chapter 2. Philatelic Joyce

1. "Philatelic Joyce," Joyce Society of New York, April 2007. This news was even more disappointing to the audience at Hamilton College later that year, who had gathered for a symposium in honor of Austin Briggs and heard another version of this talk. Many thanks to both audiences for helpful feedback, and especially to A. Nicholas Fargnoli and Austin Briggs.

2. Another literary figure in the history of the mail service is the inventor of the mailbox, Anthony Trollope, who appears quite naturally in the *Wake*, connected both to trollops ("mettrollops"—*FW* 582.34–35), "heliotrollops"—*FW* 603.28) and envelopes

("Not the phost of a nation. Nor by a long trollop. I just didn't have the time to. Saint Anthony Guide!"—*FW* 409.06–07). "Saint Anthony Guide," or "S.A.G.," is a stamped phrase a Catholic would put on the back of an envelope to send it safely on its way.

3. Thompson begins with a classically Joycean joke: "*Riddle*: What is it that the rich man puts in his pocket that the poor man throws away? / *Answer*: Snot" (Thompson 1). There is an excellent column on the idea of valuable rubbish by Patricia Yaeger, editor of *PMLA*: "The Death of Nature and the Apotheosis of Trash; or, Rubbish Ecology," *PMLA* 123 (March 2008): 321–39.

4. St. Magnus the Martyr is one of the nineteen city churches that the Bishop of London threatened to demolish in April 1920 ("April is the cruellest month"). Eliot responds to the proposed demolition as an act of violence, the final straw in the breakdown of aesthetic, secular, and sacred values following the war. To tear down a church, especially a church that he knows and loves, is a trampling of his own personal past and a desecration of the town of his poem. Far from being a poet of the fragment, as he is so often taken to be in his early work, Eliot in *The Waste Land* is a conservationist, an ordering force, a preserver of the past. The bishop's call for retrenchment was an unexpected consequence of the war, and of the influenza epidemic, and perhaps even of a loss of faith resulting from the ravages of both, though the bishop makes no reference to any of that, merely appointing a commission to inquire "into the circumstances of the ecclesiastical parishes and benefices within the City of London, and into the re-arrangements or re-grouping of parishes and benefices which might with advantage be promoted under the Union of Benefices Act, 1860, with or without the demolition of churches" (*Proposed Demolition* 3). The commission returned with the verdict that all the benefices and ecclesiastical parishes in the City be joined into four great parishes and that nineteen existing churches be removed. Six months later, in October 1920, the London County Council responded with an impassioned plea to save the London Nineteen. It is to this report that Eliot makes reference in his own notes to *The Waste Land*: "The interior of St. Magnus Martyr is to my mind one of the finest among Wren's interiors. See *The Proposed Demolition of Nineteen City Churches* (P. S. King and Son, Ltd.)" (Eliot, *Poems* 73). And if you were to follow Eliot's directions and consult this pamphlet, you would find that Eliot is actually correcting the views of G. Topham Forrest, the architect of the London County Council and coauthor of the *Proposed Demolition*, who, though he admires St. Magnus the Martyr as "one of the most beautiful of all Wren's works" (*Proposed Demolition* 18), finds the interior to be "disappointing," exhibiting "faults of design which are probably due to the restoration in 1760" (*Proposed Demolition* 19). Eliot will have none of this: no superlative is enough for the interior of St. Magnus the Martyr, because this is the object that Eliot's poem is explicitly attempting to save.

5. This is a rich site for further study, as note 4 above is intended to show. Another critic who has looked at modernism and material culture, with an eye to how objects transform over time, is Douglas Mao (*Solid Objects*). See also Vike Martina Plock's "'Object Lessons': Bloom and His Things," and Paul Saint-Amour, "Symbols and

Things." Not to be ignored is the seminal work of Angela Banner, *Ant and Bee and the ABC*, in this regard: when Ant and Bee go off in search of Bee's lost umbrella they fly over a billboard marked "Lost Things Saved in Boxes" (Banner 30–31). "Lost things saved in boxes": that's as good a description of modernism as any.

6. The church of St. Magnus the Martyr, oddly enough, originally held an "Inviolable splendour of *Corinthian* white and gold" (*TWL* 36, italics mine). Eliot was first remembering the wooden altar-piece, which has elaborate Corinthian columns, rather than the white and gold columns of the interior, which are indeed Ionic. When I mentioned this fascinating detail to the verger at Magnus Martyr (as Eliot called it), he demurred, saying that the president of Dulux Paints had been in for a funeral and roundly criticized Eliot for the final version of this famous line. "'White and gold is all wrong,' he said—'anyone can see that those columns are Grecian Grey.'"

7. Cf. Fritz Senn in *Joyce's Dislocations*: "Out of Bantam Lyons' unintelligible 'I'll risk it' at the end of Lotus Eaters (*U* 86 [5.541]), even the most perspicacious reader can make no sense, and fairly little out of 'Potato I have' (*U* 57 [4.73]). Such items [. . .] have to be kept in mind till further orders. That one central symbolic connection (by 'throwing together') should be built around variations of 'throw away,' reveals something about the method of com-position: nothing should ever be wasted in Joyce's ecological universe. A late paragraph in Ithaca recalls and assembles the various scattered elements in an exemplary nucleus of 'previous intimations' and delayed 'coincidences.' That Bloom and the reader had been tantalized by 'the language of prediction' (*U* 675.76 [17.322–41]) we learn as an *after*thought" (Senn 79–80, italics in original).

8. Samuel Beckett, "Dante . . . Bruno. Vico. . Joyce," in Beckett et al., *Our Exagmination* 14. See also "Translation as Approach," in Senn 1–23.

9. See Catherine Gubernatis, "All The World's In Want and Is Writing a Letters," a dissertation written under my direction on epistolarity in Joyce and the modernist period. Ph.D. dissertation, Ohio State University, 2007.

Chapter 3. *Finnegans Wake* for Dummies

1. "Running Out of Patience" was revived at the Cornell Joyce Conference in 2005, with the inestimable Blake Hobby, from the Department of Literature and Language at the University of North Carolina at Asheville, accompanying.

2. See Jerzy Kosinski, *Being There* (New York: Harcourt Brace Jovanovich, 1971) and *Being There*, dir. Hal Ashby, screenplay Kosinski (1979).

3. Thanks to the jeu d'esprit of Sean Latham, the editor of the *James Joyce Quarterly*, the original napkin is reproduced in the *James Joyce Quarterly*, where a version of this chapter was first published. See Sebastian D. G. Knowles, "*Finnegans Wake* for Dummies," *James Joyce Quarterly* 46 (Autumn 2008): 97–112.

4. *Popeye*—"popeyed" (*FW* 189.10); *King Kong*—"Kingable khan" (*FW* 32.02); *teddy*—"teddybearlined" (*FW* 208.17); *Kit Kat Club*—"kitcat" (*FW* 89.24); *Seabiscuit*—"Seabeastius" (*FW* 104.06); *No, No, Nanette*—"Nan Nan Nanetta" (*FW* 567.15); *Hell's Angels*—"Hillsengals" (*FW* 601.10); *Tweety Bird*—"twadgedy" (*FW* 61.07);

JFK—"hind the knoll" (*FW* 267.06). The students also found references to the following: *Hogwarts*—"hogwarts" (*FW* 296.19); *Tiger Woods*—"tigerwood" (*FW* 35.07); *Nike*—"Nike with your kickshoes on" (*FW* 270.24); *gameboy*—"Gameboy" (*FW* 451.24); *e-mail*—"Emailia" (*FW* 410.23); *bluetooth*—"bluetoothed" (*FW* 387.08); and *Google*—"googling" (*FW* 620.22). See chapter 8 for more on the connection between the Red Sox and *No, No, Nanette*. Regarding the assassination of JFK, Edmund Epstein points out as "meat for conspiracy theorists" that Lee Harvey Oswald was questioned by "an FBI agent named James Hosty Jr." (Edmund Epstein 291).

5. The map is reproduced as the back cover of the *James Joyce Quarterly* 46, no. 1 (Autumn 2008) with kind permission from Dr. Michael Meagher, associate professor and chair of Secondary Education at Brooklyn College, CUNY.

6. *Accepted as the easiest*: Glasheen xxxvii; *a good place to start*: Bishop, intro. xviii.

7. The legend for the cover of the *James Joyce Quarterly* reads: "The 'tunc' image is from the *Book of Kells Stained Glass Colouring Book*, Dover Press, 2006, with colors chosen by members of Sebastian Knowles's *Finnegans Wake* graduate seminar, Ohio State University, Spring 2004" (*James Joyce Quarterly* 46 [Autumn 2008]: frontispiece).

8. James Joyce, "From Work in Progress," *transatlantic review* 1 (Apr. 1924): 215–23.

9. The idea of reading *Finnegans Wake* in compositional order is suggested by Richard Brown in *James Joyce: A Post-Culturalist Perspective*. "Since the *Wake* is a snake with its tail in its mouth" (Richard Brown 106), an ouroboric approach to reading the book is called for: "By this means, in broad outline, the reader's experience of reading the book would follow Joyce's experience of writing it, with attention drawn to the early sketches that, with good Brunonian sense, Joyce incorporated at terminal points in the book. The search for meaning might be more closely tied to the genetic study that, with the *Wake*, so often accompanies it, giving the modern intentionalist critic a good grounding for his or her reading and allowing the narrative of the book to be realigned with the contexts in which it was produced" (Richard Brown 107).

Chapter 4. The True Story of Jumbo the Elephant

1. Satisfying except for the dropped *l* from "genteman" in the 1961 edition (*U-61* 333), a classic blunder in the "steelyrining" tradition (*U-61* 256). Bloom is nettled by a similar, but authorized, *l*-drop from the *Telegraph*'s funeral report: "L. Boom" (*U-61* 647, *U* 16.1262).

2. For someone who has spent the better part of two decades studying "Sirens," the question strikes a particular chord.

3. See Bowen, *Comic Novel* 18–19, and Bakhtin, *The Dialogic Imagination* 58.

4. Those who have been fortunate enough to visit the Jumbo Museum at Tufts University will be able to attest to the veracity of this observation: a copy of this photograph, along with other Jumbo memorabilia, is proudly displayed in Barnum Hall.

5. Austin Briggs reminds me that Carker is killed by a train in *Dombey and Son*, and in Mrs. Gaskell's *Cranford* a character is killed as he crosses the tracks, too absorbed in

reading *Pickwick* to notice the oncoming train. The St. Thomas train wreck of 1885 then joins a long literary line of tragic railway accidents, from Dombey to Dumbo to Duffy.

6. The name of the Grand Trunk Railway Line is nearly as good a joke as Lenehan's, though it can only be a cosmic accident. Barnum indulges in a similar pun in a letter to an unidentified correspondent of 7 March 1882: "All my thoughts & cares at present are locked up in two *trunks*—one of which belongs to Jumbo [. . .]" (Saxon, ed. 223).

7. Prior to its ill-fated move to Tufts College, Jumbo's hide was also exhibited at the American Museum of Natural History. Carl Akeley, a taxidermist there, was so appalled by the craftsmanship involved in Jumbo's preservation that he devoted his subsequent life to making improvements in the taxidermist's art. See Jay Kirk, *Kingdom under Glass: A Tale of Obsession, Adventure and One Man's Quest to Preserve the World's Great Animals* (New York: Holt, 2010). Thanks to Jeffrey Wood for bringing this to my attention.

8. From [H. G. Wells], *Boon*: "'It is a magnificent but painful hippopotamus resolved at any cost, even at the cost of its dignity, upon picking up a pea which has got into a corner of its den. Most things, it insists, are beyond it, but it can, at any rate, modestly, and with an artistic singleness of mind, pick up that pea' . . ." ([Wells] 110).

Chapter 5. Death by Gramophone

1. Sousa's dissatisfaction with the machine age is mirrored in E. M. Forster's 1909 dystopia, "The Machine Stops," written as a corrective to H. G. Wells (though in *Maurice*, written in 1913–1914, the pianola is received with Wellsian enthusiasm). One of the earliest supporters of the gramophone from the world of the arts was Sir Arthur Sullivan, who records on a private cylinder sent to Edison in 1888 a priceless assessment of the terrors and delights of the new Pandora's box: "For myself I can only say that I am astonished and somewhat terrified at the result of this evening's experiment. Astonished at the wonderful power you have developed, and terrified at the thought that so much bad music may be put on record forever. But all the same I think it is the most wonderful thing that I have ever experienced and I congratulate you with all my heart on this wonderful discovery" (*The Art of the Savoyard*, GEMM CD 9991).

2. For more on Paddy Dignam's reenactment of Little Nipper's recognition of his master's voice, see Thomas Jackson Rice, "His Master's Voice and Joyce," *Cannibal* 106–26, particularly for its connections to the great unsung novelist of the 1920s, Hugh Lofting.

3. This point is well made by Rice: "Ostensibly hailing the mass mechanical reproduction of art as the cultural equivalent and harbinger of the Marxist political evolution toward a classless society [. . .] Benjamin nonetheless mourns that which is lost through this leveling process. His word choice makes this sense of loss clear: 'Even the most perfect reproduction is *lacking*' in uniqueness and 'authenticity,' the original 'is always *depreciated*,' and the "'aura'" of the work of art 'withers'" (Rice, *Cannibal* 106, italics Rice's).

4. For Proust, the circumstances of war writing were different than for Joyce and Mann, in that the war thrust itself in on him as he wrote. *Swann's Way*, which was

completed before World War I, expresses the same technological horror as the other reactionary writers in this chapter: "How horrible! I exclaimed to myself. Can anyone find these motor-cars as elegant as the old carriage-and-pair?" (Proust 603–604).

5. Proust's sentence beautifully mirrors the mellifluous line of Chopin's right-hand melodies, which so often curve upon themselves in wilder and more time-defying arabesques, only to return with crystal precision to the place of origin: as the clauses build, it becomes clear that Proust is aspiring to the condition of music.

6. A parallel use of the gramophone as an Orpheus in an aboveground underworld is found in Peter Weir's *Gallipoli*, where an officer brings a portable gramophone to Suvla Bay and listens to the duet from *The Pearl Fishers* over a glass of wine as the shells burst in the night sky.

7. Much the same thing happened with e-mail, which began with a great deal of promise but soon degenerated into a curse and a snare. Compare also the initial enthusiasm for the CD, which helped put records out of business in the 1980s, only to see vinyl return with a vengeance thirty years later. In a crowning irony, the LP, that enemy of modernist authenticity, became identified with the organic infidelity it had worked so hard to suppress.

8. Frank Andrews, the man who discovered the photograph of the original painting in 1972, also makes this point: "the phonograph was the more likely instrument to reproduce an ordinary person's voice than the gramophone. For the dog to be listening to His Master's Voice on the gramophone it would require that either His Master was a recording artist or His Master had privately recorded his voice at a recording studio" (intro. to Petts 2). For more on the subject of Little Nipper's various incarnations, see Leonard Petts, "*Nipper,*" and Frederick Barnum, "*His Master's Voice" in America*. For more on the development of gramophones in general, see Timothy Fabrizio and George Paul, *The Talking Machine: An Illustrated Compendium: 1877–1929*.

9. The mulberry tree no longer exists: an attempt to uncover his remains from a parking lot in 1950 found only sheep bones (Petts 40, 55).

10. See also Gregory Castle, *Modernism and the Celtic Revival*. Isak Dinesen and Joseph Conrad present separate challenges to Rivers' claim: gramophones are introduced to a farm outside Nairobi and the Malay Archipelago in *Out of Africa* and *Almayer's Folly*, respectively, without any apparent negative side effects upon the indigenous population.

11. Each letter is dated by Eliot at the beginning of the text a month earlier: thus the December 1922 "London Letter" begins with the date "*November, 1922.*"

12. "The Possibility of a Poetic Drama," published in the *Dial* in November 1920, refers briefly to the music-hall comedian as the best hope for a new art form (Eliot, "Possibility" 447). "Extinction" is Eliot's own phrase (Eliot, "London," Apr. 1921: 453).

13. Eliot's idealization of the lower class has been usefully taken up by David Chinitz, Robert Crawford, and Amy Koritz, all of whom reach vastly different conclusions.

14. This kind of artistic slumming was a favorite aristocratic pastime. Arthur Symons wrote some dreadful poems about the music hall, and George Bernard Shaw

has a wonderful parody analysis of Lottie Collins' "Tara-ra-ra-boom-de-ay" in *Music in London*: "The dance refrain, with its three low kicks on 'Ta-ra-ra' and its high kick on 'Boom' (with *grosse caisse ad lib.*), is the simplest thing imaginable, and is taken in even a more deliberate *tempo* than the preceding verse." Shaw identifies the tune as "a configuration of the common major chord," found also in "the last movement of Mozart's finest pianoforte sonata in F, in the opening *allegro* of Beethoven's Septuor, and even in the first movement of Mendelssohn's Violin Concerto" (*Music in London*, 11 May 1892, qtd. in Green 52). See also David Deutsch, *British Literature and Classical Music: Cultural Contexts 1870–1945* (New York: Bloomsbury, 2015).

15. George Morris clearly identifies the primary source for this voice as Marie Larisch, who lived on the Starnbergersee and was in fact a cousin of Archduke Rudolph. But the well-read Marie, like the compound ghost in "Little Gidding," is "one and many" (Eliot, *Poems* 203). See Sebastian D. G. Knowles, "'Then You Wink the Other Eye': T. S. Eliot and the Music Hall," *ANQ* 11 (Autumn 1998): 20–32.

16. David Chinitz has brought to my attention the possibility that Marie Lloyd's arrival in New York City in 1913 may have inspired the turning of the key in "What the Thunder Said," for in Daniel Farson's *Marie Lloyd and Music Hall*, Lloyd is quoted as follows: "'I shall never forget my feelings when the key was turned on me at Ellis Island'" (qtd. in Farson 100).

17. This argument is also made by North, "The Dialect in/of Modernism," and Sanders, "*The Waste Land*: The Last Minstrel Show?"

18. A third song of Lloyd's with the loss-of-virginity-as-train-ride trope is "I've Never Lost My Last Train Yet" (Davison 106–07). "A Painful Case" similarly ends with a sexualized railway: the goods train is "like a worm with a fiery head," and we hear "the rhythm of the engine pounding" (*D* 113) in Mr. Duffy's ears.

19. In this way, with the deliberately obfuscating attempt at being academically helpful, Eliot is most nearly like Joyce. Compare "The collocation of these two representatives of eastern and western asceticism, as the culmination of this part of the poem, is not an accident" (Eliot, *Poems* 74) with "Megapenthus: the Cocklepicker" (*JJA* 12:174a).

20. Some versions of "Oh, the Moon Shines Bright" replace Charlie Chaplin and his boots with Mrs. Porter and her daughter. The rhyme of "water" and "daughter," interestingly, appears in another music-hall song that Eliot knew, "One-Eyed Riley," as sung in *The Cocktail Party* (Eliot, *Complete Poems and Plays* 309–10): the song is reproduced musically by Mary Trevelyan at the back of that book (Eliot, *Complete Poems and Plays* 388).

21. Though London in *The Waste Land* is three times called an "Unreal" City (*TWL* 136, 140, 145), it was as much a real city to Eliot as Dublin was to Joyce, and the text everywhere displays an easy familiarity with its surroundings. "The Fire Sermon," for instance, takes us on a river tour, "along the Strand" (by Waterloo Bridge) and "up Queen Victoria Street" (by Blackfriars, on the way to St. Paul's), past Mr. Eugenides, presumably still at the "Cannon Street Hotel" (the next bridge over, Southwark), down "Lower Thames Street," where there is a bar, a fishmarket, and a church (Old Billingsgate and

St. Magnus the Martyr, next to London Bridge), and then sweeping out with Elizabeth and Leicester "Down Greenwich reach / Past the Isle of Dogs" all the way to Margate Sands, where the last of the three maidens says, "I can connect / Nothing with nothing" (*TWL* 141–43). And all the while the river Thames carries the section: "Sweet Thames, run softly till I end my song" (*TWL* 140).

22. Also deleted from the version published in *Selected Essays* (Eliot, "Marie Lloyd," *Essays* 405–408) is an oblique reference to another of Marie Lloyd's songs: "The cage was open," says the reporter, "but the old cock linnet had flown" (qtd. in Eliot, "London," Dec. 1922: 660). The song is "Follow the Van" (Green 261); Eliot's image is further suggestive of "In the Cage," the original title of "A Game of Chess," in which the nightingale sings "'Jug Jug' to dirty ears" (*TWL* 11, 137).

23. Here one is reminded of Kittler's memorable remark about another typist of the modern period, Eliza Doolittle: "Women who have been subjected to phonographs and typewriters are souls no longer; they can only end up in musicals" (Kittler 27)—or, in Eliot's case, in a 433-line vaudeville act. Tiresias is the gramophone of the text: the prophet's voice sounds in the grooves, reduced to rigid quatrains, as mechanized and soulless as the scene he records.

24. Eliot wrote to Gilbert Seldes on 1 December 1922 that he was congratulated by a friend "a fortnight ago on having received the *Dial* prize" (Eliot, *Letters* 604).

25. Paula Marantz Cohen has traced much the same decline on the other side of the Atlantic in *Silent Film and the Triumph of the American Myth*. At the 1893 World's Columbian Exposition in Chicago, for instance, the featured acts included a fledgling Harry Houdini, Little Egypt the belly dancer, and the World's Congress of Beauties; by the time of Marie Lloyd's death in 1922, all these had been usurped by forms of mechanical reproduction: "The movies, which in 1893 were a mere technological curiosity tucked away on the other side of the Columbian Exposition, would come to dominate mass entertainment by 1920, appropriating the body for its own purposes and eventually usurping even Houdini, the consummate live performer of his age" (Cohen 46).

26. Bloom turns to Sir Robert Ball's description of parallax in desperation, as a way to push aside the thought of Boylan giving his wife a venereal disease: "Some chap with a dose burning him [. . .] Fascinating little book that is of sir Robert Ball's. Parallax" (*U* 8.101–110). Bloom's choice of adjective to describe Ball's *The Story of the Heavens*—"Fascinating"—directly recalls his previous rejection of Boylan's intrusion into his thoughts, when Boylan's straw hat is sighted from Corny Kelleher's funeral carriage: "Mr Bloom reviewed the nails of his left hand, then those of his right hand. The nails, yes. Is there anything more in him that they she sees? Fascination. Worst man in Dublin" (*U* 6.200–202). The two moments of Boylan-induced false fascination are then brought into parallax, a nail in the left hand ("Fascination") and a nail in the right ("Fascinating little book"). Furthermore, Bloom's fingernails stand in parallel with the stigmata of "Iron nails ran in" (*U* 5.374): Bloom has been nailed to Boylan's cross. See also "Parallax: The Text Asquint," in Knowles, *Helix* 8–11.

27. Charles Ives grumbles in a similar way to Constant Lambert and John Philip

Sousa in his *Memos*: he speaks of composers "copying down those slimy grooves and thinking they are creating something—helping music decline—dying—dying—dead" (Ives 136). To many modernists, the gramophone is an enemy because it represents mass culture: John Carey cites both Arnold Bennett's intellectual Matthew Park in "The Paper Cap," who "shrinks from mass vulgarity and gramophones," and George Orwell's extremely refined anti-intellectual George Bowling, equally disgusted by a childhood world that now "pulses with the din of gramophones" (John Carey, *Intellectuals* 157, 42). The most extreme form of gramophobia comes from the film comedian Karl Valentin, the Charlie Chaplin of Germany, whose *Im Schallplattenladen* [At the record shop] is quite literally a record-breaking film.

28. The French philosopher Jean-Marie Guyau wrote in 1880 of the parallels between the operation of memory and the operation of the gramophone, in that both are reproductions of analogous vibrations, concluding that the brain is "a conscious phonograph" (see Kittler 33). Kittler brilliantly connects this observation to Rilke's analogy of the needle on a recording cylinder with the coronal suture of the skull.

29. The pageant audience in *Between the Acts* understands that the gramophone is the enemy, as the church bell rings them out: "To return to the meaning—Are machines the devil, or do they introduce a discord . . . Ding dong, ding . . . by means of which we reach the final . . . Ding dong . . ." (Woolf, *Acts* 139–40). In *Three Guineas*, Woolf also compares the march to war to a broken record. Human nature, "like a gramophone whose needle has stuck" grinds out a familiar tune, reminding us incidentally of the burial site of Little Nipper: "'Here we go round the mulberry tree, the mulberry tree, the mulberry tree. Give it all to me, give it all to me, all to me. Three hundred millions spent upon war'" (Woolf, *Guineas* 59).

30. In the live reading of this section, which was originally given as an inaugural lecture at Ohio State University in 2000, I asked my then five-year-old daughter to close her eyes and shut her ears. Some moments in literature—"God damn you, you little bitch" (Greene 179), "Do it to Julia!" (Orwell 289), "Done because we are too menny" (Hardy, *Jude* 410)—are not for the ears of children.

31. "Full frequency range recording," or "*ffrr*," did not, however, make an appearance until after World War II. Decca's *ffrr* recordings are highly prized by vinyl enthusiasts for their striking realism: the recording method was a spin-off from a high-fidelity machine, known as a hydrophone, which was capable during the war of identifying individual German submarines by the frequency of their engine signal.

32. If the sixty-nine-year-old Krapp starts playing the tape at point A, and then cuts to points B, C, and D, in growing frustration, he then rewinds to a point in between C and D—call it C prime (C')—and plays the tape from there through point D to point E, which is nearly the end. Only after making his own tape for Box 9 does he return to the tape from Box 3, rewinding to yet another point between C and D (C double prime, or C") to hear the recording out to its final line (point F). These kinds of mental gymnastics are familiar to any reader who has spent time poring over the sucking stones in Molloy's pockets, or the permutations of ginger biscuits in *Murphy* (Beckett, *Murphy*

96). And these kinds of unexpected demands on an actor, who has suddenly to be aware of microseconds as the tape counter or other indicator flashes by, are also familiar to anyone who has tried to master the opening stage directions for Clov in *Endgame* or the hat trick in *Waiting for Godot*.

33. Compare also Alfred Jarry's poem to the phonograph: "They have taken my head, my head—and put me into a tea tin!" (qtd. in Kittler 28).

34. *Body electric*—Walt Whitman, *Leaves of Grass* 80; *filament of platinum*—Eliot, "Tradition and the Individual Talent," *Essays* 7; *radiant gist*—William Carlos Williams, *Paterson* 109; *metaphors for poetry*—W. B. Yeats, *A Vision* 8.

35. The new Mrs. Bundren is actually bringing a graphophone, a Columbia brand name originally coined by Alexander Graham Bell. As Cecelia Tichi points out in *Shifting Gears* (Tichi 37), Faulkner values the products of the machine age elsewhere in *As I Lay Dying*: Tull says that the brain is "like a piece of machinery [. . .] It's best when it all runs along the same" (Faulkner, *Dying* 71). But Mrs. Bundren's luggage bodes more ill for her new family.

Chapter 6. Siren Songs

1. Cf. Lewis and Short, "*taceo*," though the etymology from an Indo-European root is given as dubious. No etymology is provided for *sileo*, though there is an equivalent in Gothic, "silan."

2. Italics mine. Seamus Heaney translates this as "Gods who rule over souls! Shades who subsist / In the silence! Chaos and Phlegethon, O you hushed / Nocturnal expanses [. . .]" (Heaney, *Aeneid* 28–29).

3. The active erotics of silence are also in play, once again, in *Krapp's Last Tape*, in a reverie very similar to the Blooms' mutual recollections of the Hill of Howth. As Krapp remembers the woman in the punt opening her eyes to "Let me in," he pauses the tape and says, "Past midnight. Never knew such silence" (Beckett, *Krapp* 28). In this case, the recollection of earlier tranquility—"We lay there without moving" (Beckett, *Krapp* 27)—leads to a heightened emotion in the present. As with Mr. Duffy before the newspaper and Bloom before Rudy, Krapp utters his words *Secreto*: "*Pause. Krapp's lips move. No sound*" (Beckett, *Krapp* 28).

4. See also "goodbye sweetheart *sweet*heart he always sang it not like Bartell DArcy sweet *tart* goodbye" (*U* 18.1295–96).

5. "Silent, O Moyle!" is not usually glossed here: the more obvious reference to that song in *Ulysses* is "Lir's loneliest daughter" (*U* 9.314). Neither Don Gifford nor Zack Bowen considers the "silent roar" (*U* 11.936) to echo the roar of the Moyle, preferring to reinforce George Lidwell's connection to "What Are the Wild Waves Saying" (*U* 11.949, Gifford 305, Bowen, *Musical Allusions* 191).

6. *Do, Ben, Do*—11.39; *ray of hope*—11.710; *Sorrow from me*—11.673; *Far. Far*—11.1185; *That that was so*—11.817; *Sonnez la*—11.404; *a fulldrawn tea*—11.126; *Do, do*—11.993.

7. *Slog*—Dan: struck; *tittit*—Dan: peekaboo; *Unser*—Ger: our; *fort*—Ger: away; *forain*—Fr: open-air; *aude*—Lat: hear; *sluagh*—Ir: army. See McHugh 500–501.

8. "And then the garboard-strake began to leak. / The canned baked beans were only a putrid stench. / Two men came down with gleet" (*TWL* 57). Think of these lines the next time you say something unkind about Ezra Pound.

9. The caret before "quadrilinear" indicates a later insertion. Though the handwritten addition misspells "boustrophedontic" as "boustrephodontic," the errant vowel switch is corrected in all editions.

10. The rejection of semantic parallels between music and language is categorical for Jackendoff: "whatever music may 'mean,' it is in no sense comparable to linguistic meaning; there are no musical phenomena comparable to sense and reference in language, or to such semantic judgments as synonymy, analyticity, and entailment" (Lerdahl and Jackendoff 5). For more on the interplay between music and text in "Sirens," see Knowles, "Introduction," *Bronze by Gold* xxvii–xlii. The best work I have read on "*fuga per canonem*," Thomas Gurke's 2014 dissertation from Heinrich-Heine-Universität Düsseldorf, reads "*fuga*" as flight and puts "Sirens" through its rhetorical, mathematical, and philosophical paces to come up with a convincing case that Joyce is imitating musical affect. See Gurke, "*Fuga per canonem*: A Flight through the Canon; Music Aesthetics and Affect in James Joyce," Ph.D. dissertation, Heinrich-Heine-Universität Düsseldorf, 2014. The metaphor of the signal and the noise comes from Alex Ross, *The Rest Is Noise* (2008).

11. Another object in literal counterpoint in the episode is the actual counter from which Miss Kennedy transposes the teatray ("he banged on the counter his tray of chattering china. And /—There's your teas, he said. / Miss Kennedy with manners transposed the teatray down" (*U* 11.90–92), but this suggestion of a fugal countersubject is as much a tease as the teas themselves. See also Gurke 247.

12. Bloom remembers Martha's mistake—"Other world she wrote" (*U* 11.871)—as he tambourines with his fingers, writing that it is "utterl imposs" to write today (*U* 11.862), further combining his music and her text.

13. Joyce writes this letter on 6 August 1919, and an earlier one on 20 July 1919, in defense against Harriet Shaw Weaver's sense that "the episode seems to me not quite to reach your usual pitch of intensity" (qtd. in *JJ* 460). Like any fox when cornered, Joyce bares his teeth ("Since I wrote the *Sirens* I find it impossible to listen to music of any kind" / "the passages you allude to were not intended by me as recitative"—*Letters* I.129), but his Bach is worse than his bite.

14. For a fuller discussion of Bloom's final sound effect, see chapter 7. Liszt's Hungarian Rhapsody no. 2 has two additional distinctions: its enduring cultural relevance in accompanying Tom's pursuit of Jerry on Saturday morning cartoons and the fact that it is deliberately plagiarized in a song about plagiarism. Tom Lehrer's "Lobachevsky" turns to Liszt at the moment of the singer's theft of another's work: "And then I write / By morning, night / And afternoon, / And pretty soon / My name in Dnepropetrovsk is cursed, / When he finds out I publish first!" (Lehrer 48). This is the same Lobachevsky, of course, who makes his way via Poincaré into the "Ithaca" notesheets:

the paper plagiarized by the singer is on "analytic and algebraic topology of locally Euclidean metrization of infinitely differentiable Riemannian manifold[s]" (Lehrer 47).

15. Three notes are longer than a single line, accounting for the discrepancy in notes (59) and line numbers (62). For those following along in the 1961 edition, there are three fewer notes in that version. The corrected text puts "Imperthnthn thnthnthn" on its own line, as it does with "Horrid! And gold flushed more," "O rose! Castile," and "All gone. All fallen," adding four notes on that side. But in the 1961 edition, "Black. Deepsounding. Do, Ben, do" breaks in two after "Black" (*U-61* 256–57), bringing the total to fifty-six in that edition.

16. This section follows notes from a lecture/recital given in Dublin on 17 June 1992, with Zack Bowen (tenor), president, critic, page turner, and songwriter, and the author (bass) on keyboard. Its inspiration was the old LPs of Flanders and Swann; it will not escape students of Michael Flanders that there are several gambits here that have been lifted directly from *A Drop of a Hat*. Any parallels between the stately, plump Michael Flanders and his bluff and diffident accompanist Donald Swann and the comedy team of Bowen and Knowles are purely superficial.

17. See Heath Lees, who sets the opening line to *The Art of the Fugue* (Lees 47), and Margaret Rogers, who hears in the same line an E minor triad in second inversion: *B-E-G* (Rogers 15–18). Lees does usefully point out that "Sirens" originally opened with an acrostic that anagrammatizes the name of *The Art of the Fugue*'s composer, **B**ronze, **C**hips, **H**orrid, **A**nd (Lees 47), though the new line given to "**I**mperthnthn thnthnthn" (*U* 11.02) in the Gabler text bitches up this argument. Ebenezer Prout, the doyen of Novello Editors, had a useful sideline in setting lyrics to Bach Fugues: "Oranges, tomatoes, lemons and potatoes" went one familiar theme (the second phrase of the Little Fugue in G minor, BWV 578), "Oh Ebenezer Prout, you are a funny man / You make Bach Fugues as funny as you can" was another (the opening phrase of the "Great" Fugue in G minor, BWV 542). I suppose he's the *fons et origo* of my obsession with words and music.

18. Ruth Bauerle's invaluable collection, *The James Joyce Songbook*, is the source for all of the song lyrics printed in these pages and performed in the recital version.

19. For more on Dolores, and on her possible connections with Swinburne, see Crumb 239–45.

20. "[D]oth" is also switched out for "*did*": as with "*seas*" for "*sea*" and "*O*" for "*Oh*" in "The Shade of the Palm," this is another trivial adjustment that Joyce makes to his song texts in "Sirens."

21. Friedrich von Flotow, "M'appari," *Martha*, in Bauerle 399–403. English words by Charles Jeffrys. There are as many different versions of the words as there are editions; this text is particularly corrupt, with variant spellings of "graceful," and what can only be generously described as vocal punctuation.

22. James Joyce, Letter to Harriet Shaw Weaver, 1 May 1925 (*Letters* III.120). Morel began his translation of "Sirens" four years earlier: on 3 April 1921 Joyce wrote to Weaver

that "About a week ago Mr Auguste Morel took *The Sirens* to translate for a French review" (*Letters* I.161). Nevertheless, Ellmann writes that the late request was "Presumably to help Morel with the translation of the *Sirens* episode" (*Letters* III.120n).

23. From Joseph Prescott, "James Joyce's ULYSSES as a Work in Progress," qtd. in Bowen, *Musical Allusions* 354. It is surely irrelevant that the name of a third tenor, the lead singer of the "Commodores," is also concealed in this progression.

24. Lady Harriet and Nancy are then shades of Mrs. Bellingham and Mary Driscoll in "Circe." The counterassaulting chambermaid—"I had more respect for the scour-ingbrush, so I had" (*U* 15.892)—is connected to Mrs. Bellingham not only by virtue of appearing together at Bloom's trial but also by vice—as Sousa would say—of originally appearing in nineteenth-century sado-masochistic soft pornography. Mrs. Bellingham as "a Venus in furs" (*U* 15.1045–46) takes us to Leopold von Sacher-Masoch, and Mary Driscoll leads us to *The Way of a Man with a Maid*. Bloom refers to this latter book in "Sirens"—"Better give way only half way the way of a man with a maid" (*U* 11.1191–92)—immediately after "The Last Rose of Summer" appears in the barroom conversation.

25. Hübner speaks particularly of occasions when the musical rhythm serves to underscore the dramatic situation, listing examples as follows: "'Vornehme Langeweile' (wiegendwohlklingende, einförmige 6/8-Melodie); der eitle Nichtstuer Lord Tristran (bombastisch grotesker Marsch); 'Spinnrad' (schnurrendes Motiv); das hurtige Treiben und das Durcheinanderschnattern der Mägde auf dem Markt (Jagdmusik); die 'Verlobung' des Buffopaares (mit einer altväterlich gezierten Gavotte beginnend) und vieles andere" ["noble tedium" (mostly melodic, uniformly 6/8), the idle wastrel Lord Tristran (bombastic grotesque march), "spinning wheel" (purring theme), the nimble movement and chatter of the maids at the market (hunt music), the "engagement" of the *buffo* couple (with a tender baroque Gavotte) and many others] (Hübner 619).

26. Franz Schubert, "Gretchen am Spinnrade," words by Johann Wolfgang von Goethe, in *Goethe-Lieder* 12–21. What Wilhelm Hübner calls the "schnurrendes Motiv" [purring theme] (Hübner 619) is a familiar trope for female sexuality, as in the magic web of the Lady of Shalott and pre-Raphaelite paintings of her. Roland Barthes remarks of Schubert's song in *The Responsibility of Forms* that "his first great song, *Gretchen at the Spinning Wheel*, utters the tumult of absence, the hallucination of the return" (Barthes, *Responsibility* 289). The "hallucination of the return" is precisely the tumult at the heart of Rudy's reappearance, the return of Stephen's mother and Bloom's father, and the botched and thwarted reunion between the three protagonists at the book's close. Barthes is more clearly Joycean, in Richard Howard's translation, when discussing Gretchen in *A Lover's Discourse*: "the Spinning Songs express both immobility (by the hum of the Wheel) and absence (far away, rhythms of travel, sea surges, cavalcades)" (Barthes, *Discourse* 14). The only other place where "sea surges" and "cavalcades" go side by side is "Sirens," which expresses both "immobility" (Bloom is unable to return home during the episode) and "absence" ("Sirens" acts as a cover for the book's most absent scene).

27. The words of this sentence have been set to the beginning of Schubert's "Gretchen am Spinnrade": see Knowles, "That Form Endearing" 221.

28. The score is from Flotow, act III. The musical text in figure 6.3 differs from Glover's version, printed in *The James Joyce Songbook*, in several respects. First, it is in F, the actual key of the performance, rather than D, the key in which Dedalus first plays the song. Second, it is a piano reduction of the full orchestral score rather than an arrangement for drawing-room piano; Flotow's introduction foreshadows the modulation in "*But, alas!' twas idle dreaming*," and has a long-drawn line on solo winds that Glover replaces with a breathless pause. Glover's version is the one heard on most recordings of the piece made for Joycean purposes, perhaps because it is easier to sing. I have amended the syllabification of the text printed here in order to bring it into line with the English translation. The English translation is as printed earlier (see earlier discussion for variant spellings). For the musical examples in figure 6.3, the 1961 edition of Joyce's text is preferred (*U-61* 273–76): significant differences between editions are discussed in the notes.

29. "Piano again" is a reprise of a reprise: just before Dedalus is urged to perform, Bloom thinks "Piano again. Cowley it is" (*U* 11.573). "Stopped again" similarly recalls Cowley's truncated performance of "Love and War": "Bad breath he has, poor chap. Stopped" (*U* 11.561). "Tuned probably" anticipates the coming of the blind stripling, and "than last time I heard" is an advance warning of the words of the coming song. The musical narrator (A_1) scavenges this line from Bloom (T_2) later with "sorrow from them each seemed to from both depart when first they heard" (*U* 11.677–78).

30. If Cowley is playing during the persuading of Dedalus, then Simon's speech can be usefully considered a form of recitative; Cowley presumably knows that is easier to convince reluctant singers with the music rolling. "If you will lend me your attention" is possibly a gloss on "If you give me your attention I will tell you what I am," King Gama's song in Gilbert and Sullivan's *Princess Ida*. If so, this is the only identified reference to *Princess Ida* in Joyce's works.

31. "Harping" presumably refers to the arpeggiated accompaniment in the strings, played by the left hand in measures 1–7 and by the right hand from measure 17 (the English word "bar" for "measure" is of course far more appropriate here in the Ormond Hotel saloon). The "chord longdrawn," broken off in Glover's version, is the C_7 chord held in measures 15–16.

32. I take "human" here to be a separate noun rather than an adjective qualifying "heart," allowing all six parts of the body to be represented in the F major chord, repeated exactly six times from measures 17–22.

33. The leaves can be heard falling in the melody in measures 23–24, as marked in the musical example. "[S]trings" and "reeds" refer to the original orchestral accompaniment, and "troubled double" refers to the doubling of the bass note in the octave.

34. This elastic band, lashing Odysseus to the mast next to the deaf waiter, establishes "M'appari" as the central Siren song in *Ulysses*. "Fourfold" may show Bloom's awareness of Flotow's use of the four-measure phrase throughout the piece.

35. Note the anagram ("to flow") of the composer here. The flow is Martha Clifford's flower that consoles Henry Flower ("Flower to console me and a pin cuts lo. Means something, language of flow"—*U* 11.297–98), the flow of language, the opening of the sexual floodgates in this paragraph, and Flotow himself. Thoughts are moving rapidly in this section—the whole section from "Glorious tone" to "Language of love" (*U* 11.695–709) takes place in the timespan of three measures (measures 44–46), during which the singer also experiences a sensation of *durée*: "*And the dream too soon hath flown.*" Taking the "fuga" of *fuga per canonem* to mean flight, as Thomas Gurke does, this is the moment when the text begins to achieve lift-off.

36. According to Mabel Worthington, this may possibly be an allusion to the fairies "Tripping hither, tripping thither" in Gilbert and Sullivan's *Iolanthe* (Worthington 212). The text looks forward to *Finnegans Wake* here: "The joy the feel the warm the" (*U* 11.707–08) anticipates the cadence of "A way a lone a last a loved a long the" (*FW* 628.15–16). Love, music, and language join hands in this paragraph, becoming the three Graces of the Joycean world: *Finnegans Wake* continues their dance.

37. In performance of this woven text, the transition from the sung "*ray of hope*" to the spoken "Beaming" at measure 48 is an enormous fall. But the word in the song is actually "gleaming": either Dedalus or Bloom is getting it wrong. Neither is it clear why Bloom should have criticized Dedalus for "Singing wrong words" (*U* 11.696) earlier—all the italicized words in the section are in standard translations of the text, except for the extra "*Ah*" in "*Ah, Martha!*" (*U* 11.735), which he hasn't heard yet.

38. In measures 49–53 the text opens to meet the music: "squeak scarcely hear so ladylike the muse unsqueaked" (*U* 11.711–12) is in direct metrical parallel with the dotted rhythms of the song. The correction of "ray of hope" to "ray of hopk" is one of the least satisfying emendations in the Gabler edition: *U-61* has "unsqueaked a ray of hope" (*U-61* 275), as given in the musical example, and both the manuscript and the typescript have "unsqueaked a cork" (Rosenbach P263–64 L353–54 N274–75, *JJA* 13:70). The change from "unsqueaked a cork" to "unsqueaked a ray of hopk" is made between the first and second page proofs (*JJA* 24:191, 207). Besides concealing the unscrewed cork, "hopk" may anticipate Bloom's difficulties with the burgundy and cast a glance at the master of sprung rhythm, Gerard Manley Hopkins.

39. Both the text and the song stop dead on the word "Coincidence" (*U* 11.713), just as Bloom registers the name of the opera and Lionel registers his fall from grace, sliding slowly in measures 53–54 from a G, the fifth in a C_7 chord, to a $G^\sharp$, the leading tone for the third in a return to F major.

40. As in a game of "Musical chairs" (*U* 11.726), the music here changes abruptly, the first indication that the second verse will be different from the first as the left-hand chords wind downward (measures 63–66). This is a "Quick round" (*U* 11.726), in that the gap between the two moments of sung text is just three measures (measures 68–70), during which the entire memory of Bloom's first meeting with Molly is replayed in his mind.

41. "Lioneleness" is another anagram, this time of "loneliness" (*U* 11.738). Note also the use of the dominant (C major) in measure 76, exactly when Bloom thinks of Lionel's cry as "dominant to love" (*U* 11.736–37), and the deepening/rising chord progression of measures 69–77. The "Ah" of "Ah, alluring" (T₂) forces its way into Simon's singing (S₁): there is no "Ah" in Flotow's text at this point. "Ah" comes later with the high A at measure 87. "Here there try there here all try where" (*U* 11.739) fits exactly into the blocked chords of measures 70–77, as indicated here.

42. Joyce's added hyphen ("la-amp") by the time the word reaches the placards (*JJA* 18:111) may in this case be evidence of little more than frustration with the failure of the printer to realize his intentions.

43. In the typescript, the comma of the second line was dropped for good, leaving the first comma to dangle by itself all the way into the 1990 edition. The three dots, originally an afterthought as the struck exclamation point suggests, were then removed from "*Come . . . !*," never to return until the corrected text, and a total of seven dots were added after "endlessnessnessness" (*JJA* 13:71), of which only three remained in *U*-61 (276) until all seven were fully restored by Gabler. By the first version of the page proofs, in September 1921, the second *o* of "*Co-ome*" had been lost (*JJA* 24:192), as had been the case earlier for the second *a* of "la-amp" (*JJA* 18:111).

44. Though there are no handwritten corrections to the first page proof of this section of "Sirens" (*JJA* 24:192), comparison with the second page proof (*JJA* 24:208) indicates the two changes recorded here. "In cry of passion" is reinserted in the second page proof by hand, since the phrase was accidentally dropped from the first page proof. The repetition of the word "chords" is struck at the next iteration, and "martha" is recapitalized (*JJA* 24:224); both corrections are ignored by the Gabler edition. The repeated word "chords" is the result of a typescript error: "rising chords" ends one page and "chords of harmony" begins the following one (*JJA* 13:70–71).

Chapter 7. Seeing the Joe Miller

1. See Knowles, "Introduction," in Knowles, Lernout, and McCourt, eds., *Joyce in Trieste: An Album of Risky Readings* 1–9.

2. You don't think *langue* is the right word? How can you be Saussure?

3. The man with the Macintosh was Michael Groden; no one has done more than Groden to take advantage of the possibilities of the digital media in advancing the study of Joyce's work. See also chapter 9.

4. The real author of the original *Joe Miller's Jests* (1739) was John Mottley: the book came out after the eponymous comedian's death in 1738, adding jokes with every new edition. By the eighth edition, in 1745, the number of jokes had more than doubled from the original 247 (Hutchinson xv): like Dublin, it is "doublin [its] mumper all the time" (*FW* 3.08–09). The 1865 edition, which became the standard for nearly fifty years, contained 1,286 jests; by 1903, when a bumper edition was released in America, the book was nearly as long as *Ulysses* (Hutchinson xv).

5. There is a grand tradition of nonlimericks. One of the very best examples of this deservedly obscure genre is as follows:

There was a young man from Dundee,
Who was horribly stung by a wasp.
When asked, "Does it hurt?"
He replied, "No it doesn't,
I'm so glad that it wasn't a hornet!"

There is also the nonpalindrome, two examples of which should suffice:

Able was I ere I saw . . . Albuquerque Zoo.
Madam, I'm . . . not Merle much.

Freud classifies these frustrations of conceptual expectations as "nonsense jokes" and gives a particularly illustrative example: "'Life is a suspension bridge,' said one man.— 'Why is that?' asked the other.—'How should *I* know?' was the reply" (Freud 139). This excellent nonjoke makes an interesting comparison to Stephen's joke about the Kingstown pier as a "disappointed bridge" (*U* 2.39), about which more in a moment.

6. "Old Ollebo, M. P." is a nonanagram, missing an *o*, as "Bollopedoom" (*U* 17.408), the even worse attempt that immediately precedes it, is missing an *l*. The cryptogram is meant to be "boustrophedon[t]ic" (*U* 17.1800), but the last line fails to go from back to front as it should if it were following the path of an ox plowing a field (see Knowles, *Helix* 19–23 for more on the dropped *t* from "boustrophendontic" [*U-61* 721] and other matters relating to the Dolphin's Barn cryptogram). "Meatpot" and "Plumtree" are first anagrammatized into the legitimate "Peatmot" and "Trumplee," but then degenerate into the bastard forms "Moutpat. Plamtroo" (*U* 17.604–05). All of these are examples of the deliberately flawed language games in *Ulysses*.

7. Kenner ends with the hope that "Eventually we may be finding Stephen comic also" (Kenner, "Comedian" 194)—but Roy Gottfried had already done so in *Joyce's Comic Portrait* (2000), a much-needed restoration of the principles of comedy to what is too often read as a dour and unfunny book. Gottfried points out that the word "laughter" appears in some form in *Portrait* "more than eighty times" (Gottfried, *Comic Portrait* 14) and reminds us of Moynihan's immortal remark, following from the lecturer's allusion to *The Mikado*: "What price ellipsoidal balls! Chase me, ladies, I'm in the cavalry" (Gottfried, *Comic Portrait* 4, *P* 192). The line "ran like a gust through the cloister of Stephen's mind" (*P* 192): following the neural analogy, the "cloister" is the left posterior temporal lobe, which cloisters our stored expectations, as too many lifeless readings of Dedalus' world have cloistered our sense of the brightness and gaiety of *A Portrait of the Artist as a Young Man*.

8. "What is wit?" is one of the most dreaded questions at any graduate student's general examination: having fluffed this question horribly at my generals (the answer is found in Pope's "Essay on Criticism"), I asked the same question to an unsuspecting

graduate student of my own. His memorable (and witty) answer was "the opposite of what's happening now."

9. "Before I go on with this short history, let me make a general observation—the test of a first-rate intelligence is the ability to hold two opposed ideas in the mind at the same time, and still retain the ability to function" (Fitzgerald, "The Crack-Up" 69). Truer words were never spoken.

10. See Knowles, *Helix* 6, for possible answers to these and other insoluble puzzles in *Ulysses*.

11. Continuing the *Hamlet* parallel, Stephen's sally mirrors the play on "offence" in the Queen's closet: "*Queen*: Hamlet, thou hast thy father much offended. / *Ham.*: Mother, you have my father much offended" (III.iv.09–10).

12. See Freud, *Jokes and Their Relation to the Unconscious*, especially section V (The Motives of Jokes—Jokes as a Social Process).

13. Margaret Atwood follows this reasoning in *Oryx and Crake*—the designer of a new utopian life-form realizes that all jokes are malicious and writes them out of his program: "For jokes you need a certain edge, a little malice. It took a lot of trial and error and we're still testing, but I think we've managed to do away with jokes" (Atwood 306). See also Hamlet's throwaway as he watches *The Mousetrap*: "poison in jest—no offence i' th' world" (III.ii.234–35). The relative benignity of "The Owl and the Pussycat" and the complete works of P. G. Wodehouse may suggest another line of argument, but the malice that Koestler and others require is still there in a more innocent form: Bertie Wooster and Edward Lear engage in prolonged pillow fights with their chief adversaries, order and language. (And anyone who thinks that pillow fights are entirely innocent hasn't had brothers.)

14. Joyce is reported to have said to Frank Budgen, "The Holy Roman Catholic Apostolic Church was built on a pun. It ought to be good enough for me" (qtd. in *JJ* 546). Beckett ascribes to a similar logotheology: Murphy says, "In the beginning was the pun." Murphy gives a "clonic" example of the genre, containing four alcoholic puns: "'Why did the barmaid champagne?' [. . .] 'Because the stout porter bitter'" (Beckett, *Murphy* 65, 139). See also "the uncondensed milky way" (*U* 17.1044) and "who precisely wrote them like *Hamlet* and Bacon" (*U* 16.783), two absolute corkers in the Joycean collection.

15. "Stately" is a word of art and attitude, describing bearing; "plump" is a word of the flesh, describing a waistline. There is a long tradition in Joycean scholarship that considers these words to be essentially contradictory, a tradition that Bowen recounts and to which he provides a classic rejoinder: "In the mind of imposing, corpulent Zack Bowen, there has never been the least contradiction, tension, or ambiguity between two terms that to normal people should follow as night after evening" (Bowen, *Comic Novel* 115).

16. One of the funniest jokes in "Circe," for those with a particularly depraved sense of humor, takes place during Bloom's political campaign: "(*he takes part in a stomach race*

with elderly male and female cripples) Come on, boys! Wriggle it, girls!" (*U* 15.1613–15). This sick joke may appear to be directed at the disabled, but the real targets are Bloom, Parnell, and all people running for political office at all periods in human history.

17. The wordplay joke is everywhere in *Joe Miller's Jests*, of course—here's a Joycean example of the genre, which like Bloom's Lazarus joke also has a brush with death as its theme:

> #599. Two gentlemen were walking in the High Street, Southampton, one day, about that hour which the industrious damsels of the mop and brush usually devote to cleansing the pavement before the door. It happened that the bucket used upon such occasions was upon the stones, and one of the gentlemen stumbled against it. My dear friend, exclaimed the other, I lament your death exceedingly! My death! Yes, you have just kicked the bucket. Not so, rejoined his friend, I have only turned a little pale. (Bellew 122)

Since it's possible that his readers missed the punchline, the editor thoughtfully adds "(pail)" at the end of the joke.

18. Individual letters receiving particular discussion in *At Fault* have been indexed separately for convenience. For more on this kind of thing, see Roy Gottfried, *Joyce's Iritis and the Irritated Text*.

Chapter 8. Performing Issy

1. Though this has not been our general practice, the first three episodes and the second three episodes may also be read simultaneously, each pair starting at the same time in two different rooms, to tighten the parallax between Stephen and Bloom.

2. When students came to the house in the spring of 2016 to read "Circe," we were chanting, "Htengier Tnetopinmo Dog Drol eht rof, Aiulella!" (*U* 15.4708) in unison as my son came back from his soccer game. "Is this some kind of cult?" he asked, and of course he was right.

3. See the final line of Eliot's poem "The *Boston Evening Transcript*": "Cousin Harriet, here is the *Boston Evening Transcript*" (Eliot, *Poems* 20). Tindall identifies "another heily innocent and beachwalker" (*FW* 110.35–36) as J. Alfred Prufrock and finds in "euchring the finding of the Ardagh chalice" (*FW* 110.34–35) a reference to Madame Sosostris and the Holy Grail (Tindall 102).

4. For those keeping score at home, the innings played are as follows:

Top of 1st–*FW* 260	Bottom of 1st–*FW* 261
Top of 2nd–*FW* 262	Bottom of 2nd–*FW* 263
Top of 3rd–*FW* 264	Bottom of 3rd–*FW* 265
Top of 4th–*FW* 266	Bottom of 4th–*FW* 267
Top of 5th–*FW* 268	Bottom of 5th–*FW* 269
Top of 6th–*FW* 270	Bottom of 6th–*FW* 271
Top of 7th–*FW* 272	Bottom of 7th–*FW* 273

Top of 8th–*FW* 274	Bottom of 8th–*FW* 275
Top of 9th–*FW* 276	Bottom of 9th–*FW* 277
Top of 10th–*FW* 278	Bottom of 10th–*FW* 279

5. Though night baseball games were held under artificial illumination in the 1880s, the first floodlit game, between the Reds and the Phillies, did not take place until May 1935. The term "Night Baseball" is also a kind of stud poker with an absurd number of wild cards in the deck.

6. I owe a considerable debt of gratitude to John Gordon, who read this piece in an earlier version, identified the split-fingered fastball, and pointed out the many other places where I was "obviously off-base." Other efforts to link Joyce to baseball include Kenneth Lash, "Finnegan Wakes at Yankee Stageum," *New Yorker*, 9 Apr. 1984: 41, and the cover of the *James Joyce Quarterly* 20 (Spring 1983), which has a mash-up of Joyce in a catcher's uniform and the anonymous byline: "James JOKER JOYCE played for the Philadelphia Phinnegans and the Washington Wakes. A blazing punner, he would often stretch an ordinary single into a Dublin."

7. The Brooklyn Dodgers were originally known as the Trolley Dodgers, something that Bloom must do in Nighttown: "Close shave that but cured the stitch" (*U* 15.199). Complicating the argument that the Red Sox represent the evil empire are two factors: 1) that the Yankees currently own that distinction, and 2) that the Red Sox have been historically associated with the Irish Catholic population of Charlestown, Dorchester, and the South End of Boston, and so make for unlikely redcoats.

8. See Dan Shaughnessy, *The Curse of the Bambino*. Though the financing of *No, No, Nanette* is generally held responsible for the sale of the "bombinubble puzzo" (*FW* 181.11), the blame lies with the stage play on which that musical was based, *My Lady Friends*: *No, No, Nanette* was actually a hit.

9. Though this be madness, yet there is method in it. "All the world" (*FW* 274.n4) gives us Shakespeare via "All the world's a stage" (*As You Like It* II.vii.139), and "jelly" (*FW* 274.n4) can only refer to Cornwall's description of Gloucester's gouged-out eyes: "Out, vil[e] jelly!" (*King Lear* III.vii.83). "Bare forked animal" is reached via "*Shakefork*" (*FW* 274.L4) and is Lear's description of Edgar reduced to nothing on the heath (*King Lear* III.iv.107–108).

10. "[T]he diminitive that chafes our ends" (*FW* 278.n1) takes us to Shakespeare again: "There's a divinity that shapes our ends, / Rough-hew them how we will" (*Hamlet* V.ii.10–11). This may be an early reference to the hedge clipping that became necessary in the Wrigley outfield after the growth of the ivy-covered wall (see note on "out of left field" below).

11. "For this relief much thanks. In *Hamlet* that is" (*U* 13.939–40), thinks Bloom after the fireworks. Shakespeare's line originally referred to a player coming on in early relief, as Francisco is relieved by Barnardo (who, incidentally, has struck out twelve): "*Bar.:*' Tis now str[uc]k twel[ve]. Get thee to bed, Francisco. / *Fran.*: For this relief much thanks" (*Hamlet* I.i.07–08).

12. "1918 Spring Training." http://www.1918redsox.com/games/0407.htm. Accessed 9 Sept. 2016.

13. The distinction between "out in left field" (locative) and "out of left field" (ablative of origin) is instructive here. The former means "certifiable" or out of touch with reality; the latter means "zany" or unexpected. Cook County hospital was behind left field at the first home of the Chicago Cubs, from which inmates could be heard yelling things at the players, leading to the phrase "way out in left field"; a throw that comes from the wide expanse of the left fielder's territory ("out of left field") still finds its target, coming as a surprise. See William Safire, "Word-Watchers At Work," *New York Times*, 10 May 1981.

14. See Derrida, "Plato's Pharmacy," *Dissemination* 63. Roland Barthes' term for the holographic nature of musical meaning, *"signifiance,"* also captures Joyce's idea of middle as muddle, and word as woid: "By music we better understand the Text as *signifying* [*signifiance*]" (Barthes, *Responsibility* 312, editorial brackets in original).

15. Though Satchel Paige didn't play in the major leagues until after Joyce's death, he did play in an exhibition game in Yankee Stadium in 1934.

16. Jen Shelton provides a very different gloss on the "halt for hearsake" footnote in *Joyce and the Narrative Structure of Incest* (Shelton 112–16).

Chapter 9. In Conclusion: A Series of Forewords

1. Bloom shares his admiration for water in all its forms with St. Kevin, who is also "Hydrophilos" (*FW* 606.05); Stephen, by contrast, is "hydrophobe" (*U* 17.237), perhaps indicating in his aversion to water a lack of the generosity of spirit, even of genius, that characterizes Bloom.

2. Since September 2016, two more books have appeared in the Florida James Joyce Series: *Up to Maughty London: Joyce's Cultural Capital in the Imperial Metropolis* (2017), by Eleni Loukopoulou, and *Joyce and the Law* (2017), edited by Jonathan Goldman. A complete list of current titles is found at the back of this book.

3. See Cóilín Owens, *James Joyce's Painful Case* (Gainesville: University Press of Florida, 2008), and Roy Gottfried, *Joyce's Misbelief* (Gainesville: University Press of Florida, 2007). Since then, Geert Lernout's *Help My Unbelief: James Joyce and Religion* (New York: Continuum, 2010) has further expanded the argument.

Works Cited

Abraham, Matthew. Rev. for *Portside*, 30 Mar. 2106. http://portside.org/2016-03-30/ fall-faculty-rise-all-administrative-university. Accessed 22 May 2016.

"Adam Lay Ybounden." Sloane Manuscript 2593. British Library collection.

Adams, Henry. *The Education of Henry Adams*. Boston: Houghton Mifflin, 1961.

Adorno, Theodor. "Culture Industry Reconsidered." In *Reading Popular Narrative*, ed. Bob Ashley, 43–48. Leicester: Leicester University Press, 1997.

"An Affair to Remember." *Newsweek* 29 (Oct. 1990).

Amis, Martin. Rev. of *There Is Simply Too Much to Think About: Saul Bellow's Nonfiction*. *New York Times Book Review*, 27 Apr. 2015.

Armstrong, Alison. *The Joyce of Cooking: Food and Drink from James Joyce's Dublin*. Barrytown, N.Y.: Station Hill, 1986.

Atwood, Margaret. *Oryx and Crake*. New York: Anchor, 2003.

Auden, W. H. *The English Auden*. London: Faber and Faber, 1977.

Bakhtin, Mikhail. *The Dialogic Imagination*. Austin: University of Texas Press, 1981.

Ball, Sir Robert. *The Story of the Heavens*. London: Cassell, 1900.

Banner, Angela. *Ant and Bee and the ABC*. Illustrated by Bryan Ward. London: Edmund Ward, 1966.

Barnum, Frederick. *"His Master's Voice" in America: Ninety Years of Communications Pioneering and Progress*. Camden, N.J.: General Electric Company, 1991.

Barthes, Roland. *A Lover's Discourse*. Trans. Richard Howard. New York: Farrar, Straus and Giroux, 1978.

———. *The Responsibility of Forms: Critical Essays on Music, Art, and Representation*. Trans. Richard Howard. Los Angeles: University of California Press, 1985.

Bauerle, Ruth. *The James Joyce Songbook*. New York: Garland, 1982.

Beach, Sylvia. *Shakespeare and Company*. New York: Harcourt, Brace, 1959.

Beckett, Samuel. *Krapp's Last Tape and Other Dramatic Pieces*. New York: Grove, 1960.

———. *Murphy*. New York: Grove, 1957.

Beckett, Samuel, et al. *Our Exagmination Round His Factification for Incamination of Work in Progress*. New York: New Directions, 1972.

Beckman, Richard. *Joyce's Rare View: The Nature of Things in* Finnegans Wake. Gainesville: University Press of Florida, 2007.

Beja, Morris, and David Norris, eds. *Joyce in the Hibernian Metropolis*. Columbus: Ohio State University Press, 1996.

Bell, Robert H. *Jocoserious Joyce: The Fate of Folly in* Ulysses. Gainesville: University Press of Florida, 1996.

Bellew, Frank, ed. *Joe Miller's Jests, with Copious Additions*. New York: Office of the Northern Magazine, 1865.

Benjamin, Walter. *The Arcades Project*. Trans. Howard Eiland and Kevin McLaughlin. Cambridge, Mass.: Belknap, 1999.

———. *Illuminations: Essays and Reflections*. Ed. Hannah Arendt. New York: Harcourt, Brace and World, 1955.

Benstock, Shari. "The Letter of the Law: *La Carte Postale* in *Finnegans Wake*." *Philological Quarterly* 63, no. 2 (1984): 163–85.

Berressem, Hanjo. "The Letter! The Litter! The Defilements of the Signifier in *Finnegans Wake*." In *Finnegans Wake: Fifty Years*, ed. Geert Lernout, 139–64. Amsterdam: Rodopi, 1990.

Bible, The Holy. Oxford: Clarendon University Press, [1908].

Bishop, John. *James Joyce's Book of the Dark*, Finnegans Wake. Madison: University of Wisconsin Press, 1986.

Bishop, John, intro. *Finnegans Wake*. By James Joyce. London: Penguin Books, 1999, vii–xxvii.

Bowen, Zack. *Musical Allusions in the Works of James Joyce: Early Poetry through* Ulysses. Albany, N.Y.: SUNY Press, 1974.

———. "Our Way." *James Joyce Literary Supplement* 24, no. 2 (Autumn 2010): 20.

———. "Plato, Homer, and Joyce: Involving Orientalism, a Smidgeon of Smut, and a Pinch of Perverse Egotism." In *Joyce in Trieste: An Album of Risky Readings*, ed. Sebastian D. G. Knowles, Geert Lernout, and John McCourt, 54–64. Gainesville: University Press of Florida, 2007.

———. Ulysses *as a Comic Novel*. Syracuse, N.Y.: Syracuse University Press, 1989.

Bradley, Bruce, S.J. *James Joyce's Schooldays*. Dublin: Gill and Macmillan, 1982.

Britten, Benjamin. *War Requiem*. London: Boosey and Hawkes, [1986].

Brown, Bill. "Thing Theory." In *Things*, ed. Bill Brown, 1–22. Chicago: University of Chicago Press, 2004.

Brown, Richard. *James Joyce: A Post-Culturalist Perspective*. London: Macmillan, 1992.

Browne, Christopher. *Getting the Message: The Story of the British Post Office*. Stroud: Alan Sutton, 1993.

Browning, Robert. "Rabbi Ben Ezra." In *Robert Browning's Poetry*. New York: W. W. Norton, 2007.

Bryan, J., III. *The World's Greatest Showman: The Life of P. T. Barnum*. New York: Random House, 1956.

Buck-Morss, Susan. *The Dialectics of Seeing: Walter Benjamin and the Arcades Project*. Cambridge, Mass.: MIT Press, 1989.

Campbell, Joseph, and Henry Morton Robinson. *A Skeleton Key to* Finnegans Wake: *Unlocking James Joyce's Masterwork*. New York: Harcourt Brace, 1944.

Carey, John. *The Intellectuals and the Masses: Pride and Prejudice among the Literary Intelligentsia, 1880–1939*. Chicago: Academy Chicago Publishers, 2002.

———. *The Unexpected Professor: An Oxford Life in Books*. London: Faber and Faber, 2014.

Carey, Peter. *Oscar and Lucinda*. New York: Harper and Row, 1988.

Carroll, Lewis [Charles Dodgson]. *The Annotated Alice: Alice's Adventures in Wonderland and Through the Looking Glass*. Intro. and notes by Martin Gardner. New York: Clarkson N. Potter, 1960.

Castle, Gregory. *Modernism and the Celtic Revival*. Cambridge: Cambridge University Press, 2001.

Cheshire, D. F. *Music Hall in Britain*. Newton Abbott: David and Charles, 1974.

Chiaet, Julianne. "Reading Literary Fiction Improves Empathy." *Scientific American*, 4 Oct. 2013. http://scientificamerican.com/article/novel-finding-reading-literary-fiction-improves-empathy. Accessed 7 Nov. 2016.

Chinitz, David. "T. S. Eliot and the Cultural Divide." *PMLA* 110 (March 1995): 236–47.

Citino, David. "The World Without." Columbus, Ohio: Logan Elm, 1993. Keepsake edition; privately owned.

Cohen, Paula Marantz. *Silent Film and the Triumph of the American Myth*. Oxford: Oxford University Press, 2001.

Cohn, Robert Greer. *Toward the Poems of Mallarmé*. Berkeley: University of California Press, 1965.

Collini, Stefan. *What Are Universities For?* London: Penguin, 2012.

Conley, Tim. *Joyces Mistakes: Problems of Intention, Irony and Interpretation*. Toronto: University of Toronto Press, 2003.

Crawford, Robert. *The Savage and the City in the Work of T. S. Eliot*. Oxford: Clarendon, 1987.

Creasy, Matthew, ed. *Errears and Erroriboose: Joyce and Error*. European Joyce Studies, 20. Amsterdam: Rodopi, 2011.

Crumb, Michael. "*Sweets of Sin*: Joyce's *Ulysses* and Swinburne's 'Dolores.'" *James Joyce Quarterly* 28 (Autumn 1990): 239–45.

Dachy, Marc, ed., and intro. *James Joyce: The Complete Recordings*. CD. Booklet includes "James Joyce," by Eugene Jolas. Sub Rosa: Aural Documents SR60.

Davis, Herbert. "Inaugural Address." In "The Inauguration of Herbert John Davis as President of Smith College." Smith College Program. 17 Oct. 1940: 17–31.

Davison, Peter. *Songs of the British Music Hall*. London: Oak Publications, 1971.

Day, Robert Adams. "Joyce's AquaCities." In *Joyce in the Hibernian Metropolis*, ed. Morris Beja and David Norris, 3–20. Columbus: Ohio State University Press, 1996.

Dent, Edward, ed. *Martha*. By Friedrich von Flotow. London: Oxford University Press, 1941.

Derrida, Jacques. *Dissemination*. Trans. Barbara Johnson. London: Athlone, 1981.

———. *The Post Card: From Socrates to Freud and Beyond*. Trans. Alan Bass. Chicago: University of Chicago Press, 1987.

———. "Ulysses Gramophone: Hear say yes in Joyce." Trans. Tina Kendall, with emendations by Shari Benstock. In *A Companion to James Joyce's* Ulysses, ed. Margot Norris, 69–90. Boston: Bedford Books, 1998.

Deutsch, David. *British Literature and Classical Music: Cultural Contexts, 1870–1945*. New York: Bloomsbury, 2015.

Devlin, Kimberly J., and Christine Smedley, eds. *Joyce's Allmaziful Plurabilities: Polyvocal Explorations of* Finnegans Wake. Gainesville: University Press of Florida, 2015.

Dickens, Charles. *Dombey and Son*. Harmondsworth: Penguin, 1986.

———. *Oliver Twist*. Harmondsworth: Penguin, 1988.

Donoghue, Frank. *The Last Professors*. New York: Fordham, 2008.

Drouin, Jeffrey S. *James Joyce, Science, and Modernist Print Culture: "The Einstein of English Fiction."* New York: Routledge, 2015.

Duszenko, Andrzej. "The Joyce of Science: Quantum Physics in *Finnegans Wake*." *Irish University Review* 24 (Autumn/Winter 1994): 272–82.

Dyer, Geoff. *Zona*. New York: Pantheon, 2012.

Eagleton, Terry. "The Slow Death of the University." *The Chronicle Review*, 10 Apr. 2015: B9.

Eco, Umberto. *The Island of the Day Before*. Trans. William Weaver. New York: Harcourt Brace, 1995.

Eliot, T. S. *Collected Poems, 1909–1962*. London: Harcourt Brace Jovanovich, 1971.

———. *The Complete Poems and Plays, 1909–1950*. London: Harcourt Brace Jovanovich, 1980.

———. *The Letters of T. S. Eliot*. Vol. 1: 1898–1922. Ed. Valerie Eliot. New York: Harcourt, 1988.

———. "London Letter." *Dial* 70 (Apr. 1921): 448–53.

———. "London Letter." *Dial* 70 (Jun. 1921): 686–91.

———. "London Letter." *Dial* 73 (Dec. 1922): 659–63.

———. "The Possibility of a Poetic Drama." *Dial* 69 (Nov. 1920): 441–47.

———. "Preface." *Transit of Venus: Poems*. By Harry Crosby. Paris: Black Sun, 1931.

———. *Selected Essays*. New York: Harcourt, 1950.

———. "Ulysses, Order, and Myth." *Dial* 75 (Nov. 1923): 480–83.

———. *The Waste Land: A Facsimile and Transcript of the Original Drafts*. Ed. Valerie Eliot. New York: Harcourt Brace Jovanovich, 1971. (*TWL*)

Ellison, John (Jay). https://chicagomaroon.com/2016/08/24/university-to-freshmen-dont-expect-safe-spaces-or-trigger-warnings/. Accessed 29 Aug. 2016.

Ellmann, Richard. *James Joyce*. Rev. ed. Oxford: Oxford University Press, 1982. (*JJ*)

Emerson, Ralph Waldo. "Self-Reliance." In *Ralph Waldo Emerson: The Major Prose*, ed. Ronald A. Bosco and Joel Myerson, 127–51. Cambridge, Mass.: Harvard University Press, 2015.

Epstein, Edmund Lloyd. *A Guide through* Finnegans Wake. Gainesville: University Press of Florida, 2009.

Epstein, Josh. *Sublime Noise: Musical Culture and the Modernist Writer*. Baltimore: Johns Hopkins University Press, 2014.

Fabrizio, Timothy, and George Paul. *The Talking Machine. An Illustrated Compendium: 1877–1929*. Atglen, Penn.: Schiffer, 1997.

Farson, Daniel. *Marie Lloyd and Music Hall*. London: Stacey, 1972.

Faulkner, William. *As I Lay Dying*. New York: Random House, 1990.

———. *The Sound and the Fury*. New York: Random House, 1990.

Fitzgerald, F. Scott. "The Crack-Up." Feb. 1936. In *The Crack-Up, with Other Uncollected Pieces, Note-Books and Unpublished Letters*, ed. Edmund Wilson. New York: New Directions, 1945.

Flotow, Friedrich von. *Martha*. With an English translation by Natalia Macfarren. New York: Schirmer, 1901.

Forster, E. M. *Howards End*. New York: Random House, 1989.

———. *A Passage to India*. Harmondsworth: Penguin, 1956.

Fraser, James Alexander. *Joyce and Betrayal*. London: Palgrave, 2016.

Frazer, James. *The Golden Bough: A Study in Magic and Religion*. Abridged edition, 1922. Harmondsworth: Penguin, 1996.

Freud, Sigmund. *Jokes and Their Relation to the Unconscious*. Ed. and trans. James Strachey, 1960. New York: Norton, 1963.

Füger, Wilhelm. "'Epistlemadethemology' (*FW* 374.17): ALP's Letter and the Tradition of Interpolated Letters." *James Joyce Quarterly* 19 (Summer 1982): 405–13.

Gelatt, Roland. *The Fabulous Phonograph: From Tin Foil to High Fidelity*. Philadelphia: Lippincott, 1955.

Gifford, Don, with Robert J. Seidman. Ulysses *Annotated: Notes for James Joyce's* Ulysses. 2nd ed. revised and enlarged by Don Gifford. Berkeley: University of California Press, 1988.

Gill, Rosalind. "Breaking the Silence: The Hidden Injuries of the Neoliberal University." In *Secrecy and Silence in the Research Process: Feminist Reflections*, ed. Rosalind Gill and Róisín Ryan-Flood, 228–44. New York: Routledge, 2010.

Gillespie, Michael Patrick. *The Aesthetics of Chaos: Nonlinear Thinking and Contemporary Literary Criticism*. Gainesville: University Press of Florida, 2003.

———. *James Joyce and the Exilic Imagination*. Gainesville: University Press of Florida, 2015.

Ginsberg, Benjamin. *The Fall of the Faculty: The Rise of the All Administrative University*. Baltimore: Johns Hopkins University Press, 2013.

Glasheen, Adaline. *Third Census of* Finnegans Wake: *An Index of the Characters and Their Roles*. Berkeley: University of California Press, 1977.

Goldman, Jonathan, ed. *Joyce and the Law*. Gainesville: University Press of Florida, 2017.

———. *Legal Joyce. James Joyce Quarterly* 50 (Summer 2013). Special issue.

Gordon, John. Finnegans Wake: *A Plot Summary*. Syracuse, N.Y.: Syracuse University Press, 1986.

Gottfried, Roy. *Joyce's Comic Portrait*. Gainesville: University Press of Florida, 2000.

———. *Joyce's Iritis and the Irritated Text: The Dis-Lexic* Ulysses. Gainesville: University Press of Florida, 1995.

———. *Joyce's Misbelief*. Gainesville: University Press of Florida, 2007.

Graham, Jorie. *The Errancy*. Hopewell: Ecco, 1997.

Green, Benny. *The Last Empires: A Music Hall Companion*. London: Pavilion, 1986.

Greene, Graham. *Brighton Rock*. Harmondsworth: Penguin, 1980.

Gregerson, Linda. *The Reformation of the Subject*. New York: Cambridge University Press, 1995.

Groden, Michael. Ulysses *in Focus: Genetic, Textual, and Personal Views*. Gainesville: University Press of Florida, 2010.

Gubernatis, Catherine. "All the World's In Want and Is Writing a Letters: The Epistolary Form in Twentieth-Century Fiction." Ph.D. dissertation, Ohio State University, 2007.

Gurke, Thomas. "*Fuga per canonem*: A Flight through the Canon. Music Aesthetics and Affect in James Joyce." Ph.D. dissertation, Heinrich-Heine-Universität Düsseldorf, 2014.

Hardy, Thomas. *Jude the Obscure*. Harmondsworth: Penguin, 1978.

———. *Tess of the d'Urbervilles*. New York: Oxford, 1988.

Hart, Clive. *Structure and Motif in* Finnegans Wake. London: Faber and Faber, 1962.

Hayman, David. "Forms of Folly in Joyce: A Study of Clowning in *Ulysses*." ELH 34 (1967): 260–83.

Heaney, Seamus. *Aeneid Book VI: A New Verse Translation*. New York: Farrar, Straus and Giroux, 2016.

Henke, Suzette. *Joyce's Moraculous Sindbook: A Study of* Ulysses. Columbus: Ohio State University Press, 1978.

Herr, Cheryl. *Joyce's Anatomy of Culture*. Chicago: University of Illinois Press, 1986.

Herring, Phillip F. *Joyce's Uncertainty Principle*. Princeton: Princeton University Press, 1987.

Herring, Phillip F., ed. *Joyce's* Ulysses *Notesheets in the British Museum*. Charlottesville: University Press of Virginia, 1972.

Holt, Jim. "Punch Line." *New Yorker*, 19, 26 Apr. 2004: 184–90.

Howell, Michael, and Peter Ford. *The True History of the Elephant Man: The Definitive Account of the Tragic and Extraordinary Life of Joseph Carey Merrick*. New York: Penguin, 1980.

Hübner, Wilhelm. "Martha, Martha, Komm Doch Wieder!" *Musik und Gesellschaft* 13 (1963): 619.

Hughes, Robert. *The Shock of the New*. New York: Knopf, 1980.

Hutchinson, Robert, intro. *Joe Miller's Jests or, the Wits Vade-mecum*. By [John Mottley]. Facsimile of 1739 edition. New York: Dover, 1963, v–xix.

Huxley, Aldous. *Point Counter Point*. Dublin: Dalkey Archive, 1996.

Hynes, Samuel. *The Auden Generation: Literature and Politics in England in the 1930s*. New York: Viking, 1976.

Israel, Nico. *Spirals: The Whirled Image in Twentieth-Century Literature and Art*. Modernist Latitudes Series. New York: Columbia University Press, 2015.

Ives, Charles. *Memos*. New York: Norton, 1972.

Jolas, Eugene. "James Joyce." In *James Joyce: The Complete Recordings*, ed. Marc Dachy. CD. Sub Rosa: Aural Documents SR60.

Jones, Ellen Carol, and Morris Beja, eds. *Twenty-First Joyce*. Gainesville: University Press of Florida, 2004.

Joyce, James. *Dubliners*. With an introduction and notes by Terence Brown. London: Penguin, 1992. (*D*)

———. *Finnegans Wake*. Intro. John Bishop. London: Penguin, 1999. (*FW*)

———. "From Work in Progress." *transatlantic review* 1 (Apr. 1924): 215–23.

———. *James Joyce: The Complete Recordings*. CD. Booklet includes "James Joyce," by Eugene Jolas. Ed. and intro. Marc Dachy. Sub Rosa: Aural Documents SR60.

———. *Letters*. Vol. I. Ed. Stuart Gilbert. New York: Viking, 1966. (*Letters* I)

———. *Letters*. Vol. II. Ed. Richard Ellmann. New York: Viking, 1966. (*Letters* II)

———. *Letters*. Vol. III. Ed. Richard Ellmann. New York: Viking, 1966. (*Letters* III)

———. *Occasional, Critical, and Political Writing*. Ed. Kevin Barry. Oxford: Oxford University Press, 2000. (*OCP*)

———. *A Portrait of the Artist as a Young Man*. London: Penguin, 1976. (*P*)

———. *Ulysses*. The Corrected Text. Ed. Hans Walter Gabler, with Wolfhard Steppe and Claus Melchior. New York: Random House, 1986. (*U*)

———. *Ulysses*. Reprint of 1922 edition. Ed. with an introduction by Jeri Johnson. Oxford: World's Classics, 1993. (*U-22*)

———. *Ulysses*. Vintage International Edition. New York: Random House, 1990, copyright renewed 1961. (*U-61*)

———. *Ulysses, A Facsimile of the Manuscript*. Ed. Clive Driver. With a critical introduction by Harry Levin. 3 vols. New York: Octagon / Philadelphia: Philip H. and A.S.W. Rosenbach Foundation, 1975. (Rosenbach)

———. *Ulysses, A Facsimile of Manuscripts and Typescripts for Episodes 10–13*. The James Joyce Archive. Prefaced and arranged by Michael Groden. New York: Garland, 1977. (*JJA* 13)

———. *Ulysses, A Facsimile of Manuscripts and Typescripts for Episodes 17–18*. The James Joyce Archive. Prefaced and arranged by Michael Groden. New York: Garland, 1977. (*JJA* 16)

———. *Ulysses, A Facsimile of Notes for the Book and Manuscripts and Typescripts for Episodes 1–9*. The James Joyce Archive. Prefaced and arranged by Michael Groden. New York: Garland, 1978. (*JJA* 12)

———. *Ulysses, A Facsimile of Page Proofs for Episodes 7–9*. The James Joyce Archive. Prefaced and arranged by Michael Groden. New York: Garland, 1978. (*JJA* 23)

————. *Ulysses, A Facsimile of Page Proofs for Episodes 10 and 11. The James Joyce Archive.* Prefaced and arranged by Michael Groden. New York: Garland, 1978. (*JJA* 24)

————. *Ulysses, A Facsimile of Page Proofs for Episodes 16–18. The James Joyce Archive.* Prefaced and arranged by Michael Groden. New York: Garland, 1978. (*JJA* 27)

————. *Ulysses, A Facsimile of Placards for Episodes 7–10. The James Joyce Archive.* Prefaced and arranged by Michael Groden. New York: Garland, 1978. (*JJA* 18)

————. *Ulysses, A Facsimile of Placards for Episodes 17–18. The James Joyce Archive.* Prefaced and arranged by Michael Groden. New York: Garland, 1978. (*JJA* 21)

Kenner, Hugh. "Jim the Comedian." In *Joyce in Trieste: An Album of Risky Readings*, ed. Sebastian D. G. Knowles, Geert Lernout, and John McCourt, 191–94. Gainesville: University Press of Florida, 2007.

————. *Ulysses.* Baltimore: Johns Hopkins University Press, 1987.

Kershner, R. B. *Joyce, Bakhtin, and Popular Literature: Chronicles of Disorder.* Chapel Hill: University of North Carolina Press, 1989.

Kershner, R. B., ed. *Cultural Studies of James Joyce.* Amsterdam: Rodopi, 2003.

————. *Joyce and Popular Culture.* Gainesville: University Press of Florida, 1996.

Kift, Dagmar. *The Victorian Music Hall: Culture, Class and Conflict.* Trans. Roy Kift. Cambridge: Cambridge University Press, 1996.

Kipnis, Laura. *Unwanted Advances: Sexual Paranoia Comes to Campus.* New York: Harper, 2017.

Kirk, Jay. *Kingdom under Glass: A Tale of Obsession, Adventure and One Man's Quest to Preserve the World's Great Animals.* New York: Holt, 2010.

Kittler, Friedrich. *Gramophone, Film, Typewriter.* Stanford: Stanford University Press, 1999.

Knowles, Sebastian D. G. "Death by Gramophone." *Journal of Modern Literature* 27 (Autumn 2003): 1–13.

————. *The Dublin Helix: The Life of Language in Joyce's* Ulysses. Gainesville: University Press of Florida, 2001.

————. "*Finnegans Wake* for Dummies." *James Joyce Quarterly* 46 (Autumn 2008): 97–112.

————. "A Memorial Tribute to Zack Bowen." *James Joyce Quarterly* 46 (Spring/Summer 2009): 423–24.

————. *Seeing the Joe Miller: Humor Detection in* Ulysses. National Library Monograph Series, no. 12. Ed. Luca Crispi and Catherine Fahy. Dublin: National Library of Ireland, 2004.

————. "The Substructure of 'Sirens': Molly as *Nexus Omnia Ligans*." *James Joyce Quarterly* 23 (Summer 1986): 447–63.

————. "That Form Endearing: A Performance of Siren Songs; or, 'I was only vamping, man.'" In *Joyce in the Hibernian Metropolis: Essays*, ed. Morris Beja and David Norris, 213–36. Columbus: Ohio State University Press, 1996.

————. "'Then You Wink the Other Eye': T. S. Eliot and the Music Hall." *ANQ* 11 (Autumn 1998): 20–32.

————. "The True Story of Jumbo the Elephant." In *Twenty-First Joyce*, ed. Morris Beja and Ellen Carol Jones, 97–111. Gainesville: University Press of Florida, 2004.

Knowles, Sebastian D. G., ed. *Bronze by Gold: The Music of Joyce*. New York: Garland, 1999.

Knowles, Sebastian D. G., Geert Lernout, and John McCourt, eds. *Joyce in Trieste: An Album of Risky Readings*. Gainesville: University Press of Florida, 2007.

Koestler, Arthur. "Humour and Wit." In *Janus: A Summing Up*, 109–30. New York: Random House, 1978.

Koritz, Amy. "Disappearing Acts: Ideology and the Performer in T. S. Eliot's Early Criticism." In *Gendering Bodies / Performing Art: Dance and Literature in Early Twentieth-Century British Culture*, 137–53. Ann Arbor: University of Michigan Press, 1995.

Kosinski, Jerzy. *Being There*. New York: Harcourt Brace Jovanovich, 1971.

Kupke, Tanja. "*Où Sont Les Muses D'Antan?*: Notes for a Study of the Muses in the Middle Ages." In *From Athens to Chartres: Neoplatonism and Medieval Thought*, ed. Édouard Jeauneau, 421–36. Leiden: Brill, 1992.

Lacivita, Alison. *The Ecology of* Finnegans Wake. Gainesville: University Press of Florida, 2015.

Lambert, Constant. *Music Ho! A Study of Music in Decline*. London: Faber and Faber, 1937.

Lash, Kenneth. "Finnegan Wakes at Yankee Stageum." *New Yorker*, 9 Apr. 1984: 41.

Lawrence, D. H. *Collected Poems*. London: Secker, 1932.

Lees, Heath. "The Introduction to 'Sirens' and the *Fuga per Canonem*." *James Joyce Quarterly* 22 (Autumn 1984): 39–54.

Lehrer, Tom. *The Remains of Tom Lehrer*. Warner Bros. Records and Rhino Entertainment Company, 2000.

Leonard, Garry. *Advertising and Commodity Culture in Joyce*. Gainesville: University Press of Florida, 1998.

Lerdahl, Fred, and Ray Jackendoff. *A Generative Theory of Tonal Music*. Cambridge, Mass.: MIT Press, 1983.

Lernout, Geert. *Help My Unbelief: James Joyce and Religion*. New York: Continuum, 2010.

Leys, Simon. *The Hall of Uselessness*. New York: New York Review Books, 2013.

Loukopoulou, Eleni. *Up to Maughty London: Joyce's Cultural Capital in the Imperial Metropolis*. Gainesville: University Press of Florida, 2017.

Lowe-Evans, Mary. *Catholic Nostalgia in Joyce and Company*. Gainesville: University Press of Florida, 2008.

Lyons, F.S.L. *Charles Stewart Parnell*. London: Collins, 1977.

Mackay, James. *A History of Modern English Coinage*. London: Longman, 1984.

Mallarmé, Stéphane. *Collected Poems*. Trans. and with a commentary by Henry Weinfield. Berkeley: University of California Press, 1994.

Mander, Raymond, and Joe Mitchenson. *British Music Hall*. London: Gentry Books, 1974.

Mann, Thomas. *The Magic Mountain*. Trans. John E. Woods. New York: Random House, 1995.

Mao, Douglas. *Solid Objects: Modernism and the Test of Production*. Princeton: Princeton University Press, 1998.

Mathieson, Eric. *The True Story of Jumbo the Elephant*. New York: Hamish Hamilton, 1963.

McClurkin, Eleanor. *How to Make Hand-made Greeting Cards for Fun or Profit*. Melrose Park, Ill.: Lamp, 1959.

McCracken, Grant. *Culture and Consumption*. Bloomington: Indiana University Press, 1988.

McEwan, Ian. *Nutshell*. New York: Doubleday, 2016.

McHugh, Roland. *Annotations to* Finnegans Wake. Baltimore: Johns Hopkins University Press, 1991.

McMorran, Ciaran. "Geometry and Topography in James Joyce's *Ulysses* and *Finnegans Wake*." Ph.D. dissertation, University of Glasgow, 2016.

Miller, Arthur. *The Crucible*. Harmondsworth: Penguin, 1986.

Mitchell, Andrew J. "Writing the Fortunate Fall: '*O felix culpa!*' in *Finnegans Wake*." *James Joyce Quarterly* 47 (Summer 2010): 589–606.

Moran, Joseph M., Gagan S. Wig, Reginald B. Adams Jr., Petr Janata, and William M. Kelley. "Neural Correlates of Humor Detection and Appreciation." *NeuroImage* 21 (2004): 1055–60.

Morris, George. "Marie, Marie, Hold on Tight." *Partisan Review* 21 (1954): 231–33.

[Mottley, John]. *Joe Miller's Jests or, the Wits Vade-mecum*. Facsimile of 1739 edition. Intro. Robert Hutchinson. New York: Dover, 1963.

Newton, H. Chance. *Idols of the 'Halls.'* London: Heath Cranton, 1928; repr. British Book Centre, 1975.

Norris, Margot. "Risky Reading of Risky Writing." In *Joyce in Trieste: An Album of Risky Readings*, ed. Sebastian D. G. Knowles, Geert Lernout, and John McCourt, 36–53. Gainesville: University Press of Florida, 2007.

North, Michael. "The Dialect in/of Modernism: Pound and Eliot's Racial Masquerade." *American Literary History* 4 (1992): 56–76.

———. *Reading 1922*. Oxford: Oxford University Press, 1999.

Oestreich, James. "A Lady-in-Waiting Goes Slumming." Rev. of *Martha*, *New York Times*, 15 Oct. 1990.

Orwell, George [Eric Blair]. *Nineteen Eighty-Four*. New York: Harcourt, Brace, 1949.

Oxford English Dictionary, The. Online database. Accessed 25 May 2017.

Owens, Cóilín. *Before Daybreak: "After the Race" and the Origins of Joyce's Art*. Gainesville: University Press of Florida, 2013.

———. *James Joyce's Painful Case*. Gainesville: University Press of Florida, 2008.

Petts, Leonard. *The Story of "Nipper" and the "His Master's Voice" Picture Painted by Francis Barraud*. Bournemouth: E. Bayly, 1983.

Pichaske, David. "Reclaiming the Author, Recovering the Text: Its (*Sic*) Time." In *Walking on a Trail of Words: Essays in Honor of Professor Agnieszka Salska*, ed. Jadwiga Maszewska and Zbigniew Maszewski, 151–63. Lodz: University of Lodz Press, 2007.

Plato. *Republic*. In *Great Dialogues of Plato*, trans. W.H.D. Rouse, ed. Eric H. Warmington and Philip G. Rouse, 118–422. New York: Mentor, 1956.

Plock, Vike Martina. *Joyce, Medicine, and Modernity*. Gainesville: University Press of Florida, 2010.

———. "'Object Lessons': Bloom and His Things." *James Joyce Quarterly* 49 (Spring/Summer 2012): 557–72.

Pound, Ezra. *The Cantos*. London: Faber and Faber, 1981.

———. *Gaudier-Brzeska*. New York: New Directions, 1970.

Power, Arthur. *Conversations with James Joyce*. Ed. Clive Hart. New York: Harper and Row, 1974.

Proposed Demolition of Nineteen City Churches, The. By the London City Council. London: P. S. King and Son, 1920.

Prose, Francine. "Hers; Bad Behavior." http://www.nytimes.com/books/00/04/16/specials/prose-behavior.html. Accessed 26 Apr. 2015.

Proust, Marcel. *Swann's Way*. Vol. 1 of *In Search of Lost Time*. Trans. C. K. Scott Moncrieff and Terence Kilmartin, rev. by D. J. Enright. New York: Modern Library, 2003.

Quignard, Pascal. *The Roving Shadows*. Trans. Chris Turner. London: Seagull Books, 2011.

Rabelais, François. "Pantagruel." In *Oeuvres Complètes*. Paris: Editions Garnier Frères, 1962. Vol. 2.

Rasula, Jed. "*Finnegans Wake* and the Character of the Letter." *James Joyce Quarterly* 34 (Summer 1997): 517–30.

Rice, Thomas Jackson. *Cannibal Joyce*. Gainesville: University Press of Florida, 2008.

———. *Joyce, Chaos, and Complexity*. Urbana: University of Illinois Press, 1997.

Rivers, W. H. R., ed. *Essays on the Depopulation of Melanesia*. Cambridge: Cambridge University Press, 1922.

Rogers, Margaret. "Decoding the Fugue in 'Sirens.'" *James Joyce Literary Supplement* 4 (Spring 1990): 15–18.

Ronson, Jon. *So You've Been Publicly Shamed*. Oxford: Picador, 2015.

Ross, Alex. *The Rest Is Noise: Listening to the Twentieth Century*. New York: Picador, 2008.

Roth, Philip. *The Human Stain*. New York: Houghton Mifflin, 2000.

Ryan, Dennis. "Marie Lloyd and the Last 'London Letter': T. S. Eliot's Transmutation of Ideology into Art in *The Waste Land*." *Yeats Eliot Review* 10 (1989): 35–40.

Safire, William. "Word-Watchers at Work." *New York Times*, 10 May 1981.

Saint-Amour, Paul. "Symbols and Things." In *The Cambridge Companion to* Ulysses, ed. Sean Latham, 200–215. New York: Cambridge University Press, 2014.

Sanders, Charles. "*The Waste Land*: The Last Minstrel Show?" *Journal of Modern Literature* 8 (1980): 23–38.

Saxon, A. H. *P. T. Barnum: The Legend and the Man.* New York: Columbia University Press, 1989.

Saxon, A. H., ed. *Selected Letters of P. T. Barnum.* New York: Columbia University Press, 1983.

Schubert, Franz. *Goethe-Lieder.* Kassel: Bärenreiter, 1971.

Schumacher, E. F. *Small Is Beautiful: Economics as if People Mattered.* New York: Harper, 1973.

Scott's Standard Postage Stamp Catalogue. 1969. 2 vols. New York: Scott Publications, 1968.

Sebald, W. G. *Across the Land and the Water: Selected Poems, 1964–2001.* Trans. Iain Galbraith. London: Penguin, 2011.

———. *Austerlitz.* Trans. Anthea Bell. New York: Modern Library, 2001.

Senn, Fritz. *Joyce's Dislocutions: Essays on Reading as Translation.* Ed. John Paul Riquelme. Baltimore: Johns Hopkins University Press, 1984.

Shakespeare, William. *As You Like It.* In *The Riverside Shakespeare,* ed. G. Blakemore Evans et al., 365–402. Boston: Houghton Mifflin, 1974.

———. *Hamlet.* In *The Riverside Shakespeare,* ed. G. Blakemore Evans et al., 1135–97. Boston: Houghton Mifflin, 1974.

———. *King Lear.* In *The Riverside Shakespeare,* ed. G. Blakemore Evans et al., 1249–1305. Boston: Houghton Mifflin, 1974.

———. "Venus and Adonis." In *The Riverside Shakespeare,* ed. G. Blakemore Evans et al., 1705–19. Boston: Houghton Mifflin, 1974.

Shaughnessy, Dan. *The Curse of the Bambino.* New York: Dutton, 1990.

Shelton, Jen. *Joyce and the Narrative Structure of Incest.* Gainesville: University Press of Florida, 2006.

Short, Ernest, and Arthur Compton-Rickett. *Ring Up the Curtain.* London: Herbert Jenkins, 1938.

Shulevitz, Judith. "The Best Way to Address Campus Rape." *New York Times,* 8 Feb. 2015.

Silverman, Kaja. *The Subject of Semiotics.* Oxford: Oxford University Press, 1983.

Sonzogni, Marco. "All Black Joyce." *Times Literary Supplement,* 19 Oct. 2012: 15.

Sousa, John Philip. "The Menace of Mechanical Music." *Appleton's Magazine* 8 (Sept. 1906): 278–81.

Spoo, Robert. "Injuries, Remedies, Moral Rights, and the Public Domain." Special Issue. *James Joyce Quarterly* 37 (Spring/Summer 2000): 333–65.

Stevens, Wallace. *The Collected Poems.* New York: Random House, 1990.

Sullivan, Arthur. *The Art of the Savoyard.* GEMM CD 9991.

Sullivan, Arthur, and W. S. Gilbert. *Iolanthe.* New York: Schirmer, [195?].

———. *The Mikado, or The Town of Titipu.* New York: Schirmer, [1979].

———. *Patience, or Bunthorne's Bride.* New York: Schirmer, 1982.

———. *Princess Ida.* London: Chatto and Windus, 1911.

Svevo, Italo. *Confessions of Zeno*. Trans. Beryl de Zoete. New York: Vintage, 1958.

Szczeszak-Brewer, Agata. *Empire and Pilgrimage in Conrad and Joyce*. Gainesville: University Press of Florida, 2011.

Tennyson, Alfred Lord. "Ulysses." In *The Poems of Tennyson*, ed. Christopher Ricks, 560–66. London: Longmans, 1969,.

Thompson, Michael. *Rubbish Theory: The Creation and Destruction of Value*. Oxford: Oxford University Press, 1979.

Tichi, Cecelia. *Shifting Gears*. Chapel Hill: University of North Carolina Press, 1987.

Tindall, William York. *A Reader's Guide to* Finnegans Wake. Syracuse, N.Y.: Syracuse University Press, 1969.

Van Boheemen-Saaf, Christine. *Joyce, Derrida, Lacan, and the Trauma of History: Reading, Narrative and Postcolonialism*. Cambridge: Cambridge University Press, 1999.

Verlaine, Paul. *Oeuvres Poétiques Complètes*. Paris: Gallimard, 1948.

Vonnegut, Kurt. *Player Piano*. New York: Dell, 1979.

Wagner, Richard. *Tristan und Isolde*. Karl Böhm, conductor. With Birgit Nilsson, Wolfgang Windgassen, Martti Talvela. Libretto. Deutsche Grammophon 1966. CD 449–772–2.

Warner, Marina. "Learning My Lesson." *London Review of Books*, 19 Mar. 2015: 8–14.

Weaver, Meg. "Human History on Display at Pompeii." http://intelligenttravel.national geographic.com/2010/04/14/human_history_on_display_at_po/. Accessed 18 Apr. 2015.

Weiner, Jon. https://www.thenation.com/article/what-makes-ohio-state-most-un equal-public-university-america/. Accessed 31 Oct. 2016.

[Wells, H. G.]. *Boon, The Mind of the Race, The Wild Asses of the Devil, and the Last Trump*. Prepared for publication by Reginald Bliss. New York: George H. Doran, 1915.

Weninger, Robert K. *The German Joyce*. Gainesville: University Press of Florida, 2012.

Whitman, Walt. *Leaves of Grass and Selected Prose*. Ed. Sculley Bradley. New York: Holt, Rinehart and Winston, 1949.

Williams, William Carlos. *Paterson*. New York: New Directions, 1958.

Wilmut, Roger. *Kindly Leave the Stage! The Story of Variety, 1919–1960*. London: Methuen, 1985.

Woolf, Virginia. *Between the Acts*. Harmondsworth: Penguin, 1953.

———. *Jacob's Room*. London: Hogarth, 1990.

———. "On Not Knowing Greek." In *The Common Reader*. 1st Series. New York: Harcourt Brace Jovanovich, 1984, 23–38.

———. *A Room of One's Own*. New York: Harvest, 1981.

———. *Three Guineas*. New York: Harcourt Brace Jovanovich, 1966.

———. *To the Lighthouse*. London: Hogarth, 1930.

Wordsworth, William. *Selected Poems and Prefaces*. Boston: Houghton Mifflin, 1965.

Worthington, Mabel. "Gilbert and Sullivan in the Works of James Joyce." *Hartford Studies in Literature* 1 (1969): 209–18.

Yaeger, Patricia. Editor's Column. "The Death of Nature and the Apotheosis of Trash; or, Rubbish Ecology." *PMLA* 123 (March 2008): 321–39.

Yeats, W. B. *A Vision*. New York: Collier, 1966.

Index

Page numbers in *italics* refer to illustrations.

Dies Irae, 82, 244. *See also* music: requiem
  Mass
Dillon, Bernard, 125
Dinesen, Isak, 251
dogs, 1–2, 107, 111; fox terrier, 105, *114*; re-
  triever, 206. *See also* Little Nipper
Donoghue, Frank, 43, 245
Dostoevsky, Fyodor, 47
doubt, 6, 21, 43, 144–45; encouraged by read-
  ing, 49; failure to prize, 221
Dream of the Red Chamber, 48
Drinkwater, John, 117–18
Drouin, Jeffrey S., 242–43
Dubliners
—characters in: Mr. Alleyne, 30; Mr. Browne,
  120; Little Chandler, 129; Gabriel Conroy,
  8–9, 13, 18, 29–30, 119, 175, 237; Gretta Con-
  roy, 10; Bob Doran, 5; James Duffy, 4, 51,
  129; Eveline, 51; Mr. Farrington, 30; Father
  Flynn, 4; Michael Furey, 10, 30; Ignatius
  Gallaher, 129; Mrs. Kearney, 30; Lily, 29;
  Mahony, 4; Mrs. Mercer, 51, 53–54; Mrs.
  Mooney, 5; Emily Sinico, 4, 98
—objects in, 51; orange tie, 65; overripe
  apple, 51–52; rusty bicycle-pump, 51, 53;
  used stamps, 51–53
—stories in, 79; "The Sisters," 1, 4, 8, 154;
  "An Encounter," 4; "Araby," 3, 11–12, 29, 33,
  52; "Two Gallants," 139; "The Boarding
  House," 5; "Counterparts," 50; "A Painful
  Case," 252; "A Mother," 50; "The Dead,"
  9–10, 12–13, 18, 24, 148, 223, 260
Duette Photographers (Boston), 100
Duffy, Enda, 234, 246
Duszenko, Andrzej, 242
Dyer, Geoff, 242
dynamo, 7–9, 13, 21, 24, 112, 115, 130

Eagleton, Terry, 41
Earth, 13
eBay, 59–60
Eco, Umberto, 113, 188–89
Edison, Thomas, 104–5, 114–15, 133, 250
education, as speculative venture, 40. *See also*
  teaching

Edward VII, King of England, 10, 89
Eliot, George [Mary Anne Evans]: *Middle-
  march*, 116
Eliot, T. S., 26, 28, 104, 106, 130; Bel Esprit,
  127–28; "The *Boston Evening Transcript*,"
  209, 264; "Burnt Norton," 127, 142; *The
  Cocktail Party*, 252; "The Dry Salvages,"
  65, 75; "East Coker," 228; "Fragment of an
  Agon," 116; "Hamlet and His Problems,"
  117; "Little Gidding," 118–19, 218, 252; "London Letters," 108, 115, 117–19, 123–28, 251,
  253; "The Love Song of J. Alfred Prufrock,"
  80, 131, 135, 264; "Marie Lloyd," 115, 253;
  "Portrait of a Lady," 127; "The Possibility of a Poetic Drama," 251; "Prufrock's
  Pervigilium," 105; "Sweeney Agonistes,"
  122; "Tradition and the Individual Talent," 117–18, 136, 255; "Ulysses, Order, and
  Myth," 117, 154; "William Blake," 117
—*The Waste Land*, 17, 26–27, 50, 120–29, 136,
  217, 229; drafts of, 143–45, 256; notes to,
  62, 247, 252; as tour of London, 252–53; as
  vaudeville act, 253
Eliot, Valerie, *74*, *75*
Ellison, John (Jay), 45, 246
Ellmann, Richard, 6, 75, 165, 200, 233, 258
Emerson, Ralph Waldo, 21, 243
Emmet, Robert, 34, 50, 133, 148, 231
empathy, 49–50, 233, 246; absence of in university processes, 39; Empathy Quotient,
  49, 206
empire, British, 22, 33, 35, 94–95, 101–2, 203,
  209
England, *91*, *93*, 127, 163, 232; John Bull, 101. *See
  also* empire, British
engraving, as negative image, 5, 108
entropy. *See* chaos
Epstein, Edmund, 78, 225, 249
Epstein, Josh, 141, 143
equanimity, 11
Erasmus, 38
error, 2, 81, 145; anachronistic, 3, 162–63, 211,
  213–14, 249; coincidental, 242, 250, 258;
  genetic, 3; human, 3–5, 9, 245; hypercor-
  rection, 173, 201; institutional appreciation

Trollope, Anthony, 246
"Trust Not Appearances" (Joyce), 39
Tufts College (Medford, Massachusetts), *100*,
    101, 249–50
Tutankhamun, 128

Ulysses, 136; book of shades, 138; book of
    sums, 191; as centrifuge, 7–25; character,
    importance of, 2; history in, 2; language of
    outlaw in, 1–7, 203; midsummer panto-
    mime, 188; moral force of, 8; music in, 2,
    110, 188 (*see also* music; songs in Joyce);
    nothing fixed about, 5; as olfactory extrava-
    ganza, 1; as parable of the penultimate, 16;
    plot, feeble excuse for, 187, 214; Plumtree's
    incompleteness theorem in, 16, 136, 243; six
    keys to reading, 2; transubstantiation in, 2;
    universe of, 9
—characters in: the blind stripling, 33, 259;
    Milly Bloom, 11, 14, 62, 162, 243; Blazes
    Boylan, 11, 50, 149, 158, 176, 253; Cissy Caf-
    frey, 16, 29, 102; Private Carr, 13, 205; The
    Citizen, 30, 50, 89, 197; Biddy the Clap, 13;
    Martha Clifford, 16, 29, 55–56, 162; Bella
    Cohen, 12, 206–7; Father Cowley, 2, 5,
    33, 159, 259; Garrett Deasy, 4, 16, 49–50;
    Dilly Dedalus, 14, 243; Simon Dedalus, 28,
    67, 139, 161; Paddy Dignam, 8–9, 99, 102,
    106–7; Reuben J. Dodd, 10; Ben Dollard,
    2, 34, 159; Lydia Douce, 34, 116–17, 129,
    140, 146–50, 155–56, 160; Cashel Boyle
    O'Connor Fitzmaurice Tisdall Farrell, 33;
    May Goulding, 102, 242; Richie Goulding,
    32; The Hue and Cry, 2, 40, 207; Cunty
    Kate, 13; Mina Kennedy, 140, 146–50,
    160, 256; Tom Kernan, 21, 34; Lenehan,
    1; Lynch, 1; Bantam Lyons, 183; Gerty
    MacDowell, 2, 10, 15–16, 29, 194; Gerty
    MacDowell, and the boy that has the bi-
    cycle, 89, 102; Professor MacHugh, 5–6, 111,
    184; The Man in the Macintosh, 2, 179; The
    Man in the Macintosh, identified as John
    Philip Sousa, 106; Mario, 162; The Mob,
    5; Buck Mulligan, 13, 50, 186–88; Nymph

of the Bath, 237, 241; Jack Power, 21;
    Theodore Purefoy, 106; Tom Rochford,
    116; Rudy, 2, 36, 68, 102, 129–30, 175, 206;
    Sargent, 1, 4, 28; Hester Stanhope, 179;
    Major Tweedy, 55–58, 60; Virag, 14, 16–17,
    206. *See also* Bloom, Leopold; Bloom,
    Molly; Dedalus, Stephen
—editions of, 128, 204, 227, 249; 1922, 14;
    Gabler, 173–74, 201, 260–61; Vintage
    International, 173–74, 201, 260. See also
    James Joyce Archive; *Little Review*; Rosen-
    bach manuscript
—episodes in: "Telemachus," 8, 11, 19;
    "Nestor," 1–2, 16, 28, 216; "Proteus," 3,
    16; "Calypso," 57–58; "Lotus-Eaters," 9,
    55–56, 160; "Hades," 8, 10, 67–68, 103, 108;
    "Aeolus," 5–7, 15–16, 65; "Aeolus," as bal-
    let, 143; "Lestrygonians," 12; "Scylla and
    Charybdis," 37, 189; "Wandering Rocks,"
    13–14, 23, 33, 50; "Wandering Rocks,"
    as music-hall revue, 122; "Wandering
    Rocks," as obstacle course, 116; "Sirens,"
    2, 7–8, 22, 146–77; "Sirens," conductor
    of, 8, 154; "Sirens," "The Croppy Boy"
    in, 30–37; "Sirens," final notes of, 34, 100,
    133, 139, 187, 194, 199–200, 256; "Sirens,"
    narrative irregularities in, 33–34, 156, 260;
    "Sirens," opening keyboard to, 152, 163,
    257; "Cyclops," 15, 17, 22, 95; "Cyclops,"
    "Croppy Boy" parody, 34–36, 93–94; "Cy-
    clops," "Love loves to love love" parody,
    89, 102; "Nausicaa," 10, 15–17, 29, 154;
    "Oxen of the Sun," 15, 96, 204, 210; "Oxen
    of the Sun," notesheets to, 19, *20*; "Circe,"
    1–2, 9, 11, 14, 17, 21, 39, 101; "Circe," panto-
    mime origins of, 121; "Circe," reading in
    performance, 44, 203, 205–7; "Eumaeus,"
    129, 186, 204; "Ithaca," 12, 16–17, 19, 21,
    103; "Ithaca," black dot in, 13–14, 83, 242;
    "Ithaca," Bloom Cottage, 58, 61; "Ithaca,"
    Bloom's library, 61; "Ithaca," final kiss in,
    138, 195, 200; "Ithaca," notesheets to, 14,
    20, 242–43, 256; "Ithaca," suitors in, 68;
    "Penelope," 7, 18, 57, 69, *179*

—objects in, 23; bits of paper, 54–55; Bloom's drawer, 17, 54, 57, 62, 64, 136, 145, 243; Bloom's hat, 58, 66; bottle of Bass, 55, 194–95, 200, 219; Bransome's coffee advertisement, 54–55; cocoa, 12, 219; fireworks, 15–16; florin, 10–12, 17, 184, 193, 220, 242; flower, 55–57; hourglass, 17; jujube, 222; kettle, 219; kidneys, 1, 185, 205, 241; Lucifer matchbox, 65; moustache cup, 219; parrot, 61, 192; postage stamps, 17, 55–58, 59, 60–61, 69, 220; postcard, 179–80, 187, 193; potato, 61, 206, 248; snot, 17, 247; soap, 1–2, 199, 241; strawberries and cream, 205; throwaway, 182, 220, 248

—riddles in, 2, 21; A. E. I. O. U., 187, 193, 199; disappointed bridge, 2, 184, 190, 262; fox burying his grandmother, 184, 187, 191; I. H. S., 29, 199, 244; I. N. R. I., 192, 199–200, 253; Man in the Macintosh, 2; *Rose of Castile*, 187, 193; U. P., 197

Union Jack, 11

university, 103, 244–46; abdication of value of learning in, 40; abuse of workplace protections by, 40, 42, 46; administrative lack of empathy in, 39; at fault, 26–50; betrayal of students by, 28, 47; collegiality in, 220–21; crisis of conformity in, 21, 26–28, 45, 215; dangers for untenured professors in, 44; and institutional cowardice, 220; shadow justice system of, 39–43, 46. *See also* administrative implacability; error: institutional appreciation of; fraud

Valentin, Karl, 254
van Boheemen-Saaf, Christine, 14
van Rijn, Rembrandt, 221, 226
velocity, 8, 15, 26; omega velocity, 9, 13, 17, 34
Verdi, Giuseppe, 113, 244
Verlaine, Paul, 125, 180
Vico, Giambattista, 80
Victoria, Queen of England, 10, 53, 59, 89, 93, 99, 102, 105
Villona, François, 231
Virgil, 137, 222, 255

Virgin Mary. *See* Catholicism
Vonnegut, Kurt, 245
vortex, 8, 32

Wadham College (Oxford), 49
Wagner, Richard, 27, 141, 245; *Die Meistersinger*, 40, 200; "Ride of the Valkyries," 44; *Tristan and Isolde*, 3–4, 82
Ward Ross, Andrea, 49
Warner, Marina, 41–42, 245
Way of a Man with a Maid (anonymous), 258
Weaver, Harriet Shaw, 148, 161, 209, 256–57
Weaver, Meg, 244
Weidenbenner, Nathan, 53
Weinfield, Henry, 243
Weir, Peter, 251
Wellington, Duke of (Arthur Wellesley), 70, 212
Wells, H. G., 101, 103, 250
Weninger, Robert K., 229–30
Whitman, Walt, 136, 255
Wiener, Jon, 245
Wiesel, Elie, 46
Wilde, Oscar, 71
Williams, William Carlos, 136, 255
Wisden's Almanac, 211
Wodehouse, P. G., 263
Wood, Jeffrey, 250
Woods, Tiger, 249
Woolf, Virginia, 106, 127; *Between the Acts*, 131–32, 254; *Jacob's Room*, 142; *Mrs. Dalloway*, 48; "On Not Knowing Greek," 104; *A Room of One's Own*, 27; *Three Guineas*, 254; *To the Lighthouse*, 62–63, 136; *The Voyage Out*, 229
Woolsey, Judge John M., 89, 226
wordplay, 164, 264; acronyms, 133, 199; acrostics, 82, 201, 236, 257; anagrams, 124, 184, 222, 231, 257, 260–62; cryptograms, 144–45, 184, 243, 262; limericks, 1, 109, 183–84, 222, 262; palindromes, 262; word golf, 235. *See also* jokes; puns
Wordsworth, William, 16, 38, 242
"Work in Progress," 19, 68

Sebastian D. G. Knowles is professor emeritus of English at Ohio State University and editor of the Florida James Joyce series. He is past president of the International James Joyce Foundation and the third editor of the Florida James Joyce Series, after Bernard Benstock and Zack Bowen. Previous works include *A Purgatorial Flame: Seven British Writers in the Second World War*; *Bronze by Gold: The Music of Joyce*; and *The Dublin Helix: The Life of Language in Joyce's* Ulysses, which won the ACIS Michael J. Durkan Prize.

Sebastian D. G. Knowles is professor emeritus of English at Ohio State University and editor of the Florida James Joyce series. He is past president of the International James Joyce Foundation and the third editor of the Florida James Joyce Series, after Bernard Benstock and Zack Bowen. Previous works include *A Purgatorial Flame: Seven British Writers in the Second World War*; *Bronze by Gold: The Music of Joyce*; and *The Dublin Helix: The Life of Language in Joyce's* Ulysses, which won the ACIS Michael J. Durkan Prize.

Joyce and the Narrative Structure of Incest, by Jen Shelton (2006)

Joyce, Ireland, Britain, edited by Andrew Gibson and Len Platt (2006)

Joyce in Trieste: An Album of Risky Readings, edited by Sebastian D. G. Knowles, Geert Lernout, and John McCourt (2007)

Joyce's Rare View: The Nature of Things in "Finnegans Wake," by Richard Beckman (2007)

Joyce's Misbelief, by Roy Gottfried (2008)

James Joyce's Painful Case, by Cóilín Owens (2008; first paperback edition, 2017)

Cannibal Joyce, by Thomas Jackson Rice (2008)

Manuscript Genetics, Joyce's Know-How, Beckett's Nohow, by Dirk Van Hulle (2008)

Catholic Nostalgia in Joyce and Company, by Mary Lowe-Evans (2008)

A Guide through "Finnegans Wake," by Edmund Lloyd Epstein (2009)

Bloomsday 100: Essays on "Ulysses," edited by Morris Beja and Anne Fogarty (2009)

Joyce, Medicine, and Modernity, by Vike Martina Plock (2010; first paperback edition, 2012)

Who's Afraid of James Joyce?, by Karen R. Lawrence (2010; first paperback edition, 2012)

"Ulysses" in Focus: Genetic, Textual, and Personal Views, by Michael Groden (2010; first paperback edition, 2012)

Foundational Essays in James Joyce Studies, edited by Michael Patrick Gillespie (2011; first paperback edition, 2017)

Empire and Pilgrimage in Conrad and Joyce, by Agata Szczeszak-Brewer (2011; first paperback edition, 2017)

The Poetry of James Joyce Reconsidered, edited by Marc C. Conner (2012; first paperback edition, 2015)

The German Joyce, by Robert K. Weninger (2012; first paperback edition, 2016)

Joyce and Militarism, by Greg Winston (2012; first paperback edition, 2015)

Renascent Joyce, edited by Daniel Ferrer, Sam Slote, and André Topia (2013; first paperback edition, 2014)

Before Daybreak: "After the Race" and the Origins of Joyce's Art, by Cóilín Owens (2013; first paperback edition, 2015)

Modernists at Odds: Reconsidering Joyce and Lawrence, edited by Matthew J. Kochis and Heather L. Lusty (2015; first paperback edition, 2020)

James Joyce and the Exilic Imagination, by Michael Patrick Gillespie (2015)

The Ecology of "Finnegans Wake," by Alison Lacivita (2015)

Joyce's Allmaziful Plurabilities: Polyvocal Explorations of "Finnegans Wake," edited by Kimberly J. Devlin and Christine Smedley (2015; first paperback edition, 2018)

Exiles: A Critical Edition, by James Joyce, edited by A. Nicholas Fargnoli and Michael Patrick Gillespie (2016; first paperback edition, 2019)

Up to Maughty London: Joyce's Cultural Capital in the Imperial Metropolis, by Eleni Loukopoulou (2017)

Joyce and the Law, edited by Jonathan Goldman (2017; first paperback edition, 2020)

At Fault: Joyce and the Crisis of the Modern University, by Sebastian D. G. Knowles (2018, first paperback edition, 2021)

"Ulysses" Unbound: A Reader's Companion to James Joyce's "Ulysses," Third Edition, by Terence Killeen (2018)

Joyce and Geometry, by Ciaran McMorran (2020)

Panepiphanal World: James Joyce's Epiphanies, by Sangam MacDuff (2020)

Language as Prayer in "Finnegans Wake," by Colleen Jaurretche (2020)

Rewriting Joyce's Europe: The Politics of Language and Visual Design, by Tekla Mecsnóber (2021)

CPSIA information can be obtained
at www.ICGtesting.com
Printed in the USA
JSHW030951130221
11877JS00002B/17